Darlingji

Kishwar Desai has been a television anchor and producer for over twenty years. She has worked with NDTV, TV Today and Doordarshan. Her last job in television was as Vice-President, Zee Telefilms. She has written an award-winning play, *Manto!*, and scripts for various documentaries. She has just completed the script for a feature film to be directed by Shyam Benegal. She is currently working on a biography of Saadat Hasan Manto.

Darlingji

The True Love Story of Nargis and Sunil Dutt

KISHWAR DESAI

<small>INTRODUCTION BY LORD MEGHNAD DESAI</small>

HarperCollins *Publishers* **India**

First published in India in 2007 by
HarperCollins *Publishers* India

Copyright © Kishwar Desai 2007
Introduction copyright © Meghnad Desai 2007

'Hey There' on page 432, as sung by Johnnie Ray, written by R.Adler/J.Ross © 1996 Sony
Music Entertainment (UK) Ltd.

ISBN 978-81-7223-697-7

Third Impression 2013

Kishwar Desai asserts the moral
right to be identified as the author of this work.

HarperCollins *Publishers*
A-53, Sector 57, Noida, Uttar Pradesh 201301, India
77-85 Fulham Palace Road, London W6 8JB, United Kingdom
Hazelton Lanes, 55 Avenue Road, Suite 2900, Toronto, Ontario M5R 3L2
and 1995 Markham Road, Scarborough, Ontario M1B 5M8, Canada
25 Ryde Road, Pymble, Sydney, NSW 2073, Australia
31 View Road, Glenfield, Auckland 10, New Zealand
10 East 53rd Street, New York NY 10022, USA

Typeset in Sabon10.5/13
Mantra Virtual Services Pvt Ltd.

Digitally printed and bound at Bhavish Graphics.

For my parents, Padam and Rajini Rosha
and children, Gaurav and Mallika Ahluwalia
For all the love you have always given me

CONTENTS

INTRODUCTION

Indian cinema is, or at least ought to be, a national monument on par with the Taj Mahal and the Qutab Minar. It is older than Hollywood and bigger in terms of the films made. It is commercially successful not just in India, but around the globe, and not only among the Indian diaspora but across many countries in the Middle East, Africa, Latin America and lately in the developed world as well. It uses imported equipment to this day, yet it is not the hardware but the software—the story, dialogue, songs and dances—that Indian talent brings to cinema, which gives it its unique position. It is not the oldest but definitely one of the most successful modern industries India has created for itself.

Of course I can only speak of Hindi commercial cinema, Bollywood, as it is misleadingly though unavoidably called now. But Hindi cinema—and even this is problematic because the language it uses is not Hindi but what used to be called Hindustani, an amalgam of Hindi and Urdu—is the most widely watched across India in Hindi and non-Hindi speaking areas. This cinema in its talkies phase is now more than 75 years old.

When I was growing up, films were at the heart of all conversations with friends and relations. We saw as many films as our parents would let us and often more. We talked about the stories, remembered large chunks of dialogue and worshipped the stars. Among men there were the great three—Dilip Kumar, Raj Kapoor and Dev Anand. But among the women there was only Nargis. None could match her star status. Kamini Kaushal got married and retired from films. Suraiya fell by the wayside by the early 50s since playback singing devalued a singing star and Madhubala, though very beautiful, got lousy parts until Guru Dutt discovered her talent for light comedy in *Mr and Mrs 55*. Meena Kumari was a starlet in Wadia's mythological films

until the mid-1950s when Bimal Roy gave her a break with
Parineeta.

From 1947 to the day she retired from films after her marriage,
Nargis was at the top. She was the 'Woman in White', dignified,
glamorous, fashionable and talented. See her in *Andaaz* as a spoilt
Westernized femme fatale, and in *Jogan* as an austere yet beautiful
sadhvi, two films made just a year apart, and you see the range
of her acting. Her films with Dilip Kumar—*Mela, Babul, Deedar*
and of course *Andaaz* and *Jogan*—made us all cry since one or
the other, or both (*Mela*), had to die or be blinded (*Deedar*).
Tragedy was Dilip Kumar's forte in those days and she matched
him frame by frame. Like many of my generation, I watched
each of these films several times.

She was paired with Raj Kapoor, and they became the idols of
the young. In their films *Barsaat* and especially *Awara*, they
portrayed romantic young love to the limit that the film censors
would permit. They also made many indifferent films together, as
well as some that count as memorable for various reasons, like
Anhonee where she played a double role and *Chori Chori* for the
Shankar-Jaikishen score. By the time they made *Shree 420*, her
roles were shrinking, but even there we have the unforgettable
duet 'Pyar hua ikrar hua' with the two standing in the rain under
an umbrella. Our romantic sensibilities were shaped by Nargis's
films. When she was awarded the Padma Shri, I recall the headlines
in the Bombay newspapers. She after all belonged to India but
even more so to Bombay, we thought. Then one day we read to
our surprise that she had married Sunil Dutt.

The young actor Sunil Dutt was so shy that he blushed on
screen in his romantic scenes with Meena Kumari in *Ek Hi Raasta*
where I first saw him. He was a gentle and handsome Bengali
bhadralok hero in *Sujata,* and then there is my favourite Sunil
Dutt film *Ek Phool Char Kaante* with Waheeda Rehman, which
displays his talent for light comedy. When Mehboob cast him as
Birju, he saw in Sunil Dutt what no other director had seen so
far. This was the other Sunil Dutt, the smouldering, wronged
man fighting against all forces for justice or simply revenge. This
was after all the role Mehboob had first offered Dilip Kumar,

who wanted to play the father as well since otherwise Nargis had the bigger role. (Dilip Kumar's version of *Mother India* is *Ganga Jamuna,* with two brothers, one good and one bad, but with the mother's part scaled down.) Sunil Dutt fulfilled his promise in that film and, of course, won the heroine's heart.

This is the story that Kishwar Desai tells us. India is ill-served in terms of the biographies of its cinema greats. What passed for biographies for years were often collections of unverifiable gossip and vignettes sans attribute, with film stills their selling point and often an inadequate filmography of the subject, or worse, none at all. Stars were lucky to have some biographies; directors, producers, cameramen, music directors, art directors and the rest hardly ever figured on the bookshelves.

Kishwar Desai has been assiduous in gathering primary material—diaries, letters, interviews, archival material—to construct this account of their lives. It will surprise many and dispel some myths. Nargis is romantically associated in popular imagination with Raj Kapoor. Yet it is her love for Sunil Dutt and her tenacity in convincing him of her love which will replace the older myth once you have read this book.

Kishwar and I met when I was writing my book on Dilip Kumar and she was my managing editor. I also fell in love and was lucky to win her love and we got married. Our plan was to write a book on Nargis together and we met Sunil Dutt who promised to read and contribute towards this promised biography of Mrs Dutt, as he always insisted on calling her. Yet, within six months of our meeting, he too was gone on a day when, as it happened, Kishwar and I were watching *Mother India* in our London home. It eventually became Kishwar's solo effort, but it is one which I have watched grow with fascination and read with delight. I hope you do the same.

Meghnad Desai

Hazaaron saal nargis apni benoori pe roti hai
Badi mushkil se hota hai chaman mein deedavar paida

(For thousands of years the nargis languishes in the wilderness
Waiting for the connoisseur's eye to light upon it)

—*Mohammad Iqbal*

Prologue

The young man bent over the notepad was tall and good-looking. His dark eyes were thoughtful and he was frowning as he wrote. The quiet village of Umra lay outside his room, where a few months earlier a blazing fire had raged during a film shoot. But his thoughts were elsewhere, with a woman whose face and name were known to almost everyone.

Her fame was the problem he was struggling with. He wished she were an ordinary woman, and not a star; for him, she was simply the woman he loved. But he could not talk about their love, for there were many who would be against their relationship. The press would create a scandal.

In secret, they wrote to each other; in his letters he called her 'Pia', not Nargis. And with her irrepressible sense of humour, she called him not Sunil Dutt but 'Hey There!' from the first line of a song they liked: 'Hey there...you with the stars in your eyes...' At other times he called her Marilyn Monroe, and she called him Elvis Presley.

Now he sat by himself, putting together memories of the months just past. He wanted to collect in one notebook all the letters they had written to each other, all the notes, all the special moments they had shared. He was sentimental about every little thing, quite unlike most men in his profession.

He wrote:

I DEDICATE THIS BOOK IN MEMORY OF THAT FIRE;
WHICH PURIFIED OUR BODIES AND SOULS AND
ENABLED US TO FIND EACH OTHER.

He wrote on the next page:

IT WAS FRIDAY THE 1ST MARCH 1957,
UMRA 35 MILES AWAY FROM BILLIMORA,
AT THE BANK OF THE AMBIKA RIVER...WE
EMBRACED RED FLAMES
TODAY 9 A.M. AT THE SAME PLACE
SAME SURROUNDINGS...IT IS FRIDAY ALSO
BUT I AM ALONE TO-DAY...NO FLAMES...
THE PERSON, WHO HAS LIT THE UNDYING FIRE
IN MY HEART, IS NOT BY MY SIDE. I START THIS
BOOK AND THE WORDS IN IT WILL KEEP THE FIRE
IN MY HEART BURNING TILL ETERNITY
HEY THERE
14.6.57
UMRA

Their relationship began with an accidental fire during the shooting of *Mother India*. It was a scene in which Radha (Nargis) had to search for her son Birju (Sunil Dutt) in the midst of burning haystacks. Nargis had rejected the use of a double. All precautions had been taken to ensure her safety, when suddenly the direction of the wind changed, and the fire raced towards her. While the cast and crew looked on aghast, only Sunil had the presence of mind to rush to her rescue. He pulled her out, but they were both badly burnt by the fire.

Her hand was burnt, while his whole face, chest and hands were charred. That an actor would risk losing his good looks, his ticket to fortune, was unusual. But then Sunil Dutt was an unusual man, as Nargis was to find out.

As they recuperated together in the quieter precincts of Billimora, 35 km from the film sets, he found she had 'lit the undying fire in his heart.' She was the only woman he would ever love—and surprisingly for some—he was the only man she ever truly cared about.

Strangely, very few believe the story of their love. People said, and still say, that she didn't really care for him, that she had no choice but to marry him after her affair with Raj Kapoor went wrong. Others thought he was marrying her for her star status.

As is often the case, the gossipmongers were wrong. Nargis wrote in her diary on 16 March 1957:

As I have always felt that if ever things happened, the drums would beat for me—well the drums really did beat for me on the 1st of March 1957; but thank God they did not reach a crescendo and stopped to a dead silence, as I always feel they will the day I die. I or rather I should say we, Sunil and myself—we escaped death by just a hair's breadth. It was the shooting of 'Mother India' and the Fire sequence was being filmed. In the shot I got engulfed in walls of flames and there was no way out. I had lost the sense of direction— I could hear a voice in the distance asking me to get out, but I also heard a very strong voice within me urging me to stay for 'He' was coming and, upon not finding me, 'He' would be disappointed—I was in an ambiguous state of mind; when I felt a hand clutching at my garment—my brain was absolutely numb.

All I knew was in a matter of seconds we were out of the flames, safe, alive and laughing. The terrible happenings of those few seconds is still just a dream to me. I sometimes wonder; but I also believe that (after) all the tortures that I went through in physical pain, I have found peace, my mind seems to be at rest, I feel that I have burnt my past, Nargis the complex woman died. There is somebody new that is living and desperately wants to live—wants to laugh and know life in its truthfulness. Like a newborn baby my life seems to be pure, washed with the eternal fire of truth and love.

All the same we were brought home and given pathedine injections, which relieved us of pain and put us to sleep. A sleep which did not allow our subconscious to take hold of us. At least this was my condition. I used to get up startled every hour or two, but found myself too weak to exercise my limbs. The moment anybody came near me I would ask how Sunil was. I knew he must have been more restless than myself.

By this time I had developed definitely a strong fondness for him. I felt myself at all occasions wanting to look after him and I also did look after him in my own capacity, the best that I thought. As a matter of fact I felt it my duty, and duty not with any bondages or strain—but with love.

On the 2nd of March, I went to see Sunil in his room and to my great shock I found him quite burnt—his face, his stomach, and hands and I could see he was in agony. I stayed with him the whole day and found for myself that he could not be left alone as he was liable to hurt himself in his sleep...

She kept awake all night, sleeping for half an hour, if at all, and keeping vigil over Sunil.

I started looking after him as if he was a part of me. When he cried out with pain, my heart would miss several beats and I took a vow that he must get well. I was to do everything on earth to bring peace to him and happiness if possible. Days and nights I spent tending to his wounds, day by day as he showed improvement, I was feeling satisfied and immense happiness could be seen in my eyes. During this illness Sunil and I came very close to each other. My tormented soul cried out for help and I shared all my miseries with him. I did not hide any incident of my life.

At last she felt she could be honest because:

...his shoulders were always there for me to cry on, and I also knew his garments will absorb my tears and not scatter them out for people to make fun of me. If it were not for him, perhaps I would have ended my life before the 8th of March. For I alone know the turmoil that was going through me. What storms within me were trying to destroy me. 'I want you to live,' he said and I felt I had to live. Begin all over again.

As 'Hey There' began to reciprocate her feelings, Nargis, strangely, tried to dissuade him, saying that she was not the woman for him.

I remember he said 'I am too far gone. I can't go back.' You don't know how happy these words made me feel. I knew he was mine and I loved him very much. I just did not care for any one else. I had found 'Him' and I won't let him go. I clung to him, I kissed him, I did not want to be away from him even for a moment. I used to feel my life following him, wherever he went. Those wonderful days that we spent together alone just for each other, are the happiest days of my life and I will cherish them forever.

I was young once again, one could see love in my eyes. I could not hide the fire in my eyes from anyone. We were like two little children romping around doing all sorts of things, laughing at odd times, looking at each other just without any reason. I used to stare at him for ever so long. Everything in him I felt belonged to me...

Nargis left for Bombay on 16 March. In the sixteen days they had spent together recovering from their burns, they had exchanged promises of love. They played their favourite records and even danced together, and she taught him how to rock 'n roll. She dreamt of being with him—not of making films together, but of

> ...a home with a red roof surrounded by fields of our own where he will work, I dreamt of our children going to school.
>
> I would work in a small home for poor women. But I would be loving him and looking after him the most. All those other dreams that I used to dream once were dead and buried. I used to think it is a sin even to think of such dreams but here I am dreaming them again. Not only dreaming them but feeling them. I feel I can just stretch my hands and touch them.
>
> I simply adore him. I can't help it. I love him like I have never loved anyone else before. This is a fact. I think of him all the time that I am away from him...
>
> Lord give him strength to bear my love and give me in return his love...let him respect my feelings for him. For it is for him now that I have decided to live.

Mindful of her unhappy past, Nargis decided to tell Sunil Dutt all about herself and her family: about her grandmother Dilipa, her mother Jaddanbai, her father Mohanbabu, her two stepbrothers, Akhtar and Anwar, and Raj Kapoor. Everything. She said she was 'shameless' in wanting him to know the truth about her, because she wanted to vanquish all the demons of her past. In turn, Sunil, normally very reticent, opened up his own turbulent life to her gaze.

This, then, is the true and never-before-told story of 'Pia' and 'Hey There', 'Marilyn' and 'Presley', Nargis and Sunil Dutt, before and after the fire, told by them and by those who were close to them.

Dilipa
1880-1900

It was the last quarter of the nineteenth century and terrifyingly for Dilipa Devi, she was a widow at thirteen. Instead of starting a new life with her husband—perhaps even before the marriage was consummated—her hair was shaved off, and her young body was draped in a loose white saree to mark her widowhood. There would be no more toys or trinkets, no songs, no meals with the family. There would be a separate space for her in the house, and even her shadow was not to fall on anyone, especially during celebrations or on festive occasions. There would be no bangles on her arms, nor slippers on her feet, and she would sleep on the floor. She would have to trudge miles to fetch water and do whatever menial chores were assigned to her. She was inauspicious, and worse, for the rest of her life she would be a non-person.

The Brahmin community was especially harsh to its women, following archaic religious rules in an attempt to uphold centuries of male superiority. Many of these beliefs had, of course, to do with property rights. It was easier to disenfranchise a widow than to give her part of her husband's property. For the attractive widows, life became a living hell. Social opprobrium did not allow them to remarry even though widow remarriage had been legalized in 1856. So they became easy prey for the lustful men in the house, and though usually the victims, they were chastised for being temptresses.

'Look at the crowds of widows in the prime of life who are forbidden to remarry, and who are only too ready to yield to the temptations by which they are assailed. Modesty and virtue place no restrictions upon them; their only fear is that their misconduct may be found out. Consequently, abortion is their invariable resource to prevent such a contingency, and they practice it without the slightest scruple or remorse...' wrote the scandalized Abbé J.A. Dubois in his *Hindu Manners, Customs and Ceremonies*, the product of a thirty-year sojourn in India during the late eighteenth and early nineteenth centuries.

Not unusually, the other women in the house would treat the young widow with deep suspicion, and her sexuality was constantly under surveillance. There could be no confidantes. In many parts of India, sati, the ancient custom of burning the widow with the dead husband, was sometimes seen as the simpler solution by a male-dominated society. And, in thrall of their own futures, the women in the family would dress the widow like a bride, feed her opium, and sing marriage songs of eternal union with her husband as she was led to the pyre.

Dilipa's life, fortunately, took a different turn. In the beginning she continued to live in the house of her dead husband, where she had been trapped as the result of another ancient custom: child marriage. The Age of Consent Act of 1891 was yet to come and girls, especially in rural areas, were married young. So Dilipa, a widow and a non-person, was dependent on others for every crumb. Going back to her parents' home was not an option.

Dilipa was a fair, good-looking and not unintelligent girl, but the odds were stacked against her. Like most girls in her time, she was illiterate and spoke in the peculiar dialect of the province in which she had grown up. She had not been brought up to do any particular work and knew nothing of the outside world. Her husband's home was in Baliya. In those days, the region was divided into a number of princely states and its economy was based mainly on agriculture.

The politics of India's freedom movement would not have touched Dilipa, either. The Indian National Congress was still to be founded and the freedom movement, after the 1857 mutiny, was yet to coalesce into a force to be reckoned with. In fact, to the British rulers there did not appear to be any serious threat to the empire. To their mind, there wasn't even an entity that could be labelled India. Sir John Strachey lectured Cambridge undergraduates that 'there is not, and never was an India or even any country of India...no Indian nation, no "people of India" of which we hear so much...that men of the Punjab, Bengal, the North-West Provinces and Madras, should ever feel they belong to one great Indian nation, is impossible' (Sumit Sarkar: *Modern India: 1885-1947*). The tremors of the freedom movement were yet to be felt, and in Baliya, certainly, the social structure and life generally were unaffected by the politics of empire.

There is, however, one uncorroborated story that Dilipa was related, albeit distantly, to Mangal Pandey, one of the mutineers who instigated the First War of Independence (as it came to be known), which began as a mutiny of three regiments in Meerut, on 10 May 1857. Though it was brutally suppressed, initially the movement had some success: within twenty-four hours Delhi was occupied and Bahadur Shah Zafar was proclaimed the Emperor of India. Most of North India, the Gangetic valley and Oudh, though not the Punjab, rebelled. Unfortunately for the mutineers, there was no central command, and once the British recovered from their initial shock, they were able to overcome the rebellious forces. While Dilipa was too young to have witnessed the mutiny, her family is said to have relocated to a village near Allahabad to escape the wrath of the British.

Whether she was related to the brave soldier or not, Dilipa was certainly to display a great deal of courage following the death of her husband. For it was only a matter of time before the young widow understood that life would not improve as long as she lived under the tyranny of her in-laws.

The seemingly helpless young girl managed to find a rather unusual escape route. One version of the story is that she was at the village well when a stranger asked her to draw some water for him. She was astonished, as her clothes gave away her widowhood and most people would have considered it inauspicious to accept food or drink from her. It turned out that the man was a Muslim and since the concept that some people are unclean, circumstantially or by birth, is a uniquely Hindu one, he did not care or notice. They struck up a conversation, and the man offered the young girl refuge in his home in Chilbilla, a village in the United Provinces.

Another version is that after a vain attempt to kill herself, Dilipa stumbled into the home of a sarangi player, Sheikh Miajan, in Chilbilla. It is possible that he was a member of a troupe of musicians passing through the village, whom Dilipa met while washing clothes at the village well. Whatever the truth, in a short while, though Miajan was probably married, Dilipa and Miajan were living as man and wife. Undoubtedly, it was unconventional and very brave of a Brahmin widow to marry a Muslim. It was also a step that would have alienated her from her strictly Brahminical world forever. But for Dilipa, most of these barriers would have been meaningless, as she was already living in a world without stable relationships. Her decision to seek refuge with a stranger who offered her shelter may have been one of desperation, but it brought her back to life.

The ability to make life-affirming, positive decisions was a trait all the future women in her family were to inherit from her. And interestingly, in every generation, there would be a woman who married outside her religious community: her daughter Jaddanbai, her granddaughter Nargis, and more recently, her great-granddaughter Priya. In a country where it is not unheard of, even today, for young people to be persecuted for marrying outside their caste, marrying outside one's religion is a courageous act. It was even more so a hundred years ago when Dilipa stepped into Miajan's home.

From all accounts, Miajan played music for gaanewalis or songstresses. Though today our perception of these performers is largely fuelled by Bollywood (this tribe of extremely talented and entrepreneurial women having more or less died out), gaanewalis were usually very accomplished women, trained in the art of music, and some in dance as well. Their patrons were from the royal or noble classes, as only the rich had the time and money for such indulgences.

Like the 'nautch' (i.e. 'naach' or dance) girls who performed at the Mughal court and for the White Mughals or European sahibs, these women were also groomed in court manners and etiquette. Their lives weren't easy: many of them were exploited sexually by the nobles who paid to see them perform.

Despite their often sordid and difficult personal struggles, these performers kept the culture and music of the period alive and flourishing. A few went on to become legendary singers. Jaddanbai, Dilipa's daughter, was to be one of them. Begum Akhtar (also known as Akhtaribai), one of the greatest singers India has ever produced, was another. In southern India the devadasi tradition which was centred on the temple rather than the court had much the same contours: one of the greatest Carnatic vocalists, M.S. Subbalakshmi, was its product.

It was only in the early twentieth century that there began to be attached a deep sense of shame to being employed as a singer or a dancer. Those who earned their livelihood from music and dance and entertained in public were edged out of polite society. A carefully constructed form of music and dance which was acceptable to the 'respectable' middle class was put together instead. Thus classical music and dance as approved high art began to flourish while the memories of those talented, independent women who preserved much of this art began to be suppressed. An older feudal society had been openly admiring of these women; now, the new hierarchy concealed its admiration to match the hypocrisy of the age.

Towards the turn of the century, when Dilipa sought shelter with Miajan, the tradition of the gaanewalis was on the decline. The advent of the British meant that the nobility and royals were no longer in a position to entertain or support these women. Also, a new puritanism was making itself felt among the Indian elite and middle class, influenced as they were by the British. Simultaneously, the British White Mughal was also feeling the pressure of Victorian values.

As Pran Nevile writes in his book, *Nautch Girls of India*, 'While Mughal India saw the advent of the Nautch girl on the cultural landscape of the country and her rise...the annexation by the British of Awadh (1856) in the north and Tanjore in the south (1855)—the two dominant centres of art and culture—foreshadowed her decline and fall. For the Nawabs of Awadh, eccentric and flamboyant as rulers, were also among the last of the great patrons of dance and music. Besides the loss of support of the nobility and later of the early English sahibs who, bored with their lonely life in a strange land, had found in the nautch girl a means of lively entertainment and aesthetic satisfaction, there were several other factors responsible for her downfall.

'As the 19th century wore on, the spread of Engish education brought in a new petit bourgeois class which, influenced by Western ideas, got alienated from the art and cultural traditions of the country.' Apart from that, as more British women arrived, the patronage provided by the Mughals and then the British also began to die out.

From then on, their marginalization was swift. British women, social reformers, puritans and missionaries considered the singing and dancing girls a vice.

'In 1892,' writes Nevile, 'they started an "anti-nautch" movement at Madras which spread to other parts of the country. This movement was in a way inspired by the Madras Christian Literature Society which had launched virulent propaganda against nautch girls invited by the local gentry to perform in honour of the British dignitaries. A nautch performance was held for the Prince of Wales during his visit in 1875. He was even welcomed among others, by the Devadasis of the Srirangam temple. However, in 1890 when Prince Victor Albert was entertained to a dance recital, there were loud protests from various quarters...'

Aggrieved purity organizations like the Punjab Purity Association came into being. This particular outfit launched an all-out drive and published a booklet which contained Keshub Chandra Sen's description of a nautch girl: 'a hideous woman...hell is in her eyes. In her breast is a vast ocean of poison. Round her comely waist dwell the furies of hell. Her hands are brandishing unseen daggers ever ready to strike the unwary...' Hardly the portrait of a nubile and luscious temptress.

Ironically, however, while Her Majesty's Government refused to ban or prohibit the nautch (after the Indian mutiny, the British were generally reluctant to interfere in matters of Indian culture), Indian social reformers kept up their war cry till the dancing girls were pushed out of public view.

'In the North, (they) were compelled to eliminate the dance

element from their performances.' (Nevile) Even this did not prevent their being socially ostracized.

Yet they retained an audience. Only, now it was less from the nobility and more from among wealthy landlords, and well-employed, educated young men.

In the company of Miajan, Dilipa must have become familiar with the world of gaanewalis, who were often very wealthy in their own right.

Saleem Kidwai notes in his very perceptive paper 'The Singing Ladies Find a Voice', that from the time that official data is available, these were 'the only women listed as property owners and the only ones paying income tax.'

According to Kidwai, 'the gaanewalis were perhaps the best educated of women. The more talented also trained under the best music and dance ustads, even if only for a brief period. In fact they were valued patrons of poets, scholars, holy men, and most importantly, talented male musicians and dancers who were willing to teach them for a pittance in return for good meals and a place to stay...'

According to some accounts, Dilipa adapted to her new circumstances and managed to relocate to Agra, where she and her husband worked for a while. Agra was the first step towards an urban life for the simple, rustic Dilipa. It was the former capital of the Mughal empire and so retained much of its courtly culture and impressive monuments. Living there would have entailed a drastic change in lifestyle. Gone were the white sarees, now Dilipa would have to dress in finery. Nothing is known about her ability to sing, but if the account of her becoming a gaanewali is correct, she must have had to unlearn her Brahmin ways. The lesson of financial independence, too, would have been learnt from harsh experience.

Since attending mehfils in the evening was still a romantic and even respectable thing to do, many young men visited gaanewalis to listen to good music, in the same way that we go to concerts today.

According to one account, the recently widowed Motilal Nehru, father of India's first prime minister, was a patron of the arts. Men like him would have been more than welcome at a mehfil, and there would have been few strictures about an evening of music and poetry.

Motilal was a Kashmiri Brahmin born in Agra on 3 May, 1861. (We can safely assume that Dilipa was a few years younger. When her daughter Jaddanbai was born in 1897, she would have been around thirty.) Though he was a Hindu, he displayed a strong Persian influence in his dress and manners. After his parents' death, his two older brothers Bansidhar and Nandlal brought him up. He lived with Nandlal for the first ten years of his life, which may have led to his aristocratic ambitions later on, as Nandlal began as a tutor to the raja of the small princely state of Khetri and ended up as his chief minister.

Educated in Kanpur first, Motilal shifted to Allahabad where Nandlal set up his legal practice. It was the profession Motilal was to join. After passing his lawyers' examination with distinction, he went to Kanpur for a three-year apprenticeship, and then moved back to Allahabad in 1886 to practice in the High Court with his brother.

The paths of Motilal and Dilipa would cross by sheer coincidence. When she accompanied Miajan (who was by then playing the sarangi for a gaanewali called Vazirjaan) to Allahabad, they lived in the western wing of a haveli. It is said that Motilal Nehru lived in the same haveli after his return to Allahabad with Nandlal. This led to the speculation later on that Dilipa and Motilal knew each other, but it would not have been unusual for a young man about town to know about a local artiste anyway.

'My father told us the story,' confirms Zahida Sahaya, Dilipa's great-granddaughter, a graceful and beautiful woman who epitomizes the best of the women in the family. 'Motilal Nehru was our neighbour. They (Dilipa and Motilal) were in the same building in Allahabad.'

For Dilipa, Allahabad would have been a great change from both Chilbilla and Agra. Within fifteen years of the 1857 mutiny, Allahabad had grown into a European township. It was the capital of the United Provinces of Agra and Awadh, complete with a high court, a secretariat, a cantonment and the Muir

College. Founded in 1872, the college would grow into the first university of the province. The best-known English language newspaper of the time, the *Pioneer*, was published from here. The population of the town was just over 1,72,000 in 1901, but there was a large European presence and the divide between the Indian elite and the less privileged was growing. Dilipa may have needed to learn some social graces in order to survive here, but for an upwardly mobile young man like Motilal, Allahabad provided endless opportunities for growth.

And grow he did. Nandlal had died leaving behind a widow with seven children. Motilal had also remarried. It would have been difficult for a young lawyer with a large family to lead a comfortable life, but luckily Nandlal had left behind substantial savings. Motilal made good use of these, looking after his brother's family and managing his own early years at the Bar. (He was to refund the money with interest to his brother's family.) By 1896, Motilal was one of the four leading advocates in the High Court, earning Rs 2000 a month, and by 1905 his income had multiplied five times.

But would such a man have had the time for musical evenings? It appears unlikely, because as his fortunes improved, Motilal became more and more anglicized and by 1900 he was living in Anand Bhawan, which boasted a swimming pool and tennis courts. He is known to have imposed the English language upon his family, which resulted in 'long spells of silence'. He did encourage an eclectic mix of cultures, though the inner sanctum of the house, presided over by his orthodox wife, was strictly Hindu. The children were taught by an English governess as well as a maulvi and a pandit, and the food in the house, prepared in three different kitchens, catered to European, Hindu and Muslim tastes. Apart from swimming and tennis, wrestling bouts were organized. Wrestling was 'Motilal's favourite sport'. Certainly, none of this even faintly evokes the image of a great lover of poetry or music.

Perhaps gossip prevailed because, very much like his famous son many years later, Motilal did not enjoy a happy marriage. Swaroop Rani was often in a state of 'morbid depression', overwhelmed by her husband who urged her to learn English and adopt Western ways, advice she rigidly ignored. Neither did she change her orthodox lifestyle. While Motilal was 'domineering, rational, modern', she remained sensitive and traditional. (B.N. Pandey: *Nehru*)

Eight years after Swaroop Rani gave birth to Jawaharlal, Jaddanbai was born to Dilipa. (The birth dates of both Dilipa and Jaddanbai are unconfirmed. Jaddanbai may have been born earlier than 1897.) T.J.S. George provides us with another twist to the story in *The Life and Times of Nargis*, where he writes that Jaddanbai was acquainted with the household of a Kashmiri aristocrat in Allahabad. He adds in a footnote, 'There were not many Kashmiri noble houses in Allahabad in the first two decades of the 20th century. Certainly the best known was Motilal Nehru's clan.' What may be true, however, is the additional note in the book, 'Quoting elders in his family, Anwar Hussain's son Sarwar told this writer (George) that Jaddanbai had made a rakhi brother of Jawaharlal Nehru who must have been about ten years her senior.' Whatever the facts, after Miajan's death in 1906, it appears that Dilipa returned to Chilbilla with her son and daughter.

One of the reasons for this speculation about the links between the Nehru clan and the Dutts is that in later years, Indira Gandhi and Nargis, the children of Jawaharlal Nehru and Jaddanbai, were friendly with each other. It was a unique friendship between two equally strong-willed women. The veteran actor Ashok Kumar once noted wryly that even while on a film set Nargis would sit in a corner writing letters to Jawaharlal Nehru and his daughter Indira. There was obviously a close bond between the two families.

Dilipa's return to Chilbilla must have been a fairly traumatic event in a life that had never been calm. She was almost forty and her career was nearly over. She would need financial support to keep the family going and so she, ever pragmatic, encouraged the young Jaddanbai to train in the arts. The girl was reportedly taught music by the legendary Ustad Moijuddin Khan, the doyen of the Benarsi thumri.

He was probably a fine and disciplined teacher, because Jaddanbai grew into a superb singer. She had a deep mature voice and perfect control, whether she was singing popular poetry written in the local Braj bhasha or the superior Urdu of Ghalib. Her training and voice were apparently an inspiration for Begum Akhtar. Jaddanbai's other guru was reputed to have been Ustad Barkat Ali Khan, the younger brother of Bade Ghulam Ali Khan of the Patiala gharana. The training was rigorous and would reap rich dividends.

In the first decade of the twentieth century, there were only a few cities where singers were still appreciated. One of these, which has always welcomed artistes and where performers like the famous shehnai player Bismillah Khan lived till recently, was Benares. It was probably here that Jaddanbai made her public debut, in the hometown of her guru Ustad Moijuddin Khan.

Kashi-Varanasi-Benares has always been a rich cultural centre. From the time of the Vedas, the city is supposed to have echoed with music. Its presiding deity is Natraj, or Shiva. What better way is there to celebrate him than with constant song and dance? It is also a city of scholarship. Therefore, Jaddanbai, despite her youth, began her career in an auspicious city. And her talent did not go unnoticed. Soon invitations began to arrive for her to sing in the homes of rich patrons and noblemen.

While Dilipa begins to fade into the background at this point, she remained a part of Jaddanbai's life. In fact, many years later, when Jaddanbai came to Bombay and set up home in Marine Drive, her mother was with her. She had become a plump middle-class matron, though she occasionally displayed the spark that had pushed her out of Baliya into an adventurous new life. Those who remember her say she would sit on a rope charpoy outside Château Marine, a posh building on the Marine Drive sea-face, and keenly observe passersby. Next door was another matron who would also take out her rope charpoy and sit glaring at Dilipa. They would then roundly abuse each other, Dilipa still speaking in her village dialect. The trouble was that the other woman was a Hindu who could not bear to see a Muslim sit outside on equal ground with her. This was the greatest irony of all, that Dilipa, who was born a Brahmin, had to eventually rescind every part of her background. Her grandchildren do not even remember her singing or listening to music.

Rehana Amarjeet Singh, her eldest great-granddaughter, recollects life in Château Marine. 'Mutki Dadi (Dilipa) would put her khatiya outside and make all the lafangas who came to see my father also sit outside. She would smoke a hookah and wear a lungi and jhabla. She would irritate us. We had a radiogram and every time we put on the music, she would take out the record and say, *"Hamare namaz ka* time *hai* (It's time for my namaz)."* She did namaz five times a day, sitting in a chair.'

But, as we all know, in India the Hindu-Muslim divide is never very rigid and Dilipa slipped easily in and out of the grey area where rituals co-exist comfortably.

Rehana remembers: 'She would also do pitrupaksh (a Hindu ritual to appease one's ancestors, understandable for a woman whose family had disinherited her), perhaps because she was a Hindu who had converted to Islam. She would give food to the crows. When she was served, she would put some on the parapet and would eat only after the crows had eaten. She ate very little, and in a thali.'

Dilipa's Hindu beliefs appear to have occasionally outweighed her Muslim beliefs. 'She died before the birth of my last sibling. She had said that she would be reborn in the house. Because my mother, Iqbal, had served her so well, she said she would come back to her. She said you people, being Muslims, do not believe in reincarnation, but I do. She showed a birthmark on her body to my mother.'

Iqbal, meanwhile, had had a tubectomy and was safe in the knowledge that she would not have any more children. So her pregnancy came as a total shock. When Najam, her last son, was born, the family thought he looked like an old woman. Amazingly, there was a birthmark on his back, just like the one 'Mutki Dadi' had.

Though Dilipa was forced to struggle most of her life, before she died she saw her daughter settle all scores for her. Not only did Jaddanbai win back respectability, she married a man who rejected Brahminism and the religion that had driven Dilipa out of her home.

Jaddanbai
1910-1930

Like her mother, Jaddanbai was a determined woman with a great sense of self. She was also very intelligent, and was gifted with a versatile voice. Even in the days before singers began recording for gramophone companies (in the early 1900s), or singing on radio (by the 1930s), Jaddanbai's talents were publicized by word-of-mouth. She received invitations to sing at special mehfils and her popularity grew. It helped that her mother knew from her own experience how to handle the arrangements for a public performance.

Jaddanbai was strikingly elegant, with an oval face and long black hair. She had inherited her mother's fair complexion along with her chutzpah. As her granddaughter Zahida points out, Jaddanbai was trained in court manners and how to entertain nobility. While her mother was still speaking the village dialect, she developed a lively style of conversation, using both chaste Urdu and rather colourful abuse, depending on the company. In everything she did, her ambition was apparent: she had no intention of remaining a small-town girl.

Because she wanted to improve herself, Jaddanbai began to learn more thumris, ghazals, and even Punjabi folk songs. Her grasp of the thumri must have been quite remarkable because, as her grandson Arif Hussain remembers, many years later, when she was in Bombay, Begum Akhtar came to her to ask about a thumri which she said she wanted to learn from her.

Hers was however an itinerant existence. There was no place she could call home and all the relationships she formed, especially with men, would be fragile. While nothing is known of Dilipa's musical abilities, early recordings of Jaddanbai confirm a superb talent. From a young age, therefore, she must have supported her mother and her brother, as well as the musicians she travelled with. There was little privacy in her life: at each performance, custom demanded that she sing as well as interact with her admirers. Social norms were becoming increasingly puritanical, and in order to perform in front of an audience of strangers, almost on a daily basis, women in the profession learned to be both bold and quick-witted, often having to fend off unwelcome advances.

These were not ticketed performances, after all. Traditionally, after a song was over, appreciation would be shown in the form of money or valuables like jewellery, depending on the status of the kadardaar, or admirer. In the audience could be some who wanted a less public demonstration of their admiration.

Rajnikumar Pandya, in *Aapki Parchchaiyan,* gives a graphic account of how among the first admirers Jaddanbai took seriously was the wealthy Narrottam Das, also known as Bachchubhai, who said he loved her. (Marathi writer Shashikant Kinikar, in his biography *Nargis,* claims that it was an admirer in Benares called Bansibabu who first attracted her attention.) Perhaps she believed him, being barely in her early twenties then. But after her son Akhtar Hussain was born, the man slunk away in the face of opposition from his family. Today, his existence has been wiped out of the family's memory. In fact, some members of her family think that Jaddanbai's two sons were born of the same father, as was Nargis. However, some of her friends confirm that Nargis was aware that her siblings were her step-brothers.

Not long after, Jaddanbai once again got into a relationship, perhaps out of loneliness and insecurity. Only this time it was closer home. Master Irshad Hussain, also known as Mir Khan, played the harmonium for her. It was a repeat of her mother's life, and an unequal relationship. Mir Khan was dependent on her. The graceful, husky-voiced singer was the main attraction at their performances. The couple separated after Anwar Hussain was born. Again, there is no clear record of their marriage or separation. Soon afterwards, Jaddanbai left for Lucknow and then Calcutta.

Her visit to Lucknow turned out to be pivotal. During one of her performances, she found a man staring at her, entranced. He had come from Rawalpindi and was planning to go to England to become a doctor. He began to attend her performances regularly, and then one day, rather dramatically, he proposed to her. Half-jokingly, she asked him whether his family would agree. He said he would return to Rawalpindi and speak to them. He did not come back, and Jaddanbai went on to Calcutta with her entourage of her mother, two sons and various musicians.

Calcutta in the 1920s was still the jewel of British India and a growing centre of the arts. After losing his kingdom, the Nawab of Awadh, Wajid Ali Shah, had retired to Calcutta with his court and become a major patron of music and dance. Calcutta thus acquired its status as the residual legatee of Muslim splendour, not something the puritanical British cared for.

Music and dance were also encouraged by the feudal bhadralok who aspired to a Nawabi lifestyle. In the popular literature of the period, such as the immortal story of Devdas by Sarat Chandra Chatterji, the courtesan/singer was celebrated as an integral part of a young man's life. Spending an evening being entertained by a singer was almost a necessary rite of passage. The character of Devdas was based on real people, the scions of landed and wealthy families who dissipated their youth and spent their family fortunes as patrons of various singers and 'ladies of talent'. One famous courtesan, Gauharjaan, drove a horse and carriage through the city and was quite the toast of the town.

Women like her had rich patrons who held regular musical soirées. One such wealthy industrialist became Jaddanbai's patron in Calcutta. It was while performing at one of his musical evenings that she noticed the man who had proposed to her in Lucknow, once again sitting rapt in the audience.

The man was Uttamchand Mohanchand or Mohanbabu, son of Lala Dalbirchand Mohan and Ramdevi Mohan. He was obviously still enamoured of the singer, and this time he was determined to woo and win her. Earlier, when he had gone home to tell his family about his plan to marry Jaddanbai, he had been admonished for wanting to marry a gaanewali and packed off to Calcutta. The coincidence of her arrival in Calcutta may have helped make up his mind, for Hindus are great believers in destiny. He decided to go ahead and propose once more.

Why would a well-to-do Brahmin, on his way to becoming a doctor, want to marry a gaanewali? From her early photographs, Jaddanbai appears to have been an attractive, self-confident woman. She would not have had her mother's rustic demeanour, for she had grown up in cities for the most part. Besides, her exposure to mehfils and royalty would have given her at least a veneer of sophistication. She was also ambitious and used to adulation. In some of the early photographs, she appears slim, dreamy-eyed and draped in a saree: perhaps she wanted to look respectable, as she hoped one day to be. She was always a quick learner and soon after arriving in Calcutta, she had been able to create a niche for herself in a competitive environment.

Being a cultural hub, Calcutta had a variety of composers and voices to offer, from the plebian to the intellectually stimulating, such as the music and songs of Nobel laureate Rabindranath Tagore. It was a thriving city with a strong British presence and for a newcomer to create a name for herself so quickly was unusual. It is believed that even K.L. Saigal, who was then a struggling government clerk, attended her mehfils and was impressed by her.

Jaddanbai had to now decide whether to accept the young man's proposal or not. Mohanbabu was four years younger and seemed besotted with her. Should she consider the effects of marriage on her career or should she just give in to the emotional appeal of having a loving partner by her side?

However sceptical Jaddanbai may have been about Mohanbabu's proposal, she couldn't possibly have spurned him, for the chances of finding someone who wanted to marry her were rapidly diminishing: she was already thirty and the mother of two children.

None of Jaddanbai's objections seemed to matter to Mohanbabu. Though generally described as a gentle soul, he was in love and determined not to be thwarted. He decided not to go to England for further studies in medicine, a decision he may well have regretted later.

When Mohanbabu seemed unmoved by her objections, Jaddanbai raised her last one: how could he marry a Muslim? After all, he was a Mohiyal Brahmin. Mohanbabu then had his horoscope made. It turned out that the first part of his life was going to be completely different from the second half. He interpreted this to mean that he was destined to live half his life as a Hindu and the other half as a Muslim. It may have been a frightening thought that half his life was already over (he was not yet 30), but Mohanbabu promptly decided he was going to convert to Islam. He changed his name to Abdul Rashid. Interestingly, Maulana Abul Kalam Azad carried out the conversion. Could it be that Dilipa used her connection to Motilal or that Jaddanbai contacted Jawaharlal? Maulana Azad was already a well-known Congress leader, a Muslim scholar well versed in Arabic and Persian, a theologian as well as a fiery journalist of international repute.

Jaddanbai and Mohanbabu were married in 1928. Mohanbabu was promptly and unceremoniously disinherited by his family. It would take many years for the insult to be forgotten, but there was some reconciliation in the future. In the 1940s, when Jaddanbai and Mohanbabu were living in Bombay, his brother and his wife moved in with them.

The marriage did not quite transform Jaddanbai's life. She had merely acquired one more permanent dependant. Mohanbabu did not have a job or the prospect of one. The only source of income was Jaddanbai's profession. So, despite the marriage, the mehfils continued. Yet, now there *was* a difference. With the marriage, and that too to a man from a very respectable family, the real conversion of Jaddanbai from a gaanewali to a respectable matron began.

Meanwhile, Mohanbabu tried his hand at various money-making ventures. To begin with, he made one more attempt to

study medicine. Jaddanbai and he went to Lucknow and K.N. Singh, the actor, remembered meeting the couple there. He was somewhat bemused at Mohanbabu introducing Jaddanbai as Jayadevi, thus giving her a Hindu name. It either meant that Mohanbabu had not truly forgotten his Brahminical origins, or it may have been yet another attempt by the couple to reinvent themselves. In a new city, Jaddanbai could shed her uncomfortable past and become an ordinary wife and mother.

Significantly, Mohanbabu was never known as Abdul Rashid and he was to give his daughter a dual name: Fatima/ Tejeshwari. She was free to use either name, an indication of how easily the family moved between Islam and Hinduism.

Unfortunately, their attempt to start life anew in Lucknow was short-lived. The couple returned to Calcutta and it was here that Fatima Abdul Rashid, also known as Tejeshwari Mohan, was born on 1 June 1929. She would grow up to become the iconic film star, Nargis.

At the time, however, a life in cinema would have seemed very remote. The couple was still trying to find a foothold in some respectable profession. If Mohanbabu were not to be the sole breadwinner, Jaddanbai would have to find regular work too. The only option was to continue as a singer, though in a healthier environment if possible.

There is no doubt that women like Jaddanbai—singers, dancers, entertainers, and the most marginalized of women—played a very important role in the development of the arts in India. After being forced to give up dancing as nautch girls, only those who could sing survived, but even they found that patronage was dying out partly due to the new puritanism and partly due to the freedom movement that had taken over the lives of many young people. The women moved with the times. Instead of singing in kothas, they turned to radio, or became gramophone artistes. Many were encouraged by Mahatma Gandhi to lend their talent to the freedom struggle by singing for 'azaadi'. As they were trained singers, they could supply a readymade repertoire and talent. A few joined the growing film industry, which mainly produced silent films in the 1920s. They were practised performers, and their expressive faces were much sought after.

Once cinema shifted to the talkies in the 1930s, these women reinvented themselves yet again. As a matter of fact, Hindustani cinema developed its musical orientation partly due to these 'singing ladies'. Their ready-made talent created a unique genre that proved to be popular, and remains so, as is evident from the many song-studded films Bollywood continues to produce.

Because they were also natural entrepreneurs, having supported a floating population of family, children and hangers-on, the women were intuitively inclined to the profession of cinema where a motley collection of people would get together to produce a film. In fact, Indian cinema is unusual for the number of women who contributed in various ways, at an early stage, to its evolution. Jaddanbai was soon to be one of them.

Sangit Movietone
1930s

In the same decade that Jaddanbai was born, there took place a different sort of birth—of cinema in India.

The craze for cinema spread like a virus. After the first screenings at Watson's hotel, in Bombay on 7 July 1896, the excitement of the new medium grabbed the imagination of a few amateur cinematographers who took off on a shooting spree. All kinds of subjects were filmed—H.S. Bhatavdekar even shot a wrestling bout in Bombay's Hanging Gardens.

Recorded sound made an independent appearance in eastern India, also in the late nineteenth century. In Calcutta, Hemendra Mohan Basu imported Edison's 'phonograph' and made the first indigenous cylindrical records, known as Bose's records. Tagore reportedly recorded his rendition of *Bande Mataram* on one of these. The Gramophone and Typewriter Company Ltd, Belgatchia was in business by 1898.

Details about the first recorded song by a professional singer are less clear. According to one version, the German inventor of the disc record, Fredrick Gaitsburg, arrived in Calcutta on 27 October 1902 to record some local songs, purely as a business enterprise. The glorious Gauharjaan, the well-known courtesan of Calcutta, was one of the talents he tapped. Another version is that the singer Sashi Mukhi of Classic Theatres recorded the first song, from the play *Sri Krishna* also in 1902.

Whatever the reality, the commercial possibilities of cinema and song were already apparent. Major Warwick established the first cinema theatre in Madras by 1900, and by 1904, the Touring Cinema Co was operational in Bombay, showing two reels called

The Life of Christ; religion was to remain a crowd puller in theatres.

Occasionally, the turbulent political situation in the country lent itself to an increasingly adventurous camera lens. By 1905, the freedom struggle had gathered momentum. The Congress was involved in the Swadeshi movement and confrontations between the nationalists and the repressive British regime became more frequent. Lord Curzon and Andrew Fraser, the new Governor of Bengal, announced the partition of Bengal. Immediately spotting an opportunity for drama, the founder of one of India's most prolific studios, J.F. Madan, became a producer with Jyotish Sarcar's film of a protest rally against the partition of Bengal.

Entrepreneurs continued to enter the fray. By 1912, *Pundalik*, possibly India's first feature film, was released. It was produced jointly by N.G. Chitre, the manager of the Coronation Cinematograph in Bombay and P.R. Tipnis, later a major producer. Almost certainly based on a stage play, *Pundalik* was a film about the Hindu saint, shot on location on Bombay's Grant Road.

In 1913, Dadasaheb Phalke's film *Raja Harishchandra* was screened in Mumbai, marking a new era for Indian cinema. Through a skilful combination of mythological content and clever editing, Phalke created magic on screen, and gave the fledgling new medium a distinct Indian identity. He also went on to screen his first three features, *Raja Harishchandra, Mohini Bhasmasur* and *Satyavan Savitri,* in London. By 1918, Phalke had set up Hindustan Cinema Films.

The action had begun to spread to other parts of the country as well. *Bilwamangal,* also known as *Bhagat Surdas* and probably the first Bengali feature film, was made by Rustomji Dotiwala for Madan Theatres. In the same year of 1919, Ardeshir Irani launched his first studio, Star Film Co, and *Nala Damayanti* became the first international co-production, with Italy. By 1921, the lure of silent films had spread to the south, and R.S. Prakash launched the Star of the East film company in Madras.

The political situation was grim, with frequent and bloody encounters. The brutal massacre of Sikhs at Jallianwala Bagh, Amritsar, ordered by General Dyer in 1919, was followed in 1920 by the non-cooperation movement, which was finally called off by Gandhi after the killing of 22 policemen at Chauri Chaura.

However, because of the strict censorship policy now advocated by the British government for home-grown cinema, films could not be made on nationalist themes and continued to revolve around mythological and romantic stories. And, of course, religion: the first Indo-German co-production by Himanshu Rai, *The Light of Asia* (1925), based on the life of the Buddha, was an outstanding silent film of international standards.

These early developments in cinema did not involve Jaddanbai but, unknown to her, the stage was being set for her entry. Till the 1920s, she was still pursuing her profession as a singer in the United Provinces. By that time, in her search for security, she had ended up as the mother of two sons. Fortunately, her marriage brought her back to Calcutta, which had become the home to a number of well-established studios. She discovered that cinema was being viewed and discussed, and talented artistes were actively sought after. It was a thriving industry.

Then, inspiration came in the form of another enterprising woman, Fatma Begum, regarded as India's first woman producer and director. In 1925 Fatma started her own production company and directed *Bulbul-e-Parastan* which was released the following year.

By another serendipitous twist of fate, Lahore opened up as a film production centre with the setting up of the Punjab Film Corp, among others, and a few years later in 1928, Abdul Rashid Kardar launched the United Players Corporation. This was the origin of Playart Phototone—the company which would lure Jaddanbai to Lahore and start her career in cinema. Kardar's partner Hakim Ramparshad had heard her sing in Calcutta and was impressed enough to offer her work.

Thus Kardar and Jaddanbai began a professional relationship which was to last her entire life. When her son Anwar began looking for work, Kardar would be the one to give him his first role in a film.

Meanwhile, the first radio program, which ran for three years, was broadcast privately by the Madras Presidency Club Radio in

1924. By 1930, the Department of Industries and Labour had taken over the radio operations and started the Indian broadcasting service in Bombay and Calcutta. This was wonderful news for Jaddanbai because it was closer home, and singing for the radio was far more acceptable than singing for an invited audience of her chaahnewale.

While some singers reinvented themselves and exchanged the 'Bai' in their names for 'Begum', Jaddanbai retained the suffix. In any case, her luck was turning and finally there was hope that she could leave the itinerant world of public performances and find a career in cinema, or radio, or as a gramophone artiste. Of the three, she chose to take cinema seriously, and began to withdraw from her image as a 'songstress'. By the time the first talkie, *Alam Ara*, was released, Jaddanbai was already on her way to Lahore with her family.

Alam Ara, advertised as 'all talking all singing all dancing' was produced by Ardeshir Irani for Imperial Movietone. It was released on 14 March 1931, just squeaking past *Shirin Farhad*, produced by Madan Theatres, which had also been working overtime to release its first talkie.

Imperial Movietone won the race and had a runaway hit. The song-studded *Alam Ara* (it had seven songs) was based on a popular Parsee play written by Joseph David, and told the story of the king of Kumarpur and his two wives, Navbahar and Dilbahar. It was the first 'all talking' lost-and-found story in which the heroine Alam Ara is taken away from the palace and brought up by gypsies. She is then identified by a charm around her neck. It is easy to see where a thousand other Indian films got their inspiration from.

But it was the actress playing Alam Ara who was the cynosure of all eyes. More than a decade younger than Jaddanbai, Zubeida, born in 1911, was reportedly the daughter of the Nawab of Sachin and Fatma Begum. Sachin was in Surat district, and it is assumed that the lovely Zubeida, like her sisters Sultana and Shehzadi, was a princess, though this claim is thrown into doubt by Christopher Buyers, who says that Nawab Sidi Ibrahim Muhammad Yakut Khan III (1887-1930) 'is supposed to have left three daughters by the Bollywood actress and first female director, Fatima Bai (b.1903 ; died 1983)...Even if true , there is no record of a marriage or contract having taken place between the Nawab and Fatima Bai. Equally no record exists of the Nawab having recognized any of her children as his own, a prerequisite for legal paternity in Muslim family law.' He also points out that if Fatma was born in 1903, she would have been eight years old when she gave birth to her second daughter Zubeida.

However, as in Jaddanbai's case, the date of birth shifts according to convenience, for most personal history at this time was recorded in memory, not on paper; all contemporary accounts of Zubeida say that the Nawab was her father. Certainly, her dubious origins had no impact on her popularity.

Zubeida acted in her first film *Veer Abhimanyu* when she was supposedly just 10 years old. With an ambitious mother and two sisters who were also actresses, Zubeida may have had a lot to cope with. But she acted in over 70 films, both silent and talkies, including her mother's films *Bulbul-e-Parastan*, *Heer Ranjha* and *Milan Dinar*. In 1934, she set up Mahalaskhmi Cinetone in partnership with Nanubhai Vakil, another legendary film maker. It was an interesting life, and one which would appeal directly to Jaddanbai's creative instincts.

With the arrival of the talkies, there was a growing demand for actresses who could speak Hindustani and sing. The time was finally right for Jaddanbai.

Though the women who worked in early Indian cinema (with a few exceptions like Devika Rani and later, Durga Khote) were usually from 'disreputable' backgrounds, they quickly earned enough money to catapult themselves into respectability.

In his book *Indian Film Stars* (1933), journalist Bodh Raj Oberai provides a detailed list of all the contemporary actors, with short write-ups on each of them. According to Oberai, the actresses came from very different cultural and religious backgrounds. While about 40 per cent of the women were Hindu, 30 per cent were Muslims and the others were of mixed Indo-European parentage, including Jews and Christians.

It was certainly unusual, anywhere in the world, for so many Muslim women to be on screen and out of purdah. It was even more unusual to have them setting up film production companies. In fact, that feat from the 1930s has never been repeated. Immediately after Independence there were still a few prominent Muslim actresses, especially in the 1950s and 1960s—Nargis, Suraiya, Madhubala, Meena Kumari—but over the years the numbers have declined considerably. Perhaps the best known in recent times are Shabana Azmi and her niece, Tabu.

The other unusual aspect about the women mentioned in the 1933 book is that most of them (regardless of religion) identified themselves as singers or dancers. Most of the Anglo-Indian actresses would have had European fathers—posted in India by the British Raj—and so blue eyes and blonde hair were not uncommon. Some of them, like Patience Cooper and Ermiline, became extremely popular, though they were usually given Hindu names to ensure public acceptance. For instance, Miss Winnie Stuart became Manorama, Miss Gasper became Sabita Devi, Miss Renee Smith became Sita Devi, and Miss Stella Green became Shyama.

In the silent era these Anglo-Indian actresses did very well, but very few of them were able to make the transition to speaking roles in the talkies on account of their anglicized Hindustani. One of the best known, who managed to work steadily from 1925 to 1975, was Sulochna (though the roles became smaller with each film). Her real name was Ruby Myers. A former telephone operator, she was hugely successful with *Wildcat of Bombay* (1927), which was later remade as *Bambai ki Billi* (1936). In the film she played eight roles, including that of a European blonde, a gardener and a banana seller! Like Fatma Begum, she also launched a production company, Ruby Pics, in the mid-1930s.

What possibly helped the entry of women from diverse religious and social backgrounds was the fact that cinema of that early period did not belong to any one region of India but was being produced all over the country. Therefore there was neither a regional hegemony nor the desire to produce predominantly any one kind or genre of cinema (as happened till very recently when the maximum number of films were produced in Mumbai, and there was an overt and covert pressure to create cinema which was acceptable to the dons of the industry. Now, with professional companies funding small entreprenuerial cinema projects, the environment is changing again.) Films were being produced in the west in Lahore, Calcutta in the east, and beyond, in Rangoon as well. They were also being made in Poona, Kolhapur, Indore, Bangalore and Bombay—wherever there was the initiative to put together a team, a story, and the finances.

According to the 1935 annual issue of *Filmland,* the impact of the talkies was tremendous: '14th March (1931) is the Red letter Day in the History of Indian Talkies for on that day was released India's First Full-length Talkie "ALAMARA"...'

The magazine noted that there were 86 film producers listed in Bombay alone and ten more in Poona and Kolhapur, out of which 27 had their own studios, and 13 more had 'Sound-proof Studios and possess Lighting Equipment.' It also noted that 'Lahore has 23 concerns, Delhi 12, Peshawar 1, Amritsar 3, Karachi 7, Ajmer 3.' Calcutta had fourteen 'concerns' in 1935. Burma, it seems, had produced three Hindi talkies: *Carvan* by Wallison Movietone, *Shane Subhan* by Brahma Film Company and *Chandrajit* by Burma Imperial. There were four studios in Madras. Of course, some of the production houses listed never got around to completing a film or even starting one, but there was a boundless enthusiasm for entering the world of cinema, because it was clear that there were profits to be made.

Filmland pointed out, 'An average talkie (its length must not be less than 1400 ft) costs somewhere from Rs 45,000 onwards.' Whereas silent films had been sold (all India) from anything between Rs 9000 and Rs 28,000, the talkies were being sold usually for twice the amount—and that too only for North India. This was a considerable jump. Some Sulochna starrers such as *Indira MA* were sold for Rs 90,000 and went on to become huge hits. The top five talkies in terms of the number of weeks they ran were '*Shyamsundar* (25 weeks), *Amrith Manthan* (20 and onwards), *King of Ayodhya* (16 weeks), *Puran Bhakt* (15 weeks) and *Lale Yaman* (14 weeks).'

But in terms of collections, the top five talkies are listed as *Shirin Farhad, Alam Ara, Maya Machchindra, Toofan Mail* and *Yahoodi ki Ladki.* Most of these were costume dramas.

The top heroines of the period were Sulochna, Gohar and Madhuri. Among the men the top spot was shared by E. Billimoria, Gul Hamid and Saigal. Most of the actors, regardless of rank, were employees of a studio. In a few cases, the actors remained with a certain production house or studio and were responsible for the growth or decline of that studio. But often, actors and technicians were drawn by the lure of fame and fortune to work in different parts of the country.

Abdul Rashid Kardar who, along with his partner Hakim Ramparshad had persuaded Jaddanbai to come to Lahore, was one of them. He had a chequered career as a painter and still photographer, before returning to Lahore to join B.R. Oberai's Pioneer Productions as an actor (this was probably the same conscientious Oberai who painstakingly put together *Indian Film Stars* and ran a magazine as well). Unfortunately, Playart Phototone did not make any really successful films. Jaddanbai's debut film *Raja Gopichand*, produced in 1933, was among their more forgettable creations. Nonetheless, Jaddanbai's acting career (though she was pushing 30 by then) progressed rapidly. Her latest mentor was Moti Gidwani. Born in Karachi, he was one of the few film directors who had actually studied filmmaking in the UK. After a somewhat shaky start—his first film bombed at the box office—he managed to establish himself. He is said to have helped with the making of *Alam Ara* and then collaborated with Dalsukh Pancholi on the successful *Khazanchi*. Gidwani was to direct Jaddanbai in Lahore in *Insaan Ya Shaitan*, another film that sank with hardly a trace.

Yet her move to cinema had not gone unnoticed. In a stunning but unglamorous photograph published in the 1935 *Filmland* annual, she sits with her eyes closed, in a plain white saree and blouse (quite reminiscent of her daughter in later years when she played the part of an ascetic in the film *Jogan*), her hair in a long plait, strumming a tanpura. The pose is of a serious artiste— quite unlike the other women featured in the same magazine with their pancake make-up and come-hither smiles. The caption reads, 'Here is the famous Indian songstress Jaddan Bai who so long persistently refused offers from the Screen. At last she has

succumbed to the lure of talkies and has joined Mr Hakim Ramprasad's Playart Phototone Corporation, Lahore.'

Jaddanbai had now begun to be recognized as a cine artiste, apart from being a singer, and was featured in other articles, even in English magazines, as well as in listings of cinema actors. Bodh Raj Oberai writes in his entry about her in *Indian Film Stars*:

> Miss Jaddan Bai is a famous songstress of India, and is one of the few best reputed musicians residing in Calcutta.
>
> She was born in 1902 in the district of Allahabad. She is thin, of middle stature and has attractive features. She has black hair and black eyes.
>
> She knows Urdu, Hindi, Bengali and Persian as well. She began her career as a dancing girl at the age of six or seven and when she was thought to be quite proficient in the art of singing, she left Allahabad and went to Calcutta –where she acquired name and fame. She joined films in 1932, and played the leading role of the mother of Raja Gopichand in 'Gopichand' produced by the Playart Phototone Corporation of Lahore. She has played an important role in 'Bhuk Ka Shikar' produced by M.U. Malkani at the Imperial Studio, Bombay.

There is no mention of either her husband or her three children, and her age has been reduced by five years. Only those aspects of 'Miss Jaddan Bai' which would be useful for her film career are mentioned.

Imperial Studios, mentioned in the write-up, had been set up by Ardeshir Irani in 1926. It was her work at Imperial Studio that brought Jaddanbai to Bombay, where she finally came face to face with Zubeida. They both acted in *Seva Sadan* (1934), directed by Nanubhai Vakil who had co-founded Mahalakshmi Cinetone with Zubeida. Naturally, she was the star of the film, playing opposite Shahu Modak, the Marathi Christian cine star. His claim to fame was his enactment of the role of Krishna in 29 mythologicals, in Marathi, Hindi and Bhojpuri.

Around this time, Jaddanbai began composing film music (as in *Raja Gopichand*) and this may have also encouraged her to think of moving permanently to Bombay. Her real goal was clearly to acquire the lifestyle of Begum Fatma and Zubeida.

Towards that end, in 1934 she launched her own five-year-old daughter as a child actor in the ironically named *Naachwali*. Interestingly, Jaddanbai did not give her daughter any serious training in music or dance. Was it because of a perceived lack of talent, or was it that Jaddanbai wanted to close a certain door to her past forever?

Meanwhile, unaware of the plans being formulated for her future, the little Fatima, called Baby Rani in her early films, played with her dolls and dreamt of becoming a doctor.

At this point, it made perfect business sense for Jaddanbai to move from Lahore to Bombay. None of her three films had done particularly well, and if she wanted to start her own production house, she would need support and rich patrons, who were probably easier found in Bombay than Lahore. Once again, she relocated to a new environment.

It was a shrewd and prescient move because after Partition, Lahore was to decline as a film centre, while Bombay would surge forward despite the trauma of Partition and the migration of some major artistes to the newly formed Pakistan.

Glimpses of the glorious years ahead were visible already in

1936: Bombay was becoming the hub of Hindustani cinema. The number of cinema halls in the country had risen from 148 (1921) to 675 (1932). But more importantly, of the 1515 talkies produced between 1931 and 1940, 927 were in Hindustani, and the most prolific companies were all based in Bombay—Imperial, Ranjit, Sagar and Wadia. In fact, Calcutta saw the sad decline of many pioneering studios such as Madan, East India and Kali Films. Only New Theatre continued to flourish.

Jaddanbai's ability to project herself as a cinema star when she was already reaching her mid-thirties was due to the success of other very popular matrons who dominated the screens of the 1930s. Proof of their popularity may be found in the success of Ranjit Film Company, later to become Ranjit Movietone.

Ranjit Movietone was run by Chandulal J. Shah, who had set it up in partnership with Gohar, a plump, round-eyed actress. One of her greatest hits, *Gun Sundari* (a remake of Shah's eponymous 1934 silent film) was the story of the persecuted but diligent wife who rescues her good-for-nothing husband and his family. It was a winning formula, and was employed again in the next film, *Barrister's Wife*, another melodrama about the persecuted wife who—what else?—rescues her family from disaster. Shah and Gohar had a long-lasting successful partnership, though the stout Gohar was an unlikely choice for a screen siren.

Many of the films being made at the time were heroine-centric, some more dramatically so. While Shah and Gohar were taking the more traditional view of femininity, others such as Fearless Nadia, along with Homi Wadia, were creating a new action-oriented persona of a superwoman riding a horse called Punjab ka Beta and beating up villains of all shapes and sizes. *Hunterwali* (literally, the woman with a whip) may have held a masochistic appeal for men, while women aspired to be the blonde bombshell. But for Jaddanbai, it was the more traditional aspects of womanhood, the 'Gohar' model, which made financial sense.

Arriving in Bombay, she rented a flat close to where she would eventually move—Château Marine. Having settled her family there, she began to get in touch with some of her old contacts. These were the patrons who had appreciated her performance in earlier days, and perhaps could sponsor her next project. In the meantime, she was also acting in a film: *Insaan Ya Shaitan*.

Jaddanbai set up Sangit Movietone in 1936, and in quick succession produced five films: *Talash-e-Haq, Hridaya Manthan, Madam Fashion, Jeevan Swapna, Moti ka Haar*. Not only did she produce and direct the films, she wrote the story and dialogues and composed the music as well. Apart from acting in the films, of course. These films were also unique in that they were home productions in every sense of the word—most of the family participated in them. Apart from Jaddanbai, they included her son Akhtar Hussain, and her young daughter, who was still known as Baby Rani.

The films were usually morality tales, and they voiced 'Bai' Jaddanbai's concern about a society rapidly degenerating due to 'Western' influences. They also served as a veiled gesture of support for swadeshi values. Perhaps it was the only way in which filmmakers of the period could fight a subversive war against British colonialism and censorship. Jaddanbai must have followed the political triumphs and travails of Jawaharlal Nehru in the struggle for independence. And she would certainly have been aware of the freedom movement, especially now that she was in Bombay, where the Congress leaders often met.

The quaintly named *Madam Fashion* typified the East-meets-West formula. The story is about the troubled life of Sheeladevi (Jaddanbai), the wife of the wealthy Seth Amarnath (Ansari). After her world travels with her husband, Sheeladevi is now a slave to fashion. Even though her husband has helped her become 'fashionable and a society lady', he is unable to withstand her wild demands for ever more 'dance dinner and races'. She meets up with the villainous Mister Jagdish (Yaqub), whom she had first encountered in Germany, at the races. He loans her money so she can place some bets. Needless to say, their friendship makes Amarnath very jealous—especially after he spots them together, leaning on the railing of a ship. For him this is an open admission of promiscuity. So Sheeladevi leaves her home, but not her fixation with 'fashion' which also includes (shock and horror!) imbibing liquor. Quite soon, she is evicted by the bailiff for not

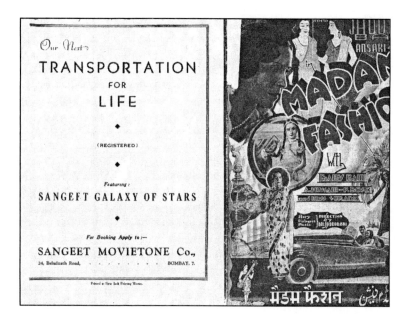

paying her dues and spending all her money on another pile of fashionable clothes. There is also a complicated sub-plot in the film, involving the villainous Mister Jagdish.

Akhtar Hussain plays Jaddanbai's son, as she sensibly always wrote roles for herself in which she could play the mother of children. Baby Rani once again plays Jaddanbai's daughter, and seems to have quite a pivotal role: she wanders around lost, looking for her mother, and towards the end is kidnapped by Mister Jagdish. This was the first of a series of life-threatening situations in which the unsuspecting Baby Rani would be placed in all Sangit Movietone productions. The shrewd Jaddanbai knew that nothing gets an audience more tearful and tense than the sight of a helpless child faced with cruelty or worse.

Given that it was made by a woman who had spent most of her life looking after her family (she was a 'dancing girl' at the age of seven—just a little older than Baby Rani), with little time for meaningless leisure, *Madam Fashion* paints an almost wistful picture of the lives of the rich and careless.

Jaddanbai herself enjoyed an occasional flutter at the races. She smoked cigarettes and may have had an occasional drink, but she knew that the Indian audience would prefer her not as a punter but as an upholder of tradition.

While she cast around for another film project, Mohanbabu also started going to the races. It was a good strategy: the couple could make contacts and look for business opportunities while rubbing shoulders with the cream of Bombay's elite. Not that Mohanbabu, still happy-go-lucky and gentle, had much luck at making money. He had tried various enterprises, including some with Akhtar Hussain, none of which were particularly successful.

Jaddanbai's granddaughter Rehana remembers, 'He did a lot of business with my father to earn money. Buying and selling of commodities; then, when there was a profit in the buying and selling of oil, he did that. He was also a bookie, used to get a lot of tips from Aziz Ahmedbhoy who had a lot of racehorses. We all were members of the Turf Club, mainly to mingle with the top society. In the members' enclosure we would meet everyone.'

It was not long before Jaddanbai launched another film: *Call of the Soul—Hridaya Manthan*. It had an equally complicated plot and was supposedly based on a real story. The publicity leaflet for the film promises that its hero 'in the flesh and blood could be found today wandering in the bylanes of Calcutta, a sad wreck of humanity broken by drink, privations and suffering—a victim of Society's cruel laws. The heroine for her part, is living the degrading life of a "daughter of joy".'

The film portrays a married but misunderstood woman, Nirmala Devi (Jaddanbai), who is forced to leave her home because her husband suspects that she is 'impure', even though she was the victim of a kidnapping. It is the story of Sita retold, of course, and is complete with an agni pareeksha at the end when the young Baby Rani is trapped in a burning house—yet another life-threatening situation!—from which Nirmala Devi rescues her.

In a brave departure from the norm, part of the film was shot in Sonagachi, the red light area of Calcutta, where Nirmala Devi 'sits and sings as the popular songstress Kanti Bai'. Jaddanbai tries to portray how innocent women are sometimes forced into professions by 'Society's cruel laws'. A large slice of life indeed, and something she could identify with.

Jaddanbai's son 'A. Hussain' is in the film too, and plays her brother-in-law. Perhaps he sang some of the songs, for he is billed as 'A.Hussain THE GOLDEN VOICED'. Unfortunately, no copies exist, of the film or music, either with the family or at the National Film Archives of India, so it is difficult to confirm whether Akhtar actually sang any of the songs.

It appears that Akhtar was the only one among Jaddanbai's children to have inherited her talent. According to the family, he sang very well. He was his mother's favourite son, but like his stepfather, he was unable to pursue an independent career, outside the home productions and later, his sister's films.

None of Jaddanbai's films were box-office hits, but they did establish her as someone who understood all aspects of cinema. She was shrewd enough to keep an open house and was a phenomenal net-worker. Almost anyone who hoped to make it in cinema one day would make at least a few visits to Jaddanbai's house.

It seems that she would help anyone who needed it, without looking for anything in return. Once when the neighbouring family was short of money, and there was no food in the house, she quietly sent across whatever was required. Her large-heartedness was legendary.

Their lifestyle was not grand, but it was certainly a life of plenty. Apart from her mother, her three children and her husband, the house often overflowed with relatives. Château Marine, the building she would finally move into and where her grandchildren and great-grandchildren still live, is a five-storey art deco style structure on the sea-face of Bombay; the flats are large and spacious. She rented the ground-floor apartment. All the rooms in her time were usually full—and if relatives arrived, charpoys would be placed in the corridor for the newcomers to sleep.

Her kitchen staff readily provided hot meals to all visitors and the popular image of Jaddanbai was of a generous, though often foulmouthed soul. No one minded her colourful language: it was part of her changed persona, from a sylph-like singer to a stout woman of the world, a film producer and entrepreneur. The ability to pepper her conversation with language not normally heard in the drawing rooms of dowagers was a trait she shared with her mother and also passed on to her daughter.

The world that Jaddanbai created in Château Marine was totally different from her own childhood in the village of Chilbilla. But it was what she had dreamt of and it gave her the opportunity to sit amidst high society as an equal. Fortunately, as Bombay was still evolving, cinema offered an entry point to a wide variety of people who came with nothing but could became millionaires. (As cinema became more competitive in post-Independence India, and the Nehruvian age of idealism died with him, politics began to offer the same facility for ambitious wannabes who wanted to make a quick buck.)

*

While Jaddanbai groomed her daughter into a sophisticated English-speaking film star, far away in Khurd, in Jhelum district (now in Pakistan), a young boy was growing up, whose life would one day intersect with Jaddanbai's in an unexpected way. He was a simple but fiery-tempered child with a strong sense of fair play, used to settling his battles with his fists.

Balraj Dutt was the son of a land-owning farmer, and he had no idea that his destiny was tied to the family settling down to a life of glamour in Château Marine in Bombay. While he played in the dust with his friends, his future wife Baby Rani was also playing make-believe games, but on celluloid. She was groomed and coiffed and made up even at the age of five. When she was not on screen, she was sent to study in a convent school. His world, on the other hand, comprised of a rustic though large home, a village school of indifferent standards, and a mother who was soon to be widowed.

The two worlds could not have been more different—the Hindu world of Balraj, who would grow up to become Sunil Dutt, and the world of Baby Rani, born in an ostensibly Muslim household, who would grow up to be Nargis. But within two decades they would meet and become inseparable. Theirs was the story of India itself: of a country changing rapidly and beyond recognition, through personal ambition and forced migration.

Balraj Dutt
1930-1947

Dewan Raghunath Dutt was a Mohiyal Brahmin, as was Jaddanbai's husband before his conversion to Islam. According to legend, the Mohiyal Brahmins (also known as Hussaini Brahmins), had shown great valour in defending Prophet Muhammad's grandson at the battle of Karbala, and were highly respected by Shia Muslims.

Unlike the mild Mohanbabu, Raghunath was earthy and aggressive. He had been given the title of Dewan in recognition of his status as an owner of substantial farmland, in and around Khurd. Like the other landlords, he lived in the Dewanon-ka-mohalla in the village. At the time, Khurd had a large community of Hindus who co-existed peaceably with the majority Muslim population.

Dewan Raghunath was a tall, good-looking and somewhat regal figure in his turban and loose salwar kameez, much admired as he rode by on horseback to supervise work on his land. He reportedly cut such a dashing figure when he attended weddings that he was often mistaken for the bridegroom. Meanwhile, his young wife Kulwantidevi (also called Mangala), stayed home for the most part, looking after their children: Balraj, Rani and Som.

Tragedy struck in the 1930s, when Balraj (born on 6 June 1929) was still very young. His father died suddenly and mysteriously. As was his routine, Raghunath had woken up early, bathed and walked to the nearby halwai's shop to drink sweetened and thickened milk. He died soon after drinking the milk, causing speculation that he had developed a fatal allergy to some ingredient in it, or had been deliberately poisoned.

At the time, Kulwantidevi was visiting her parents in Gujarat (now in Pakistan) with Som, who was only a few months old. Balraj and Rani had stayed behind in Khurd with their grandmother Lakshmidevi.

Balraj, who was fond of reading, was sitting under the trees outside the house, looking through his books, when a distraught Lakshmidevi called him in. They set out to collect Raghunath's body in a horse carriage but midway encountered the entourage bringing it home. A telegram was sent to Kulwantidevi. According to tradition, the older son Balraj lit his father's funeral pyre. The young boy was visibly trembling with emotion, but he forced himself to go through the ceremony without crying. The memory of this crisis so early in life was to serve him well.

After Raghunath's death, the children and their mother became dependent to some extent on those relatives who could offer help. Lakshmidevi was also a widow and of her three sons, two had died before the age of 35. She cried often for her dead sons and her husband, much to the distress of her grandchildren.

The young Balraj still had his father's impressive bearing unforgettably stamped on his memory. He once saw a newspaper photograph of Jawaharlal Nehru on horseback and excitedly took it to Kulwantidevi, asking whether his father had looked like Nehru. She replied that his father had been even better looking. However, the memory of the two good-looking men on horseback conflated in his mind and Nehru was to become a surrogate father figure for him, as indeed he was for so many young men growing up in that idealistic age.

Meanwhile, school distracted the two older children from dwelling on the loss of their father. Balraj and Rani studied up to Class V in the local school. Though he always topped his class, Balraj was determined to improve himself and would study late into the night by the light of an oil lantern.

When Lakshmidevi complained that he was using up all the oil in the house, he would chide back, 'You are old, so you go to sleep—I will finish another bottle of oil and then sleep.' His mother did not scold him, because she was convinced that he 'would become someone or achieve something. No one has to tell him to study, he does it on his own.' She was proud of him, and suffered his stubborn behaviour and their fierce spats in silence. The bond between mother and son would remain strong throughout their lives. Balraj never allowed himself to forget that as the older son, he was responsible for looking after his mother and his siblings.

A fiercely independent boy, he hated being told what to do. He would not allow anyone to touch his books or help him get ready for school. Since bound books were not available at the time, the pages had to be sewn together, and he insisted on doing this himself, struggling with the thick thread and even thicker needle.

The village school only taught children till Class V; they would have to go to school in a neighbouring village if they wished to continue their lessons. Rani was not permitted to go so far away, but Balraj was insistent and rode several miles every day on horseback to the Khalsa school. His grandmother suggested he travel with an adult companion, but he resisted, and sat behind the man, pinching and kicking him until the family agreed to let him go alone. The horse, Bhagwani, and child soon became a familiar sight in the area.

The road to school was not easy. There was tall grass all around, and a stream to negotiate. At times, there were unpleasant encounters with miscreants, or other children looking for a fight, but Balraj successfully resisted all attempts to provide him with a chaperone.

Once, when Bhagwani was not well, he borrowed his uncle's mare which was known to be dangerously rebellious. 'A boy took a bet with him for one paisa and dared him to jump the mare over a wall,' Rani remembers with a laugh. 'He immediately did it, even though the mare was tough to control. But the boy did not pay up. Balraj did not forget either, and every day the boy would submit to a thrashing for not giving him the one paisa. Finally, his father who was a doctor came to complain to my uncle, Ramlal. But my brother explained that actually he was the aggrieved party because the doctor's son owed him one paisa!'

Balraj was certainly not a docile child. He meant well, but did things his own way. He upset his mother so much by arguing all the time that she gave up trying to discipline him and often locked him out of the house. He would then throw pebbles at the door, disturbing their neighbours who would have gone to bed by seven in the evening. In sheer embarrassment she would be forced to let him in.

His grandmother was another victim. She was almost blind by now, and her one comfort was her hookah. She would smoke, seated on a charpoy parked securely behind the door. But she could not smoke in peace if Balraj was around. He would remove the tobacco or the water, and sneak away before she could nab him. Another favourite prank was to try and break open her wooden trunk. He provoked her by saying he wanted to see her hidden khazana. The poor woman would flail around the room helplessly while he skipped and dodged her.

His mother and grandmother secretly enjoyed his arguments and antics. The boy's high-spiritedness livened up a sombre household which had sunk into gloom with too many early deaths. But when he courted physical danger, the two women became hysterical. He would climb all the way down into the village well to bathe, making his grandmother weep. 'I am already half dead, this boy will kill me,' she would lament. (Many years later, Balraj's wife would use the same words about their son, Sanjay. But by then the mischievous prankster in Balraj had sobered into respectability, and no one remembered the frights he used to give his own mother.)

The village games outside the house were simple: 'dhoop chaon', 'luka chippi', kabaddi. They would play hide-and-seek on moonlit nights. It was a world far removed from the political turmoil which characterized India at the time.

The freedom movement had been given a firm direction under Mahatma Gandhi by now, but the concept of a new country called Pakistan, carved out of India, had already come up for discussion in the early 1930s. Under continuous pressure, the

British agreed to give partial autonomy to the undivided country, and selective elections were held in 1937. The harmony was shortlived—all the elected Congress ministers resigned at the start of the Second World War as war had been declared without consulting Indian leaders. However, it was their profound belief that both imperialism and fascism had to be fought, and so with the willing collaboration of the Congress Party, Indian soldiers were sent to fight alongside the British.

In 1942, Singapore fell to the Japanese and many Indian soldiers were taken prisoner. Subhash Chandra Bose had escaped from India and after a meeting with Hitler, he had gone to Singapore where he founded the Indian National Army. In the same year, the Congress started the Quit India movement, after rejecting Sir Strafford Cripps's proposal of Dominion status. Later still, in 1946, a Cabinet Mission was sent to India by the Labour government in the UK which had won the 1945 election. The Mission suggested an alternative political formation: a loose confederation of India's provinces in which individual states could form regional groupings. Basically, it meant that the Muslim majority areas in India, in the east and the west, would have a chance to form quasi-autonomous regions. The people and the states could then choose whether they wanted to remain where they were or shift their allegiance. It was a difficult concept to accept for the nationalists, and it led to growing fears among the Muslim politicians that they would not get a fair deal in a Hindu majority India. Yet, it was their last chance to avoid partition.

The Mission failed to garner support among the political parties and by August 1946, when the Muslim League launched Direct Action Day, the partition of India began to look unavoidable.

None of this seemed to disturb the quiet, gentle pace of life among the Hindu and Muslim villagers in Khurd, or of the Dutt household, where life went on as usual.

Family support helped. Hansraj Chhibar, Balraj's uncle, often stayed with them and supervised the lands. When Balraj misbehaved, his uncle would break a branch off the ber tree, cut away the thorns and bellow for the boy. This was Balraj's cue to change into a black dhoti which helped him hide in the fields, especially in the dark. Or he would creep onto the terrace, jumping from roof to roof, till his uncle gave up. Sometimes he did get caught and was whipped, and this would make Rani cry. To her annoyance, he appeared to enjoy her distress if *she* ever got punished, and this is something that still puzzles her: why did he tease her when she was being chastised?

There was a softer side to Balraj as well, and his sister remembers him lying beside her on the terrace and singing folk songs celebrating the harvesting season:

Kankaan diyan faslan pakiyan ne
Pakwan pakandiyan jattiyan ne
Vaadi da mausam aya hai
Har passé noor savaiyan hai

(The wheat fields are golden and ripe
All the women are cooking dishes to celebrate
The weather feels glorious
And everywhere you can see a heavenly glow)

It was at rare moments like this that the young and quite naïve girl felt close to her precocious brother. Usually she was inarticulate and overwhelmed by his protectiveness. Balraj had already internalized the patriarchal order in which they lived. She remembers how strict he could be with her: she had to cover her head, she could not visit her friends' homes—they would have to come over. The village boys turned away when they saw her coming down the road with her friends, murmuring that 'Balraj's sisters are coming'. They were petrified of being beaten up by Balraj if they looked towards her or her friends.

Another childhood passion was fireworks. Around Lohri, celebrated in mid-January to mark the end of the coldest month, he would spend a week with the other village children, making crackers out of hollow reeds and gunpowder. Then he and his friends would gather at the gurudwara and fling lit crackers at each other. Once, a cracker caught fire in his pocket and he was burnt on the side. The scar was to remain for the rest of his life.

After Class VIII at Khalsa College, where he accumulated trophies for singing as well as for academics, it was time to move to Rawalpindi. He lived for a year with his mother's older sister, Lajwantidevi, who was also a widow. Then he shifted to DAV High School, Jhelum and probably stayed in a hostel until matriculation. A certificate (most likely a provisional certificate, dated 14 April 1948) states:

'This is to certify that Bal Raj, son of L. Raghu Nath Datta, of the D.A.V. High School Jhelum passed in the First Division the Matriculation Examination of the Punjab University held in March, 1945.
Passed also in ONE additional subject.'

Balraj wanted to study further, but his uncle insisted he join the army. Reluctantly, he went to Meerut for a medical check-up.

In 1946, Balraj was barely 16 and looked much younger than his age. The inspector at the army camp asked him seriously if he had run away from home. In any case, he was accepted as a clerk in Lucknow.

It was the first time Balraj was living so far away from home. By the time he came back to Khurd for a holiday, the mischievous boy had been replaced by a responsible army clerk laden with gifts of fruits, clothes and brightly coloured embroidered sandals. His mother kept aside her red sandals for his future wife, because as a widow she could not wear anything in an auspicious colour.

Meanwhile, Lakshmidevi had died. Rani was permitted less and less freedom, and had to be content with her crotchet and knitting. The youngest, Som, took no interest in school and spent most of his time playing with the other village boys. Unable to redeem the situation as yet, and tied down to his job, Balraj went back to work.

Lucknow, in the Muslim heartland of the United Provinces, had always been a city inhabited by the cultural cognoscenti, where Urdu shair-o-shairi flourished. Attracted by the richness of the language, Balraj developed a lifelong love for mushairas or poetry reading sessions, a relatively inexpensive pastime.

Slowly a more cosmopolitan culture began to envelop him. He made new friends and his horizon expanded. He started thinking of studying further, in a larger city, perhaps Bombay. But he needed to save money before he could take the plunge.

Balraj's fledgling dreams were overtaken by political events. Unable to reconcile the growing schisms between the Congress Party and the Muslim League, a victorious but debilitated British government, drained by the Second World War, appointed Lord Mountbatten in 1947 as the Governor General of India. He was to be the last Viceroy. The British had acceded to the demand to quit India, and on 3 June 1947, Mountbatten announced the partition of the country. With the creation of East and West Pakistan came the largest migration in the history of the world—around 12 million people, divided by religion, were to cross the new borders to their new homes. An unprecedented carnage followed, in which over two million people lost their lives, as each community massacred the other.

It was August 1947 when news of the newly formed state of Pakistan reached Khurd. Almost overnight, Kulwantidevi and her two children found themselves living not just in a separate state, but in a different country from Balraj. It was a frightening realization. They had to reach him quickly before the border closed.

They watched their Hindu neighbours wrap up their silver and jewellery and leave their homes in frighteningly vulnerable caravans. Slowly the Dewanon-ka-mohalla emptied out, as did the other Hindu areas of the village. Kulwantidevi felt she could not leave the house and the farms, and so they stayed on.

Soon looters arrived at the empty homes, and news of massacres in the surrounding villages reached them. Kulwantidevi was told that Khurd would be attacked next. A terrified Som was informed by his Muslim 'friend' that he would be the first to cut him up. Fortunately, before anything untoward happened, their relatives in Jhelum sent trucks with Sikh soldiers to protect and guide them out.

Apart from Kulwantidevi's family, others had to be evacuated as well—especially the elderly from neighbouring homes. They were all squeezed into the trucks, with very few possessions. As they settled down, Kulwantidevi told Hansraj that she had put all the family jewellery into an earthern pot and buried it in the grounds of the house. Her uncle said he would go back and look for it.

When he reached the house, he realized that his Muslim neighbours were suspicious at his reappearance. The haveli had rooms full of harvested crops and grain, and very soon, a few of them came over with large sheets and took away most of it. Realizing he could not trust his neighbours, Hansraj called in the farm labourers. They were also Muslims, but he felt he could rely on them since they had worked for him. He asked them to find the earthen pot and bring it to him later in Jhelum.

Meanwhile, the family was relocated to a relative's home in Jhelum. It was a large haveli with its own well, which meant they did not have to step out even to fetch water. The situation was still very tense. Kulwantidevi and her family were worried that Hansraj had not joined them. Finally, one day he did arrive, and within a fortnight the labourers arrived with the jewellery.

Outside the house was a rapidly filling refugee camp from where the frequently heard cry of 'Allah-O-Akbar' would chill their bones. As the situation worsened, Hansraj said that if the Muslims attacked, he would first slit the throats of Rani and her cousins, Pushpa, Santosh and Sundar (Ramlal's daughters) and then fight the enemy. There were many others like him, Punjabi men who felt compelled to slaughter their women like animals rather than have them raped by a mob.

Rani and her cousins clung to each other and wept. They could not imagine that their uncle who loved them so much could actually kill them. To make matters worse, news came of the massacre of Hindus on a train en route to India. They also learnt that a similar train was being prepared to evacuate them from Jhelum.

It was another uneasy day—Kulwantidevi lay ill, and Som was also sick—when the door burst open and a contingent of fierce Baluchis barged in. The family was roughly ordered out. Rani still remembers the chapatti left baking on the stove as they all stumbled out. A petrified Kulwantidevi forgot all about her jewellery, once again. They were to lose it forever.

Outside, men stood on either side of the road with guns, naked swords and knives, ready to attack. The family had to leave as they were, without taking anything from their homes. It was a stream of tremulous and disarmed Hindus that began the long journey to the invisible border, beyond which lay their future homes.

As the refugees began the long interminable march to the train, Ramlal was taunted by some of the Muslims with swords. 'Why don't you leave the girls behind? Why are you taking them?'

Somehow, half-fainting and sick with fright, the family boarded the train. It was as though they were waiting to be attacked—perhaps then, or perhaps when the train was moving. They froze with fear when an armed soldier climbed onto the train and looked around. It turned out that he had come from India to specially escort the Hindus. Probably to reassure them, he said there were 600 soldiers on the train and they had enough ammunition to fight for a week. A ripple of relief ran through the crowded compartments.

In Lucknow, the initial euphoria over India's independence had changed to grief for Balraj who was desperately worried about his family. He, the son of a Dewan and the rightful owner of his father's farmlands, still did not know that the moment India was partitioned, he had lost his entire inheritance, forever. Apart from his small salary, he was now a pauper.

The train carrying Balraj's family slowly reached Attari, and then finally Amritsar. With typical Punjabi generosity, people waited at the station with baskets full of paranthas and freshly cooked arhar daal, along with buckets of water. 'Bole So Nihal', chanted the waiting crowd and the trainload of passengers replied in tearful gratitude, 'Sat Sri Akal'. They were finally out of harm's way, after weeks of terror.

The displaced family longed to see Balraj, but they knew it would be difficult to go to him immediately. They would first be taken to a refugee camp and would have to wait till the situation was conducive for travel.

The train finally halted at Ambala and the family disembarked. Rani remembers that Ramlal's father-in-law was an official with a huge bungalow where everyone took shelter. They were fed, clothed and looked after with great generosity. A community kitchen was opened and large quantities of meat were cooked, and baskets of fruit distributed. Kulwantidevi stayed there for three months with her children, though she begged her cousin Ramlal to write and ask Balraj to fetch them. Because of the turmoil the family still hesitated to contact him. They couldn't be sure that their letter would reach him and they feared for his life, should he set out in search of them.

For Balraj, the entire episode was a nightmare. It had such an impact on his psyche that long after Partition, all his life in fact, he referred to himself as a 'refugee', even on the front page of his bio-data when he became a member of parliament.

During those three months, he listened anxiously to the radio and read the newspapers for any information about the trains coming in, but he had no idea where his family had disappeared, or how he could contact them. He hated the feeling of helplessness. He hunted for them in the ever increasing number of refugee camps, hoping that he would suddenly see his mother's smiling face, or his sister would run towards him, or that he would spot his brother playing. But none of this happened.

In interviews he gave years later, he said that he found his family at the refugee camp in Ambala entirely by accident. Even though, according to Rani, they did not suffer too much and were actually quite well looked after, it could not have been more humiliating for them: from a self-respecting, financially secure family, they were now at the mercy of strangers, forced to beg for shelter.

It was a very emotional reunion. Balraj took them to Lucknow and rented a three-bedroom house. But it was soon obvious that they were going to face severe financial problems. Though Balraj did not want to stay in the army, he bought some books to help him study for the post of lieutenant, so he could earn more money.

He also thought of joining the Air Force. In May 1948, he received a letter from the Short Service Commission recruiting officer at the Air Force station, Kanpur. It was addressed to Mr Balraj Dutt, Pratab Bagh Aliganj, Lucknow, and asked for a certificate stating that he was unmarried, in reference to an interview he had given on 15.5.48 at Kanpur.

He was now obsessed with getting a new job which would bring him a higher salary. And he knew for certain that his ambition to study further was slipping further and further away from him every day.

Then came the good news: the recently appointed governments of India and Pakistan had launched a policy of compensation and rehabilitation for those who had lost their property and homes during the forced migration. Tarlok Singh, a graduate of the London School of Economics, was appointed the Director General of Rehabilitation. It was a gigantic and unparalleled land resettlement made all the more difficult by the fact that approximately 2.7 million hectares had been abandoned by Hindus and Sikhs in West Punjab, whereas only 1.9 million hectares had been left behind by Muslims in East Punjab. By the time Tarlok Singh completed his work in November 1949, he and his team had made 250,000 land allotments. Balraj and his family got their allotment as well. But their land in West Punjab had been rich and fertile and now, like many others in India, they discovered that they had lost twice over: the land they were allotted was inferior and less than what they had owned.

His uncle Ramlal wrote to say that they had been allotted two houses with farmland in Mandoli (now in Ambala district, Haryana) as compensation for what they had lost in Khurd. The family quickly boarded a train and left for Mandoli.

While his family settled down, Balraj went out to look for work with a Sikh friend who ran a transport business at Etawah, near Kanpur. After a few months, he returned despondent. He still wanted to go to college, but he couldn't because he thought it was his responsibility to arrange a marriage for his sister. He told his mother, 'Every time I try to plan something for myself, she comes in front of me like a wall—I can't do anything until I get her married.'

Balraj turned to his relatives for help, but most of them were still recovering from the trauma of Partition, and organizing a wedding was the last thing on their minds.

He went then to Delhi, probably to some distant relatives. There was great excitement at the Mandoli home when his all-important letter arrived. By then Rani had learnt to read Urdu. She opened the envelope, and the photograph of a handsome young man fell out. The name at the back, written in English, Hindi and Urdu, was Balkrishan Bali. He was to marry Rani. The 19-year-old Balraj had found a husband for his sister!

Upon his return to Mandoli with the proposal, Balraj leapt around with joy. The only hitch was that the boy refused to 'see' the girl (a euphemism for the engagement ceremony). The usual ritual of the girl serving tea to the intended groom was done away with because Balkrishan Bali told Rani's mother and uncle that he did not need to see her. He had met Balraj Dutt and that was enough. She must look like her brother, he said, and the matter was left at that. He was actually right—both brother and sister looked a great deal like their mother.

Within three months, the couple who had never seen each other got married. No one was happier than Balraj. He tried on Rani's entire trousseau, teasing her all the while.

Even though he was ecstatic that his sister was settling down, Balraj was a sentimental man at heart. It rained on the day of the wedding, and Balraj wept the most. When asked why, he said he would miss her: 'Now whenever I come home she won't be there.' Though they did not know it then, Rani would remain close to him throughout his life.

With his mother now settled in Mandoli amidst her family, and Rani married, he felt Kulwantidevi was happy at last. A country woman, she loved nurturing her crops, tending her cows, drinking in the fresh air. Life had snatched everything from her and then miraculously, some of it had come back. Like her son, she was a free spirit, more than capable of looking after herself and Som. Within a few months, Balraj realized that there was nothing to hold him back any more.

Ever conscious of his 'refugee' status, he had got a 'character certificate' from his senior officer a few years earlier.

It read:

Character Certificate

This is to certify that No. 3939 Civ. Clk. Balraj Datta s/o Raghu Nath Datta a Refugee from West Punjab (Jhelum) is personally known to me.
He comes of a respectable Mohyal family and is a promising young man with good physique and excellent character.
Dated 18 Mar. 48
Signed by Lt Colonel
Comd. R.T.A.S.C. Records (MT)

This was the only recommendation he had, but it was as though his sister's marriage had lifted a huge burden from his shoulders, and he could concentrate on building a career, though he still had no idea what it would be.

A new decade had started: it was 1950, he was twenty years old; he must have felt that it was time to move on. His mother gave him all the money she had: fifty rupees. With that, and a small bundle of belongings, he took a train to Bombay.

Château Marine
1930s-1940s

While Balraj and his family were being forced apart and then miraculously reunited, Fatima was growing up into a self-confident young woman, studying at Queen Mary's Convent in Bombay.

Jaddanbai by now was a well established matriarch of Bombay, renowned for her knowledge of music and her cultural soirées. The family continued to live well, though given the vagaries of film production, there were times when Jaddanbai's career would plummet. At such difficult moments she toyed with the idea of leaving Bombay forever.

'There was a time after the family came to Bombay when they did not get the sort of response that they were looking for, and it was difficult for them to survive,' says Zahida, quoting her father Akhtar Hussain. 'So Jaddanbai said, "*Chalo bhaiya shaayad boriya bistra baand kar kahin doosra shahar dekhen? Yahan to mamla jam nahin raha.* (Shall we just wrap up our belongings and go elsewhere? Nothing seems to be working out here.)"

'There was a nice *sone ka kada* (a golden bangle) on her hand. She pulled it off and said, "Go off and sell it." The money came. She called the servants and said, "All the important people I know in town"—and she knew all the best people—"I'll call them over. There will be a party at our home."'

It was a masterful strategy. When the guests arrived, she announced sadly that the family was leaving Bombay the next day, and had decided to have one last mehfil. The guests, who

were rich and used to requests for money, succumbed to the
more subtle ploy. They asked with concern, '*Bibi kyon ja rahi
hain, kyon* pack *kar rahi hain?* (Why are you packing up and
leaving?)' 'No, no, we cannot stay here,' she replied. 'Nothing is
happening for us here. We will go back to our village...'

The guests, predictably, were aghast. How could she, a patron
of the arts and so talented herself, go away and live in a village?
'You cannot leave Bombay,' they declared. '*Aap bataiye ki kya
karna hain* (Tell us what we can do).'

'I am thinking of launching a film company and making a
film,' she replied.

'*Theek hai*, we will finance it,' came the reply. And Jaddanbai
was back in business again.

'That is how things were done. She would try to manouevre
(her way), because they went through lots of ups and downs,'
says Zahida.

None of the films launched by her production house created
a storm in the Arabian Sea, but they brought in enough money
to keep the family afloat. In any case, they were not dependent
on her talent alone any more; her sons had grown up. The 'golden
voiced' Akhtar was attempting to get a foothold as an actor and
director; the younger son, Anwar, was soon to get a break as an
actor. And Mohanbabu was ever ready to work on any business
offered to him.

In the 3000 sq. ft flat in Château Marine, the first bedroom
belonged to Jaddanbai, Mohanbabu and Nargis; Akhtar Hussain,
his wife Iqbal and their seven children were in the next room.
Anwar Hussain with his wife Rashida and their five children
were further down in the third room. Apart from these 19 people,
there was a constant stream of guests.

Rehana remembers, 'One day, we saw a ghoda gaadi arrive
with 8-10 people in it. We were very young, and we saw what
we thought were some "natives" coming to the house with some
funny-looking suitcases—village folk. Everyone asked, who are
these candidates? And they said actually they were relatives from
Chilbilla.'

It goes to show how much Jaddanbai's lifestyle had changed,

that her granddaughter referred to the relatives from Chilbilla (they were Jaddanbai's brother and his family) as 'natives'.

Jaddanbai had told her older son in 1946, '*Ai Akhtar, humko hamara bhai bahut yaad aa raha hai, to jake gaon se apne mamu ko le aao* (I am missing my brother a lot, so go to the village and bring your uncle here).' Akhtar set off for Chilbilla as there was no phone connection to the tiny village in Uttar Pradesh.

'So he took the train to Allahabad and landed in Chilbilla. Your sister is missing you very much, he said, and Mamu said he was also missing her very much. So Zulkadar mamu and Bismillah aunty and their sons Asghar and Kaisar, and the bahus and Asghar's son Salim, all came in the tonga with their suitcases,' recounts Rehana.

The arrangements made for them were simple: seven more charpoys were laid out at night in the corridor outside the bedrooms, and cleared away in the morning.

As the family fortunes improved, separate cooks were hired for Mughlai and Western food, reminiscent of the arrangements in Motilal Nehru's house. At one point, the family owned eleven cars and employed seven chauffeurs. Except for another family which had a Buick, no one else in the building owned a car.

'(We did not) call out for the servants. They would stand at the door, awaiting orders. She turned around, and they would run up to ask, "Ji Bibi?" Everyone called my grandmother Bibi,' recalls Zahida.

When Pandit Nehru came to Bombay, Jaddanbai asked for an appointment with him. Instead of the perfunctory five minutes allotted to her at the Raj Bhavan, he spent two hours with her. As Zahida points out, they must have had a lot to catch up on, for this was the first time they were meeting since the Allahabad days.

Château Marine continued to echo with music even though Jaddanbai did not sing any more. She had stopped performing in public many years ago, and now she quit singing for films altogether, saying her voice was no longer what it used to be. The family believes that jealousy drove someone to mix sindhoor in her drink, thus wrecking her voice forever. Music was still heard at home though, because Nargis was taught the sitar by Vilayat Khan, and Akhtar sang, mostly for pleasure. He organized large mehfils at which Jaddanbai's friends, including Bade Ghulam Ali Khan, Allah Rakha and Amir Khan—little known at the time—performed in front of a specially invited audience.

In years to come, these artistes would become internationally known musicians and singers, but in the early 1940s, only a true connoisseur would have recognized their talent and potential. In those days, most artistes were forced to live on the edge of poverty. After Partition, Muslim performers and singers had to struggle even harder to receive state assistance and patronage. On the other side of the border, Pakistan did very little to preserve this largely extempore style of singing. The music was taught through an oral tradition and there were no written texts. If the guru of a certain gharana died or could not sing any more, much of the musical tradition he represented was lost with him.

Jaddanbai could empathize with these performers and welcomed them warmly, even providing food and shelter if they needed it.

The actress Shammi (her real name is Nargis Rabadi) is a Parsi who was brought up in a very conservative environment. She was young and naïve when she first met Jaddanbai, while looking for work: 'I met her in a production office. She was a very friendly person, but started warning me about the person I had gone to meet. She said, "Don't do this film, this fellow will do this and that," and started abusing him. I was so shocked I didn't know what to do. Then she asked me if I liked music. We chatted a bit. She said, "Okay, you must come to the house for a function." I was so frightened of her, I couldn't say no. I went. It was the first time I met everybody (in the film industry). The mehfils were quite popular and went on until two in the morning. She (Jaddanbai) knew all the artistes who performed on a friendly basis. (That is, they were not paid for their performance.) Everyone used to be frightened of her, even her elder son Akhtar.'

According to Shammi, by the time she met Jaddanbai, Mohanbabu was no more. From all accounts she severely missed her soft-spoken spouse who had stood by her through all the hard times, but she was a modern woman who refused to become a recluse: the evenings of music and song continued. Throughout her life, it was music that had sustained her, so why would she abandon it at this critical juncture?

The renowned Hindustani vocalist Pandit Jasraj got to know her well, as he told her grandson Ishrat. He and his brother Pandit Pratap Narain met Jaddanbai when they were very young. They had arrived in Bombay looking for work after their father's sudden death. Pandit Motiramji had been a talented vocalist trained in the Mewati gharana. He was often invited to sing in the presence of royalty.

The two brothers had no work or money and sometimes no food. Someone advised them to go to Jaddanbai. She recognized them and inquired about their father. When they told her about their search for work, she summoned her driver, Kasam, and took the two young boys to a studio. Pandit Jasraj remembers her accosting a stout businessman there, and asking him to give them work. Obviously used to such requests, he said, '*Achcha bibi*, when our film starts I will give them work.' But she refused to move, insisting that he give them work straight away. Succumbing to her strident persuasion, he called the manager and hired the young Jasraj for Rs 40 and his older brother for Rs 100.

Château Marine was a gathering place for many future cinema legends, then just starting out, such as Kamal Amrohi, Amanullah Khan, K. Asif and Dilip Kumar. Zahida recalls that none of the men had the temerity to sit beside Jaddanbai on the sofa. Instead, they would sit around her deferentially. When Kamal Amrohi, who would go on to make the classic *Pakeezah* and marry the legendary Meena Kumari, turned up penniless from Amroha, Jaddanbai immediately sized up the situation. She ordered Iqbal, '*Akhtar ka pyjama-kurta nikaalkar inhe deejiye. Jaiye miyaan, nahaiye dhoiye, pet bhar khana khaiye*. (Give him Akhtar's pyjama-kurta. Please go, bathe and eat to your stomach's content.)' Then after he had bathed, she asked, '*Haan miyan, sunaiye, kya likha hai* (Yes, now tell me, what have you written)?' She was obsessed with the idea of nurturing talent.

Other film artistes like B.R. Chopra, Ramanand Sagar and Majrooh Sultanpuri worked at Jaddanbai's Rangmahal Studio in Dadar. Chopra was still a journalist and used to come to Rangmahal to collect information for his stories and articles. Akhtar helped with the home productions and the general running of Rangmahal Studio.

But not a leaf moved without Jaddanbai's permission.

Even the household revolved around her. While her daughters-in-law, or 'dulhans' as she called them, had to look after the 'choolha chowki' (the domestic chores), she kept herself free to pursue her work in films and music. The elder dulhan, Iqbal, was encouraged to remain indoors and in purdah. Fortunately, Iqbal acquiesced. Though she was educated and was conversant with both Persian and Urdu, she preferred to remain in the background.

While Jaddanbai did not discriminate between her daughter and her daughters-in-law in material things, she could not be as liberal with her bahus as she was with Fatima. She realized that in most 'good' homes, the daughters-in-law were discouraged from working or stepping outside the house.

Kusum Sethi, a neighbour, was six and a half years younger than Fatima, but became her good friend: 'After Partition, in 1947, my uncle Amrit Lal Sethi came to Bombay from Lahore. My mother was a widow, so all of us, my brother, sister and I, came with him. The Jaddanbai clan used to live across the floor from us. I was in school, in Class VI. I used to come from school and would still be in my uniform, when Fatima (or Fatty, as I called her) used to come from shooting. She had started acting in films while I was studying at the Cathedral School.' It must have been difficult for Fatima to see her new friend pursuing a normal education. She had loved her own school, but her attendance had become erratic. She continued to learn on her own, and became a voracious reader but increasingly, other demands were being made on her time.

Kusum says, 'Her mother was also very strict with us. She would tell us in the holidays, "Learn how to cook, how to knit." You won't believe it, but Fatty was a marvellous cook. She learnt from Iqbal, who was a very good cook. She looked up to Iqbal a lot. They were very fond of each other. She was like a second mother to her because Jaddanbai was busy with her movies. And Iqbal was a lovely lady, which is why you find her children are very good. They are not pompous. They are very family-oriented." Iqbal, though only nine years older than Fatima, treated her like a daughter, and seemed to fit Jaddanbai's definition of a dulhan perfectly.

Rehana says, 'My mother was 15 when she got married and Nargis was around six (perhaps closer to seven). My father was 18. My mother's parents used to live in Bhindi Bazaar (in Bombay). My grandmother was a Kashmiri and my grandfather was Afghani. They probably lived in Amritsar and before that, in Rawalpindi."

Obviously they did not have as much money or the same social standing as Jaddanbai. But she did not mind at all as she climbed four storeys up to their flat, drawn by the desire to find an attractive, 'innocent' girl for her son.

A marriage broker had suggested the match. Akhtar was handsome, but says his daughter Rehana, 'a big flirt, flirting with all his film heroines.' Jaddanbai was concerned about his 'affairs' and wanted a bahu like 'Pearl S. Buck's heroine in *The Good Earth*.' She must have heard of the book, perhaps even read it or seen the film, which was a 1937 MGM release.

She herself was nothing like the traditional housewife. Well-groomed, she wore sleeveless blouses and was often spotted with a box of cigarettes in her hand. She was a member of the Turf Club and a keen punter. Her children went to English-medium schools. In fact, she could have been the inspiration for *Madam Fashion*. Yet she was determined to get a docile, pretty bahu for her son, so that he would stop philandering and settle down. It was important that he did not stray because Jaddanbai still wanted to make films using in-house talent and, as far as possible, she wanted all hands on deck.

A curious Fatima had gone with her mother to meet the prospective bride who had been described as being very lovely. Iqbal lived with her parents and sister in a cramped two-room flat, and was cooking in the back room when Jaddanbai and Fatima arrived. There were no servants in the house.

After Jaddanbai had seen her, Fatima also went in to meet 'this beautiful vision, completely white, wearing a salwar kameez, chunni on her head, making chapattis on the tawa.' Fatima held her chin and tilted up her face to ask, 'Are you my bhabhi?' Iqbal took the young Fatima on her lap and hugged her. Within four days, Iqbal and Akhtar were married.

It was to be a long and sometimes painful relationship since Akhtar still had a number of women friends. But, as Jaddanbai had correctly estimated, Iqbal's prayers and her pious nature kept her from rebelling. Not only that, she actually rose to Akhtar's defence even in arguments with her beloved Fatima. Her acceptance of her fate helped to bind together a family that might have scattered under different circumstances.

In any case, Akhtar was the favourite son, and in Jaddanbai's eyes he could do no wrong. He always had a role in her productions. Anwar too acted in films, but these were usually outside the home banner.

Akhtar's son Arif says of his uncle, 'He was introduced to films by A.R. Kardar, our neighbour on Marine Drive…Jaddanbai gave a break in all her films to Akhtar as a hero. She was biased towards him, perhaps because he was the first-born. So Anwar complained to me that "he is the golden boy and I am nothing".'

'Yet he was spoilt too. A great raconteur, he enjoyed the good life as much as his brother, pursuing macho interests such as body building and going for shikar in these huge imported cars we used to have—Buicks and Chryslers—to Bhopal or wherever there were game reserves, with his friends, a bunch of actors like Yaqub, Suresh and Agha.'

Rehana adds, 'Anwar was a *dil phek aashik* (he wore his heart on his sleeve) and very charming, especially with women. He called every woman "darling". This darlingfying everybody would irritate his wife. But he was a good actor, and did a very good play called *Pathan ki Musibat*, which was staged in Bombay at the Opera House. It completed golden and silver jubilees all over the country.'

Nargis would later joke that her son Sanjay was more like her two lafanga brothers, and less like the straitlaced Sunil Dutt. Thanks to them, she had observed situations where men and women mingled freely and romance was just a jingle of the bangles away. Among Akhtar's many girlfriends was Reba Gupta, Protima Bedi's mother. She would tease him into singing duets with her and then tell Iqbal that it was only because Iqbal was so nice that she was not going to steal him away. The actress Mumtaz's mother, Naaz, though married, also adored Akhtar, and often regretted that she had to address him as 'Akhtar bhaiya'.

Anwar had married young but was firmly attached to the company of his girlfriends, including Begum Para, Shammi and Protima Dasgupta, whom he had worked with. These may have been completely innocent relationships, says Shammi, but were often misunderstood; realizing the truth, Jaddanbai restrained herself from being too censorious.

It was Anwar's first wife Shehzadi who Jaddanbai disapproved of very strongly. Anwar and Shehzadi lived together for only a year, during which their son Sarwar was born. It was an unhappy time, and ultimately Shehzadi took the battle to court, but Jaddanbai won the case and kept custody of her grandson.

Rehana remembers, 'My mother Iqbal had just had a stillborn baby. Sarwar was nine months old, so my mother nursed him. As a result, he always addressed my mother as Badi Amma and my father was Bade Abba. Then Jaddanbai said, "*Main Iqbal ki bahen ko laaongi,* my *Good Earth ki bahu* (I will bring Iqbal's sister to be my daughter-in-law. After all, she is my *Good Earth* bahu)."'

She believed that Iqbal's sister Rashida would be just the kind of stabilizing influence Anwar needed, since Iqbal had turned out to be a perfect daughter-in-law.

Delicate, beautiful Rashida was very young at the time and still played simple children's games with Fatima. Hell-bent on reforming her son, Jaddanbai ignored all well-meaning advice. Rashida's mother pointed out that she was not ready for marriage but Jaddanbai used all her negotiating skills, insisting, 'I want a girl from your house.'

The nikaah was read out. But it was soon obvious that the two were very different from each other: Anwar was used to a carefree life, and liked to party, smoke and drink, while Rashida was a child. The stress of having a husband who wanted a glamorous lifestyle, and the later responsibility of five children took their toll. As Rashida grew older, she slowly withdrew from reality.

Rehana says, 'She still lives with us, and is very subdued sometimes, very aggressive at others. She was diagnosed as schizophrenic. Anwar Uncle took her to the best psychiatrists, but nothing helped.'

For once, Jaddanbai had miscalculated.

Shammi says, 'Rashida has not been all right for as long as I have known her. Bibiji used to go to all the astrologers to find a remedy. We used to try everything, even *jadu tona* (spells) because we hoped that she would be all right.' Shammi, who accompanied Nargis to some of these jadu tona sessions, says they invariably ended in giggles over the shaman while Rashida showed no improvement.

So, despite the men getting married, nothing really changed. While Akhtar continued to enjoy the cool sea breeze with his friends on the steps of Château Marine, Anwar would race his friends down the open stretch of Marine Drive on a motorcycle. They did not have regular jobs, but they were talented and life was full of promise.

Growing up in this luxurious but unconventional household, Fatima still had time for normal activities.

Kusum says, 'We were like two peas in a pod. We did everything together. There were just three or four girls in the building. Apart from us, the others were very studious. There were 15 boys, including more than half a dozen of the Hussains. We would play with the boys, and what a hammering we would get! Her mother (Jaddanbai) would say, "You are girls, so live like girls." And she would fight with my mother. My mother was rather meek. She would answer, "Bibiji, you tell them, they don't listen to me." We were tomboys. We even played French cricket since there was no room in the building to play proper cricket, so when you hit the ball you swung the bat around you. That was how you took runs.

'There was only one maidan nearby and I remember that sometimes we would go off with Akhtar to play football with the boys. We would have great fun. Or we would sit outside Château Marine and crack the smuttiest of jokes. No one who walked by Château Marine escaped our remarks. People would be scared to pass by, they would say, "These girls will tease us." We also used to hire cycles for 4 annas an hour and go cycling with friends on Sunday morning. There was hardly any traffic on Marine Drive. It was great fun. We were always being blasted by our parents to be more lady-like. "You behave like boys!" they would scream. But we would have a ball.'

Rashida was withdrawing into her own world, and Baby Fatima, or Baby as she was fondly called, began helping out with her brothers' children. She was especially close to Akhtar's daughters whom she got to indulge even more after she became an actress with money of her own.

As she became financially independent, Zahida says, 'She did so much for us. She looked after us. The three of us sisters were her responsibility. She educated us, fed us, clothed us. She would even carry me on her shoulders into the pool at the CCI and toss me in and say, "Learn to save yourself." She was an excellent swimmer, a graceful diver, wonderful with knitting, handicraft, and a polyglot—she spoke Punjabi, Gujarati and Marathi. So talented. She looked small but she was larger than life.'

They idolized their aunt; in their eyes, she could do no wrong. Yet, she was the first to realize that the atmosphere at Château Marine was far from ideal for growing girls, and they were sent off to boarding school for a short spell. Her nieces would call their aunt 'Hitler' but were happily resigned to her discipline.

Of her generosity, Zahida says, 'Amongst us brothers and sisters, Rehana was my mother's favourite. So for Rehana's birthday, clothes and gifts would be distributed but on mine, I would be told I couldn't have a party. My mother would say, "I have no money, so you will have to wear Rehana's old clothes."

'My aunt would then buy me the most beautiful dress, with

ribbons and shoes and socks, and order sandwiches and chips and a cake from Bombelli's. At lunch break, she would send a servant to school with a note saying, "Call your friends for a tea party, it's your birthday!" It was all very last minute, so only a couple of friends would show up, and a lot of the food would be wasted.' This did not deter Fatima from doing the same thing the next year, all over again.

She was particularly keen to give them a good childhood because it was something she herself never had. She had worked very hard as a child actor and then, at 14, she'd had to abandon school to begin her acting career as an adult film star.

Like Balraj, Fatima was keen to carry on with her education. After all, she was the first girl in her family to go to an English-medium convent school, and remembering her father's abandoned ambition, she dreamt of being a doctor. This was in 1943, in pre-Partition India, when it was very unusual for a girl from her background to have such aspirations. As it turned out, fate—and her family—had other plans for her.

Nargis
1940-1950

It was billed as 'An artistic picturisation of the will of Providence bursting with mirth and music.' The film, ironically, was called *Taqdeer* and it changed Fatima's life completely.

Cinema, strangely enough, had never seemed an attractive option to the young girl. She was to say later, with unconcealed regret, 'It all started way back when as a child I acted in my mother's films. I was a happy carefree girl with lots of friends. Suddenly I noticed that my classmates had begun to avoid me.

'One day, I cried to my teacher, "Nobody wants to play with me!" The Principal of the school called me in and gave me a lecture on the evil influence of films. She said she hoped I would not besmirch the name of the school and that she would pray for me.

'Pray for me? But what was wrong with me? I was not in any trouble and I had not committed any sin. Why then, should anyone pray for me? I could not understand until I learnt that my best friend—we were neighbours—was not allowed to play with me.

'And then I knew. It had something to do with my working in films. It was something bad. And I cried till I could cry no more. But when the tears were exhausted, I began to think. I thought, my mother works in films. But she is not bad. She is the most wonderful woman in the world...' (*Filmfare*, 1 January 1960)

For a brief period of five years, between the ages of seven and twelve, Fatima could concentrate on school and carry on being a tomboy, swimming, cycling and playing cricket. She had acted as Baby Rani in her mother's films, such as *Talash-e-Haq* and *Hridaya Manthan*, but now she could slam the make-up box shut because she was too old for 'baby' roles and too young to be a heroine.

In 1942 she reportedly acted in *Tamanna* and *Pardanasheen*, but clearly, neither film made much of an impact, because little information survives about them. But it was only a matter of time before one of the many visitors to her mother's house, always on the lookout for fresh faces, spotted Fatima, ending her carefree childhood forever.

Mehboob Khan, one of India's most successful directors, and the man who gave Nargis her iconic role in *Mother India* fourteen years later, was a good friend of Jaddanbai's. He was one of those who often dropped in at Château Marine to sit around discussing various dreams and projects. As a teenager with the less romantic name of Ramjan Khan, he had run away from his home in Billimora (Gujarat) to join the film industry. Not disheartened by his early experiences as an extra, he learnt the trade and eventually set up his own company, Mehboob Productions, in 1942. Earlier, in 1935, he had acted with Jaddanbai in *Naachwali*.

Mehboob's films were an interesting pastiche of social realism, representing a changing nation moving towards modernity while still mired in the feudal past. His opening montage of a hammer and sickle was accompanied by the words '*Muddai lakh bura chahe to kya hota hai, vahi hota hai jo manzoore khuda hota hai* (Man may wish any evil but that alone happens which God wills).' It was a spiritual counterpoint to the Communist icon but then, such a mix of the rational and the religious has never been unusual in India, especially in the world of cinema.

By the time he decided to cast Fatima, Mehboob had directed close to a dozen films, some of which, like *Ek Hi Raasta* and *Aurat*, presented heroic women trying to outwit their gender-driven destiny. *Aurat*, starring Sardar Akhtar, was the precursor to *Mother India*. It was the story of Radha (Sardar Akhtar), a simple villager and single mother struggling to pay off her debts, ward off natural disasters and bring up two sons, one of whom is a serial delinquent. The 'impressively languid' (as she is described in the *Encyclopaedia of Indian Cinema*) Sardar Akhtar was an

Urdu stage actress who later married Mehboob.

Ali Raza, a screenplay writer who worked with Mehboob on some of his best films, including *Andaaz* and *Mother India,* remembers how Fatima was persuaded to act in *Taqdeer*: 'Mehboob sahib was looking for a new actress for his film. In those days there was a beautiful partnership between Mehboob sahib and Aga Jaani Kashmiri (the legendary screenplay writer). He had a great role in establishing Mehboob Productions. The first film that Mehboob produced, *Najma,* and later *Taqdeer* and *Humayun,* he wrote them all. He was an ustad (master), my mamu (mother's brother).

'So Mehboob was looking for a girl. It was the monsoon season. Mehboob and my mamu were passing by Marine Drive, the roads were flooded with water, and so was the car. They wanted shelter from the rain and ran into Jaddanbai's house. There they spotted Nargis. And they decided this was the girl... I didn't ever regard her as very beautiful, but they may have noticed her vivacity. It was more eye judgement than a screen test.'

Fatima was persuaded by her family to go to the studio with Mehboob. Casually, he asked her if she would like to see herself on screen. She agreed, and was told to sit on a sofa, given a piece of paper and asked to say the lines. To her surprise, when she finished, everyone started clapping and said, '*Pede lao.* New heroine *mil gayee.* (Bring some sweets to celebrate. We've found the new heroine.)' Then Mehboob took the young girl aside and said there would be a huge financial loss if she refused the role. Tricked into submission, she tearfully agreed. (Interview in *Filmfare,* February 1978)

When they returned to the house in the evening, Mehboob announced that he had found his heroine for *Taqdeer*. The fourteen-year-old would act opposite Motilal, a suave 33-year-old actor. Akhtar was thrilled: there was going to be a new star on the Jaddanbai firmament. Also another source of income for the family whose fortunes were always fluctuating dramatically. There were often more than 30 dependants (including the domestic staff) in the house and usually only one earning member. Now the young Fatima would become part provider too.

Mehboob was not very happy with Fatima's name, however. He thought names beginning with 'n' were lucky; it may have been because his first film under his own banner was called *Najma*. He finally chose the name Nargis, and it did suit her, especially in her later, more elegant, white-sari-clad years.

Taqdeer was a film from the lost-and-found genre of Hindi cinema. It was set in the Kumbh Mela, the world's largest religious gathering, held every 12 years. The Kumbh has been made notorious by Indian film scriptwriters as the place where families accidentally lose their children. (As it happens, families do deliberately 'lose' unwanted members like ageing relatives and parents in the chaos, though mainstream Hindi films, of course, prefer to ignore this reality.)

Taqdeer begins with just such an unhappy accident: the daughter of Justice Jamnaprasad is lost at the festival. To console the distraught mother, the father adopts a young boy. In one of the hilarious asides in the plot, the foster mother continues to think of the little boy as her 'daughter' and even addresses him as 'beti'. Meanwhile, the real daughter grows up into Shyama

(Nargis), a glamorous dancer trained by her impresario foster father. By another coincidence, Jamnaprasad's adopted son Babu (Motilal) wanders into the theatre and falls in love with Shyama. The rest of the film focuses on disentangling the plot until everyone ends up with their correct identities and Shyama and Babu can be allowed a life together.

Despite the hackneyed plot, the film did quite well. *Filmindia* gave it a good review:

> 'Taqdeer' Becomes a Purposeful Entertainer!
> Nargis Makes a Brilliant Screen Debut!

The reviewer picks a few holes in the story and the music direction, and then goes on to say, 'In Nargis, the picture introduces a new girl to the Indian Screen. Realising that she appears on the screen for the first time, she could be said to have done excellently, especially so in the emotional situations of the story wherein she has gamely responded to the demands of her director and has at places done better than several of our seasoned stars put together. Her success is the triumph of Mehboob, who has in addition photographed her very carefully and thus helped a lot to glamourise her.'

This was the sort of review that any newcomer would have died for. The truth was that Nargis was too young for the role. Watching the film now, one can appreciate her composure and charm, which at times offsets her stiff recitation of dialogues that were obviously beyond her years. Romancing a man old enough to be her father also put her in an awkward predicament; his prancing like an eager young colt is even more unconvincing because of her youth. Nargis was never an accomplished dancer, so she was at a distinct disadvantage in her very first film as an 'adult' actress. The clumsiness that she managed to sometimes cover up in later films is very apparent in her tiny, hesitant schoolgirl gestures.

But Nargis had Jaddanbai's chutzpah, and by the time she signed *Humayun*, her next film with Mehboob, she had polished her skills in *Ismat*, a Fazli Brothers film, and *Anban*. Despite her initial awkwardness on screen, she had youth on her side, and a clear Urdu diction. The other heroines of the time may not have been much older, but they were already beginning to look jaded. Many of them had annoying affectations and were handicapped by unimpressive dialogue delivery, though a few were very good singers. Nargis was pitted against actresses like Leela Chitnis, Renuka Devi, Kanan Devi, Vanmala, Sitara Devi, Shanta Apte, Sadhana Bose, Nurjehan, Shanta Hublikar, 'Fearless' Nadia, Mumtaz Shanti, Shobhana Samarth, Khurshid, Naseem Banu, Suraiya and Durga Khote. It was a formidable list, but the only actress who might have truly challenged her over time was Nurjehan, who had opted to go to Pakistan after Partition. The other great beauty, Naseem Banu, chose early retirement.

Suraiya was another competitor. She and her mother lived very close to Château Marine. A common friend and neighbour was Shanti Mahendroo, the daughter of the legendary Rai Bahadur Chunilal, who set up Filmistan.

Shanti remembers, 'Nargis was 14 years old and was already in the movies. I could not get too close to her; the trouble was that I was very friendly with Suraiya, and Nargis's mother did not like that because there was competition between them. Suraiya was our next-door neighbour, and she was already in films. She came from Lahore. Mumtaz Begum, her mother, was very pretty, with light eyes. A very majestic woman, the way she used to dress up, she had a lot of style. She was also a singer from Lahore. I met Suraiya when she was 15. Her mother used to tell me, "Why don't you join films? You have good features..." She always said that Suraiya didn't have a proper chin.'

The popular press stoked the rivalry between the two actresses by comparing them constantly, down to the cars they owned. Nargis bought a low-seated Riley sports car and had it painted black and white. Not to be outdone, Suraiya got herself a custom-made American Cadillac and painted it orange and white. Then she had curtains strung up so that no one could peer in.

Their attire was equally remarked upon: while Nargis would appear off-screen sans make-up and wearing a white saree and two plaits, Suraiya would be thickly made-up and dressed like a Mughal princess, loaded with diamonds. Since they both lived on Marine Drive, crowds would begin to gather at the time of the day that they were expected to leave for the studios.

Their love affairs were tracked with equal zeal. The popular number from their hit film *Barsaat* became the leitmotif for the romance between Nargis and Raj Kapoor:

Jiya bekaraar hai
Aayee bahar hai
Aaja mere balma
Tera intezaar hai

(My heart is impatient
Spring is here
Why don't you come, my love
I am waiting for you)

Whereas Suraiya's romance with Dev Anand inspired the following ditty on the streets of Bombay:

Jiya bekarar hai
Suraiya bimar hai
Aaja Doctor Dev Anand
Tera intezar hai

(Her heart is impatient
Suraiya is unwell
Come over Dr Dev Anand
She is waiting for you)

(Adi Katrak, 'Nargis and Suraiya: The Legend Continues', *Filmfare,*
7 March 1975)

The one big advantage that Suraiya had, chin or no chin, was her ability to sing. However, she lost this edge over Nargis with the advent of playback music, and Lata Mangeshkar. Once the legendary composer Naushad had helped brush up her Urdu diction, Lata became the voice of several heroines for more than sixty years, starting in the early 1940s. She was a boon for actors like Nargis who simply could not sing. Soon, playback singers became the norm and the importance of the actor-singer declined.

Nargis had a few years to establish herself before the real competition showed up in the form of Madhubala, Geeta Bali and Meena Kumari. Madhubala, with her dazzling smile and perfect features, was to make her debut as an adult actress only in 1947, with *Neel Kamal*, when she was fourteen years old. Incidentally, she starred opposite Raj Kapoor.

Geeta Bali, all curly locks and natural grace, started her film career at 12. She was 18 when she won recognition in *Suhaag Raat* (1948). Meena Kumari, who played the tragic heroine to perfection, was perhaps the best actress among the four. She had acted as a child but was only taken seriously after *Baiju Bawra*, in 1952. She was 19 at the time.

None of these three had the sort of enterprising family that Nargis had. When other producers were not filming with her, her own brother Akhtar Hussain would launch a film with her. Though Madhubala, Geeta Bali and Meena Kumari all supported their families financially, none of their families had the clout of the family at Château Marine.

The clout was important because films—good, bad, indifferent—kept coming Nargis's way. Some were torn to shreds by the critics. *Nargis* was one of them. Produced by Famous Pictures Ltd in 1946, the film starred Nargis and Rehman, who had recently made his screen debut. One review in *Filmindia* said: '*Nargis* has no story in it. It has bits from many pictures. There is one suicide in it; two attempted suicides; a precocious child; a court trial; a theatre sequence; some dacoits and their artificial caves...We are told that one of the dacoits loved a girl called Nargis.'

Worse, the review called her the 'Girl With Papaya Face'. it complained that the performance by Nargis was not up to expectations and 'She is, in addition, photographed so unsympathetically that her papaya face looks exceptionally long in this picture giving her an odd appearance.'

No one can deny that Nargis had unconventional looks. The imperfections, like the gap in her front teeth, seemed to identify her as a fallible human being, and helped her melt into her roles. She was never the 'film star Nargis' in the parts that she played, whether it was that of a sophisticated woman of the world, or a village simpleton. But whenever she worked with a skilled director and cinematographer, she looked dazzling on screen.

Indeed, in one poll conducted by a film magazine of the time, she was voted the most lovely 'screen siren'!

It also helped that very early in her career, she acted opposite established heroes. After Motilal in her first film, the next big star she worked with was Ashok Kumar, again in a Mehboob film, *Humayun* (1945). By now she was sixteen years old, and the veteran of four films in an adult role. Ashok Kumar was 34 and remarkably successful, despite being an accidental actor. He had acted in about 20 films by then, and was a self-assured, mature actor not given to histrionics. It may have been daunting for Nargis, but she actually was able to hold her own in all the scenes in which she appeared with him. The film, however, was a complicated, idealistic mess—possibly Mehboob's attempt to shape the future, given that the partition of India seemed imminent.

The story had two main strands. One was clearly devised by Mehboob to promote communal harmony. For this purpose, the plot introduced an unlikely romance into the life of the first Mughal emperor, Babar (Nawaz). Babar asks the daughter (Veena) of a defeated Rajput to treat him as a surrogate father. This leads to a feud between Babar's son Humayun (Ashok Kumar) and the Rajput husband of the princess. The two remain sworn enemies till the final, though fatal reconciliation.

The secondary plot had Humayun falling in love with a haughty Persian princess, Hamida Bano (Nargis), only to be firmly rejected by her. However, after his defeat at the hands of Sher Shah, when he is in exile, impoverished and much humbled, she meets him again and reciprocates his love.

By elaborating on the tender hearts and minds of the Mughal dynasty, Mehboob hoped to evoke nostalgia for the Mughal rule at a time when communal tensions were on the rise. Most of the 'history' in the film was, of course, pure fantasy, but *Humayun* still made an enormous impact with its grand imperial sets. Some of this splendour would be echoed much later in K. Asif's *Mughal-e-Azam*.

In her elaborate Mughal costumes, Nargis was filmed exquisitely by Faredoon Irani in *Humayun*, and Mehboob as always helped with his meticulous eye for detail. She looked slightly more mature and very lovely. Nargis had finally 'arrived'.

Her brother Akhtar Hussain was quick to realize her potential, and set up Nargis Art Concern. At the head of this production house, he made seven films spread over two decades, all with Nargis.

Zahida says, 'My father did exactly seven films as an actor. Seven was his lucky number. He had seven children; he was the hero in seven films; he produced seven films. He was stuck with the number seven. He was a very young man, only 25, when he became the owner of a studio, my grandmother's studio, Rooptara or Rangmahal as it was called in those days, based in Dadar.'

Among the films produced were *Romeo and Juliet*, *Anjuman* and *Pyar ki Baten*, all of which were period dramas. (Contemporary themes appeared much later in his cinema, such as in the unforgettable *Raat Aur Din*.) Akhtar had an inexplicable penchant for swashbuckling heroes whipping out swords in some fantasy land; both his mother and he seemed to be rather fond of this genre. Perhaps it was the influence of Hollywood costume dramas. In attempting to recreate Shakespeare, no doubt the mother and son team felt they had reached the highest echelons of intellectual respectability. The singer from Chilbilla had indeed come a very long way.

The new production house was launched with *Romeo and Juliet* (1948), and Anwar got a role in a family production at last. The film, according to *Filmindia*, saw the transition of Nargis from her 'awkward, gawky old self into a smart, sophisticated and poised young lady of today.' She was cast opposite Sapru who, the reviewer complained, could have injected a little more fire into the romantic scenes. William Shakespeare's name appears in the credits along with that of Kamal Amrohi, who wrote the 'screenplay and dialogue'.

In the *Filmindia* review, Akhtar receives his share of accolades even though his film was a copy of the MGM version with Norma Shearer—made with far fewer resources, of course. 'His effort and achievement are not negligible,' says the review. As part of the film's publicity, Norma Shearer was quoted as saying how much she liked Nargis's portrayal of Juliet.

Hindi adaptations of Shakespeare are not unusual today

(*Maqbool* and *Omkara* being two very recent attempts), but Akhtar Hussain was clearly ahead of his time.

The two brothers never forgot their own importance, even when they were behind the camera. The brochures for the 1951 film *Pyar ki Baten*, describe Nargis as 'never so stubbornly poutingly beautiful as when she acts the Princess Nadira in PYAR KI BATEN. This glamorous queen of emotions, and heart-throb of millions proves again that she is an artiste of rare calibre, yet unequalled on our screen.' Akhtar Hussain unblushingly describes himself as: 'the young and handsome hero of yesteryear hits, and now enterprising promising producer of ROMEO AND JULIET, ANJUMAN and DAROGAJI, his many hits does it again in PYAR KI BATEN.'

Anwar Hussain, who did not even act in the film, is the 'tall dark and handsome, dashing cavalier of a heap of hits...stalwart mate to his elder brother in making PYAR KI BATEN. His MERCUTIO of the immortal ROMEO AND JULIET will live as long as good character portrayal lives on our screen.'

Bombast, unfortunately for them, was not enough to conquer the box office. Like his mother, Akhtar could not really hit the jackpot with Nargis. He was able, though, to raise money to make the films, as she was now a bankable star. Further, the money she earned from her other films went mostly into the family coffers. Some of it was invested in property and jewellery, and the rest was spent in maintaining the lifestyle the family had got used to.

A few family members deny that she contributed anything substantial, but it is hardly likely that a girl of fourteen would have been in a position to sign her own contracts or negotiate terms. Those who maintain that she did not support the family will find themselves contradicted by the letters she wrote in later years, when she was trying to quit cinema and get married. These letters give ample evidence of a girl who grew up working for and giving to others. Right until the end of her career, she was unable to stop signing films because she worried about what would happen to her 'children'—the children of Akhtar and Anwar Hussain.

Initially, Jaddanbai drove Nargis's career. In 1949 she wrote *Anjuman* and Nargis starred in it with Jairaj and other actors from their circle of family and friends, including Anwar, Neelam and the redoubtable Durga Khote. The *Filmindia* reviewer who vacillated between giving Nargis a good review and tearing her apart seems extremely upset with the film: '*Anjuman* is a monumental waste of celluloid. It has an idiotic story of a marriage tangle of two rich brothers with the usual tyrannical mother who puts a lot of emphasis on family status and lends a deaf ear to the prayers of love from her eldest son, Prince Yousuf...Prince Yousuf falls in love with Anjuman, the daughter of his own aunt who is poor in worldly possessions...'

Nargis played Anjuman and according to the reviewer, 'This excellent artiste has been virtually murdered by her brother. She fails miserably in her amateurishly developed role and for the first time gives a very poor performance.'

Even worse, the reviewer added, 'The story of this picture was written by Bai Jaddan Bai who died recently of heart failure. This picture is disappointing enough to give anyone a heart attack and it was probable that Bai Jaddan Bai, the author of the story, could have been seriously affected by the unholy mess that *Anjuman* has become...'

Jaddanbai's death could not have come at a worse time for Nargis. She had been an adult actress for barely five years and was only 19. Her father had died the year before, and it seemed as if her resolute mother had decided that she would join him quickly on the other side. She died within nine months of his death.

Nargis wrote later that at one o'clock 'at night she died in my arms and was buried the next day.' At times of despair, her mother's soul would 'call her' and she would go to the graveyard 'to see her'. In the publicity booklet for *Pyar ki Baten*, released in 1951, Akhtar, Nargis and Anwar wrote alongside the photographs of their parents:

'Their memory will always remain fresh in our mind, they were separated from 18th November 1948 to 21st July 1949. Now they are united forever...But they have left us at a very tough spot. God help us and may their souls rest in peace…'

Nargis had a few challenging roles in hand at the time. One was *Aag*, directed and produced by the son of Prithviraj Kapoor, the blue-eyed Raj Kapoor. The others were *Anokha Pyaar* and *Mela*. These were her first films opposite the legendary actor Dilip Kumar (born Yusuf Khan). Dilip was a regular visitor at Château Marine and was very close to Jaddanbai. He was about 25 and extremely well-spoken. The son of a fruit merchant, a Pathan from the North West Frontier Provinces, he was constantly trying to improve himself. At this time, he had worked in fewer films than Nargis.

Dilip talks about Jaddanbai as a commanding presence: 'In the house there was Nargis, Jaddanbai, her mother, Nargis's brothers and a lot of visitors. There were meetings and conversations all the time. Jaddanbai was larger than life, *bhari bharkam, zinda dil*. She was very proud of the Urdu language and Urdu shayars would come to her frequently. We met regularly. If I did not go for four-five days, she would phone me herself. "*Kya haal hai* Prince (How are you)?" She used to call me Prince. "Are you alive?" I would say, "*Haan hum bhi samundar ke kinare hain* (I am also here, by the sea shore). How is your health?" "Don't ask about me, tell me about yourself," she would reply. So there would be conversations like this, about our interests, but you had to have the ability to converse with her with finesse. I had never seen her films, but I had heard some of her songs. They were songs of an earlier period, ghazals.'

Dilip Kumar has a sensitive, melodious voice and he sings a haunting ghazal which recalls his time at Château Marine, ending with the lines:

Zindagi ke lutf aur bandanawazi ke mazey
poochh us bande se jo bande ka banda ho gaya.

(All the joy of life and pleasure from relationships
you can only ask that person who belongs to someone)

'This was her style of singing. She liked my singing too, and often encouraged me to become a professional singer, to sing for the movies. I said speaking these film dialogues is no less of a strain, *kya kam aafat hai*. I told her you always say these nice things and I find myself flying high.'

Dilip remembers Nargis, not much younger than he was, mingling with the guests who often included K. Asif, Mehboob, and sometimes Ashok Kumar.

He says, 'Before I acted with her, you know in the market there is always a buzz when a new artiste enters, there were rumours that Raj Kapoor was also making a film. Anyway without much discussion, Asif and Naushad said, get her to do this film, and because we used to go to Nargis's house very often there was no obstacle in talking about it. And we found that she was a very carefree girl, involved with her brother's family, and also with her mother, and her mother's friends. She would chat with Mehboob and us as well. She would talk to me in English, because she had studied in an English-medium school.

'So if she wanted to say anything about anyone, or speak against someone, for instance if there was a writer who was a *badtameez* according to her and she wanted to be critical, she would say in English—you know, that man actually is a rascal. Others would not understand.'

Dilip Kumar and Nargis managed to capture the imagination of the public with their first two films. With the wounds of Partition still raw, tragedy spoke to the public psyche, allowing the audience to weep with the lovers destined for unhappiness.

Anokha Pyaar, with music by Anil Biswas, was scripted by Zia Sarhadi. It was a conventional triangular love story with Ashok (Dilip Kumar) falling in love with a doctor's daughter, Geeta (Nargis), while a flower-seller, Bindiya (Nalini Jaywant), is secretly in love with him. The dilemma forces Ashok to contemplate suicide, but Bindiya beats him to it and kills herself instead.

Filmindia was once again extremely critical, announcing:

'Anokha Pyar' Presents an Old Story!
Bad Recording Kills the Music!

Surprisingly, the reviewer was critical of Dilip Kumar, saying he could have done a better job. Of Nargis, he writes that she 'is very well photographed and gives a subdued performance as

Geeta.'

The second film, *Mela*, a Wadia film directed by S.U. Sunny, had memorable music by Naushad and lyrics by Shakeel Badayuni. '*Yeh zindagi ke mele duniya mein kam na honge, afsos hum na honge*' (The festivals of life will carry on undiminished; pity, we may not be there to enjoy them) was a song among many others which became, and have remained, very popular. *Mela* was another tragic story in which Mohan (Dilip Kumar) is to marry his childhood sweetheart Manju (Nargis), but on the eve of the wedding, he has an accident in a nearby town. Manju waits for him, and then to save his pride, her father marries her off to a 70-year-old man who already has children. Manju returns to meet her lover after the death of her husband, but dies in an accidental fall. Mekhoo (Jeevan), the villain, accuses Mohan of her murder and he is sentenced to 20 years of imprisonment. Though innocent, Mohan does not want to defend himself because he wants to protect their love. (Dilip Kumar often played the relentlessly self-sacrificing hero.) After completing his term, he returns to the spot where Manju had died and kills himself.

Mela was soaked in misery, and *Filmindia's* reviewer was suitably enraged, calling it an unprogressive anti-social and reactionary film; he blames the Parsi producers for not understanding Hindu sentiment. However, he does admit that Dilip Kumar has done a good job and that 'Nargis plays her part well, especially in pathetic scenes, though she looks unconvincing in sequences of her synthetic motherhood.'

Nargis and her family were not very selective about the films she signed, which was one reason why Dilip Kumar acted in just seven films with her. 'I did very few films with her, because like Suraiya she used to believe in quantity, whereas from my point of view films in which there was a certain calibre required, of the language, those films were better. But for them, whoever came, gave the money, the film was made.'

Yet he remembers her fondly. 'She was a nice girl. I don't know why she got into that...'

As Dilip Kumar's expressive voice trails away, one senses a certain sadness that most people who were close to Nargis felt about her involvement with the new kid on the block, Raj

Kapoor.

Nargis met Raj in a year when she was already feeling vulnerable, for her father had just died. Many of the films she was working in were sombre and dark. Her life so far had been an endless cycle of work with little other distraction. Most of the people she knew were either much older or much younger. And the death of her mother would soon deprive her of the one anchor she had in life.

She needed something uplifting and youthful, an exciting diversion. When it came, she was fairly defenceless to resist. For Raj Kapoor had charm in abundance. He was young, talented, and very ambitious; it is quite likely that Nargis had never met anyone like him. He was also very good-looking. It was an irresistible combination.

The first meeting between Nargis and Raj Kapoor has been immortalized by him in his film *Bobby*. Many of their private moments emerged in some form or the other over many articles, or as scenes in films. But all that would come later. For now, Nargis could not resist the invitation in Raj's twinkling blue eyes.

Balraj/Sunil
1950

U nlike Jaddanbai, who came with her family and knew exactly what she wanted, Balraj Dutt arrived in Bombay all alone. He didn't know anybody in the city, and had nothing more than the fifty rupees his mother had given him. He had not come here to try his luck in the film industry like most migrants from small towns. Unsophisticated, yet eager to learn, he just wanted his BA degree and some sort of employment, preferably a regular office job. For this, he was willing to even sleep on the pavements and go without food. He had very few possessions and just two pairs of white kurta-pyjamas which he washed and wore on alternate days.

His major anxieties were not about himself, but about his mother, sister and younger brother. Though they were now settled in Mandoli, and his sister was married, Balraj still felt the burden of responsibility. He had to get a good job, and to acquire one, he would first have to get a higher educational degree. He could not imagine any other way of self-improvement as he had no contacts or rich patrons.

Fortunately for him, with the influx of refugees from Pakistan, special facilities had come up around the city for them. Balraj learnt that Jai Hind College had started morning classes for refugee students, and enrolled there. His nights were spent at the Simla Hair Cutting Saloon at Kala Ghoda in the heart of downtown Bombay. It was open for business from 7 a.m. to 9 p.m., and he slept on the floor once the last client had been shaved and clipped.

He also found an evening job at the BEST (Bombay Electricity

Supply and Transport) bus depot as a clerk. He was a time keeper who clocked in the buses for a salary of Rs 120. He could now afford to share a small room. For a while, his roommate was a rugged young man called Rajendra Kumar. Rajendra had also come to Bombay to work, but in cinema. He eventually became the incredibly successful 'Jubilee Kumar'. Their lives remained very closely linked. Not only did they become good friends and act together in *Mother India*, their children later fell in love and married.

Meanwhile, in college, not surprisingly, the tall, slim and handsome Balraj attracted attention, but remained slightly aloof. Many of the students came from fairly wealthy backgrounds and could not fathom this nice-looking boy who would quietly do his work and was reluctant to participate in any of their activities.

Actually, Balraj couldn't afford any extra expenditure and so avoided anything frivolous. He would not take part in the colour-throwing at Holi either, because he had only two kurta-pyjamas and if these were spoilt, his entire wardrobe would be wrecked.

While he struggled to make Rs 120 last a month, literally around the corner from his college was Château Marine, where Nargis lived as one of the industry's highest paid actresses. His only encounter with her was through film posters. He could not even hope to see any films till he met Krishen Lal Narang, who became his constant companion. Krishen's relative Khairati Lal Sethi worked at the Empire Theatre, and organized tickets so the three friends could watch movies.

Krishen remembers, 'My brother was a captain in the army. We came to Bombay after Partition and stayed with my brother in Colaba. Balraj and I were both very hard up. Balraj was working in BEST, and I was working in central excise. The college which we joined in 1950 was Jai Hind. We would study from 7 to 10, and after that if there was some job, we would do that. T.M. Advani, who later on became the vice-chancellor of the Bombay and Kashmir universities, was the principal at the time. Initially they had no building of their own. They hired the Elphinstone

College building at Kala Ghoda, and our classes used to be conducted there in the morning. We were both studying arts, and graduated in it.

'On the sixth of June 1950, I still remember, when I entered the college I found that most of the students were Sindhis and from other communities, and there were a few Punjabis. I was looking for someone from my community and I found Dutt sahib wearing his trademark kurta-pyjama, so I thought he was related to Prithviraj Kapoor, because Prithviraj Kapoor used to wear a white kurta-pyjama and a chador like his. I went up to him just out of curiosity and said, "Are you related to Prithviraj Kapoor?" He said, "I don't know him." We introduced ourselves and started talking.

'Then we found a common friend who was working in Empire Theatre, opposite VT Station. I said he is related to me, and we started meeting at his place. Khairati Lal Sethi was very jolly and he used to make all of us laugh. He was a booking clerk. We used to meet at an Irani restaurant, we would sit there for hours and then go for a movie. '

Balraj, says Krishen, was always interested in his studies. 'I found Dutt sahib to be a very intelligent person, because if the professor made a mistake, he would point it out. Everyone started liking him.'

The biggest problem in Balraj's life in those days remained accommodation. The arrangement at the Simla Hair Cutting Saloon allowed no privacy or quiet moments. It was important to have a semi-permanent place at least, so he could study, but he had little money to spare.

Krishen says, 'He said to me he had no place to stay. He was now sharing a place at Kurla, in another chawl. Unfortunately for him, the wife of his co-tenant was on her way back from Allahabad, and he had been given a month's notice to find alternative accommodation, or else he would be evicted. All his worldly possessions were in a single suitcase.'

Krishen could not help Balraj because he lived with his brother in the military area of Bombay. The brother had just been transferred out of Bombay and Krishen and his mother, father and sister also needed a home urgently. Luckily, Krishen's brother managed to arrange space with one of his colleagues in the outhouses. But even then they couldn't help Balraj. It was a desperate situation and one day a sheepish Balraj told Krishen that his suitcase had been thrown out, because the long awaited wife had arrived.

Though life was very difficult for them, the Punjabis in Bombay were a close-knit community, ready to help each other. Though they had lost everything during Partition, they still retained their inherent open-hearted generosity. They attempted all kinds of employment, and thanks to their natural enterprise, took loans or sold their family heirlooms to set up industries and small manufacturing units. Some of them did extremely well, but they never forgot those dark days. One great bonding factor amongst them was the Punjabi language, which helped them to identify one another in the unfamiliar city.

Krishen continues, 'I said, I also have no place but I will do something for you. I took him in a bus to a friend and said, "*Iske liye kuch karo* (Do something for him)." A friend was staying at Esplanade Court, near Kala Ghoda, right next to Elphinstone College. He had a small room, and there he accommodated him. But he was quite a strange chap. He used to throw Balraj out every now and then, just say "Get out". Since he did not have anywhere else to go, he continued to stay there. On many occasions he had to sleep on the veranda. I have seen it myself because I used to get up early and pick him up on the way to college, which started at 7 a.m.'

Because of the insecure environment, the two friends studied in the Asiatic Library. It was well lit and open till late. Sometimes they visited another friend, who worked in the railways and had a small room. Krishen says he used to study till 6 a.m. and could barely scrape through, while Balraj, who would be asleep by 1 a.m., did much better.

Throughout this period, Balraj had to be extremely frugal and keep his earnings somewhere safe. So he began to hand over his entire pay of 120 rupees to Krishen, and would then take 10 or 20 rupees from him as and when he needed it. Invariably, his salary would run out by the twentieth of the month and he would have to borrow money. It was usually very small sums, but even if he borrowed two rupees or eight annas, he wrote it down, and at the beginning of the month, the money would be returned. Krishen tried to brush the debt away, telling Balraj to forget about it, but Balraj always paid it back. It became a lifelong habit: to repay any outstanding amount immediately upon getting the money in hand. As a result he never had a huge burden of debt, though he went through some really difficult times.

Krishen insists that the reason why Balraj stood out in college, even as a penniless refugee, was because he was like 'a *giddadh singhi* (magnet). Once he became a friend, you could not forget him, or leave him. If you ever left him, you would try to look for him. Although he had no money in his pocket, we would hunt him out because he was excellent company. He was very nice to speak to, and he was very up-to-date with all contemporary information. You could discuss anything with him, any current topic in those days—and he was just a matriculate.'

Jai Hind was a co-educational college with plenty of extra-curricular activities. Balraj began to be drawn towards theatre and started writing comic plays. Some were satirical, such as *Mr Liberty and Mr Metro*, which was a comment on the increasingly modern lifestyle of urban India. He was often annoyed at the fast-changing social norms around him. For instance, he could not look any of the girls he studied with in the face, though some of them were very interested in him. Years later, he would explain, 'I kept thinking, what if she was my sister? Would I like it if anyone stared at my sister like that?' He didn't realize that such old-fashioned chivalry appealed to the girls. The more he tried to steer clear of them, the more they seemed intrigued by him. Of course, there was also a practical reason behind his overt shyness: he could not afford to take anyone out or spend money on them.

One of his friends from college, who later became a well-known character actor, Mack Mohan, remembers: 'We organized a picnic from college and he said that he would not come because he had only one kurta-pyjama. I had a checked shirt which I

gave him and said that he must come, else our group would
break up. He wore that shirt and came with us. He was as thin
as me, at that time. He kept the shirt for many years. He was
quite sentimental about these things.'

Since money and food were always in short supply, Krishen
asked Balraj to write a special scene into his plays for him: a
party scene in which a lot of food would be consumed. All their
favourite snacks, like samosas, would be included. Though now
serious-minded and dour, the mischievous boy who used to tease
his grandmother in the Khurd days still lurked in Balraj, so he
often obliged Krishen with this 'party' scene, making him a happy,
well-fed man.

These theatrical activities meant Balraj was now part of a
group developing creative ideas all the time. The boy who had
come to Bombay without a single friend or acquaintance soon
found he had a lively social life.

Mack Mohan recollects, 'Our group—with Sudhir (who also
became a character actor), Balli (as Balraj was known), I and
four-five other friends were always together. In the college canteen
the first two tables were reserved for girls so you couldn't sit
there, but our table was the last one, it was reserved for us. Balraj
was the drama secretary (Sudhir was his chief assistant). We did
a play together which we staged in Ulhasnagar, Balraj and I, and
after that I did a play in college called *Hakimji.* '

The worlds of theatre and film were intimately connected in
Bombay. At this time in the film industry, Punjabi actors,
directors and musicians were becoming prominent. While there
is little doubt that the Muslim community (whether from Punjab
or elsewhere) had been extremely powerful before Partition, their
influence had begun to wane after talented figures like Nurjehan,
Zia Sarhady and Saadat Hasan Manto moved to Pakistan.
Others such as Mehboob, K. Asif, Dilip Kumar and Jaddanbai
had stayed behind. But now it was time for the non-Muslim
Punjabis to start asserting their authority. New alignments
began to be formed. One of the rapidly rising stars, apart
from Raj Kapoor, was Dev Anand, who had launched
Navketan studios with his brother Chetan Anand in 1949. Sudhir,

Balraj's friend, was an ardent admirer of his. And through him, Balraj was introduced to cinema.

Sudhir, who is now a veteran actor of many films, says of his college days, when he was a star-struck, good-looking young Punjabi with the kind of face that Hindi film producers were on the lookout for, 'I was very fond of Dev Anand. I was a fan of his, and I went to see him. Amarjeet Singh was his Public Relations Officer, and we used to meet on the local train. And he said, "You come along and meet us, you remind me of Dev Anand. Let me talk to Dev sahib about you." He called me, and so I went. At that time they were shooting *Taxi Driver*. It was a nightclub scene. Sheela Ramani was dancing and Dev Anand was playing cards. Amarjeet was showing me around, and then this voice came, "Who is that, *baith jaao, baith jaao* (Sit down)." I sat down. Then Amarjeet said, "Now everyday you have to appear, because you are in the shot." It became a joke, and everyone started making fun of me. Later we went to see the film...'

Living in Bombay, it was difficult for anyone to not take an interest in cinema. In the 1950s the city was a thriving film production centre. This was partly due to the rising cost of raw film stock, and the destruction of business houses in some parts of the country after Partition. Films had become very expensive to produce, and it was more economical to work in a city where all the facilities were available. During this period, filmmakers and technicians began to drift naturally towards centres where employment was more secure. One such big centre was Bombay; the other was Madras.

Despite the glamour attached to the stars, many of the actors, like Dilip Kumar, could be spotted around the city in restaurants and clubs like normal people. The carefully orchestrated media frenzy came only in the later 1960s with the rise of the superstars. If anyone wanted a glimpse of film actors in the 1940s and 1950s, it was an easily indulged desire.

Balraj and Krishen would stroll down Marine Drive, and as Krishen says, 'We used to walk and look at the girls. You know how young boys are. There were a lot of good restaurants there.

At the place where there is a restaurant called Talk of the Town today, there was the Parisian Dairy. A lot of film stars used to go there. We could not afford to go there but in front of that there was an Irani restaurant so we would have tea there because it would cost one anna, and at the Parisian Dairy it would have cost eight annas or one rupee. One anna was a very big thing for us. We used to watch all the film stars, mainly we used to see Dilip Kumar, and another actor called Shyam.' (Shyam was a leading actor and made many films with Suraiya. He died at the peak of his career when he fell off a horse during a shoot.)

As Balraj began to settle down in Bombay, he was involved in the usual college activities, but in many ways he was a little different from the rest of the crowd. He was driven by a peculiar idealism and a desire to do something for his country, a patriotic streak that lay very close to the surface. While it made his fellow students admire him, it also made figures of authority seek him out as an example for the others.

Krishen remembers one incident clearly: Dr Radhakrishnan, the vice president, had been asked to inaugurate the newly constructed building of Jai Hind College. The college principal specially instructed Balraj Dutt to be in the forefront, in his trademark white pyjama and kurta, to receive the vice president. It was a great honour. It may have been that the principal decided to give him a chance because he always came forward and seriously complained to him if he felt that the college discipline or prestige was at risk. Or perhaps the principal felt that Balraj with his strict values was the right person to represent the college, because he would even reprimand his friends if needed.

After all, this was the Nehruvian age of idealism, and like many at that time, Balraj was a devoted follower. He believed that he and others of his generation had to build a new India, for which he had to be disciplined in his lifestyle and Gandhian in his values.

His friends had no such illusions. They were young and careless compared to Balraj. Mack Mohan, who was a cricketer and somewhat of a lad, says, 'I had a book called *Wife for Sale*. I had put it in my hip pocket with the title jutting out so people could see it, especially the girls. The principal saw it, and he said, "What is this? You should not be carrying such books in the college." I said someone had given it to me and so I had put it in my pocket. Balli pulled me up saying, "Why are you carrying this book? It is good you got caught." He had the book confiscated.'

Because he was not malicious but rather transparent in his idealism, his friends let him be. They accepted that he was fiercely protective of his value system. It was understood that when they went out into the world, Balraj would take up some boring conservative career. After all, this was a man who never even smoked or drank. Mack Mohan remembers that even on occasions when his father invited Balraj over and offered him wine to drink as 'grape juice', Balraj refused. Only a few times did he see him wistfully roll up a bus ticket like a cigarette and put it in his mouth, pretending to smoke. Naturally, there was no money to spare for cigarettes.

Then came the turning point. A popular Sindhi play called *Leela Chanisar* was staged at Jai Hind College, and Professor Panjwani who was in charge asked Balraj to give the commentary during some of the dances. A representative from Radio Ceylon happened to be in the audience, from an advertising company called D.J. Keymer and Company Limited. It had a radio and cinema publicity department, and the representative, impressed by Balraj's voice, asked about him as a possible talent. He was told that Balraj was a third-year student. The agent tracked him down later to say that they were going to start a new programme in Bombay for Radio Ceylon. It was for Lipton's, the well-known tea brand, and would involve interviews with film stars. They wanted to use Balraj's voice for the show. He would have to do the interviews if he was willing to take on the programme. Was he interested?

It was a fantastic opportunity for someone who enjoyed theatre and therefore would relish the dramatic aspect of interviewing film personalities. But he already had a permanent job at the bus depot, and there were no long-term guarantees in the Radio Ceylon offer. Tempted, but worried that it was too much of a risk, Balraj discussed his dilemma with Krishen. The new job would bring him a salary of 300 rupees, more than double of what he was earning. But what was the insurance against an uncertain future? What if they threw him out? Then he would have lost his job at the bus depot as well.

With typical Punjabi pragmatism, Krishen advised him to do both. Balraj pointed out that it was not possible as he would have to do the radio interviews whenever the film stars were available. Krishen then suggested that he ask for two years guaranteed employment.

After some more soul-searching, Balraj negotiated a two-year contract with Radio Ceylon. He had to do two programs a month, in which the highlight would be an interview with a film star. He would be accompanied by a recording engineer. The interview was to be interspersed with music. Balraj was a good writer, and as his confidence grew he sometimes ended up writing both question and answer for his more inarticulate interviewees.

Balraj now began to explore opportunities within the film industry and in the process moved closer to his own future. Once again, the catalyst was a chance meeting. Invited by Bimal Roy, he was able to do an interview with Nargis at the premiere of *Do Bigha Zamin*. But she was a major film star and he was only a lowly journalist—nothing registered between them. Then Krishen dared him to get her autograph in return for a meal at a favourite Punjabi restaurant, Sher-e-Punjab.

The strategy he devised was simple. The two friends parked themselves at the bus stop in front of Château Marine. Balraj called out to her nephew who was outside and requested him for an autograph of his famous aunt. The triumphant Sunil enjoyed his tandoori chicken without realizing that his future wife's signature had paid for it. Apart from this incident, Krishen points out, Balraj showed no interest in Nargis. But he adds on a cautionary note that Balraj was a very private person. Few people, even his closest friends, ever knew his innermost thoughts. (In later years, his daughters used to observe him carefully locking his cupboard everytime he left his bedroom. They often teased him about the valuables he was protecting so carefully. After his death they discovered it was only his personal papers that he had been safeguarding, nothing else.)

The D.J. Keymer programmes, *Voh Dekh Sitara* and Lipton's *Mehfil,* were well received, and his association with Keymer carried on for at least two years. One of the first things Balraj did was to buy a radio so that he could listen to his own show. Among his personal papers, carefully preserved for over 50 years, is the receipt for the Murphy radio, bought in 1954 for Rs 400. He could pay only Rs 100 for it immediately; the rest would be paid in monthly instalments of Rs 35 each. As Balraj had nothing to prove his bona fides when he bought it, P.V.R. Chandran, the director of D.J. Keymer, stood surety for him.

Things were beginning to improve. To begin with, Balraj's income had gone up considerably. In good months he was earning Rs 500 or more. The break-up for the month of August, as shown in his carefully maintained file, was:

Lipton's Radio Programme Production—August, 1954
No. 1 Scripting and voicing for four Filmi Khabren
Programmes for 1st, 8th, 15th and 22nd August,
1954 at the rate of Rs. 75/- each   Rs 300
No. 2 Scripting and voicing for one 'Meet the Stars'
Programme for 29th August, 1954,
at the rate of Rs 150/- each   Rs 150
No. 3 Conveyance allowance on items nos. 1 and 2   Rs 50
_____   _____

              (Rs Five Hundred Only)   Rs 500

He could now start sending money back home to his mother. Again, carefully preserved in his files are the postal order forms. Some of them are for Rs 250, which means that he was sending half his earnings home at times.

Back in Mandoli, no one knew what Balraj was doing. The family had settled down, but there were some problems which still needed to be resolved. His brother Som was one of them. He had skipped primary school in the chaos of Partition and later flatly refused to go back to school. He lacked Balraj's passion for education and says with disarming candour, 'My uncle told the masterji in the village that "I want you to put my nephew

Som into school." But I stipulated that I would only attend school if I went straight into the fourth class. Masterji objected, saying I should first complete my studies upto class three, but my uncle persuaded him saying, "At least he will get into the habit of going to school, how does it matter to you?" Finally I was admitted to the fourth class.'

He adds, unblushingly, 'Unexpectedly, one day an inspector came to the school and asked me a question. I did not know the answer, but I looked at the paper of the boy in front and answered correctly. So the inspector told Masterji, "He has answered so well, as it is he has lost the first few years, so why not let him remain here?" So if anything good has to happen, it happens.'

Luckily for Som, he was now part of a newly independent nation where language had acquired important political connotations. Almost overnight, schoolbooks were switched from Urdu or English to Hindi and the regional languages. Som was good at Hindi and eventually managed to finish his matriculation.

However, his brother Balraj, for whom constant self-improvement was essential, was disappointed at his brother's preferance for Hindi. He wrote to him from Bombay (on 23 June, 1954) after receiving a letter from Som in Hindi: 'I request that you should always try to write in English... In one of your letters, you told me to send you a handwatch, but my dear, it is called a wristwatch. I hope in future you will try to correct yourself. '

If that was not stern enough, Balraj added, 'You should always try to write simple and correct English, and to improve it write two pages of English always. About your difficulties in Mathematics, try to solve one question for about ten times and gradually you will be quite at home in these subjects, too.'

Ten times! Som had no intention of solving anything even once. Despite his high hopes that his brother would excel at academics, Balraj did not succeed in persuading his brother to study. While he wanted Som to complete his MA and become 'a very, very big man one day', Som was quite content with his laid-back existence in Mandoli. He had a loving mother and a brother who was responsible enough to solve all their problems, even if he lived very far away.

The only pressure came from his friends, who wondered how many brothers he actually had. Som remembers, 'I used to tell my friends that we are two brothers, but I don't know where the other one is. Sometimes, once in a while we would get a letter from him, and a money order for Rs 100 or 50. We had no idea where he was. I was also very carefree. Not bothered.'

Finally some exciting news arrived from the absent brother. 'One day a letter arrived saying, "I am compering programmes on Radio Ceylon." He said that he broadcast the show on such and such day. I did not even know the name of the programme. There was no radio in the house. So I regularly cycled to the nearest town, sometimes in the rain and the storm, just to listen to the radio. To hear my brother's voice.'

Meanwhile, Balraj's contacts in the film industry grew through his radio programmes. It helped that the film producers were very co-operative; they appreciated the free publicity provided by the show which had fans in both East and West Pakistan, apart from India. Publicists such as Amarjeet Singh became close friends. The Radio Ceylon programmes were also very crucial for cinema at the time as the Indian government had taken a rather puritanical view of film songs and cinema after Partition. Film music was practically banned on All India Radio. Dr B.V. Keskar, the Minister for Information and Broadcasting, had decided that Hindi (actually Hindustani, as it was a mix of Hindi and Urdu) film music was 'harmful' for listeners and that All India Radio should play only classical music. Cinema was looked down upon as morally corrupt—except that it filled the state coffers via the entertainment tax.

Balraj played an important role in popularizing stars and film music at this time. As a result, he received many invitations from eager producers. One still in his files is from Bombay Talkies, dated 7.6.54, inviting him to the release of *Baadbaan* at Roxy Theatre. The letter says courteously, 'I am sure you will extend your co-operation by covering the opening. I am sure it will be a successful film.' Balraj returned the compliment by ensuring that he gave good mileage to the film on his programme. He was also frequently asked by listeners to send them photographs of certain film stars. This led to more interaction with the film world.

He began to help in arranging publicity for film stars, which would not have been unwelcome. As he wrote to a colleague about arranging a publicity shoot: 'I spoke to Kalpana Kartik about her pictures... She is not shooting on Sunday and I hope I will be able to take her pictures at Godwyn Studios. She prefers to be photographed in Punjabi dress...'

By now, he'd had his first taste of success in a fairly demanding job. He began to realize that a regular office job was not the only way to make a good living. Because his life revolved around cinema and all its attendant glamour, his lifestyle was changing very fast. The rustic boy was growing up into a more worldly-wise man. Adding to his new-found poise was the adoring fan mail pouring in both from India and Pakistan. He was meticulous in replying to each and every one. To one young fan he wrote that he was going to attend the actor Ashok Kumar's birthday, accompanied by Shammi, Nimmi and Sunder, all established actors in the 1950s. In his chatty answer to the fan he also wrote: 'Dev and Mona are away in Ceylon. They are expected back on the 14th instant. I will try to get their pictures for you when I meet them.' Dev and Mona were, of course, Dev Anand and his wife Mona, a.k.a. Kalpana Kartik , who were his friends by now. This letter is far removed from the life of the refugee who had arrived friendless and penniless in Bombay four years earlier.

Krishen recollects that it was a busy time for Sunil. 'He took a lot of interviews, including those of Meena Kumari, Nirupa Roy and Bharat Bhushan. Bharat Bhushan used to stay in Andheri, so Balraj asked me if I wanted to come along for the interview. I was very fond of all this, so I went along. Bharat Bhushan was not at home, but his wife Ratna was there. She laid on a real feast for us and Balraj said, "It's Tuesday, so I am fasting today, I can't eat anything." I said if he doesn't eat, I'll eat. And I did.' It seemed the good times were rolling now. Not only for him, but also for his friends.

Nimmi, who created a sensation in her first film, *Barsaat*, which was shot under Raj Kapoor's banner in 1949, recalls, 'I remember the first time he came to interview me. I have always been unable to make the person who comes to meet me to feel small in any way. That was never my nature. He said he did not expect stars to be nice people. Within a few moments, we were talking very naturally and having a good conversation. It was a very normal interview, but I don't remember what he asked and what I said. That time we used to live in Churchgate Mansions near Churchgate, and he was studying in Jai Hind College close by. He came to my house for the interview.

'But he always remembered that interview. So whenever we were together at a public function, even in his last years, he would recollect that incident in his speech. He said that when he started doing interviews everyone told him to interview Nimmi because she was easy to talk to and very humble. Even when he got the Dadasaheb Phalke award in 2004, I was on the podium with him, he started his speech with the couplet he had recited during the interview, he still remembered the couplet, and recited it. I have forgotten it, but he remembered it. '

Through the early part of the 1950s, though he was still just a radio artiste, Balraj was meeting people from the film world on such a regular basis that it was only a matter of time before somebody decided to make him an offer he could not refuse.

During the shooting of Ramesh Saigal's *Shikast*, Balraj was invited to interview Dilip Kumar. The star was shooting with Nalini Jaywant in the hills beyond Panchgani. When he arrived for the interview, Dilip Kumar said, 'I have no time now, you will have to come to my place.' According to Dilip Kumar—who does not mention having given Balraj a hard time—he asked Balraj to take a trial interview before the actual one, to help the latter hone his skills as an interviewer.

Ramesh Saigal spotted Balraj and asked whether he would like to work in films. Saigal had just completed two successful films, the Dilip Kumar–Kamini Kaushal film *Shaheed*, and the Ashok Kumar–Nalini Jaywant starrer *Samadhi*. Balraj replied, 'Provided you give me a leading role.' To his credit, Saigal simply answered, 'Come tomorrow and we will see.' The next day, the clothes that Dilip Kumar had worn for the shot were handed to him. And they gave him the same scene to enact from *Shikast* with Nalini Jaywant.

When Balraj emerged from the make-up room, he looked a sight: his trousers were short and his shirt buttons were all popping wide open. Even in that strange attire, feeling like a trapped animal, he performed as well as he could. He was relieved when he could finally wash the make-up off his face and get back into his own clothes. A few days later, Saigal sent word to him, saying that he had got the job, and gave him a signing amount of Rs 150. Balraj confided to Krishen that Ramesh Saigal had told him that if he had met him earlier he may have taken him in place of Dilip Kumar.

Once again, he was undecided whether he should give up his radio job, and there was a further temptation: Chandran, his boss at D.J. Keymer, wanted to send him to the UK for training. Confused, he asked Chandran for advice, who like Krishen before him, told him to carry on with both jobs and 'let destiny take its own course.' (Interview with Bhawna Somaya, *Junior G*, March 1991). Eventually Balraj did not go abroad for training.

Meanwhile, other radio stars like Ameen Sayani also became aware of his existence. Sayani recollects, 'I was connected to Radio Ceylon's sole agency in India through its production department, since 1949. And in the '50s we got to know that there was an ad agency, D.J. Keymer's (which later became Benson's and then OBM, that's Ogilvy Benson and Mather and then Ogilvy and Mather). It was an agency that had begun independently in those days to record shows for Hindustan Lever. These were sponsored radio shows to be broadcast on Radio Ceylon. And they were routed to Radio Ceylon through our office. And through those programmes, when we heard them, a voice emerged. It was a relaxed, sincere, very friendly, very appealing voice, well-versed in Hindustani but with a marked Punjabi accent—and of course the name was Balraj.

'His main radio show was a programme called *Lux ke Sitare* and it was a series of interviews with very famous film personalities. It was produced incidentally by a man who was a very famous lyric writer, a dialogue writer in films, and also a very outstanding radio writer and producer, Mr Vishwamitra Adil. Through these programmes and through the fact that we were both working for the same station, Sunil and I—I beg your pardon, I should refer to him as Balraj when I am talking of those days—Balraj and I did meet in those days, but not very often, at film functions, parties, etc. I found that he was a very likeable person indeed. I also came to know that very soon he was picked up by a number of film producers because all the people who came to be interviewed in that programme, *Lux ke Sitare*, seemed to fall in love with this very tall and handsome, and yet rugged and gentle person who was always smiling. He had very wonderful eyes, very deep and expressive eyes which hinted of a past that was full of struggles which nevertheless had been well handled and smoothened out, and then of course we heard that Mr Ramesh Saigal had picked him up for a film called *Railway Platform...*'

By October 1954, Balraj was shooting for *Railway Platform* at Osian village, in Jodhpur. The shoot lasted an entire month.

Balraj could not have imagined any of this in his wildest dreams. He was actually acting in a film with Nalini Jaywant and Sheela Ramani. And even though he was paid a pittance, between 500 and 1000 rupees, it marked a phenomenal rise in stature. However, there was already another actor by the name of Balraj (Balraj Sahni), so he changed his own name to Sunil Dutt.

While he was at Osian, Balraj also managed to help organize a charity show in aid of the Flood Relief and Police Welfare funds. They raised Rs 7000 and the show is notable as the first of many charitable fundraisers that he was to organize in his life.

On 29 January 1955, *Railway Platform* was released. It was billed as a

Pleasant parade of passengers
Against the fireworks of turbulent emotions

It received glowing reviews.

Raaj Grover, who worked as an assistant to Sunil Dutt in many of his later films, takes a realistic view. Sunil Dutt knew

Dev Anand's publicist, the amiable Amarjeet Singh. Amarjeet decided to help his new friend.

Raaj Grover says, 'When his first film *Railway Platform* was released, the next morning he and Amarjeet were standing outside the *Times of India* office at 2 a.m. He picked up the first newspaper that came off the press. Amarjeet had clout, he was a publicity man for Dev Anand. The review was very very good, very positive. That is the day Sunil got drunk.'

Not only did the review give a glowing account of his performance, the accompanying photograph was his, not of the more senior Nalini Jaywant.

The review headline announced:

Saigal's *Railway Platform* Delightful Social Satire

It read, 'Ramesh Saigal's second picture under his own banner...produced by his brother Keval Krishan and directed by himself was premiered at the Royal Opera House on Friday night in the presence of a house packed with film celebrities, headed by their doyen and leader Prithviraj Kapoor, and fans...'

It said that Ramesh Saigal wrote the screenplay and dialogue and Sahir Ludhianvi the lyrics. The music was composed by Madan Mohan and the film was shot by Dronacharya.

The huge cast stars Nalini Jaywant with a tall and handsome newcomer named Sunil Dutt making his debut opposite her in romantic lead. Sheila Ramani heads the support with Johnny Walker, Manmohan Krishan...

The picture was given a rousing reception at the premiere, as well as at the earlier afternoon and evening shows by audiences that rocked the house with laughter and chuckled right through its length when they weren't actually rolling in the aisles in delighted appreciation of its robust and lusty humour and the subtle sparkling wit of its commentary upon the time and the conditions in which we live...

As far as the histrionics go, Johnny Walker's is the outstanding performance. He is (in a) difficult and unsympathetic role. That he has made it what it is, is a credit to his versatility and talent as an actor, and a tribute to Mr Saigal's brilliant observation and extremely clever writing and direction.

'Equally brilliant and outstanding is Sunil Dutt's performance as

Ram. For a debut, he is superb. Handsome, tall and graceful, displaying a self-possession worthy of a Thespian, completely natural in expression, appearance and movement, this young man is the discovery of the decade and makes a fine acquisition to the depleted list of our romantic heroes...'

To make the review even sweeter, the film critic points out that Nalini Jaywant warms up only 'after a shaky start in the opening scenes.'

It was no wonder then that after reading this review Sunil got drunk, and probably imagined that producers and directors would be shortly breaking down his door. When you see the film now, more than half a century later, you can tell that apart from a few awkward moments, Sunil is comfortable in his role. What does not bear much scrutiny is the film itself.

Its premise is certainly more imaginative than that of Nargis's debut film, *Taqdeer*. *Railway Platform* tells the story of 24 hours when a train breaks down in the desert, bringing out the differences between the rich and the poor and their attitude to adversity.

The film repeats the socialist message of Nehruvian India: the poor are willing to help each other, the aristocrats are concerned only with their own welfare, and the traders or the middlemen, represented here by Johnny Walker, want to make money from misery. Sunil, as the unemployed youth, is worried about his ailing widowed mother and his sister's marriage—all situations which he had already experienced in real life. Nonetheless, he plays the good Samaritan, ignoring his comfort to help others. Despite the ecstatic review, the film is quite unremarkable.

With a good start in a new career and a new name, Sunil carried on with his radio programmes. Meanwhile, as he explained to an unhappy fan in November, after he returned from the shooting in Rajasthan, one of his programmes, *Vo Dekh Sitara*, had been taken off air. But he continued broadcasting Lipton's programme at 7.45 p.m. on Sundays on Radio Ceylon.

He was also very hopeful of starting two new shows, *Music and Music Makers* and *One Act Plays*. However, neither of these ever went on air. The flow of letters from his fans cheered him up in those difficult days while he waited restlessly for a big break.

By January 1955, Sunil had shifted into a more upmarket flat, which he rented for Rs 150 a month. This tiny flat would prove truly lucky for him. It was in a building called Prithivraj Chambers, on Napean Sea Road. It had only one bedroom, was on the fourth floor, and there was no lift. But he finally had a place of his own. And every time he ran up the flight of stairs, he probably hoped for the long-awaited letter signing him up for a big film.

However, there were still two years to go in the wilderness, of making a few films that gave him a little more money and a little more security, but not the superstardom that he now craved.

Raj Kapoor
1948-1955

Nargis was glowing. No one could complain now about her gap-toothed smile or lanky figure, because her whole demeanour—the way she walked and talked, and the way her eyes shone into the camera—proclaimed that she was a woman deeply in love. The wonderful thing about her love was that when she was on screen she did not need to hide it, she wore it like a talisman, and in film after film her love ensured that she and her man were an incomparable couple. But the terrible thing about her love was that in her personal life she had to hide it, because her lover was a married man.

Their affair was to last for nearly a decade. Strangely, it started with a fire, and ended with a fire. Raj Kapoor was looking for a heroine for his film *Aag* (The Fire) when he met Nargis, and her affair with him ended, almost symbolically, when Sunil Dutt rescued her from a real fire during the making of *Mother India*. In between these two events stretched a turbulent decade of love and heartbreak.

Raj Kapoor, the son of Prithviraj Kapoor, belonged to one of the great Bombay dynasties. Just as Jaddanbai was immersed in music, so was Prithviraj passionate about theatre. They were both extremely volatile individuals; Jaddanbai was the matriach around whom everything revolved in her household, while Prithviraj was the quintessential patriarch in his home. A handsome, flamboyant Pathan, he dominated the world of cinema, and then through his three talented sons Raj, Shammi and Shashi, he created an empire that exists till today, with his grandchildren and great-grandchildren continuing the tradition.

By the 1940s, Raj, like Nargis, had already made his debut as a child actor. They both grew up in an environment where cinema was daily fare, to be constantly discussed and planned for. By the age of 23, Raj had not only been through the grind of working in theatre with his father as an actor, a production manager and art director, he had also been a clapper boy at Bombay Talkies and was now ready to produce, direct and act in his own film.

Aag was an exciting film. Even watching it today, you can sense the intensity and vision of the young Raj. It is also one of the few films ever to depict the plight of a refugee traumatized by Partition.

Jaddanbai greatly respected Prithviraj Kapoor. She always said that his family was to be held in high regard, and so she actually reprimanded the six-year-old Nargis for being disparaging about Raj. According to the journalist Bunny Reuben, Nargis first saw Raj when he was about nine or ten.

She recounted to Reuben years later, 'My mother and I were shopping for sarees across the road from the Royal Opera House. I was just a kid and didn't know then that the Royal Opera House was headquarters for the great Prithviraj and his theatre group Prithvi Theatres.

'Just then I saw a fat boy with a round face and light eyes come out not far from our car and stare at us. He was munching away at some snack or other. "Mummy! Mummy!" I exclaimed innocently, pulling at my mother's saree and pointing at the boy. "Just look at that fat boy over there, how he's staring at us!"

'My mother glanced at him then hustled me quickly into the saree shop. Once inside she remonstrated with me, "Don't say rude things like that! Do you know who that boy is? He is the son of that great actor Prithviraj!"'

Surprisingly, the two families had little to do with each other, possibly because they lived at two opposite ends of Bombay. One day, however, Raj Kapoor dropped in with an unusual request. He was looking for a studio to shoot his new film, and he wondered if Jaddanbai, who was at the time shooting *Romeo and Juliet* at Famous Studio, could tell him about the facilities available there.

He rang the doorbell at Château Marine and Nargis, who was frying pakoras in the kitchen, opened the door, a streak of besan on her forehead. He recollected the incident later (for Raj, every incident was a piece of cinema, and he would embellish the narration with laughter, hurt, nostalgia, whatever his director's heart demanded):

'She asked me who I was and I said I was Prithviraj Kapoor's son, because at the time those were the only credentials I had! She said she knew me very well because she had seen me on stage in *Deewar* (a popular Prithvi Theatre play). I enquired whether Bibi-ji...was home. She said, "No...nobody is here... I am alone in the house." And she asked me to sit down, but I said, "No, no...I must go." And I left the house, but I didn't leave her behind. Her memory stayed with me. I drove straight to Inder Raj Anand and said, "I must have this girl in my film...You must write her into the screenplay!..." That was how I met Nargis and cast her in *Aag*—with that tremendous build-up in *Aag*, my audience was waiting to catch a glimpse of her...but they could only see her in the ninth reel.' (Ritu Nanda: *Raj Kapoor Speaks*)

By this time, Raj was no longer the 'fat boy' but it still wasn't easy to sign up Nargis. She was a star. She had acted opposite the two biggest names in Indian cinema at that time, Ashok Kumar and Dilip Kumar. She was also fiercely protected by her family, who decided which films she should act in. But Raj was audacious enough to try his luck and his charm. It was a moment Nargis's family remember both with fondness and an underlying resentment. If only they had known what his chance encounter with her would bring!

Zahida recalls her father's account: 'Raj Kapoor came with 5000 rupees to my grandmother, and said *ki "Main jee Prithviraj Kapoor ka ladka hoon, mujhe Nargisji chanhiye picture mein* (I am Prithviraj Kapoor's son, and I would like Nargisji in my film)." And my dadi said, "Yes, I have respect for Prithviraj, he is a good man, does a lot of things to promote art." She loved anyone who promoted the arts.'

The fresh-faced Raj was listened to courteously and in principle, Jaddanbai acceded to his request. But Akhtar, who also worked as Nargis's secretary, decided to renegotiate the price, and reportedly asked for Rs 40,000, since Nargis was an established actress.

Aag was a complex film. At one level, it begins Raj's cinematic search for his own self. The young hero of the film, Keval (Raj Kapoor), tries to break out of his father's conservative stranglehold. The father, a judge, wants the son to study further, get a degree and a proper job, but the son rebels and wants to be in theatre. The film can be read as both an acceptance of Prithviraj's influence on his son, and an expression of Raj's deep desire to reject him and find his own voice.

The young man's passion for theatre is intertwined, in the film, with his childhood love for a girl for whom he searches constantly, after being parted from her in their schooldays. Perhaps this too was autobiographical, describing Raj's own hunt for romance, for he was married a little before he began *Aag*. It was an arranged marriage, and though Krishna was the sister of his dearest friend, the actor Premnath, the sensual, adventurous Raj would have felt as though his feet had been tied before he was ready to run. Women, especially those who acted in his films, were always in danger of being swept away by him. *Aag* was only the beginning.

In the film, Keval leaves home and finds fulfilment in the theatre company he sets up. Life seems to take on more meaning with the appearance of the young refugee girl, Nimmi (Nargis), with whom he falls in love. He trains her to become a great actor. But when he discovers that his best friend and mentor Rajan (Premnath) is also in love with her, he decides to burn his own face and destroy his good looks so that Nimmi will be repelled by him. The theatre that he has so painstakingly built is wrecked in the fire.

The fire was symbolic of Keval's quest for love and his theatrical ambition, which consumes him. *Aag* is a youthful but searing film, and Raj's talent as a director was apparent. It was the launch of his banner as well.

The review in *Filmindia* was ecstatic. The headlines screamed:

Raj Kapoor Scores Personal Triumph in 'Aag'!
Story Presents Blending of Art and Idealism!

The review lavishes praise on the film:

'Aag' is the maiden production of Raj Kapoor. He has written the scenario, directed and produced the picture, and has also played the main role in the story. And Raj Kapoor is only 23—the youngest producer in the country. But the boy has produced a picture...that takes our vote as easily the best picture of the year in art, purpose and presentation...Raj Kapoor gives a promise of a brilliant future. 'Aag' is an idealistic story. It has a dreamy biographical aspect which almost makes it the life-story of Raj himself as he would have probably like to have lived (the review here makes a somewhat oblique reference to Prithviraj's influence on Raj, and then carries on)...quite a few of Raj's own daydreams and inhibitions have found their expression in 'Aag' thus making the story all the more intimate and appealing...the spectators cannot help but identify certain sequences in the story with the unsaid episodes of Raj's own life.

Apart from the story, the review noticed the high production values: 'The camera has been used with suitable psychological effects and at places the shadows create a devastating impression on the mind.'

But the reviewer was happy only with Raj's acting, saying he 'dominates the show completely, living his role to perfection.' Nargis's inability to dance annoyed the critic who spluttered that she 'acts well only above the shoulders, especially in pathetic situations. But in the dance sequences her deformed back and squeezed up figure without any grace or contours become repulsive...' It was strong language, but then Baburao Patel (the editor of *Filmindia*) was never known for subtlety. The review continued, 'In spite of its art and idealism, or perhaps because of it, the picture has become popular also with the crowds.'

To everyone's surprise, the blue-eyed 'Pinkie' (as Nargis teasingly called him in private) had turned out a fine film. Nargis was impressed. It was something two generations of the Jaddanbai clan put together had not been able to do till then. No doubt Nargis's open admiration pleased Raj. He decided he would involve her in all his productions.

Meanwhile, things were not going very well at Château Marine. While Nargis was attracted to Raj, and he made no secret of his own interest, her family was slowly waking up to a potential problem. But before they could do anything about it, Mohanbabu died. Nargis's whole world seemed to fall apart. She was very close to her soft-spoken father, and when she was growing up he had been the confidante who got to hear of all her adolescent worries; Jaddanbai was too formidable to be confided in. As Nargis sank into depression, other issues cropped up.

Everyone at Château Marine had assumed that Mohanbabu would be buried according to Islamic rites, but others thought he should be cremated according to the Hindu tradition. Though he had supposedly been converted to Islam, Mohanbabu had retained his Hindu name, and this added to the confusion. There are those who profess, even today, that he never completely converted to Islam. In any case, while in life he and Jaddanbai could do a Hindu-Muslim mix and match, Mohanbabu's death, and later hers, led to fierce controversy.

Mohanbabu's family, which had disinherited him, had not interfered with his lifestyle so far. One of his brothers had even stayed at Château Marine for a while, but now the situation became fraught following Mohanbabu's death.

Zahida remembers: 'My father said, "*Jab tumhare babuji nahin rahe* (when your grandfather died), his Hindu family came to cremate the body, they said he was a Hindu. But we knew that Babuji had written a will stating, 'I had converted to Islam on my own and my body belongs to my wife and children, it is up to them to decide what to do with it and no one has any claim to my body.'" My dadi (Jaddanbai) was sitting there in a state of shock and when my father said, "Chachaji (Mohanbabu's younger brother) has come to claim the body," she replied, "The man I loved is not the body. If they want it, give it, let them take it."

'But my father insisted that Babuji had written a will. He went to Babuji's cupboard and said, "*Babuji kahan rakh gaye vo* will." Just then an envelope fell out—I get goosebumps telling this story—and Babuji's will was in it. My father then said to his uncle, "Either let us do what we have to do, and you can sit here peacefully, or please leave." But my grandmother was very upset. She said, "Uttam, I am following you very soon, I cannot live without you." She also died of a heart-attack, within nine months.

'Nargis was about 20. She was shooting for *Andaaz* at the time, the scene where her reel father dies. It was the same time when her father, Mohanbabu, actually died. She was very close to her father.'

The actor Nimmi had just arrived in Bombay and had met Mohanbabu earlier. 'At the time of his death, I was not yet Nimmi, my name was still Nawab Banu. I got the news from Mehboob Productions that he had died. He was very sick. I had also gone to see him. I remember there was a storm the night before, and a lot of trees had been uprooted en route.'

She remembers that his last rites were conducted according to Islamic tradition.

No doubt Nargis was devastated. If she managed to keep working, it was partly due to her newfound love, and partly due to the interesting and complex nature of the films she was now working on. She acted in a film called *Lahore*, which is worth mentioning because, like *Aag*, it is one of the few films which dealt with Partition, and the riots in Lahore. The film was banned in Pakistan, but was released in India on 6 May 1949. Nargis played the role of a Hindu girl, Lilo, who is trapped in Lahore, and Karan Dewan played Chaman, her sweetheart who is now a refugee in Amritsar. *Filmindia* lauded the courage of the producer Jaimini Dewan for 'doing something that has not been done before.' Barring a few films such as *Aag* and *Lahore*, most filmmakers avoided the theme of Partition.

Cinema history, however, was made by another film, *Andaaz*. It was a major step forward in many ways, a breakaway film that boldly spoke of a modern woman who could have a relationship with a man who was not her husband. Once again, it was Mehboob who broke the mould.

Ali Raza, who worked on the script and the dialogue, remembers the controversy which dogged the film from the beginning and ultimately was responsible for its outstanding success.

He says: '*Andaaz* was my first film. It would be incorrect to stay I made a great contribution to the film. In fact, initially when I came to Bombay I could not get an opportunity to write.

My mamu (Aga Jaani Kashmiri) was a member of the Royal Asiatic Society. I went there and read film stories all the time and dreamt up ideas for stories. The story idea for *Andaaz* came from a dramatist called Shums Lucknavi. He was very famous, and he wrote a lot of stories for V. Shantaram. The idea belonged to him but there was disagreement about the storyline.'

Ali Raza was brought in to write the screenplay as the debate on the central character played by Nargis spun out of control.

'Mehboob fell out with Aga Kashmiri because he said, "This character is a randi (a whore), how can you call her a heroine?" When the film was released in Liberty, I was a protégé of Mehboob sahib, so we were both sitting together downstairs in the theatre. Shantaram came down after seeing the film, and tore into Mehboob. "What have you done," he asked him, "what sort of a film have you made, have you gone mad? You will be ruined." So everyone had a different perspective, especially of the role played by Nargis.'

The review in *Filmindia* also has a perplexed tone. It credits Shums Lucknavi with the story and the headline excitedly proclaims:

'Andaaz' Draws Crowds at Liberty!
Dilip Kumar Gives His Greatest Performance!

But the critic could not really bring himself to agree with Mehboob on the central theme of the clash between modernity and tradition. Neena (Nargis) is a rich independent-minded woman, who dresses in Western clothes and is stylish and confident. Out horse-riding one day, she has an accident and a stranger, Dilip (Dilip Kumar), rescues her. He becomes a friend. After her father's death, Neena is traumatized and gives half the business over to Dilip, who stays on to help her. Dilip is in love with her and misunderstands her friendliness for love. In fact, she is in love with Rajan (Raj Kapoor) who has gone abroad and returns, to Dilip's dismay, and marries Neena. Neena then discovers Dilip's true feelings towards her and, unable to bear the torment, leaves her home for Simla. Neena and Rajan have a child but Rajan begins to suspect her fidelity. Ultimately, there is a confrontation when Neena and Rajan come home, and Neena fatally shoots Dilip. She is tried for murder and sent to jail.

It was a rather harsh indictment of the modern woman, but perhaps it captured the mood of the nation.

As Meghnad Desai says in *Nehru's Hero: Dilip Kumar*:

> *Andaaz* was the modern film of its time. It had superb music by Naushad and glossy camerawork by Faredoon Irani. The sumptuous sets indicate opulence of a scale not shown previously in Hindi films especially of a westernized fashion. The plot moves between a hill station (it could be Simla) and a city (it could be Bombay). There are dances and birthday parties, pianos everywhere and the houses are big. Indeed Mehboob Khan set down the grammar of staircases for all subsequent Indian films. The sweeping staircase commanding the set and the piano by the foot of those stairs faithfully copied immediately afterwards in *Awara* and then in several other films were Mehboob's lasting legacy. After *Andaaz* there was no excuse for tattiness in sets...

In terms of acting, Dilip Kumar went through the entire gamut of emotions.

> But Nargis matches him throughout the film. As he withdraws into brooding, she flowers first into a woman in love and then one haunted by her dark secret, possessive as the mother of her child, alternately happy with and estranged from Rajan as her moods fluctuate. Then, at the end, a woman fully grown up when she realizes what carnage she has unleashed on three lives without meaning to. Her confrontation with Dilip as he attacks her and then her stoic stand in the court as she refuses to defend herself after Rajan's testimony are miles away from the headstrong young woman about to go horse-riding, in the memorable scene that opens the film...

What comes through is the image of a strong woman who has relationships on her own terms, even though, as she realizes, these could culminate in great tragedy. It was an unconventional film, and stood the image of the long-suffering *bharatiya naari* in a white saree and with a demure expression, on its head. This was the heroine as a vixen, an involuntary tease, never seen before on the Indian screen, which is why Aga Kashmiri had dismissed her as a 'whore'.

Ali Raza says he grasped the underlying problem in the film

and sought to express it. 'I understood that we are all at a manzil, a stage in our lives when we are not surefooted—where should we go, this way or that? We did not know, and neither did the character of Nargis, she did not know whom she loved, this one or that one. Only at the end she grasps at her traditional values and her husband. The fact that this was about a modern woman who could be friendly with a man other than her husband, this is what made the film what it was.

'In the production the only independent actor was Dilip Kumar. Even Raj Kapoor would surrender, he was professional, he wanted to do what the director wanted. But Yusuf would be sitting there, thinking of something, rewriting the scene. Usually there was not too much rewriting, Mehboob sahib was very strict about suggestions on the set.'

Ultimately, everyone was satisfied. '*Andaaz* set the standard for social pictures and it ran a lot. No one had seen that kind of grandeur before. It is still memorable.'

Andaaz was also memorable for other reasons. Raj discovered Nimmi on the sets of *Andaaz* and she would act with Nargis in his second film, *Barsaat*. It was he who he suggested that she change her name from Nawab Banu to Nimmi. And why Nimmi? Perhaps because of the success of *Aag* and the name of its heroine, Nimmi.

Nimmi remembers her first meeting with Raj. 'I came to Bombay when *Andaaz* was being shot. It had been written by Raza sahib. Though it is really God who gives you the opportunity to do things, I got my chance to act through Jaddanbai. It was because people had a lot of respect for her.

'My mother and she were friends, but my mother had died when I was very young. So when I came to Bombay I used to go to watch a lot of shooting in Central Studio. Once when I went to the studio, they were shooting *Andaaz*. Jaddanbai was there and the chair next to her was vacant. Out of respect I kept standing, and she said, "Sit down." I sat down. I was just an ordinary girl, shy, thin and skinny, no one really noticed me.

'There was a staircase on the set and Raj Kapoor was standing on it. He saw Jaddanbai sitting across. He called out to her, "Bibiji!" in his special way. Actually, at the time, he was very worried about *Barsaat*. In his conception, in his imagination, he needed a very innocent, shy teenager and he had not found anyone. Because all the girls who would come for the audition obviously wanted to impress him, and so they would come dressed smartly and did not fit the part...He came up to us, saying "Bibiji, Bibiji" and then he saw me and asked Jaddanbai, "Who is this girl?" And Jaddanbai said, "She is someone we know, she is the daughter of a friend." He said, "I want to take her in my film." He wanted to know my name, and it took me five minutes just to tell my name.

'Then he spoke to Mehboob sahib who said, "She is like a daughter to us." I was very nervous because I had hardly seen any films and I knew nothing about Raj Kapoor. Mehboob sahib asked, "Do you know him?" indicating Raj Kapoor. So I said *jee haan*, and he said, "Prithviraj *ke bete hain*." I did not even know that, so I said *jee haan*. Mehboob sahib added, "He made the film called *Aag*." I said *jee haan* again. He said, "Have you seen it?" Without understanding anything, I just said *jee haan* once more. There were so many questions in my mind. I had come to Bombay without any diploma or degree. But I saw that girls were working everywhere and felt I must also do something.

'Mehboob spoke to my grandmother and said that "You have also worked in cinema, your granddaughter is a good girl. If she is successful, she will have a good career ahead." Then they did my screen test. And there were a few more girls there doing their make-up and I looked at them secretly to see if those girls looked better than me. Fortunately, one failed, the next failed, the third failed to pass the screen test. I had one advantage, that Urdu is spoken in our home. The script given to me had a very tragic dialogue and I learnt it really quickly. But it is difficult to describe how nervous I was. I was saying the dialogue but my mind was asking me all kinds of questions, and I was thinking that it was time for me to fail now, and that I had failed, so due to the fear of failure, I don't know or what it was, tears started streaming down my cheeks. I was really in a daze, and when I snapped out of it, I realized that everyone was clapping. I asked the assistant, "What's happened?" and he said, "You have passed." So that is how I came into the industry.'

Jaddanbai was on the sets of *Andaaz* that day, to keep an eye on Raj and Nargis. She had heard some gossip and was worried about her daughter. After all, Raj was a married man and she did not want her daughter to fall in love with the wrong man. Jaddanbai was a worldly-wise woman and she knew how long it had taken her to win respectability. She did not want her daughter to suffer the same fate.

As Nimmi says, 'From the time of *Andaaz* everyone began to feel that sentiments between Rajji and Nargisji were increasing. When I was working with them in *Barsaat*, I really began to realize it. Because our mothers had been friendly, now Nargis and I also became very close to each other. We used to go for outdoor shooting. Her mother was very strict and Nargis was always chaperoned.'

All plans to shoot *Barsaat* in Kashmir were vetoed by Jaddanbai. Instead, most of the long shots were taken in Kashmir, and the close-ups were shot in Mahabaleshwar and Panchgani. She wanted Raj and Nargis to remain under close scrutiny. If she could not go for a shoot, she would send one of her sons to keep an eye on the amorous couple.

While Nargis had grown up in the midst of the flirtatious film crowd, Nimmi was still naïve. However, she and Nargis became very friendly, and she was co-opted into a romantic subterfuge carefully planned by Raj and Nargis.

Like the others, she had begun calling Nargis by her nickname, Baby or Babes. Often she would tell Nargis's brothers that she and Babes would like to go for a walk. Once they were given permission, the two girls would stroll away.

'And then we would find Rajji's car parked on the way. These two (Nargis and Raj) would put me in the backseat, put three-four overcoats on me and make me go to sleep, and say, "Don't wake up." And we would be there for hours, or we would go for a drive, and I could hear everything that they were saying. They would say, "Nimmi, go to sleep." But it was fun. They fought quite often and then would stop talking to each other. Rajji would say to me, "Come on, Nimmi, let's go boating." But I knew I was being used in their fight and would try to resist, asking, "But what about Babes?" And he would say, "No, you come with me."

'I would go with him, but I would be worried throughout because going out with him could compromise me. She would hide and watch us. I thought, ultimately these two will get together again, but I will be in trouble! I will lose my self-respect. So I had to be very careful all the time.'

Nargis was a star, but Nimmi remembers clearly that she did not behave like one. She, Nimmi and Cuckoo, the dancer, would eat their meals together in the make-up room. Nargis and Nimmi started sleeping in the same room at night. Probably Nargis felt safe with her, as she was part of her 'secret life'. Nargis's brother and chaperone on duty, Anwar and Nimmi's cousin, slept in another room, seemingly oblivious to the nightly rendezvous.

As she did with her nieces, Nargis started giving her clothes to Nimmi even if they did not fit her. She would insist that Nimmi wear her blouses, sarees and high heels. That Nimmi was more petite did not deter her.

Barsaat was released on 10 March 1950 and made box-office

history, but Jaddanbai was not around to see her daughter's triumph. She died while it was still under production. In the last 18 months, Nargis had found love but lost both her parents. Her grief probably brought her even closer to Raj. She now started spending more and more time away from home and at the studio that Raj was building at Chembur. She found solace in making plans for the future. Raj was a good director, even brilliant at times, and she felt she could learn a lot from him. She was at a point in her life when the gossip in the press did not bother her: she was one of the industry's top heroines, and Raj made her feel special. *Barsaat* seemed to put the seal on their relationship; its success was a good omen.

Filmindia again appeared to salute what it called Raj Kapoor's 'morbid approach to life.' The headlines of the review read:

'Barsaat' Makes New Box Office Records!
Raj Kapoor's Artistic Triumph!

The best part about the film was its music. Every song was a hit. The score by Shankar-Jaikishen was melodious, and the lyrics by Hasrat Jaipuri, Shailendra, Ramesh Shastri and Jalal Mahilabadi for songs such as '*Mujhe kisise pyaar ho gaya* (I have fallen in love with someone)', '*Hawa mein udta jaaye* (It flutters away in the breeze)', '*Chhod gaye balam* (My lover has left me)', '*Jiya bekarar hai* (My heart is restless)', '*Barsaat mein humse mile tum* (You and I met in the rain)' were memorable. They set the standard for future Raj Kapoor films, in which music would play a crucial part. In later films, Raj himself could be seen playing the tambourine or the harmonica. In *Barsaat* he 'plays' the violin and uses it to woo his love. This scene became the iconic RK Studios symbol: the woman bent backwards in the arms of the man, who has her in one hand and his violin in the other. It is also the first film in which we hear the familiar Anniversary Song from *The Jolson Story* (1946) which became the hallmark of Raj Kapoor films, and was repeated very effectively, especially in *Mera Naam Joker*, the most autobiographical of his films. In *Mera Naam Joker* it was used deliberately to recall his romance with Nargis, especially the scenes in *Barsaat*.

Barsaat was a dark story about love and the peccadilloes of two friends who go to Kashmir and get romantically involved with two local women. Very often in Hindi cinema, Kashmir was shown as a paradise where the women were innocent and trusting. Pran (Raj Kapoor) falls in love with Reshma (Nargis) but loses her temporarily, while Gopal (Premnath) ruthlessly uses Neela (Nimmi). In the end, Pran is reunited with Reshma, but a pregnant Neela kills herself. The film has all of Raj's passion and is carefully constructed but sometimes, almost absentmindedly, it lapses into melodrama.

Raj was unable to disguise his feudal attitude towards women: he often showed the woman falling at the feet of her man, or taking the occasional slap from him (as in the later *Awara*). In *Barsaat*, even the *Filmindia* critic cringes: 'Neela, the Kashmiri girl, kisses Gopal's feet and sheds tears of joy on them. This procedure is probably Raj's conception of a woman's loyalty to her man.'

Nonetheless, *Barsaat* did very well and established both the RK brand and the Raj-Nargis pair. Nimmi also got her share of justly deserved praise for her 'glorious' debut. *Filmindia* specially mentions that her 'introduction is so suggestively tender and sexy that she becomes popular within a minute.'

Nimmi remembers, 'Then we came back to Bombay (after the film shooting) and of course, RK Studios was built. Both of them were still very close to each other.'

In those early years, the closeness did not prevent Nargis (as it would do later) from working in other productions. By now nearly six of her films were being released every year, and by the time Raj made *Awara* in 1951, she had a dozen more films behind her. She had matured as an actress. Not only was she slowly taking charge of her own affairs, she was also being offered challenging roles, such as Chandulal J. Shah's *Jogan*.

Jogan was not a hit, but it stands out among the films that Nargis acted in. It radiates the kind of obsessive passion that Raj had ignited in *Aag*, but is far more mature. A thoughtfully made film with a genuinely strong story, it seems to be way ahead of its time. According to Kidar Sharma, who directed it, Nargis regarded it as her best film.

Meghnad Desai notes in *Nehru's Hero*:

> One year after *Andaaz*, Dilip Kumar and Nargis were teamed up
> again in *Jogan*. In the credits of *Jogan* there is a question mark next
> to the 'story writer', but it is now well known that the story was
> conceived by Chandulal Shah who owned Ranjit Movietones which
> produced as many as 160 films in its time in the '30s and '40s. *Jogan*
> was one of the last good films he made. Kidar Sharma who had been
> trained in New Theatres as a writer and director was asked to direct
> and his claim is that he finished shooting the entire film in 29 days.
> The film was released at Liberty in Bombay on 5 May, 1950.
> *Jogan* is about the dialectics of desire and denial. In one sense it is a
> very chaste film; the hero and heroine do not even touch each other.
> Yet it releases tremendous erotic tension just because two attractive
> young people deny themselves the most obvious form of interaction.
> Vijay (Dilip Kumar) is at a loose end in his native village where he has
> returned to sell the ancestral house. Wandering by the river, he hears
> someone sing *Ghunghat ke pat khol*...and finds that it is a jogan—
> a mendicant woman who is holding her satsang in the local temple.
> The jogan (Nargis) is seen in contrasting light and shadow so that
> she is elusive and perhaps in the half darkness of the soul herself. She
> is disturbed by the sight of the stranger...'

There is very little dialogue between Surbhi, the jogan, and
Vijay. But he becomes obsessed with her. A princess who had
left her home and palace because her parents were forcing her to
marry an older man, Surbhi is tempted by Vijay's offer of a way
back to the world she has renounced, but she does not succumb.
She mortifies her flesh and starves herself to death, leaving behind
a book of poems for Vijay, signifying her more sensual self.

Nargis was possibly the only actor who could have played
the lead role; Meena Kumari had still to establish herself as a
tragedienne. Nargis skilfully portrayed a range of emotions, from
a romantic young girl being forced into marriage to a serene
jogan. She also had to portray wordlessly her inner turmoil when
Vijay comes into her life. It was a very difficult role, but she was
more than a match for Dilip Kumar.

In October the same year, the film *Babul* was released in which
she acted opposite Dilip Kumar again. *Babul*, as mentioned in

Nehru's Hero, was a pointless film but it was a huge commercial hit. Directed and produced by S.U. Sunny, the film had Nargis enacting a role similar to the one she had in *Mela*: the simple village belle who would die before she got the man she loved.

By now, Dilip Kumar ruled the screen and his forte was tragedy. In film after film, he would be deprived of love, usually at the very bitter end. Sometimes this would force him to take extreme steps, as in *Deedar* in which he gouges out his eyes. For Nargis, if she played opposite him, there would be a similarly disastrous ending. The Raj Kapoor films with their usually happy climax and the upbeat Charlie Chaplin mood, especially in and after *Awara*, must have been a welcome relief.

Babul, despite its grim ending, was a straightforward love triangle. The new postmaster, Ashok (Dilip Kumar) arrives in the village, and Bela (Nargis) the simple village girl, falls in love with him. He, however, is attracted to Usha (Munnawar Sultana), the daughter of the rich landlord. Bela confesses her love to Usha, and so Usha decides to be noble and marry someone else. If this were not tragic enough, Bela tries to mend things between Ashok and Usha, and fails. She then, in a bizarre accident, falls off a tree and dies in the arms of Ashok. Ashok (even though he still loves Usha) puts sindhoor in the parting of her hair, proclaiming that they are now married, as she is carried away, quite literally, by the spectre of death.

It was not Nargis's best performance. But *Babul* did very well. *Filmindia* exclaimed:

> 'Babul' Becomes a Beautiful Entertainer!
> Excellent in Music, Photography and Direction!

However poor the storyline, it was films like this which kept Château Marine in clover. Jaddanbai and Mohan Babu were no more and Nargis was supporting her brothers and their families, as well as the other dependents—relatives, cooks, chauffeurs, ayahs. They all had to be looked after. Sometimes Anwar managed to get work as a character actor, but Akhtar was primarily her manager, and it was he who decided who she should work with and for how much. She still took very little interest in her own money; for her it was merely a means to making everyone around her comfortable.

The discomfort at home was not due to the money, but due to the rows over Raj Kapoor. A friend who prefers to remain anonymous, but was very close to Nargis, says that initially Raj was known to be a good director and producer, but was not much in demand as an actor: certainly, Nargis was signing more films. Then, Nargis began to ask that he play the lead in all her films. It was a strategy Meena Kumari would follow later when Dharmendra, the macho Punjabi actor, came into her life.

Nargis's help meant extra income for Raj's studio. However, slowly Raj starting pressurizing Nargis to work mostly with him. Or, at least, to give preference to his work and his dates.

Nothing could have enraged Akhtar more than to see his power over his sister slipping away. He said in an interview:

> People think *ki main bura hoon*. But although I won't deny Baby's earnings fed the whole family, I did not exploit her. In fact when Raj insisted on her giving up all other films except RK's I deferred to her wishes. Raj had told her, 'We will work together and build up RK Studio. You shouldn't expect payment from RK because I've made you a partner in the studio.' However, he didn't make it official. On the other hand he stage-managed a contract which Baby asked me to sign, saying I should not object to her association with RK, in return for which I would be paid three or four thousand every month. I hated accepting the money but Baby insisted on it for my wife and children's sake. (*Super*, June 1981)

Even though she continued to act in the films he had lined up, he could see that her priority was shifting, and that she preferred now to take advice from Raj. Akhtar loved his sister, but in this matter he was as egotistical as Raj. He could not share her with anyone else. It is a fact that he never really thought about his sister's desire to get married or live independently. As the anonymous friend points out, in Château Marine most of the women worked and the men took it easy.

Zahida remembers the bitterness of the period: 'What did Raj Kapoor have to lose? He had only to gain and gain and gain. Who lost? Who lost? You know, it was such a harrowing time. I have literally seen my father beat up his sister over Raj Kapoor. He said, "Baby you are ruining your life, forget this damn Raj Kapoor, *apna kaam kaaj karo, apni mehnat karo— shaadi kar ke apna ghar sansar basaao...jab aadmi ke sitaare wahan tak pahunchte hain duniya ka har aadmi milta hai. Tum kaunsi ghalat fahmi ka shikaar ho? Kyon is chakkar mein baithi ho? Kyon apni zindagi barbaad kar rahi ho?* (Do your own work, set up your own home by getting married. When you are doing so well you can get any man of your choice. Why are you being so deluded? Why are you ruining your life?)" He was ten years older than her and had brought her up like his own child. He said when she was born, Bibiji put her in his arms and said, "*Lo tumhari choti behen hai* (Here, this is your younger sister)." We have never loved anyone the way we have loved Baby. How could he stand by and see his sister ruining her life? No, he could not. There would be violent fights because of Raj Kapoor, there was no other reason for them to fight except Raj Kapoor. And the love that lady had in her heart for Raj Kapoor was tremendous.

'It was not easy for her. Here at home she had to face the wrath of her brother, go to the studios and work, and go through whatever she would go through, and every night she would go from Marine Drive to Chembur and back again. It was not that she stayed in the cottage, the cottage was there for her to take rest. RK Studios was not ready as yet.'

By now their relationship was an open secret and the gossip magazines began to pay heed.

For Nargis, despite the problems she was facing at home, it may have been a relief to have things out in the open. And when she was in Chembur, she simply became part of the team putting the RK brand together—a very important part.

Zahida says, 'So every day she would go up and down, and then she would help RK. And there she was in his costume room, and there she was helping out, and so many of her personal things went into that studio—her personal clothes and everything. I remember the first floor, that museum, that huge place, what do you think they filled it with, where was the money to fill it?

What was RK Films giving Nargis—two thousand rupees a month? A miserable amount even in those days. She could have been making at least twenty thousand.'

Meanwhile, Nargis kept working and two more of her films with Dilip Kumar were released.

Hulchul, produced by K. Asif, was a surprisingly chaotic film. It had some very interesting characters, such as Kishore (Dilip Kumar) in a circus act. But the film was chopped and changed around till there was little meaning left. Again, Nargis did not give a great performance. Sitara, the dancer and actress, appeared in a far more memorable role. One of the reasons could have been the off-screen rivalry between the two great Pathans: Dilip Kumar who was now established, and Raj Kapoor who was spreading his wings. Once again, as in *Andaaz*, Nargis was caught between them.

Of the two, the sadder film, *Deedar*, was also the bigger hit. Again a noir film, it had Dilip Kumar at his tragic best, playing the blind singer Shamu, who has been separated from his childhood sweetheart Mala because he is poor and she is rich. He is 'cast out' from her sphere and is brought up by the poor but kind Champa (Nimmi) and her family. Champa, naturally, is in love with him, but Shamu still longs for his Mala. Coincidentally, Mala's husband Dr Kishore (Ashok Kumar) operates on him and restores his eyesight. Naturally, as happens in Hindi cinema, once Dr Kishore discovers that the object of Shamu's love is Mala, he decides to step out of the way. However, when Shamu finds out that Mala is married to Dr Kishore, he blinds himself all over again and goes off to live with Champa. The story is implausible and full of phenomenal sacrifices by all concerned. But the music by Naushad and the lyrics by Shakeel Badayuni greatly lifted an otherwise gloomy film.

Filmindia was pleased about other things. Its review headline read:

'Deedar' a Moving Love Story!
Nimmi and Dilip Beat Nargis and Ashok!

After the blazingly good performance in *Jogan* and memorable roles in *Barsaat* and *Andaaz*, was Nargis slipping into mediocrity? There is little doubt that she worked best with demanding directors. Mehboob unfailingly drew out the best in her, as did Raj. But in *Deedar*, it was the diminutive Nimmi who got the accolades. The *Filmindia* critic, who was never kind, was equally devastating here: 'One wonders whether Nargis can ever beat Nimmi given equal opportunities. Nimmi is so human and touching in her portrayals that it is difficult for an artiste used to synthetic emotions to compete with her.'

Nimmi, on the contrary, remembers that Nargis had anything but synthetic emotions.

She says: 'I worked with her in *Deedar*, there were few films with two heroines equally balanced and important. I refused to play the secondary role, but in *Deedar,* we were equally balanced, because mostly Dilip Kumar would face the camera! After that I don't think there was a similar film with two heroines.

'Even though I was a nobody she never made me feel that she was older or more famous than me. Therefore I think that not only as a good actor but even otherwise, she was a good human being. She learnt her lines very fast and in fact never used glycerine; she would weep real tears if required in a scene. I would imitate her when I started and said I must cry real tears. And when an artiste is emotional, you can sink into the scene, then tears just flow.'

The atmosphere at home had become tense, so Nargis had rented a fifth-floor apartment in Château Marine and shifted there with her nieces and nephews. This gave her some privacy and allowed her to come and go as she liked. However, during the Raj Kapoor years, even this arrangement was to prove untenable. Then she bought a flat in the next-door building, says the friend who prefers to remain anonymous, and she had it decorated in a flamboyant style. It was here that she would sometimes meet her really close friends. This was one of the very few times when she took a financial decision that was not driven by her brother. Slowly, she began losing interest in productions which did not have Raj in them or were not related to RK in any way.

Meanwhile, Raj was now ready with his next big production: *Awara*. It created waves, even more so than *Barsaat*.

While a lot of the credit went to Nargis and Raj, much of it was also due to the writer, Khwaja Ahmed Abbas. Abbas was a founder member of the Indian People's Theatre Association (IPTA), and he brought a lot of the leftist philosophy of that organization into cinema. He had written plays before he came into films and was a prolific writer, perhaps more erudite than the emotional Raj. However, both the men understood the pulse of the masses very well. Abbas wrote some of Raj's best films: *Awara, Shri 420, Jagte Raho* and *Bobby*. The first two were co-authored with V.P. Sathe. Each of the films had a clear story and broadly documented aspects of the class struggle. Raj created Raju, the little man who was to struggle against the big bad world. Raju became his alter ego and had a look and mannerisms reminiscent of Chaplin's tramp, a debt that Raj acknowledged.

What escaped Nargis's notice was that these films mainly revolved around Raju and the heroine had a minor role. By the time *Jagte Raho* (though it was not directed by him, Raj was very involved in it) was made, barely five years after *Awara*, the heroine had been squeezed out and Nargis appeared only in one short scene. Was this deliberate? It is hard to tell, but from all accounts, Raj felt Nargis was part of RK and took her participation for granted.

By the time *Awara* was filmed, RK Studios had been built and the RK team was in place. Apart from Abbas, there were the musical duo of Shankar-Jaikishen, cameraman Radhu Karmakar, and lyricists Shailendra and Hasrat Jaipuri.

For Nargis, Raj wisely returned to the image of the modern woman from *Andaaz*. In *Awara*, she is a working woman, a lawyer. He plays a more dubious character. The contrast between the two is an attempt to examine if 'the son of a thief will be a thief' and explore the question of whether it is nature or nurture that determines the goodness in human beings.

Filmindia echoed what everyone else seemed to feel:

'Awara', the Best Picture of 1951!
Raj and Abbas Share Honours!

Released at the Royal Opera House in Bombay on 21 December 1951, the film became a huge hit. Raj (Raj Kapoor) is the son of a judge, Raghunath, played by Prithviraj Kapoor. Raghunath's pregnant wife is kidnapped by a dacoit, Jagga (K.N. Singh) when she is pregnant. After her return, the judge suspects the child is not his, and she is thrown out of the house. Raghunath's son, Raj, grows up in the slums as a shoeshine boy, and slowly Jagga wins him over. Meanwhile, Judge Raghunath's ward Rita (Nargis) grows up to be a lawyer. She and Raj had been childhood friends. (Raj's obsession with childhood sweethearts took a long time to wear away.) As an adult, Raj meets Rita accidentally and they fall in love. At the film's climax, Rita defends him in court when Raj is accused of murdering Jagga and attempting to kill Judge Raghunath. Slowly, during the cross-examination, the truth emerges that Raj is actually the judge's son.

The USP of the film was definitely its casting. Finally the tension between father and son was obvious for all to see, as

Prithviraj was pitted against Raj on screen. Though Nargis had never looked so beautiful, *Filmindia* noted that she was 'outclassed' by the two Kapoors.

However, she created a sensation of sorts by appearing in a swimming costume, another ploy Raj would use in later films. Nargis was not the first actress to appear in a swimsuit (the first was Meenakshi in the film *Brahmchari* in 1938) but she was the first to do so in his films, and he did not hold back from exploiting her sexuality in other ways as well.

The song '*Dum bhar jo udhar mooh phere, o chanda* (If you look away for just a moment, o moon)' was shot on a boat with Raj and Nargis. In the lead-up to the song Raj says, '*Agar aur kareeb aogi, toh naav doob jaayegi* (If you come any closer, the boat will sink).' She replies, with a smile of total capitulation, '*Doob jaane do* (So let it sink).' The Indian audience had never seen a woman so unafraid to display her passion. It was a declaration of liberation. Till then, cinema had been content to deal with the coy, docile Indian woman. Now suddenly, Nargis changed the rules. But it was done with finesse. There was no nudity or vulgarity. She lost control, but kept her dignity. It was a hard act to follow and very few actresses have managed it.

Awara very quickly became an international film, especially popular in the Soviet Union where hundreds of children were named after Raj and Nargis. India after independence had close cultural links with the Soviet Union, partly due to the prominence of left-leaning intellectuals, with their unshakable hegeomony over India's art and culture. Their stranglehold led to the downgrading of Indian cinema for many years: unless a film was 'progressive' or 'socially relevant' or 'realistic', i.e., if it did not deal with poverty or slums in some fashion, it could not be 'art' and so was automatically deemed 'vulgar'. Luckily, some of the card-carrying members of this intellectual dictatorship happened to work in the Bombay film industry, and their films and their poetry usually got grudging recognition from the cultural czars. Some of the best poets such as Kaifi Azmi and Sahir Ludhianvi belonged to this group. So did Abbas. It was a powerful group and it had the support of the government, which was essential in the years just after independence. The backing of Abbas ensured that *Awara* was screened in the Soviet Union. And that was the start of international recognition for both Nargis and Raj, who were invited to Moscow and feted—as a couple—wherever they went. The film travelled to the Middle East and even Africa. The song '*Awara hoon* (I am a vagabond)' became synonymous with Indian cinema, and in Russia and China (where it went via Russia), it is popular even today.

Why did *Awara* capture public imagination? Like all of Raj's films, it was stylishly shot. Radhu Karmakar was the cameraman for most of his films, and in this too he used light and shade very effectively. It boasted a long 'dream sequence' shot in the as-yet-unfinished RK Studios where Nargis was once again pressed into dancing—the one skill she did not possess. Yet the stunning music and the whirling gaseous clouds taking the hero from heaven to hell made for compelling cinema. Every song was a hit and Shankar-Jaikishen outdid themselves with *Awara hoon*.

Prithviraj Kapoor was the central character in the film, around whom the whole plot revolved, but it was the theme of young love which won the film its popularity. The storyline was strong, there was plenty of humour, especially in the first half, and the romance between Raj and Nargis was more than believable. Suddenly, the audience could not think of one without the other.

None of this was very good for Nargis, who still had to face her brother's anger whenever she went home. Yet she continued to support her family and acted in eight more films (outside the RK banner) before Raj released his next, *Aah,* in 1953.

Shammi remembers the tension at Château Marine: 'She was definitely unhappy because of the atmosphere in the house, but she got out of the house at eight in the morning, and she was out the whole day in the studio, working. A stage came when she was defiant. Akhtar used to beat her, and I would only look at her and say "*Kya phir se hua* (Did it happen again)?" And she would say, "Yes." Raj Kapoor and she were working together, he was a very intelligent man, you jell with a man like that when you are very creative. He was very good-looking, hardworking, and later on, she started looking after the production work, she was spending all her time there.

'Krishna (Raj's wife) was very much there inside the home, but she was not connected with film. Nargis obviously felt guilty about it all. In a relationship of that sort you feel a sort of guilt, if you are an honest person, if you are practical and well-read, you are knowledgeable about things. She had come so much further than her own family, she could no longer get along with those people who never read, who were not on the same wavelength. So she started spending more time in the flat she had bought next door, and at RK Studios.'

Nargis acted in a total of 16 films with Raj Kapoor during this period. Only six were under the RK banner, from 1948 to 1956. Yet they were inseparable and she did not give up hope that they would marry one day.

Nimmi watched Nargis going through the agony of being the 'other woman': 'At the time she was very unhappy and insecure because she was involved with a married man. But when talk of marriage with Rajji would come up, the whole Kapoor family would gang up on one side. You are not going to get married again, they would tell him. Because his wife, Krishna, was very popular among the relatives. They used to treat her like a devi, and she was very much like one. He wanted to get married to Nargis—but it was not possible.'

Nargis confided to her young niece Rehana how difficult it was to stay within the circumscribed role assigned to her, when she wanted to participate fully in Raj's life: 'One day she told us—she could now talk openly to us—that Krishnaji had gone to Jabalpur, and she was shooting at RK Studios, when Raj's son Chintu (Rishi) became very sick. They came running to the studio and said, "Nargisji, we have to call a doctor, he is very sick." She immediately stepped forward, and then stepped back just as fast, because she thought if something happens to that child, if he dies or something, everyone will say she killed him. She wanted to go, to take him with her to the doctor, get him treatment, because she had no ill feeling towards Krishnaji and the child, and also because she had all of us 10-12 children whom she was looking after, but she was scared.'

Her brother, meanwhile, had not given up on her. In his attempt to get her to return to home productions he wrote *Bewafa* (released in March 1953), in which he took care to cast Raj as a cold-blooded heartbreaker and thief who is only after her money. To his credit, Raj took this in his stride, even though the more heroic role in the film was given to the ageing Ashok Kumar. Akhtar's game was unwittingly (or perhaps deliberately) given away in the publicity booklet, which told the story most amusingly.

SYNOPSIS

The old adage that Love in the teens lacks judgement—Was this true in the case of our young Heroine RUPA? Did she love Someone? Or Was she loved in return? OR Did someone else love her? And what was the outcome ? All this is wrapped in deep Mystery? Rupa's life began in a Chawl. She led a miserable existence with her uncle who was a drunkard, who ill treated and tortured her. RAJ her neighbour had always a playful and cajoling attitude to-wards Rupa. He even sympathised on her pitiable state and profered timely help to her which she used to accept though reluctantly. One day she was forced to leave the chawl and wanted to put an end to her life but Fate had decreed otherwise. She met Ashok, a poor and unsuccessful artist who lived in a humble room in the neighbour-hood. Ashok with a connoisseur's eye thought Rupa an ideal model for his paintings. This proved true. Ashok and Rupa became rich over-night. Rupa forgot her miserable past and was happy in her present rich environments with Ashok.

At this juncture Raj arrives on the scene—a completely changed Raj—dressed like a gentleman with aristocratic behavior and habits. Rupa was very pleased to meet Raj after such a lapse of time. She introduced Raj to Ashok—who though had not met each other before but had heard of each other. Ashok was not well impressed with Raj nor Raj with the former. Raj's intimacy with Rupa grew more and more every time they met. Ashok did not approve of this association as he thought that Raj was not good enough for Rupa and that he was more after her money. Raj on the contrary gave all the assurances to Rupa that he only cared for her and nothing else mattered to him in the world. All these developed into a conflict and misunderstanding amongst the three namely, Rupa, Raj and Ashok. How did this culminate?

Who was successful—Raj or Ashok?
Whom should Rupa wed? Raj or Ashok?
With whose views of life would Rupa agree—Raj's or Ashok's?
SEE the answer to all these on the *SILVER SCREEN.*

Bewafa was produced by Nargis, no doubt to placate her irate family, especially Akhtar. But she did not pay heed to the message in the film, and like Raj, she acted out the part, but followed the dictates of her heart. The one liberal feature in the film was that the artist and his muse could live together in the same house without being married, and draw no criticism from anyone. Not even the vagrant Raj.

While *Bewafa* was being produced, many more films were signed with them as a couple. Some were good, and some were forgettable, such as *Ashiana,* produced by Swinder Sabharwal. Once again it was the story of childhood love, adult romance and finally, death for the two lovers. The *Filmindia* review is irate and sums up the film thus:

Raj and Nargis Give Stupid Portrayals!

The film that attracted attention when it was released on 15 August 1952, at Super in Bombay, was *Anhonee*, produced and written by Abbas under his banner Naya Sansar. Once again he went back to his theme of baby switching, only this time it was with two half-sisters who looked exactly alike. Yes, it was Nargis in a double role.

The theme was familiar: one child grows up in a rich household, while the other is poor and becomes a prostitute. The twist is that it is the legitimate child who has become a whore, and the illegitimate one who is brought up in a shareef khandaan in Lucknow. The children had been switched soon after their birth.

Nargis gives a wonderful performance in the film. At last she had a role that was challenging. She plays the incorrigible Mohini with great gusto, blowing smoke rings and hitching up her saree, while as the sober Roop she is all melancholy sweetness. Raj is the struggling lawyer who falls in love with Roop and stumbles upon the well-kept secret that her father had once had a mistress. The cunning Mohini, who wants both Raj and her share of the family fortune, is killed off by the scriptwriter at the end so that Roop and Raj can live happily ever after.

Filmindia was surprisingly not very pleased:

Abbas Stoops to Produce!
'Anhonee', a 'Progressive' Stew!

The reviewer grumbled: 'Even in progressive Abbas's picture there is a gun, a piano, a triangle, duets, buffoons, and of course a car accident. We had thought Abbas could do without them...'

The tirade continues: 'It seems that Raj Kapoor didn't satisfy Abbas the way he presented Abbas's story in 'Awara.' So Abbas probably wanted to pick up the old case again and show Raj Kapoor how he would have done it. But for all that we don't think Raj Kapoor or for that matter anybody will agree with Abbas that it was worth his while...'

In those days, the double-role was still very complicated to film and it took a brave director and a very experienced actor to attempt it. It is interesting, too, that Abbas chose to create a double role around Nargis and not Raj Kapoor. Did he recognize, as did many others, that she was the better actor?

The music by Roshan and the lyrics by Shailendra, Santoshi and Sardar Jafri also helped. The first song that Raj Kapoor sings as a struggling lawyer trying to win Roop's heart, *'Main dil hoon ek armaan bhara* (I am a heart full of aspirations)' is a Talat Mehmood classic. Nargis got to sing some good songs as Mohini, both at her kotha and then at Roop's party where she embarrasses everyone by flirting openly with Raj. But good though the acting is, the film itself is a cliché-ridden melodrama.

At the time, Raj was getting ready to shoot *Aah,* which would be a watershed film for him and Nargis. They had been together for four eventful years, and after *Aah,* the agreement was that Nargis would stop acting in 'outside films'. It was the nightmare Akhtar Hussain had been dreading.

Nimmi remembers that time: 'They both enjoyed working together, and understood each other's work. She was his muse. There was a bungalow near the studio where she practically began living and she only worked with him, without doing any other outside films. She had given up all outside work because she was sentimentally involved with Rajji, and he had asked her to give up all outside work. Though she was a star, the masses could only see her in RK films. They could not see her in non-RK films any more.'

Château Marine's fortunes started to decline.

Zahida says: 'When she got into RK films, she started refusing a lot of work. And my father used to look after all his sister's work, you can say he was her secretary, everything was managed by him. He used to say, "Baby, you are an actress, you are getting such good work, why are you not taking it? RK makes one film in two years, three years, you are not in front of the public all the time. Public memory is very short-lived. And your work speaks for you, your talent speaks for you. What are you doing?" That was a phase of life when she did not want to listen to reason at all. You cannot make anyone do anything forcefully. She was at that age. My father was totally against this RK episode to begin with. He did not approve of it, he disliked it, he kept telling her that when she could have got the best man on earth, why should she waste her time with this much-married Raj Kapoor. But I guess when you are young and in love, reason takes a backseat.'

By the time *Aah* was made, the 24-year-old Nargis had acted in more than 33 films which were not part of the RK banner. She had acted in only three films—*Aag*, *Barsaat* and *Awara*—for the Raj Kapoor banner. But her involvement with Raj was so strong that it overshadowed everything else. The more they insisted that she give him up, the more she resisted. And finally one day, the breaking point came, and she announced that all decisions regarding her dates would be handled by Raj. It was the gesture of a woman who felt she must stand by her man.

Zahida says: 'Those were bad days, all our cars were sold, our staff came down to the minimum, our family jewellery was sold, our family was down in the doldrums. Bua's career was restricted to mainly RK films. She was giving all her best to RK. The family went through a very harrowing time. I would not say she was the sole bread earner, but she was definitely earning more than the rest. And when the times fell bad on the family, and she would not take films outside of RK, my father said to her, "Baby, how are we going to survive and how are we going to pull on? You have to take outside films."'

While her brother fretted and fumed, for once in her life Nargis decided to be firm. After all, she was already 24, and she wanted to do everything she could to preserve her relationship, even though she was the more insecure and unequal of the two.

Aah, the long awaited RK production, did not live up to the promise of *Awara*. Inder Raj created a complex version of *Devdas* (including the tubercular Raj Kapoor dying in a tonga en route to his beloved's wedding, complete with a song by the tongawala) without the context of the original film. *Devdas* has worked in different cinematic avatars because it is firmly rooted in the Bengali feudal world of a certain era, when the bhadralok lost themselves in drink and romance. So we have had Baruah, Saigal, Dilip Kumar and Shah Rukh Khan enact the role quite convincingly.

However, Raj was never able to do tragedy as well as Dilip Kumar could. According to the review in *Filmfare*, 'For a young man weighed down by a frustrated love affair, two infected lungs, and a sensitive tortured poetical mind, he looks surprisingly well and plump.'

The plot was akin to *Cyrano de Bergerac*. Raj is attracted to a girl called Chandra (Vijaylakshmi) after reading her letters. He discovers the truth later that they were actually written by her sister, Neelu (Nargis) who is also a poet, like Raj. They fall in love. But the moment Raj finds out he has tuberculosis, he camouflages his illness with lies and deception, even trying to make Neelu believe that he actually loves her sister. Finally he dies of consumption and Neelu marries someone else. The film was a box office disaster compared to RK's previous successes. In a later re-dubbing, the end was changed to a happy one but by then it was too late.

The *Filmfare* review is not very encouraging about Nargis either, saying that 'She is very well photographed and looks beautiful. But her flair for comedy is limited to primitive acting (by which the critic probably means that she was child-like) and director Raja Nawathe hasn't helped her any.'

Why did Raj Kapoor not direct the film himself? If he had done so, it would probably have had the intensity of *Awara* or *Shri 420*, which followed. The film had a loose clumsy look, as though it were waiting for someone to come and tighten it up.

Perhaps this was the time when Raj in real life was also suffering some personal angst. According to Shammi, at one stage he had even drawn up his divorce papers, and was ready to leave his wife for Nargis but at the very last minute, his family prevailed and the papers were torn up.

Finally, a time came when Akhtar realized that he could no longer get his sister to follow his suggestions. The break came at the start of Mehboob's film *Aan*. Nargis refused to give any dates. It shocked everyone because in many ways, Mehboob was her mentor. Ali Raza who wrote the dialogues for *Aan* remembers: 'The clash between Nargis's personal and professional life did not come in *Mother India*, but much earlier, in *Aan*. The film's mahurat was done with Nargis, but it was Raj who controlled the dates and looked after the peripherals, which Mehboob sahib did not like. Mehboob sahib wanted a lot of dates, and a lot of cooperation was required, they were to shoot continuously for forty nights at a stretch.'

Nargis did not think she had a career away from Raj, and was content to allow him to run her life. She sent a clear message to her brother about who was calling the shots. The tension escalated even further because Mehboob had given Nargis some of her best films, and now she was unable to accommodate him. The role in *Aan* finally went to Nadira. That she did not act in *Aan* would have also upset Dilip Kumar. Heroines did not usually refuse to act opposite him.

Meanwhile, preparations began in earnest for the shooting of Raj's next blockbuster, *Shree 420*. It would take nearly two years for the film to be completed. During this period Nargis, who used to work in at least six films every year, acted in only one: *Angarey*.

Shree 420
1955-1957

Shree 420 literally means a cheat. While the film *Shree 420* was highly successful, neither Nargis nor Raj was aware of how closely the film's title would come to represent their real life. She was still hoping that a miracle would enable them to spend the rest of their lives together. She wanted to settle down and have children. She even decided to meet Morarji Desai who was then the home minister of Bombay. According to Zahida, she thought he would be in a position to grant them special permission to marry. Raj and she were hopeful that there might be a way to get married without his getting a divorce from Krishna.

Morarji Desai was known to her personally. Nargis had been at the forefront of fundraising activities for a while, and he was often at these events as an important invitee or the chief guest. She had other political contacts as well. She had met Jawaharlal Nehru (quite accidentally) and kept in touch with him and his daughter Indira, having revived the contact which had been established by her mother.

Zahida says: 'Her meeting Pandit Nehru was a total mix-up. One day my father received an invitation card saying come to tea at the Raj Bhavan to meet Pandit Nehru. It was addressed to Akhtar Hussain. My aunt said, "How come you've got a card?" My father in his own right was an actor, a director, a producer, so why not? It was an invitation for Mr and Mrs Akhtar Hussain. My aunt asked, "What will Bhabhi do there?" My mother was a housewife and did not really go out very much. So Nargisji landed up at the Raj Bhavan. Everyone recognized her, of course, and she was very happy. Actually the card was meant for a Colonel Akhtar

Hussain—we found out much later. It was destiny. She got in touch with Nehru and then with Indira, and so her interaction with the family continued. And you can see that connection is still there, through Dutt uncle, through Priya.'

These political connections were a ray of hope, or so Nargis imagined. She knew the prime minister of India, she was friendly with the home minister of Bombay. She was a famous film star. Surely something could be done to help her. The intractable Morarji had just worked on the Hindu marriage laws, and she thought he would be able to guide her. But their meeting was a disappointment and nothing was resolved.

Morarji Desai was in any case rather puritanical and was identified with prohibition in Bombay. He sought to emulate his hero Mahatma Gandhi but was widely known to be unhelpful and headstrong. Many years later, he briefly became prime minister of India at the head of the shortlived Janata government which came to power after the Emergency imposed by Indira Gandhi. To turn to him for guidance was a complete error of judgement.

A friend close to her remembers her dejection at the rebuff, because she had been keen to find a solution which, she imagined, would not hurt Krishna, Raj Kapoor's wife: 'Nargis was basically a simple soul. Raj was a very good director who saw that she was a talented actress. It was a compatible professional relationship. He pursued her. And at that age, any girl, especially if you have had a very strict background, would have slipped up with all that attention.

'But she was determined that she would never spoil Raj's family life. It was always in her mind. And yet she wanted to settle down and get married to him.'

Knowing it was a problem without a solution, Raj tried in his own way to make her feel valued.

Shammi disputes the assertion that Nargis had no income from RK Studios. 'All of Raj's films were hits, so he had money. She was paid by RK—all her expenses, whenever we travelled, whatever she bought or used, all the bills would go to RK. Naturally, her earnings were not going to Château Marine now.

It may not have been very much, because in those days we were not paid in crores. When Dilip Kumar got one lakh of rupees in those days, the news was splashed in the papers. Eventually she also took one or 1.5 lakh rupees per film but that was towards the end of her career.'

Of course, film budgets were also not very big, nor were the films too elaborate. Nimmi says, 'Shooting would normally take a few months. *Andaaz* took around 60 days of shooting, with a budget of six or seven lakh rupees. That would be worth crores today. If an agreement was for one lakh we would think it was a huge amount. We used to be competitive amongst ourselves. If we heard that Dilip had signed a contract for a lakh, we would say now we must get one lakh. When I left the film industry, I had signed a film from Madras, which was never completed; the contract was worth three lakh rupees. When I started refusing films, the word spread through the whole industry, Nimmi is doing a film for three lakhs. Before *Mughal-e-Azam* came out, the competition was all between Nargis and me, not Madhubala. She was pretty, but not in the same league.'

Mughal-e-Azam was another instance of Nargis succumbing to Raj Kapoor's wishes. It was a grand period film about Emperor Akbar, the Mughal-e-Azam, and the romance between his son Saleem and a dancing girl, Anarkali. It was K. Asif's dream film. And K. Asif's dreams came in lavish proportions. He took 15 years to make the film and several lakhs of rupees were spent on it. His search for authenticity made him go to incredible lengths and he even persuaded Bade Ghulam Ali Khan to sing for the film—the only time he lent his voice to film music. To avoid saying no to the persistent filmmaker, Bade Ghulam Ali asked for a fee that was ten times what playback singers were usually paid. Asif trumped him by accepting the challenge and paid him as much. Ghulam Ali sang two memorable songs for the film.

Originally, Asif had signed up Chandramohan and Nargis. Nargis was to play the part that eventually went to Madhubala. Then Chandramohan died, after only ten reels had been shot. Asif prepared to re-shoot the reels with Dilip Kumar and Nargis. But Raj Kapoor decided that Nargis could not act in the film any more. The film Nargis refused became the iconic Indian period film of the century. It was re-released in 2005 in colour and ran to packed houses. It established forever the myth of Madhubala as the beautiful but unattainable woman.

In 1955, the same year that a gauche new actor with a Punjabi accent, Sunil Dutt, made his debut in *Railway Platform*, Raj Kapoor's slick new production *Shree 420* was released. It took the country by storm, right from its opening song—'*Mera joota hai Japani, yeh patloon Inglistani, sar pe lal topi Roosi, phir bhi dil hai Hindustani* (My shoes are Japanese, my trousers are English, my red hat is Russian, but my heart is Indian).' Raju (Raj Kapoor) is a tramp who with all his worldly belongings in a bundle makes his way to the big bad city and goes through a series of adventures in which he learns to deal with urban life. *Shree 420* keeps a rapid pace and the plot moves smoothly. The mood is no longer dark or sombre, as it was in *Aag,* or even *Barsaat,* for *Shree 420* is mainly about problem-solving. The film belongs to Raju, while the symbolically named Vidya (Nargis) is an impoverished school teacher who falls in love with him and keeps him on the right path.

Written by K.A. Abbas, the film follows the good-hearted tramp's descent into the sleazy underbelly of the city before he is redeemed. As usual the songs were woven intelligently into the film and became huge hits. For instance, the song '*Mudh mudh ke na dekh* (Don't look back)' performed by Maya (Nadira)— also symbolically named—marks the point of his fall from grace. And then there was the scene which epitomizes the Raj-Nargis romance: the two of them in the rain, under an umbrella, singing '*Pyar hua ikrar hua* (We fell in love, and accepted it)'.

One of the lines in the song was loaded with meaning for them: *Main na rahoongi tum na rahoge phir bhi rahengi nishaniyan* (I won't be there nor will you but signs of our love will live on). The shot cut from the two of them to three children huddled together in the rain, dressed in raincoats. They symbolized the children that the lovers would have, but in reality they were Raj and Krishna Kapoor's children, who had come to attend the shooting that day. The irony was, undoubtedly, a little excessive.

As theatres put up notices warning the public to dash for advance bookings because the film was sold out, it became obvious that Raj's team—music directors Shankar-Jaikishen, lyricists Shailendra and Hasrat Jaipuri, cameraman Radhu Karmakar and of course, writer Abbas—had created magic once again. Yet, for Nargis it must have been galling to share star billing with Nadira (a Baghdadi Jew, Florence Ezekiel was also discovered and named by Mehboob and she had replaced Nargis when she dropped out of *Aan*). Indeed, from *Awara* to *Aah* and *Shree 420*, Nargis found her roles getting smaller and smaller. She may have been Raj Kapoor's muse, but as his reputation grew, she dwindled in importance.

Barsaat, Awara, Shree 420. The hat trick ensured Raj's legacy as a producer/ director/ actor and no one could fault him on any of his roles any more. If he had needed Nargis initially, he certainly did not need her now. He was a star in his own right, and a bigger star than she was.

After Morarji Desai's refusal to cooperate, Nargis began to weigh her options. It was a difficult time because Krishna had two more children during the time that Raj and Nargis were an 'item'. Simi Garewal, who acted in *Mera Naam Joker* and later made a documentary on Raj Kapoor, recollects seeing love letters that Raj wrote to Krishna from Moscow, when he was travelling with Nargis.

Nargis was too decent a person to actively try and ruin Krishna's life and though the two met, she did not try to humiliate her in any way. In fact, a friend remembers how at film functions, Nargis would sit at a discreet distance. But Raj Kapoor would personally get up and bring her to sit next to him. Krishna Kapoor would be seated on his other side. Both the women knew what Raj was doing, but neither wanted to rock the boat. It was an uneasy truce.

The strain was beginning to show during the shooting of their next film together, *Chori Chori*. The film, based on the Hollywood film *It Happened One Night*, was shot in the AVM studio in Madras. Some of those present felt that Raj was beginning to take too much interest in a South Indian actress working on a set close by. Obviously, this would have been another blow for Nargis who was becoming increasingly insecure. She was now 27 and a lifetime of being 'the other woman' stared her in the face. Was there no way out?

They struggled their way through *Chori Chori* (another aptly named film). It was premiered at the Regal on 11 October 1956, and received lukewarm reviews, though it did very well at the box office. While the film has stood the test of time, and the music by Shankar-Jaikishen is superb, *Filmfare* was devastating in its criticism:

Puerile Treatment and Utterly Naïve
Direction Mar AVM's 'Chori Chori'

The critic rues: 'The story is hackneyed and its treatment grievously lacking in imagination, with not the slightest conception of characterization, or sustained credibility.'

The story is familiar: a millionaire's daughter Baby (Nargis) wants to marry a man her father thinks is a gold-digger. So she runs away from his yacht. The father announces a reward of a lakh and a quarter rupees for anyone who finds her. A journalist fallen on hard times, Suman (Raj Kapoor), meets up with her. They fall in love but when she discovers that he has been hired by her father to take her back, she returns to Daddy and he agrees she can marry the gold-digger. At the last minute, everything is resolved between Baby and Suman and the lovebirds elope on his scooter.

The film has a mélange of interesting characters as many people join the hunt for Baby, hoping for the reward. Comic relief is provided by Bhagwan and Johnny Walker, also among the bounty hunters.

Filmfare wrote that 'Raj Kapoor turns in a perfectly natural portrayal in an apt role and carries the picture on his shoulders. The whimsical touches with which he invests his performance are just enough to give life to the part. Nargis for her part does as well as she can in a poorly written and directed role. She appears definitely ill at ease in comedy... She has a few good moments, but on the whole hers is a brittle and artificial performance.' Contributing to the film were many of the usual suspects from the RK bandwagon: Shankar-Jaikishen, Shailendra and Hasrat Jaipuri, and the story was written, or more accurately, 'adapted' by Aga Jaani Kashmiri.

The best part of the film is its music, especially the three duets sung by Lata Mangeshkar and Manna Dey, which seem to uncannily mirror the romance between the stars. The first song '*Ye raat bhigee bhigee* (This mellow moist night)' has a shy pyjama-clad Nargis in her room wistfully hoping for romance while he is outside on a hammock wishing the same. The next number is a marionnette song-and-dance with the puppets changing into Baby and Suman puppets in Baby's imagination. She complains that he does not leave her alone and he protests his love: '*Jahan main jaati hoon wahan chale aate ho* (Wherever I go you follow me)'. The third song, '*Aaja sanam madhur chandni mein hum* (Come, my darling, outside in the moonlight)' has her willing and eager, while he looks annoyingly unsure.

At that point, their future was indeed precarious.

What happened to Nargis, and why did critics at the time

feel she was not at her best? Was the gossip doing the rounds affecting her performance or were the viewers themselves affected by the gossip? Was weak direction by Anant Thakur to blame? Basically, Raj was a director himself, and so could understand a role or a part without any problems. Later in life he acquired too many mannerisms to be a really great actor, but now he was at the peak of his career and very assured in front of the camera. Nargis, on the other hand, needed a strong directorial hand to turn in a really great performance.

It was sometime during the filming of *Chori Chori,* far away from Bombay, that Nargis slowly woke up from her dream and realized she had made herself uncomfortably dependent on Raj: she did not have a career independent of him, she had no films on hand, no money coming in except what she got from RK, and her family was becoming increasingly estranged from her. As far as she could see, she had no real future, either personally or professionally. The Kapoor khandaan was not going to permit any formal alliance between them. She realized that Raj was always going to stand by his wife and children.

Zahida remembers: 'So when this thing happened, and she realized that he wasn't going to marry her, then my father told her, "Baby, now what do you have to say?" And she said, "Bhaiya, get me some work. *Bhaiya mujhe kaam dilwaiye.*"'

With those words, she began to rebuild her life. There was no clean break—Raj and she carried on meeting—but she began to re-build her career and her home life.

Zahida says: 'Then my father got in touch with a couple of producers and said, "Nargisji is available." They replied that Nargis is exclusively RK property and she will not work for others. But my father told them she would. He spoke to H.S. Rawail and he signed her up for *Miss India.* Then she did *Adalat, Lajwanti, Ghar Sansar.* And then Mehboob sahib wanted to make *Mother India,* and she signed up for that. So she had all these other films.

'She was a very strong woman. Once she made up her mind, she could put him away just like that. And believe me, he went around like a man hurt, asking one and all, "*Kaisi hain vo?* (How is she?)" You know, all that rubbish, all the time. (Even in later years) he would call me up because my voice sounded like hers.

'He must have loved her—or it was his ego which was deflated totally. I don't know, the definition of love varies from person to person. But why did this man cry when he could have done something about it and did not?'

The fact that Nargis had started working on her own was a shock for Raj who had got used to her steady presence. She had helped to build the RK brand in so many ways. He never denied that fact: in his office there was always a photograph of her, as a tribute, even after she married Sunil.

The rift between them became even more obvious with the film *Jagte Raho*. From some accounts it appears that the script originally had Raj and Nargis play a simple village couple looking for water to quench their thirst in a callous and indifferent city. But by the time the film was shot, Nargis had been written out, and the film belonged to Raj, who played the mute villager to perfection. Directed by Sombhu Mitra and Amit Mitra, the film had dialogues written by Abbas. It explored the divide between the rich and the poor and, as the leftist Abbas loved to do, examined the superficiality of urban life. It managed to achieve all this mostly through pantomime and very little dialogue. It was a brilliant film in many ways, though it borrowed heavily from Chaplinesque imagery, including the sharing of food with a street dog.

Nargis appeared only in a guest role, at the end, as the devotee at a temple who gives water to the thirsty peasant. Those who sat through the first few screenings of the film recollect how the audience anticipated the shot, and kept saying, 'He will only quench his thirst when Nargis appears.' And that is exactly how it happened. In a film which was otherwise satirical and fast moving, Nargis appeared in a lyrically shot scene, wearing a Bengali-style white saree, one shoulder bare, carrying a pitcher of water, just as dawn broke. She looks luminous in that brief role. (Years later, Raj would try to recreate the look with Zeenat Aman in *Satyam Shivam Sundaram*.)

The film was not a popular hit, but it did well in the 'artistic' circles and won the Karlovy Vary award in 1957.

Nargis, who had helped in the production whenever she could, didn't quite savour the film's critical success. Instead she kept herself busy with her other projects. Unlike the popular myth that she went straight from RK Studios into the production of *Mother India*, it seems she was already discussing and signing up other projects.

Most of the new films were unexceptional. And in most of them, she played the part of a married woman. From working almost exclusively with the 'A' class of actors, she was now pushed into working with the second rung. These were good sturdy actors, but none could match the calibre of Raj who was now part of the holy trinity of Hindi cinema: Dilip-Dev-Raj.

Of her new heroes, Raaj Kumar was very new to films, and Pradeep Kumar was best known for his intense bushy-browed good looks. Only Balraj Sahni was a seasoned actor, with training and experience in theatre. He was enormously talented, but because he often played the role of a poor, oppressed person, his presence would immediately conjure up a sense of seriousness, sincerity and tragedy. He is best remembered for his role as a rickshaw puller in *Do Bigha Zamin* (1953), directed by Bimal Roy.

In another film, *Pardesi*, Nargis was cast opposite a Russian actor, Oleg Strizhenov. An extremely ambitious project undertaken by Abbas, the film was a joint production with Russian director Vassily M. Pronin and was meant to be a celebration of Indo-Russian friendship. Apart from Nargis, it featured Prithviraj Kapoor and Balraj Sahni. The film carried a strong political message of Indo-Soviet friendship—Nehru had recently visited Moscow and met Khrushchev and Bulganin in June 1955. *Pardesi* was a joint production between Abbas's production house Naya Sansar, and Mosfilms.

Abbas suitably reinvented history in the film, in which he revealed the fifteenth-century links between Russia and India through the journey of a Russian traveller, Afanasi Nikitin. The real Afanasi had set up trade between the two countries. But the 'pardesi' Afanasi has other things in mind. While travelling in India he meets a Maharashtrian peasant girl, Champa, who falls in love with him. He saves her life after she almost dies of snakebite, and then stays with her family for a while before he sets out on his travels again. Towards the end of the film, Champa has a baby and Afanasi gets on a dhow and heads back to Russia.

The film was released in India on 6 December 1957 and failed to do well. The Russian version was extremely short, and a little more successful.

As Nargis wrote later, the experience of making the film, especially the shoot in Moscow, was a nightmare: thanks to the Russian system of working in shifts, things moved extremely slowly, with the unit packing up every day on time, whether any shots had been taken or not. By this time Nargis was already out of her RK phase and desperate to come home. But all her appeals to complete the work soon fell on deaf years, and she was in Moscow for a month, often arguing with Abbas and Pronin. Her professionalism would not let her leave.

Among the more cheery films that she signed at this time was *Miss India*, written and directed by the character actor and comedian I.S. Johar. The story is about Rama (Nargis), an educated girl who is duped into marrying a crook, Anil (Pradeep Kumar). Instead of thanking her stars when the thieving Anil abandons her on her wedding night, she decides to track him down. In order to do this, she has to slip into a variety of disguises, including that of a young boy and a princess. Finally, Anil falls in love with her and her real identity is revealed. The film was a straightforward masala entertainer and did fairly well at the box office.

Miss India did not thrill the reviewers, however. One review of the film which was released at Roxy, on 31 May 1957, carried the headline:

'Miss India', More Silly Than Entertaining

But the second line in *Filmindia* read:

Nargis Saving Grace of the Picture

The review mentions that 'From the players, Nargis, of course, gives the best and most lively performance in the picture in the role of Rama. Playing a generally lighthearted role with abandon she provides some effective comedy and proves her versatility.

Pradeep Kumar as Anil is burdened with an unsympathetic role and gives a performance a shade less dull than usual.'

At least the review was better than the one she got for *Chori Chori*.

Another mediocre film lay ahead with *Lajwanti* which, very much like *Adalat*, focused on a married woman whose fidelity is falsely doubted. As in *Miss India*, the woman believes that she can be happy only when she is reunited with her husband. Though separated by two decades, these films were akin to the films Jaddanbai produced and acted in. Jaddanbai played the role of a 'fallen woman' unfairly pushed into that environment in *Talash-e-Haq*, as did Nargis in *Adalat*. The defence, in both cases, was that women found in brothels are often from 'respectable' families.

With these later films, the carefully constructed image of Nargis changed. From the short-haired, wilful, horse-riding, modern woman seen in films like *Andaaz* and celebrated in *Awara*, she was now the traditional weeping *Bharatiya naari*, begging her husband for forgiveness and a place at his feet.

Why did Indian filmmakers suddenly begin to create such characters? Nargis was not the only actress wallowing in middle-class misery on screen. It is possible that the search for an Indian identity that Raju sung about in *Shree 420* had led to a rejection of 'Western values'—the source of all evil. In a patriarchal society, it was obvious that women would be the first victims. Nargis had rejected 'Western values' once before in *Andaaz*, and now she continued to do so in films like *Lajwanti* and *Adalat*. In *Lajwanti*, for instance, she innocently hides from her husband the real reason for her friendship with an artist, and ends up being thrown out of the house. All these films had one clear message: it was time the Indian woman went back into her domestic space. Her real god was her *pati parmeshwar*. The sari-clad Nargis in these films is very different indeed from the one who joyously wore a swimsuit in *Awara*.

In the political arena, too, India was moving towards an era of well-meant but misplaced national pride through a slew of protectionist, socialist policies. Everything 'phoren' and 'Western' had to be rejected as the government tried to restrict imports and build indigenous industry. Films, naturally, were a reflection of the country's new ethos.

Not surprisingly, none of the film reviews were favourable, and neither *Adalat*, released on 21 November 1958, nor *Lajwanti*, released the following year on 13 February 1959, did very well. By the time these were released, however, Nargis's life had changed, thanks to *Mother India*. This film by Mehboob spectacularly made up for all the other mediocre films she had accepted.

According to Nimmi, 'Mehboob sahib had such a long standing relationship with Jaddanbai, he had acted as an extra in her film. Now he had also reached a pinnacle of success. Nargis could not refuse him again, she respected him a lot. The role he offered her was very attractive. But I was very foolish that I did not join Mehboob Productions for *Mother India*. Mehboob sahib asked me to do the role that Kum Kum would do eventually. (It was a small role compared to that of Nargis.) Dilip sahib had already refused the role offered to him saying they are not making *Father India*, they are making *Mother India*.'

Dilip gave up on the film only after carefully examining the script to see if he could carve out a larger role for himself by playing both father and son to Nargis. From Mehboob's point of view, this would have changed the entire concept of the film, as it revolved around the woman protagonist. Some of the ideas Dilip developed during this period would eventually be used in his own film *Ganga Jamuna* (1961).

Nimmi could not walk out that easily. 'But I could not refuse Mehboob sahib because I also had great respect for him. So I went to the journalist Baburao Patel and said, I cannot refuse Mehboob sahib, but how can I play this small part? The message was sent to Mehboob sahib through Baburao, and I refused the role."

Mother India was based on *Aurat*, which in turn was inspired by the Pearl S. Buck novel *The Good Earth*, and had shades of Brecht's *Mother Courage* too. The story was credited to Babubhai A. Mehta and the dialogues were written by Wajahat Mirza.

In Mehboob's films, the women were always stronger than the men. The men were weak and sometimes ignoble; the women were strong and courageous. *Mother India* in particular offered a wonderful opportunity for any actress, because it traced her journey from marriage to old age.

After 16 years, when he decided to resurrect *Aurat*, Mehboob had no idea that just as he had started Nargis's career, quite unwittingly, he was about to end it. In another coincidence, he was about to hire for one of the main roles in the film the man whom Nargis would fall in love with and marry.

Sunil at this time was struggling to speed up his career. He still needed one good break. Things were not too bad for him, though, because after *Railway Platform* there had been a slow trickle of offers. But he had not lost his old sense of caution and kept tabs on every paisa spent.

His sister, Rani, had come to live with him with her young son and daughter, in the little flat he rented on Napean Sea Road. While he was happy to have Rani with him, he was worried about her for she did not seem to be well. Nor did she seem very keen to go back to her husband. Somehow he had to make things right for her, and for his whole family. There were other pressures as well. He had to buy a car, move into a bigger house. Actors need to look the part and be glamorous. But he had no money.

Nimmi, who first met Sunil Dutt when he interviewed her, now helped by acting opposite him in a couple of films. She remembers: 'His first film *Railway Platform*, which was made by Ramesh Saigal, flopped miserably. But it did not discourage him, because after coming into cinema no one really wants to leave. So he was looking around. Then Ramesh Saigal's younger brother found a producer who wanted to make a film, *Rajdhani*, on a reasonable budget, and he signed up Sunil Dutt, and then he came to me.

'By that time, I was living in Worli in a bungalow which was on a hill-like rock. The producer said, "Outside on the sea-face is strolling the hero of *Railway Platform*, waiting to be told about his *kismet ka faisla* (his fate). No established heroine is ready to work with him. If you agree to work with him, then we can go ahead with the film."

'These things never worried me, that the hero is new or his film was a flop. After all, I was also new at one stage in my life. So I said, "Please tell him that I will work with him." We began to work together. Meanwhile, Sohrab Modi was also making a film, *Kundan,* and he had asked me to act in it. The film was quite miserable—Sohrab Modi's role was good, not mine. So I kept refusing. However, his wife Mehtab came to me and said, "Please act in the film, two-three of his films have flopped." His financial condition, at the time, was not good. They asked me then to do a double role, act as the mother and the daughter. I started working in the film. I was doing the mother's role, but then I also acted the part of her grown-up daughter. They needed a hero to play opposite me. So I said, "Modi sahib, there is a hero, Sunil Dutt—why don't you see him? You will like him. He is very nice." Modi sahib called him, and so Dutt sahib worked with me in *Kundan.*'

Despite Nimmi's efforts, things did not go well with Sunil in *Kundan.*

His friend Krishen remembers: 'Before *Kundan,* he had signed up for *Kismet ka Khel* with Vyjayantimala and Kishore Sahu. If you ever see *Kundan* you will think it is a wonderful picture, but you will not find Sunil Dutt's name anywhere. Kishore Sahu had told him, I am signing you with such a big star, you will have to give me preference for the dates. Unfortunately, Sohrab Modi had also kept a simultaneous shooting schedule.

'Sohrab Modi got really angry with him and said, "I will ruin your career." And then Sunil replied, "Modi sahib, I have great respect for you as you are older than me, but no one can ruin anyone else's career, that is in the hands of the Almighty." I remember this word by word. Even Nimmi chastised him later, saying, "Dutt sahib, why did you say this? If you had told me, I would have said I cannot come on that day, so you would have got a chance to accommodate both films."'

Sunil wrote formally to Sohrab Modi on 29 February 1956, about some money which was still owed to him. It is obvious from the tone of his letter that Modi had not forgiven him but Sunil, as always, was polite:

Dear Sir

REF: The Balance of my Remuneration
_____

Please let me remind you that there is still a balance of Rupees Two
Thousand Five Hundred, which you have to pay to me, while I
rendered my services as an artiste in your picture 'Kundan'.

I shall appreciate it very much if you clear the accounts at your
earliest.

I am awaiting for your immediate and favourable reply.

Thanking you,

Yours faithfully,
Sunil Dutt

Life was not easy. He had to chase money, and he had to
chase work. On 27 February 1956, he wrote to Joseph Taliath
at Citadel Studios in Madras about a film called *Payal*.

My dear Mr Taliath

I am all apologies for not contacting you while you were in Bombay.
I hope you will definitely forgive me.

Mr Taliath, I was really very upset from all sides. My picture KISMET
KA KHEL was not a success. I was very much disturbed financially
also. I wanted to invite you at my residence, but could not do that
even. I also received some very sad news from my home. These were
the conditions and reasons which kept me away from you. You were
also upset as you were for quite some time in Bombay for getting the
songs recorded, and I did not want to impose myself. I hope you will
consider my position and forgive me. Now tell me if you want the
songs recorded or not.

Please do write to me when you are going to start shooting for
PAYAL, and try to be in touch with me. I have only one picture in
Bombay, MOTHER INDIA. I was getting two pictures in Filmistan, but
I did not accept them as I want to devote full energy on these two
pictures. I hope you will try to finish the picture soon. I will not sign
any more pictures till your picture is complete.

I hope you will try to bring a good idea for the climax of the
picture. Don't put me in jail as Kishore Sahu did. The climax should
be on me and I should chase the actual murderer. Only then the
public will realize the full worth of the Hero.

Please do consider all these factors and work hard on the climax.

I want to discuss with you on the previous scenes also, which I will do when I come to Madras.

I hope you will write to me about your activities.

Yours sincerely
BALRAJ

Balraj/Sunil was obviously not modest about his aspirations, and this letter is an early indicator of his directorial ambition. He tells Taliath quite clearly that the audience must appreciate 'the full worth of the Hero'! For someone on the first rung of his career, it indicates a surprising self-confidence.

Payal did eventually get made in the same year as *Mother India*, but it vanished from the cinema houses without much ado.

An interesting, if melodramatic, film that Sunil acted in was *Ek Hi Raasta*. His character dies halfway through the film, but he shared reel space with Meena Kumari and Ashok Kumar, which immediately elevated his stature. He played the part of an honest factory manager murdered by embezzlers. His wife (Meena Kumari) and their son are then looked after by Ashok Kumar, though they have to face a lot of gossip and calumny. Sunil looks fresh and young, and exits before we can seriously evaluate his acting.

It was still early in his career, and some of his 'healthy' habits such as oiling his hair had not left him. As he was to tell his children later, he was already naturally shy, and the smell of the oil helped to keep Meena Kumari at a safe distance.

The real test of his acting skills would come later in *Mother India*. He would be directed by one of India's best-known directors, and act with one of the biggest stars of the Indian screen, Nargis. Fortunately for him, Rajendra Kumar and Raaj Kumar, the other two actors in the film, were also fairly new, so they could find comfort in each other if the going got difficult. In fact, because Rajendra Kumar and he had shared a room when they first arrived in Bombay, they became particularly good friends during the making of *Mother India*.

The difference in stature between them and Nargis can be measured in terms of their fee. The actors were signed up for ten months. Rajendra Kumar was paid Rs 5000, Raaj Kumar got

Rs 6000 and Sunil Dutt offered to work without a fee, but was given a small amount of ten or twelve rupees every month (according to an interview with Gayatri Chatterjee, quoted in her book *Mother India*). In contrast, Nargis reportedly received Rs 5000 every month for the ten months. She was very obviously the star.

In September 1955, Mehboob began shooting for *Mother India*. Most of it was on location in Gujrat. As is usual on location, the crew spent a lot of time with each other. Nargis, probably still preoccupied with her personal problems, was the remote film star for Sunil, though he was flattered when she spoke to him occasionally. During breaks, they came back to Bombay, and he would drop in to meet her at Château Marine. This time he was not an autograph hunter or an interview seeker, he was an invited guest.

Zahida remembers: 'During the making of *Mother India*, Sunil Dutt came to the house, so did Rajendra Kumar and so did Raaj Kumar. These were *garib, bhooka nanga* (poor and starving) actors. Nargis never differentiated between rich and poor but we used to notice their clothes. We never said anything to her because we were scared she would get angry. "Look at the human beings not the clothes!" she would shout. When they dropped in, she would call out to us, go to Gaylords, get chicken patties, get pineapple cakes, and I used to think, why feed these guys chicken patties and pineapple cakes? They will be happy if you tell the cooks to make them bhajiyas and send them off—why are you giving them all this? Why are you being sophisticated with these people, what do they understand? Waste of time and money, and they are coming along and eating it all, *muftkhorey* (freeloaders).'

Nargis, very much like her mother, only saw the men as artistes who deserved respect, and she would genuinely try to make them feel at home. Sunil may have absorbed some of this warmth, and began to feel more comfortable in her presence. One of his friends insists that because she was friendly, he started falling in love with her. She was definitely sympathetic, and she told her a little about his family life, especially his sister Rani, about whom he was still very worried.

In between shoots, if Sunil was away, others from the *Mother India* unit started dropping in at the Napean Sea Road flat to check on Rani. Sometimes even Sardar Akhtar would come by and later, of course, Nargis.

Sunil also began to worry about his image and realized that now he was interacting with stars like Nargis who were completely out of his league. Something had to be done about this, and as a first step, he bought himself a car, with a little help from his friend Krishen. It was the Punjabi biradari that made it possible. Almost all his life, Sunil remained a bad businessman, but he was able to depend on a few friends who always helped him out of a financial hole when required.

Krishen says, 'For his first car I got a personal loan for him, for eight thousand rupees. It was a DeSoto maroon and white double-coloured car. Dev Anand used to have a big car, a Studebaker, and so he too wanted something. Though we never had any money, we had a good circle of friends. He always said, "Krishen, you have many friends—*mujhe kuchch* loan *mil sakta hai kya?*" So I asked, *kitna.* He said, "*Dus ho to chalega, nahin to kum bhi chal sakta hai.* (Would it be possible to get me a loan? I asked, how much? He said ten thousand would do, or even less.)" I asked if 8000 would do, he said *chalega* (will do). I went to a friend who was studying in college with us and whose family was quite rich. He simply asked his mother to give the eight thousand rupees, even though eight thousand rupees then is equal to eight lakh rupees today. When Mataji came back with the money I was in tears, and said, "You never even asked why I want it." Anyway, after a month Sunil signed another film, and immediately called me and returned the money. He asked me if they would like to charge some interest. I said, "Don't insult my friends, they are not moneylenders."'

The next step was to buy a larger house. All the stars had big homes or bungalows, and he had only a tiny flat, which too was rented. He finally managed to locate a sprawling bungalow at Pali Hill. In the 1950s, that part of Bombay was quite deserted, so prices were lower. But he still had no ready cash.

Yet everything seemed to be falling into place. He had

managed to find ways in which to fund a car, someday he would be able to find the money to fund the house. He was quite certain it would happen and slowly, he began to feel a little more secure.

The person who was not feeling secure at all was Raj. He had by now begun to feel a little left out of Nargis's new life. He could not reconcile himself to her absence, nor could he allow himself to admit that Nargis wanted to move on. He wanted to keep the status quo and his special place in her life. He had started drinking quite heavily, and if his behaviour at times was inappropriate, who was there to tell him?

Despite his fondness for his family, Raj seemed a very lonely man throughout his life. His relationship with Nargis was special. And suddenly, she had gone missing. Spoilt by adulation, he could not accept that he was the guilty party.

Zahida says, 'When she left to act in *Mother India* there was no face to face confrontation or exchange of words, there was nothing like that. But, of course, in his own subconscious mind Rajji realized that he was not doing justice to her. *Unke dil mein chor tha*, a guilty conscience, so he was unable to stop her, and was unable to do anything, and then whatever destiny had in store happened.'

The young Zahida had a bizarre encounter with Raj one night during that phase. The children were staying with their aunt in her fifth-floor apartment, and their parents were on the ground floor. 'I was very fond of Rajji as a child. But the only time I remember that he came to Château Marine, without her, was when she was shooting for *Mother India*, and was in Baroda.

'It was 9.30 at night, we had gone to bed, but we were not yet asleep. And the ayah knocked and said Raj sahib *aaye hain* (Raj sahib is here). We were the only people there, we were kids, and we came out, and he was totally drunk. He said to us, "Darlings, how are my darlings, darlings, I'm very tired. Darlings, I'm very hungry—got something to eat? Darlings, I'm very tired." So I looked at the ayah and said, "Whatever there is in the kitchen, give it to him." Whatever there was she brought it, heated it up and gave it to him.

'He ate it and said, "Darling, I'm very tired, can I just go to sleep?" So I said fine. *Bua ka kamra khaali tha* (My aunt's room was empty) and I said, "Fine, go to sleep," because she was in Baroda. So he went and lay down. We had this little toy mandolin, and he said, "Darling, play it for me."

'So I was playing the mandolin, round and round, twisting the dial clockwise and anti-clockwise and I was yawning and playing, and finally I said, "Raj uncle, Raj uncle, I have school tomorrow."

'Then he said something that really scared me. He said, "Darling, you are going to die very soon, I can see that while you are playing ..." and I thought to myself, *"You* are drunk, why are you killing *me?"* And I left the mandolin and said, "Uncle, I have to go school tomorrow." I got out of there. Imagine telling a small child that you are going to die very soon. He knew Nargis was in Baroda, but he was passing by and he became so emotional that he thought he would come and see the family.

'My parents were downstairs. When we told him we will tell our parents you are here, he said, "No, no, let Akhtar sahib sleep." My father would have questioned him, "What is this, why are you coming here and disturbing my children?" He would have taken him downstairs and put him in the car and told the driver, *"Leke jaao. Mere bacchon ko* school *jaana hai.* (Take him. My kids have to go to school)".'

Had he been more honest with Nargis, perhaps life would have taken a different turn for Raj. She may even have stayed with him if she had the assurance that he would not play the field any more. But what she saw left her disheartened. She had given up everything for him, even her plans to marry. (Raj's reputation as a ladies' man was to precede him everywhere. Even Vyjayantimala Bali in her autobiography, *Bonding,* confesses that her grandmother had been extremely reluctant to allow her to act in *Sangam,* because she was worried about the rumours concerning Raj. But her own alleged romantic link with Raj, she says, was baseless and completely manufactured by the RK publicity machine.)

In an interview Nargis had given in 1953, when their romance was at its peak, she had said, 'As for my own marriage, I have more or less outgrown the thought, if not the desire. I am like the doll my mother bought for me. The doll that never reached its new home in one piece.'

She felt she had reached the point of no return: she did not think marriage was a possibility. After all, she had been with him for over nine years.

In any case, the last hope of reconciliation was to be wiped out by a blazing fire and for Nargis, Sunil and Raj, life would soon take a new direction.

Radha and Birju
1957

*M*other India* was a complex film. It came after Mehboob Productions had made three loss-making films, *Amar, Paisa Hi Paisa* and *Awaaz*, between 1954 and 1956. It was imperative for Mehboob that he regain his position in the film industry as the creator of extravaganzas like *Andaaz* and *Aan*. In fact, *Aan* had enjoyed some international success as well, and a French version of it was released in 1954 as *Mangala, Fille des Indes*. Comparisons (however incongruous) to movies like *Quo Vadis* encouraged Mehboob to make another film which would have an international audience. So the scale and scope of *Mother India* had to be grander than anything seen before, though it would be set entirely in rural India.

Mehboob hired the Mysore-born Hollywood actor, Sabu Dastagir (a.k.a. Selar Sabu), who had played the title role in *The Elephant Boy* (1937), a box office hit adapted from Rudyard Kilpling's *The Jungle Book*. In 1942 Sabu was cast in the film version of Kipling's classic as well. Sabu had started life as a fatherless mahout and went on to become India's first truly international star who worked in both the US and the UK and won accolades for his performances.

He was brought into the country by Mehboob, paid a retainer of Rs 5000 and put up at the Ambassador hotel. But the required government permissions could not be obtained in time and he had to leave. One can only speculate about the path not taken: if Sabu had been taken on board and the film titled not *Mother India* but *This Land Is Mine* to make it sound more 'international', how would the story of Nargis and Sunil have played out, individually or together?

After the initial hiccups, shooting began in the villages around Umra, mostly at the farm of a landowner called Nemani. The crew stayed at the farm while the land, animals and even homes of the villagers were used as sets or props, with adequate compensation of course.

As the publicity booklet says, 'When a producer requires 300 bullock carts, 200 farmers, scores of horses, tractors, ploughs and 500 acres of paddy fields to be flooded—not to mention the sympathy and active support of scores of villages—to produce a spectacular picture like "Mother India", money becomes a helpless instrument of negotiation.'

Every scene was carefully lit and meticulously shot. Special efforts were made to keep the film realistic—Nargis and Raaj Kumar even learnt how to plough the land to make their movements look natural. The story of *Mother India* is similar to that of *Aurat*. Nargis played Radha, a simple but resilient villager who marries Shyamu (Raaj Kumar). They have a happy marriage, till Shyamu's debts to the moneylender Sukhi Lala (Kanhaiyalal) become unbearable. After a tragic accident in which Shyamu loses his arms, he abandons his family, leaving Radha to bring up the children and work the fields. She battles all sorts of problems, including the death of a child and unwelcome advances from Sukhi Lala. Her two surviving sons grow up as completely opposite characters—Ramu (Rajendra Kumar) is sober and responsible, and Birju (Sunil Dutt) is mutinous and violent.

Birju is the son Nargis has to kill in the end because he kidnaps Sukhi Lala's daughter to extract revenge for his mother's humiliation. Sunil's role was of a man-child, someone who is aggressive and macho, yet innocent and protective of his mother and her land. It was a difficult role, and it must be said that Sunil didn't quite master the mutinous ferocity with which he had to play it. The fine character actor Yakub had played the role in the previous version and to do better than him was a challenge. Also, the adult Birju was supposed to adapt some of the mannerisms of the young Birju, who was played, rather more acceptably, by Sajid. Sajid was a child from the Bombay slums whose father was paid Rs 750 for allowing the boy to act. It is said that later, touched by his performance, Mehboob and Sardar Akhtar took care of him. There are photographs of Sajid, Sardar Akhtar, Pandit Nehru and Mehboob at some of the many functions to celebrate the release of the film.

With images reminiscent of Soviet-style propaganda, *Mother India* appealed to the Indian audience for many reasons: Mehboob's deft direction, the cinematography by Faredoon Irani, Nargis's outstanding performance, Naushad's superb music, Shakeel Badayuni's lyrics. Music has always been key to a film's success, and so it was for *Mother India*. '*Pi ke ghar aaj pyaari dulhaniya chali* (The lovely bride leaves for her husband's home)', '*Duniya mein aaye hain to jeena hi padega* (Now that we are in this world, we have to learn to live in it)', '*Nagari nagari dware dware* (In towns and villages…)', '*Dukhbhare din beetey re bhaiya ab sukh aayo rey* (Finally the difficult days are over and happy days are here again)' and the spectacularly filmed '*O jaane vaale jaao na ghar apna chhod kar* (O do not leave your homes)'. The last song evoked painful images of Partition with these lines:

O jaane vaale jaao na ghar apna chhod kar
Maata bula rahi hai tumhen haath jod kar
Thehro pukarti hai tumhari zameen tumhen
Laut aao maa ki haay lage naa kahin tumhen

(O do not leave your homes behind
Your mother calls you back with folded hands
Please stop, your land is calling out for you
Come back before a mother's sigh hurts you somehow)

Following devastating floods, the villagers abandon their homes and a long line of bullock carts begins to stream out, while Radha sings to try and stop them from leaving. According to Gayatri Chatterjee in her book *Mother India*, Mehboob had deliberately asked Badayuni and Naushad to keep the Partition in mind while composing the song.

She notes, 'It is awesome to see the submerged land and hundreds of villagers assembled for the shot. The plea in the song is caught in a time warp, impossible to respond to—nothing can actually be revised. But the impact of this plea, *don't leave*, would sear the minds and hearts of Indian audiences or anyone else who has known migration and exile. The appeal includes people outside the village—outside the narrative—encompassing cities and townships...The villagers halt, listen and stay on. If there had been a near obsessive representation of urban migration in the films from the 1930s through to the 50s, *Mother India* is unique in that it portrays a reversal of the process of migration and a desire to arrest, as it were, an event that has already happened.'

It was due to scenes like these which probed India's collective consciousness, and the personification of Nargis as Mother India or Bharat Mata, that led to the film being polled even in 2007, in a poll commissioned by the news channel NDTV, as the best film of the last 60 years.

Though Mehboob kept running out of money while making *Mother India* (Nimmi remembers lending him some to complete the film, and he also tapped Nargis for help), he was determined to make an unforgettable film. Everything, therefore, had to have a message, a personal appeal to the people of India.

The scene that was a turning point for Nargis and Sunil came towards the climax of the film. Birju hides in a haystack while running away from the mob that is out to lynch him. Radha follows, looking for him, and the villagers set the haystacks on fire to smoke him out.

By 1 March 1957, the crew had already been shooting this difficult scene for a week. Faredoon Irani was framing every possible angle to heighten the onscreen tension. The girl who was doubling for Nargis had already been injured and now Nargis had volunteered to do the shot.

Everything was going well until the wind changed direction. Suddenly Nargis was trapped inside a ring of fire. In a manner reminiscent of his daredevil days in Khurd, Sunil leapt into the flames. Strangely, Nargis had made no attempt to get out of the fire. She later said she was listening to some higher power which told her to stay there, and was 'ambiguous' about being rescued. But when Sunil reached her, she allowed him to lead her out.

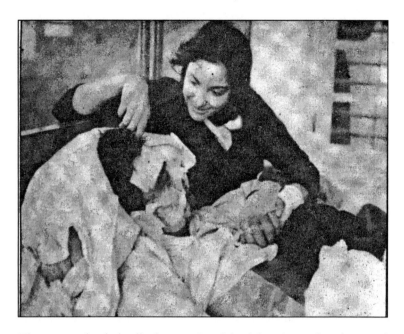

They were both badly burnt. Sunil had burns on his face and chest, and she had burns on her hands. Had Sunil not acted swiftly, Nargis could have lost her life in the fire. She was only 28 years old then.

Bombay was too far for the injured couple to travel, so Mehboob sent them to recuperate in his homestead in Billimora, 35 miles from Umra. Mehboob did not want to immediately send word to Bombay, unsure what Akhtar's reaction would be.

Once at Billimora, Nargis felt better after swallowing some painkillers, but she was horrified when she went into Sunil's room. He had high fever and was drifting in and out of consciousness. Nargis felt her inaction during the fire was responsible for his state. She sat by his side, changed the bandages, gave him his medicine and kept vigil over him.

She placed wet bandages on his fevered brow, brought him food, and sat with him throughout the night, carefully monitoring his comfort. She anxiously waited for him to open his eyes, and was surprised at the rush of relief she felt when he did.

Slowly, she began to be drawn to the man she was nursing so

devotedly. She had known him for some time, he had even visited her at home, but it was only now that she felt she was getting to know him, as his fever broke and he regained consciousness.

Sunil was deeply moved by her efforts to look after him. After all, she was a famous film star and he was still a newcomer. Yet, she was making him feel as though they had known each other for ages. His natural reticence in front of women began to recede. Soon they were talking like friends—sharing ideas, thoughts, dreams. Their fortnight in Billimora became a turning point: incredibly, they had fallen in love.

As she sat by his bedside, she realized that his courage in pulling her out of the fire had impressed her. It was a long time since someone had sacrificed anything for her. She was the one who always did things for others, whether it was for her family or Raj. Though they were both close to 30 years of age, when she looked at Sunil she saw something of the ideals she had once possessed. His shy and gentle style, quite unlike Raj's flirtatiousness, was like a balm to her. Unusually, she was spending time with a man who treated her like a normal human being.

To her own surprise, as she talked to Sunil, she realized she had stopped caring for Raj a long, long time ago. And even if she had loved him, it had never been like this. What she felt now was a powerful emotion that engulfed her and made her happy beyond belief. The depression she had been through evaporated in the face of this love. She admitted that she may have ended her life because of the 'turmoil' in it, had he (Sunil) not said, 'I want you to live.'

Raj had come into her life when she was 19 and ready for a relationship. If it hadn't been Raj, it would have been someone else; he just happened to be her first boyfriend. The relationship grew because she was able to relate to someone who was more or less her age. All her other heroes, except Dilip Kumar, were much older, such as Moti Lal and Ashok Kumar.

She was to tell Sunil, when they realized they loved each other, 'I have been a good human being, I have never hurt anybody. I have been kind and had all the virtues of a good woman, which I am proud of. I don't care what people say and think of me, for

I know I am a very strong charactered woman, I fell in love once and yielded completely to one man, and I am proud that next to that man nobody can claim in this world of loving me, even touching me. And now it is you, my love. I remember a verse from Tagore's *Gitanjali*:

Life of my Life
I shall try and keep my body ever pure
Knowing that *Thy* loving touch is upon all my limbs.'

She said she was 'shameless' in discussing every detail of her life, and was not worried because she knew 'that his (Sunil's) shoulders were always there for me to cry on—and I also knew that his garments will absorb my tears and not scatter them out for people to make fun of me.'

As the days merged into one another, Sunil discovered how difficult the last few years had been for Nargis, caught in a hopeless relationship with a man who did not care for her reputation or her future, and only wanted to exploit her. More and more he wanted to protect her and look after her forever. She confessed to Sunil that her relations with Raj had been on a 'razor's edge', and that she had been 'desperately' trying to cling to him without any response. She told him that Raj 'had started making me feel disgusting even to myself' and that before she met Sunil, she had 'no reason to be living—I was like that beautiful plant which wanted to bloom but could not because there was poison in the soil.'

With Sunil, things were different. To begin with, he was not as complicated a person as Raj. He was a straightforward, plain-speaking man with a deep respect for women. He could never put his woman on a pedestal one minute and abuse her the next. He was also far less experienced in matters of the heart. Apart from a few mild flirtations, he had never been with a woman, or even had a girlfriend. It was this naïveté that appealed to Nargis, no longer the young girl who had been swept away by twinkling blue eyes. She longed for someone steady and thoughtful. She found in him all the old values of chivalry that made her feel safe. Finally, she had met someone whom she could respect as well. And even more wonderfully, she loved him and he loved her back!

She wanted to sing and dance and laugh—and her vivacity infected the normally dour Sunil who, for the first time in his life, understood the lighthearted joy of being in love.

She said, 'I knew he (Sunil) was mine and I loved him very much. I just did not care for anyone (else). I found him and I won't let him go. I clung to him, I kissed him, I did not want to be away from him even for a moment, I used to feel my life following him wherever he went...'

She began to feel that he belonged to her and dreamt of getting married, having children and living in a house with a red roof. She thought Sunil would work in the fields (he had told her of his childhood in Khurd) and she would work in a home for poor women.

Again and again she reiterated that she 'adored him' and 'loved him like I have never loved anyone before. This is a fact. I think of him all the time that I am away from him and feel so content, when I am with him. My only prayer is to God—Oh! Lord give him the strength to bear my love and give me in return his love, that can live and not wither away. Let him respect my feelings for him. For it is for him now that I have decided to live. Oh! You love of my life.'

In her letters she was open and blunt about her affection. And within the fortnight they had decided to get married. But it would be a while before they could share their secret with the world.

Mother India was still under production, and had people suspected an affair between Nargis and Sunil, it could have led to a scandal. To begin with, she was playing his mother in the film, and Mehboob would have worried (as indeed he did later) that people would never accept the film: it would seem too much like incest.

This could damage Sunil's as yet nascent career. He would face jibes and innuendoes—as a newcomer getting involved with such a well-established actress. More importantly, if Mehboob turned against him, many doors would slam shut in his face. Third, if Raj Kapoor got to know, it could lead to unpleasantness and more gossip, as Raj was not known to keep his feelings to himself.

The fourth and most serious problem could be the reaction of Nargis's family. Akhtar was likely to go ballistic if he heard that a newcomer like Sunil had had the temerity to propose to his sister. Further, if Nargis got involved in a relationship with an actor, so soon after Raj, how would it affect her career? Akhtar had resurrected it once, but it would be difficult to do it twice. Moreover, the income at Château Marine would plummet again.

To avoid their relationship becoming public, the couple began to employ all sorts of strategies. They decided that they would not speak about it to anybody, or at least to as few as possible. As a result, even to this day, most people, even family and friends closest to them, have no idea how often they met in those early days. It was usually in secret, at night.

Since they couldn't meet openly, they constantly wrote to each other. In their letters and in the journal each one kept, they addressed each other as 'Pia' and 'Hey There'. When they sent telegrams to each other, they would sign as 'Pia' and 'Hey There'. Another set of fun pseudonyms was 'Marilyn Monroe' and 'Elvis Presley'.

On 20 March 1957, they met again in Bombay. They had been away from each other for only four days, but she told him how frightened she was that they might be separated permanently. They considered going abroad so that no one could come between them. Nargis feared that either Raj or Akhtar would ruin things.

> After so many years of miseries I have found love, I won't let it die. I can't...Now I come to think that I have never really loved anyone as I love you...Yes, I sacrificed for others—clung to my mistakes, trying to convince myself that I was in love—but now as I sit and think, that could not have been love—it was just lust and passions from the other side—and I satisfied it at the cost of my life—false vanity. What had come over me? Where were you my love? I lost so much in search of you. Life really plays a peculiar game; but with me, it cheated me for so long. It seems I was in a daze and suddenly my eyes are open and I see things clear very clear.

As the filming of *Mother India* went on, Nargis returned to Billimora in the first week of April and found she was restless without Sunil. Everything reminded her of him, and she wrote to him, 'Every day is a painful one without you and yet when the day is over it relieves me with the thought that you are coming soon and once again I will have a chance to look at you.'

During the day she would play the indomitable Radha and at night she would become a young girl, gazing at the moon, lovesick. 'I lie in bed till the moon sets—Looking at it and hoping that you must be doing the same and thinking of me—are you?' she would ask him.

She was also getting ready to leave for Russia to complete the shooting of Abbas's Indo-Soviet production, *Pardesi*. It was not a happy thought. 'Hardly any time is left—then I will leave for Russia and come back after 2 or 3 months—I just don't want to waste any time without you...when will that day come, when we will always be together?'

Her letters to Sunil echo another fear: would confessing her love so openly make him turn away from her? She told him, 'I think I'll spoil you with too much of love and affection and then you won't care for me, but I can't help (it)—how can I hide my feelings, I'm not such a big pretender—they say it is not nice to let your man know that you can't live without him—is it so, darling?'

In her correspondence with Sunil, Nargis reveals herself to be a woman hungry to show her love. Almost as though she could gaze into the future, she wrote to him, 'Darling, don't get angry, but remember even if I die, I will always be there with you spiritually. I am so much attached to you that even death can't take me away completely from you.' These lines would probably comfort Sunil much later, but right now it was the constant separation and the rumours which had him worried.

There were people who had seen them together in Billimora, and spoken about it in Bombay. Nargis wrote to Sunil, 'Lots of people in Bombay are talking a lot of nonsense. The rumours are thick...' She mentioned close friends and warned Sunil to be careful, as people were saying that at first he tried to 'hook' Madhubala and now 'found Nargis in a horrible state of mind and so he is taking advantage of her weakness and making grounds for himself for a better future in his profession.'

Already, his acting in *Mother India* was being criticized, she said, and it worried her that so many nasty things were being said.

Obviously, the rumours were beginning to disquiet Sunil. He

had planned that they would keep their relationship secret for two years, time enough for him to build a career, so no one could accuse him of marrying above his stature. He was also keen to ensure that he earned enough money to look after Nargis as well as his own family. Nargis was worried about the two-year delay because it would mean she would be 30 by the time they married.

Once the rumours about their relationship spread, things took a turn for the worse. Mehboob made his feelings about the 'affair' quite clear. He told Nargis he was in little doubt that Sunil was using her to climb the ladder of success. Nargis wrote an agitated letter to Sunil on 11 April 1957, while on her way from Bombay to Baroda aboard the Frontier Mail: 'I can't understand why Mr Mehboob is so shocked with the news that Nargis and Sunil Dutt are to be married. Is it not possible for two innocent people in love to get married? Does he think he can really keep us apart? I don't worry but I do get hurt.'

Nargis had known Mehboob since she was 14 and thought that could be the reason for his annoyance. 'I know Mr Mehboob is so very possessive about me that he can't stand anyone who gets my affections.' She mentioned another actor whom Mehboob had encouraged her to be friendly with, despite knowing that she didn't care for him. 'But about you, he knows deep down within himself that we love each other. I told you he won't like our association. Sometimes I get so fed up of this world and its people.'

It was a frustrating time for both Nargis and Sunil. She was increasingly concerned that the constant pressure on Sunil would drive him away. She even wondered if it were not better for him to just forget about her. Almost immediately on the back of that thought came the realization that she would rather die than live without him. The next day, when more gossip about them was published in the paper, she felt as though everyone was looking at her strangely, and that all sorts of thoughts, some vulgar, some jealous, were passing through their minds.

This was enough to snap her out of her morose thoughts and she decided that she had to fight back to preserve their love. She gave an interview to *Filmfare* about the fateful day, 1 March 1957, as though written by the 'Soul of Nargis'. The interview was published on 7 June.

1st of March, 1957: It was 4:30 p.m.

Preparations were being made for the fire sequence in 'Mother India'.
Nargis made up to look like an old woman, was talking to some of
  the members of the unit. Strangely enough she was talking of death
and saying how much her hands, with the make up on them resembled
her mother's hands. 'Ready for take' came a voice. Then 'Light the
fire'—and the studio hands proceeded to do so. Mr Mehboob's quiet
voice came through megaphone: 'Baby, run in!' She ran in, to embrace
the flames. The flames responded willingly. They embraced her and
planted burning kisses on her weary but determined brow. It was
soon over. Nargis was rescued. She had sustained burns. But, in the
flames she had at last found the TRUTH she had been searching for, the
truth which freed her. The old Nargis died in those flames. Nobody
knew her. No one understood her. Only I. I knew her. I am her soul.
I am the new Nargis, still childlike as the old but, after passing through
that fire, somehow happily, gratefully, satisfyingly different.

Writing in this way relieved her of the anxiety she felt, as she
wanted to reassure Sunil that the 'old Nargis was dead'. She
announced to him that 'victory will be ours' but it was obvious
that the next few months were going to be trying. She was
constantly worried that the rumour mill would grind out all
kinds of allegations about her, though she had always been 'pure'.

As far as Sunil was concerned, what had happened was in the
past. He accepted what Nargis had told him and did not question
it. It was Nargis who would mention it sometimes, as she did in
a letter on 18 April, saying that she had gone for a function
where Raj was also present, but that he was seated far away
from her, and that she left early. Episodes like these made her
want to leave Bombay forever, because she felt that 'all eyes
were focused on me and I felt very uncomfortable.'

For the first time Nargis wished that her brothers had saved
some of her money for a time like this so that she could leave the
country and not work any more. She told Sunil, 'Believe me I
don't feel like working any more and I am being forced to work
because I need the money. My heart is not in my work any more.
I feel quite fed up... I want to go away from India so badly; but
find no way.'

Sunil was under constant pressure from Mehboob to deny their affair, so he spoke to the press. Mehboob could finally breathe a sigh of relief, and so could the lovers, as Mehboob actually seemed to believe the denial. But Nargis and Sunil kept making plans, working out how to get through the next couple of years before getting married. Part of the plan involved going abroad, at least for Nargis, who wanted to study at Columbia University and had even applied there for a course in midwifery or nursing

It was a confusing time, because despite their desire to do everything the correct way, they had to pretend that they were not in love. For Nargis, it was even more draining than her relationship with Raj. Then, though everyone had disapproved of the relationship, they could at least work together and see each other often. In any case, Raj did not care what people said, whereas Sunil was far more vulnerable. She needed to spend time with Sunil, but they were forced to distance themelves from each other, at least in public. Soon she would be leaving for Moscow, the thought of which made her impatient and angry.

It was a time that she should have been celebrating. The man she loved had proposed to her, and they were to be married. Then why was everything so difficult?

'Pia' and 'Hey There'
1957

Now that the newspapers had announced there was nothing going on between Nargis and Sunil, the pressure on them began to ease a little. But in order to avoid any fresh rumours, they continued to write to each other as 'Pia' and 'Hey There'.

Film industry acquaintances continued to tell Nargis how Raj had asked about her and then cried while talking about her. Old associates from RK Studios would call up, and conversations with them would 'disturb' her. She knew the world of cinema was close-knit. News of the smallest indiscretion could spread like wildfire in a few hours. She had, after all, not done anything to hide her own feelings all these years. What if stories about her affair, about the cottage at RK, about their foreign travel, were told to Sunil? Would he still love her? Their letters and notes to each other at this time reveal passion, but also an increasing fear.

On 28 April 1957, Nargis wrote about a music director who had given her a call: 'He always upsets me, always talking about Raj and my associations. I told him that please I do not want to talk on this subject but he was like an evil shadow who would not listen to me—knowing that I am over sensitive; he was trying to play with my sentiments—I got rid of him ultimately. But he and his talk left me quite disturbed. Not for anything else, but for this reason, that why am I not left alone?'

The implication was that Raj still missed her. Sunil, meanwhile, often had to suppress his rage on hearing rude inferences about her in his presence. It was very hard, but he had to stay calm and say nothing.

In an attempt to get away from it all for at least a couple of years, Nargis wrote abroad for admission:

29-4-57
Bombay
India
Dear Sir—
I'm an Indian girl from Bombay and I'm very anxious in taking a course of specialised nursing—particularly maternity nursing or midwifery—I would be highly obliged if you could furnish me with the complete details of how many years course it is, do you accept Indian girls and what should be the qualifications of the student. Also send me Bulletin of information as soon as possible—Thanks a lot.
My address is—
Tejeshwari Mohan
c/o Sunil Dutt
80 Napean Sea Road
Bombay 6
India

Yours Sincerely
Tejeshwari Mohan

The letter was not addressed to any particular university. Later she would explain her interest in midwifery in an article she wrote for *Filmfare* on 1 January 1960: 'As a matter of fact...I had seriously thought of having a mobile midwifery unit and tour the villages with a woman doctor, rendering assistance and giving instruction to expectant mothers. My heart goes out to these women who lose their lives in childbirth, through sheer ignorance.

'When I was shooting at a village called Umra, for "Mother India" I witnessed a tragic incident. A young woman died in childbirth, leaving behind her four little ones bereft of a mother's loving care. She died only because of inadequate medical care and this incident opened my eyes to the conditions prevailing in our villages...' She goes on to write how she would feel lost if she did not do any kind of 'public work' because she never wanted to be a 'mere glamour girl.'

It is significant that she signed the application letter as

Tejeshwari Mohan. It was her first step towards shedding the identity of Nargis, one that had so often deprived her of love. She also wanted to fulfil her desire to work in medicine. She knew she couldn't become a doctor, but perhaps she could still try to be a nurse or a midwife.

With no one but Sunil to confide in, Nargis thought about her mother. 'As soon as I close my eyes, patches of colour and disturbing images appear. Do you think it is my mother's soul which is calling out to me? I haven't been able to go to the graveyard for so long to see her...'

The next day, 29 April, she went to the graveyard. She told Sunil later, 'I wanted to go to see my parents. I have just come back from the world of the dead. The graveyard has no one big or small. All their problems are or have been solved by the eternal sleep they are in. Everything was so peaceful, beautiful flowers, and incense was being burnt. There was a peculiar kind of happiness and contentment there, as if these people were more alive than us living ones. We kill ourselves with so much longing and desire, worries and so many other things. I carried your letter near my heart. I could not help crying when I reached my mother's grave. I prayed for her soul and asked for her blessings. I told her I need her, she must help me, then it was my father's grave. I became slightly hysterical I think. Because Ameena (her ayah) was asking me to control myself and I know I couldn't. Oh my love, I told him about you, I begged him to help me, for he loved me a lot and I was his favourite child...'

Some comfort could be derived from the fact that they had begun to meet at Sunil's house in the evenings, hoping that no one would find out. They were both busy with different films. Sunil had started shooting in Madras for *Payal*, the film he had written to Taliath about. Nargis still had parts of *Mother India* left to work on, and shot *Miss India* for most of the night on the streets of Bombay.

She was also trying to earn as much money as she could. She was worried that if she got married and stopped contributing to Château Marine's coffers, the children, whom she regarded as her own, would suffer.

Fortunately, producers kept coming up with contracts. On 25 April N.S. Kwatra came to sign her on (he eventually produced *Adalat*) with Rs 25,000 in cash. 'Of course,' she says, 'everyone at home wanted us to accept the money, but I said no—not until I approve of the story. Am I not strong?' She wanted him to know that she was not interested in acting any more and was working only because she had no choice. Sunil had his own family to look after and was sympathetic; at the same time, he was keeping his fingers crossed that she did not commit herself to too much work and further delay their plans.

When Kwatra came back the next day and she heard the story, she wrote to Sunil:

> I liked the story. Nothing very unusual, but a very good subject and a good role for me to play. I think Ramu (Rajendra Kumar) will once again play my son in this picture. I have said yes to them. Mr Sunny also came over and is coming with the story in a few days. Now do you believe me that I want to work, collect money and go away as soon as possible. I always try to be happy my love, but only sometimes a shadow of sadness crosses me, because I feel so lost and lonely without you...

She was worried that 'Raj Kapoor is going to shadow our life always.'

Bombay, she says, 'is an awful place, away from here with you I feel so much better than being in Bombay without you. Our love must bloom with all its purity without being polluted by the wagging tongues of the people, who never seem to be happy in any circumstances...'

> Sometimes I wish I was not a film star. I wish I was not famous. What price this popularity—incredible. This is what makes me sad—I think I have made many mistakes so I must suffer to overcome them. I have never liked people taking interest in my private life—but I suppose, the life of a film star is such that the people feel it is their right to take interest in their lives. When I go away I hope I only become a legend for people to remember with kind words. So that I should lead a peaceful life as a wife and a mother. That is what I ask of God and life. I hope this is granted to me. I wish I could probe into the future and see...

Meanwhile, Iqbal had a dream that sounded ominous. (Rehana has apparently inherited her mother's capacity to 'dream' up likely omens; everyone listens to her when she says, 'I had a dream!') Iqbal saw Nargis in a beautiful red saree and Raj in a peculiar, printed shirt. He had come to meet her but she refused to see him. In the dream, Iqbal insisted that she meet him. The two of them then disappeared for a long time. Iqbal woke up before there could be a resolution.

Compelled by her anxiety, Nargis took the dream more seriously than she would have otherwise. She tried to interpret it and reached different conclusions, that the red clothes indicated either money or ill-health or death. But she also believed that 'God can't be so cruel by giving me so much happiness and snatching it away from me. Of course we will laugh together, eat together, live together soon, very soon.'

Death often features in the letters Sunil and Nargis wrote to each other. They were full of declarations of love, and equally full of declarations that they would die if they did not receive each other's love. The melodrama onscreen seemed to have seeped into their real lives. While Sunil was away completing *Payal*, Nargis wrote long, detailed letters to him about her happiness when she was with him and what he meant to her.

She told him how 'content' she felt in the short time they had known each other, and that 'There could be no other love for me in this world but you.' She read a book called *Memories of Our Wedding* and copied out for him the vows exchanged between husband and wife:

> Thou art my life, my love, my heart
> The very eyes of me—
> And last command of every part
> To live and die for thee.

She wrote to him, 'This is the vow that I have already taken, my love.'

Nargis compares her present happiness with the dark days that had gone before.

> I have had nothing else in life...before I could not feel. What could be

my parents' love, they were snatched away from me. The dreams I
built were shattered to pieces. The love I wanted to possess was
denied to me. To the extent even in material things anything I wanted
was not mine, was always snatched away from me. I got nothing
(though) everything I gave...
Nobody can tolerate the other being happy and flourishing—they
find their bounden duty to destroy all that is good and pure. The
exceptions live and enjoy inspite of all opposition and I am proud
that we are one of those exceptions...I think I am in love with life;
because I am in love with you.

On 18 April she wrote: 'My love for you was from the very
beginning; but of course it became concrete only after our accident.
Tell me did you also love me from the beginning; but could not
possibly admit it...this love of ours has actually grown on us.' In
a long letter dated 27 April, she reiterated: 'Darling, when we
grow old, you know what people will say? We have never seen
two old people so much in love and so devoted to each other as
Mr and Mrs Dutt.'

Then she got word from Mehboob that they were about to
start dubbing for *Mother India*. By now Sunil had come back
from Madras. *Payal* was to be released on 19 May. She went to
Mehboob Studios in the evening 'and was told that you (Sunil)
were there and saw the Fire sequence—I saw it too. That shot was
there too, where we got burnt. I liked it; but felt it was short...'

Her inability to meet Sunil obviously made her restless. After
writing to him earlier in the evening, she decided to write to him
again. 'This is the only contact I have with you. While writing to
you I actually feel I am talking to you...they say I have been
loved before, but I never felt it. Now I feel that somebody loves
me. My "Hey There" wants me, wants me for his wife and mother
to his children.'

Once again sad dreams plagued her. She was not well during
this period, and neither was Sunil, both having picked up chest
infections. On 29 April, Nargis woke up early, having dreamt
that when she returned from her course in America, Sunil had
another glamorous 'society' woman in his life. She was crying. It
was seven days since they had met, because Sunil had been busy.

Throughout this intensely passionate period, there were frequent misunderstandings, followed by a desperate desire to make up. For two responsible adults, Sunil and Nargis were behaving like hormonally charged adolescents.

When they finally met again, at Mehboob Studios, she almost fainted with emotion. She wrote to him later, dramatically, but with complete and touching honesty, 'As soon as I saw you...my limbs became weak. There was no strength in me. My heart started beating hard and my entire body started shaking. It was difficult to get hold of myself. At that moment I did not know whether to cry or to be happy. Whether I should talk to you or just cling to you and be there without uttering a word.'

It is surprising that she was able to conceal such emotion from her closest friends, who did not think that she was in love at all.

Nargis was relieved that work would start soon, so she would be busy and less obsessive about their relationship. Nonetheless, even between shots for *Miss India*, she sat down to write short notes to Sunil. On 30 April, she wrote, 'I have just finished one shot. As they prepare for another, I sit and write to you... I do miss you very much and feel sad and lonely without you.'

By now, Nargis had developed a persistent cough while Sunil had a suspicious wheezing in his chest. Neither could stop working, however. Nargis was trying to wind down her career, while he had to push his forward. He probably had the harder time of it because he had to both look for work and nurture his new-found love, who was easily depressed and increasingly insecure.

Finally, they managed to meet at Mehboob Studios again a few days later, and she said to him, 'I knew you would be at Mehboob Studios, that is why I came. I couldn't stay away myself. Thank God we were together for most of the time. Before I go (she was leaving for Moscow) I don't want to miss anything. As much as I can be with you, I will be, I don't care what people say. This is a fact that I love you and I am very proud of it.'

The two-year period of waiting hung heavy for her. 'Not seeing you for days and days becomes impossible. After all, I have to be away from you for two years. Two years will be like a lifetime.'

Nargis wanted to convey to him her own feelings, but she also wanted him to feel special and wanted. And as much as Sunil wanted her to know that he loved her 'desperately', she was keen to let him know that 'You are me. (That's) what I liked in you to love you so much. I found my lost self in you. My thoughts are your thoughts. My ideals are yours. My heart beats in rhythm with yours—my eyes look into yours and find my image in them. I feel we are not two people we are one. With one common soul.' It was liberating for her to be so open and honest; she had never allowed herself this freedom before. She even told him that she would show her love for him in front of everyone, without fear. Not only did she tell him that there was no one else for her, she added that she was jealous if he put his arms around any other woman. This was the other fear haunting her: she knew how fickle men in the film industry could be. What if Sunil was trapped by some scheming woman?

In a long letter dated 5 May, she described how hurt she felt when Sunil kept his distance in front of the others and ignored her while they were at Mehboob Studios. She was totally distraught, and wrote to him at the studio, telling him how hurt and fragile she really was. It is a very touching letter, because it reveals how sensitive she was to his every gesture.

The obsession with Sunil now pushed Raj further and further into the background. Raj sent her messages and phoned her at the studio, but it meant nothing to her. 'He spoke to me very nicely, asked me about my burns—and so many other things. I told him that I do like to see him and talk to him personally and clear off a lot of things. My shot was ready so I closed the phone. After I finished my first shot, Raj's phone came again. I spoke to him very frankly all that I felt. All that I wanted to say. Of course I was very polite.' It was a difficult moment, made more difficult by the fact that she thought Sunil was not being entirely honest with her.

She imagined that because he did not acknowledge her at the studio, he was upset about something. The weight of this subterfuge nearly pushed Nargis to the edge: she thought again of the final 'release'. Fortunately, when they met later at night,

Sunil explained the reason why he had withdrawn from her. He was angry not with her, but the situation they found themselves in. For a proud, independent man, it was difficult to accept the difference in their stature: she, the megastar, he the struggling newcomer.

She tried once again to placate his wounded ego, telling him to be proud of her instead of denigrating her achievements: 'So what if I am more famous and internationally known. So what if I have moved in higher and intellectual circles. Aren't you proud of me if I am intelligent? Why is it that I love you and want to be your wife—and not the wife of all the so called intelligent and big people. Don't you find I have completely submerged myself into you? Besides my love, I have given 14 years to achieve this position—you have yet to travel towards your goal. Why should you be so disheartened so soon?'

She told him that perhaps her associations could actually be a help, not a hindrance. Even in the midst of this fracas, she could not help correcting his pronunciation, saying he is a silly 'stenograypher' and that he does not have to put 'a patrol in his car'! His Punjabi accent, also noticed by Ameen Sayani, had obviously not improved with time.

Sunil's fear that he was not as famous or as wealthy as she was would remain no matter how much Nargis smoothed his ruffled feathers. But she managed to calm him down and got both of them to relax. The next day, she looked at herself in the mirror and admitted, with satisfaction, that 'I have never looked so pretty as I did today.'

On 10 May she wrote to him that he should have saved her sooner 'from the hell I was in. Not knowing you for so many years, I feel I had not lived. I was dead. I was in a coma. And suddenly I have been brought back to consciousness. I opened my eyes and looked upon my heaven. This is true, this is real, all the rest was a horrible nightmare...'

The nightmare continued in other ways. She wrote:

> My love, you must not get upset on what Raj Kapoor or anyone else says about me. Darling they will say anything to distract you from me. They will cook up all sorts of stories—as a matter of fact it hurts

me to know that people have such ideas about me. Though I know how purely I have lived. I have been very proud of myself. I have not been like other women, who have flung themselves from one man to another. And yet some people talk about me as they would talk about a cheap woman, without any morals. I want you to have faith in me, trust me. I will never do anything by which I will bring shame to you. I love you. And I am yours forever. Mr Raj Kapoor was a bad dream. It is finished—I am not concerned with him anymore. I don't even think about him. I shudder with remembrance of those horrible nine years...Thank God, I got away before it was too late. Let us never talk about him...

Soon after this, she left for Moscow. She was lonely there, and took care to write to him everyday and send telegrams as well. So did he. He had sent her a present for her birthday on 1 June: a framed photograph of himself, which she said 'was one the most cherished presents that I have ever received in all my life.' Sunil had written a personal dedication on it. She kept the photograph on her bedside table in the room, hidden from other members of the cast and crew.

Though she was abroad, she received several telephone calls on her birthday, including some from the film unit of *Pardesi*, who also came to her room. Mosfilms, the Russian producers, sent her flowers. Abbas threw a lavish tea party for her at the Prague Hotel, where a lovely cake was baked for her. Stars from the Soviet film world, the unit of *Pardesi* and the media were at the party, which was also attended by members of the Indian diaspora, including Ambassador K.P.S. Menon, who raised a toast to her with the wish that she remain 'young, charming and loving through all (her) years.' He also appreciated the work she was doing as a cultural ambassador working to bring peace and understanding between India and the USSR. Other toasts were proposed and everyone drank champagne. There were telegrams for her from Mehboob and his wife, and even one from Raj Kapoor:

BABYJI—THIS BE YOURS FOR EVER AND IN THE QUEST OF YOURS FOR
TRUTH MAY WISDOM BE YOUR FRIEND PHILOSOPHER AND GUIDE—
WITH KIND REMEMBRANCE
RAJ

When she told Sunil about the telegram she quickly added, 'Don't worry it is you that I love and care for.' On his birthday, six days later, she sent him a long telegram, with a few coded messages that only they would be able to understand. It read:

PRESLYJI DARLINGJI LOVEJI STOP. SO THE DEVIL WAS BORN TODAY STOP I LOVE YOU VERY MUCH STOP LIVE LONG FOR PIA LIVES FOR YOU STOP I WILL BE WITH YOU TONIGHT WHEREVER YOU ARE AND WILL KISS YOU THE WAY YOU HAVE NEVER BEEN KISSED BEFORE STOP SHUTUP BHANIYAAAA
PIAJI

The telegram reached him on 6 June at 8.30 p.m. It was followed by a letter (written on 30 May), which may have made him feel insecure again. Not only had she flown at the height of '40,000 feet and at the speed of 550 miles per hour,' she had been the only woman among 47 men en route to Moscow in a jet. When she got off at Prague, there was a huge crowd to receive her. 'They clapped and cheered for me. I came to know that "Awara" is being shown here. They were calling me Rita, as that was my name in "Awara".'

Nargis was the only Indian actress then to receive such adulation from a foreign audience.

Another blow to Sunil's ego may have been Nargis's attempts to advise him on the films he should sign. At this stage, Sunil was still planning ways to fast-forward his career. He had received an offer from Anant Thakur, the director of *Chori Chori*. Nargis wrote to him from Moscow, 'My love you must not let that contract of Anand (sic) Thakur go. Take it. He is a good man. He will take your suggestion. He will discuss with you. Only you must be very friendly with him. I think the only way to get a little satisfaction in work is either to work under a very good director— or work with a man who is a duffer. We must collect money— you have a very big mission in life... Don't get worried on things like failure of "Payal" and spoil your health—everything will be alright.'

Despite Nargis's optimism, the next few months of separation were going to be worse than either of them had imagined.

Pardesi
1957

It was a lonely time for both of them. Just as they discovered each other, she had to leave. Many issues lay unresolved, and among them was Sunil's decision to wait for a few years before getting married. One evening, when the Indian crew for *Pardesi* got together in Moscow, Nargis heard Manmohan Krishan sing the gentle song composed by Madan Mohan: '*Chand madham hai aasman chup hai* (The moon is waning, the sky is silent)' and it brought back so many memories that she lost control and started crying. She wrote to Sunil on 3 June: 'Before I could realize what I was doing—I quickly wiped away my tears. They all noticed. I could not give any explanation...'

Soon after this public breakdown, she saw the rushes of *Pardesi* and was appalled. She says, 'I was highly disappointed with my role. The shots are very nice—I look nice too—but that is not everything. I have no role. They say they have added a few more scenes—what is the use, if my character has no bearing—I told Abbas in a round about way... I was absolutely shocked. For I feel I am completely wasted in this picture—and any extra girl could have done...'

She also added:

I curse the day I accepted this picture. For that I curse the day I joined films. This sort of work is not for me. I would have been happier being just an ordinary girl. I'm too modest and good. These people of the films are not for me. They take a lot of advantage of my goodness. They are happy with those sort of people who give it back to them. They don't appreciate a person who endures their nonsense. Mr Mehboob and all the others including my brother—they just know how to take the best from the person...then when the time is over—nobody even bothers to look sympathetically.

Despite her annoyance, she pointed out again that she wanted to be whisked away from it all by Sunil. 'I am already getting fed up of film making. They make me feel very important—but I feel lonely, lost, completely lost without you. I hope Mother India comes here then we will all come here together...'

To make matters worse, two days later, the sets of *Pardesi* were still not ready, and Abbas said that it would take a while longer. It upset her to think that she was in Moscow, far away from Sunil and without any work to justify the distance. Abbas told her that it would be at least a month before work on the film could be completed, and to her further annoyance, assured her that her role had been changed and scenes had been added, but that he could not tell her in detail what these changes were.

Her professionalism would not permit her to explode in anger as she longed to do. The shooting progressed at a snail's pace, sometimes with just one shot being taken the whole day from twelve different camera angles.

Luckily, there were some distractions: parties at the embassy and elsewhere. There were many who wanted to fete the crew from India which now included actors like Achala Sachdev, Manmohan Krishan, David and Jairaj. Thanks to the popularity of Raj Kapoor films in the USSR, especially *Awara*, hers was a familiar face. About going to a store to shop, she wrote, 'People don't leave me alone here, too. They know me and so a crowd started gathering. The best was to get out—and we did.'

It wasn't always easy to escape. One evening she went with the other Indian actors to the Park of Culture, where a big exhibition was on. Nargis noted ruefully, 'All young couples were dancing—singing and enjoying themselves. All of them were asking about Raj. I am fed up of answering them.'

There were also plenty of TV interviews and radio shows. She found she could not get away from the topic of Raj Kapoor, as clips from *Awara* or *Shree 420* would usually precede the interview. She would however try to steer the conversation towards *Pardesi* and especially *Mother India*.

The crew was not entirely isolated from the news from Bombay. It kept trickling in and the journalist V.P. Sathe arrived with the story that though Sunil had issued a contradiction, everyone still believed that Nargis and Sunil were married. She suspected that someone had overheard their conversation with Mehboob, when he had warned them off the relationship, and told the press.

Other people arrived from Bombay as well, with a different agenda. Madhu Achrekar, who was an art director with Raj Kapoor, came to Moscow for his art exhibition. He tried to persuade Nargis to make more films with Raj, if only as an artiste. She said frankly, 'The very idea, I told him, is ridiculous. I don't wish to get involved any more. He has the nerve to say that it is destined that one day Raj and I will work together again, even if not in RK Films maybe in some other producer's films. I told Mr Achrekar that I'm leaving work altogether so the question does not arise of my working at all...'

This did not stop Raj from trying to get in touch with her directly. He asked one of the crew members of *Pardesi*, Jairaj, to send a telegram to him about Nargis's programme. He was even prepared to come to Moscow on his way from Karlovy Vary, where *Jagte Raho* was being screened on 2 July. She quickly told Jairaj that she was leaving on 28 June for Bombay. More pressure came from Akhtar, who said she had been offered a film by another producer opposite Raj, but he was leaving the decision to her.

There were snide remarks from Abbas as well. They had read the article in *Filmfare* in which she had said that following the fire on the sets of *Mother India*, she had 'seen the truth'. Abbas and Sathe wondered whether the 'truth' she had seen was Sunil Dutt. Thinking quickly, she replied that she had seen life and death in front of her in those few seconds, and what was life if not the ultimate truth? But her defences were being worn down by the obtrusive curiosity.

Nargis suggested to Sunil that the best way to quash the rumours was to actually get married soon.

But things were not going well for Sunil. He too was feeling claustrophobic with the constant din in the media about their 'marriage', and was worried about the impact this would have on his career, apart from the emotional toll of having to keep quiet about it all.

He felt even worse when he found out that Mehboob was planning a film with Nargis and Dilip Kumar. Given all the past associations, the very thought made him nervous. After all, Nargis had known Dilip Kumar and Mehboob for much longer than she had known him. How could she refuse? The anxiety gnawed at him that he had only been with Nargis for a few weeks: they had come close to each other in March, and by the end of May she had already left for Moscow. He felt he had no real hold over her.

He sent her a telegram on 9 June, addressed c/o Mosfilms Moscow.

> HOW ARE YOU I REMEMBER YOU PROMISE NOTHING UPSETS YOU
> GUESS WHO YES YOU ARE TRUE A NEWS FOR YOU KING DECIDED TO
> STAR YUSUF AND YOU
> BHANIYAAA

The telegram was framed in their special code. However, the disjointed style of writing was not deliberate. He later confessed to her that he simply could not compose the telegram with care as his friend Amarjeet was leaving for the post office and he couldn't finish writing it properly. Given that Sunil could not be seen sending telegrams to her, he had to depend on someone who would keep his mouth shut. So while the first two lines conveyed to Nargis that he remembered her and loved her, the news was really in the last two lines, that 'King' i.e., Mehboob was going to make a film with her and Yusuf Khan (Dilip Kumar).

Much to his relief, Nargis wrote back at length, explaining to him that she did not want to star in the project. 'As for Mr King I care two hoots for him, his studio and everybody else. He also is just trying to cash in on me—by casting me with Yusuf Khan. Sorry to say but I have lost all respect for him... I shall tell him very plainly in London that I can't work in his picture as it will involve two years in the making and that I have very concrete plans about my life. Also that I have to earn money in this year.'

She was keen to get as many projects as she could in 1957 so that she could save some money for her two brothers and their children. She knew (from her earlier experience during the Raj Kapoor years) that her relationship with Akhtar especially would suffer if she stopped working, so the only way was to cushion her departure with cash.

Because she was extremely worried both about the gossip that Sunil kept hearing and about their own future, she dreamt that he was unwell. Coincidentally, Sunil had just suffered another setback. He had been promised a role in a film on the Taj Mahal by Mehboob. But according to his notes, on the Sunday that Nargis dreamt he was sick, Dilip Kumar came to Mehboob Studios and the idea of filming was dropped. 'I really thought I was dead, a part of my body had been cut... Mr Mehboob had not let me sign Bimal Roy's films because he said that if I do so he is not going to give me the Taj role. I feel I am a complete failure.'

Nargis wrote to him bluntly not to rely on Mehboob for a film. But she also told him that she would write to one of her confidantes and confess to her that they (Sunil and Nargis) were in love and were going to marry. Sunil sent her a telegram immediately to say she should not do so, as it was too soon to reveal the truth to anybody. This must have made Nargis even more impatient. However, at the worst of times, her sense of humour remained intact and so she did send a small note to the confidante, after first informing Sunil that she had done so. When a harried Sunil arrived at the mutual friend's house, the note was shown to him. It read:

WASN'T THIS A SHOCK—
HA HA HA

The situation in Moscow did not improve: the shifts were from 4 p.m. to midnight, but to Nargis's frustration only two shots would be taken in one shift. She lost her temper with both Abbas and the Russian director Vassily M. Pronin, and threatened to leave in ten days' time even if the work was not done. She wrote that the entire 'unit and Mosfilms are getting on my nerves. Am not quite well here myself. Due to too much worry have been coughing for the last three days. You are also not looking after yourself,' she complained to Sunil. She was again writing to him morning and evening and found inventive ways to send the letters. One batch was even sent through the son of the Indian ambassador, to Delhi.

Sunil was also sending her letters almost every day, but on 12 June he sent her a telegram. It was sent directly to her room: c/o Leningrad Hotel, Room No. 1506, Moscow.

FED UP OF GOSSIP MONGERS GOING UMRA TEN DAYS SHALL VISIT
THE PLACES AND DARGAHS FOR MONROE
PRESLEY

Monroe, of course, was another nickname for Nargis. She called him Presley and had given him an album of Presley's photographs for his birthday. But their plans to lie low were not working. He wrote to her that he had heard rumours about her that he found unpalatable. He was still without work, and so decided to visit the dargah of a saint in Umra to pray for their relationship. It was here that he also started keeping a record of her letters to him, carefully noting every word. On the cover of the book, he wrote:

LETTERS
FROM THE WOMAN WHO NEEDS ME AND I NEED HER
SHE
IS MY LIFE, MY ENTIRE SELF, MY EXISTENCE AND A GREAT
FRIEND
I CALL HER PIA
HEY THERE
12.6.57

He also began to keep a record of his letters and telegrams to her. Sunil's entries did not have the expressiveness or style that Nargis displayed, despite the fact that of the two, she was the one who had barely finished school, and he had, as she teased him often, completed his BA Honours. But he wrote to her with love and tenderness, and his letters improved with the passage of time.

On receiving the telegram about his leaving for Umra, Nargis wrote back the same day, 'The words clearly show that you are upset. Let them gossip, to hell with the world...I am glad you are going to Umra—monsoon must have started—and Umra will be lovely. I wish I would be there with you.'

Pardesi was moving very slowly and Nargis felt like a prisoner in her room, waiting for the films to end. There were too many breaks in the schedule, and she felt trapped. She kept going for plays, went sightseeing, visited the library, and even watched a football match, but said, 'My mental tension is turning me mad—I am so disgusted with myself. I curse my nature—why am I so timid... I don't make others feel responsible about me.' Nargis never had starry airs or tantrums and it was too late for her to start now. She did not feel she could walk out of the film, and there was little she could do to complete it any faster.

Meanwhile, Sunil was increasingly concerned about her stature as a star, and wrote to her that *Miss India* had been released and was doing quite well, whereas *Payal*, his film, was nowhere in the running. His depression must have communicated itself to her. She was a success, he was still a struggling artiste, a 'failure', in his own words. She wrote back vehemently in a telegram on 18 June:

RECEIVED LETTER DATED 4TH EXTREMELY HURT STOP SERIOUSLY THINKING NEVER TO COME BACK STOP MEET YOU IF STILL LIVING ONLY WHEN AM NOBODY OR WHEN AM WORTHY OF YOU STOP PEOPLE NEVER HAPPY WITH HAPPINESS OF OTHERS STOP WISH YOU COULD LOVE ME FOR WHAT AM AND NOT WHAT PEOPLE MAKE YOU BELIEVE STOP TERRIBLE STATE OF MIND GOD HELP
PIA

Sunil was worried about her reaction, because he felt he had to tell her everything even if it upset her. Also the month of separation was like a 'century' for him. He sent her a telegram from Mandoli on 20 June after visiting Umra:

HEY THERE SAYS UMRA BREATHES OF PIA PURITY AND PLEDGES STOP SHOULD NOT GET HURT TO READ HIS LETTERS PLEASE STOP HE IS ALONE LOST SCARED SOME INNER FEAR IS EATING HIM NO-ONE TO SHARE HIS SORROWS STOP CAN YOU SEND HIM HIS PIA AND THERE HE GOES TO VILLAGE WITH HER
PRESLEY

Sometimes there would be a hiatus in their correspondence,

and he had to wait endlessly for a reply from her. Even if it was just a week of silence, the time hung heavy, and he often thought of death: if she did not reply in time, he imagined the worst. Nargis, on the other hand, was usually quite stoic despite her own fears. After one such telegram from him, she tried to explain her own life to him.

> You know darling, my father was very much in love with my mother. My mother was a songstress. My father married her against the wishes of everyone. I'm sure he must have been told ever so many things about my mother. I'm sure these very kind of people must have associated her with so many people because her nature also was very free and intimate. I believe when she was young she was very pretty. Anyway my father never asked her about her past— never made her feel dirty and unwanted—never went on confirming her chastity from other people. The result was both my parents were inseparable till death and very much in love with each other—they had respect for each other...Mr Mehboob married a woman with a confirmed past. She even has a daughter and he knows it—Do you think he goes degrading his wife by telling her—by insulting her—by believing what people told him. He knew what he was doing and he married her. My love I am not going to force you—I don't want you to have a wife who is a shame to you...Maybe I am not that woman...I shall never dream of anything—I build up so much and then when it breaks it crushes my heart along with it...

She saw nothing but loneliness and misery ahead of her.

> Everyone left me at the time I needed them most. My parents left me at a dangerous age when I needed them the most—I trusted Raj—he after exploiting me did not bother about me—left me at the bend of the road of life—bewildered I stood looking around in darkness when someone held my hand and said 'I am the one I have always been the one, the truth you were in search of.' I clung to him with faith and love...

She thought it might be better to be separated from him at this point than shove him into an emotional hell for a lifetime. She said, 'Your words—do you remember your words—"I have made you my wife on the first night that I kissed you." Don't feel hurt but I have to compare—even Raj told me that I am his wife. Darling, I am pure in my soul, in my heart, in my thoughts. I had told you that you will not be able to bear my love. For when I love I love with my heart and soul and mind. I don't keep anything for myself.'

Back in Bombay, on 21 June, Sunil came home from a public screening of *Taqdeer*. As he said to her, 'I loved every frame... especially you,' and he found her worried message:

DARLING DON'T KILL PIA STOP LETS GO AWAY TOGETHER I DON'T CARE FOR PROFESSION STOP PIA LOVES YOU MORE THAN HER OWN LIFE STOP NOT GOING TO EUROPE COMING HOME DIRECTLY STOP WE WILL FIND EVERY HAPPINESS IN EACH OTHERS ARMS STOP I BEG OF YOU MY LIFE I NEED YOU STOP PROMISE NO WORRY PLEASE STOP IF YOU THINK OF DEATH PIA WILL JUMP 15TH FLOOR STOP I LOVE YOU MORE THAN YOU SILLY
PIA

But the worries would not go away. He had finally been offered a role in *Sadhana* but had been told that his hair was too short and they had to wait till it grew a bit. Unlike Nargis, who was working, albeit sporadically, he was basically waiting for a good film to turn up after Mehboob's offer fell through. Eventually *Sadhana* did get made and he played opposite the newly arrived Vyjayantimala, who was amused at his nervousness when it came to any physical contact. In her autobiography, *Bonding,* the actress remembers that when he had to touch her, his hand would be visibly shaking. 'He was very quiet and wouldn't talk much, just do his work, listen to the director and intently follow the instructions. A very methodical and diligent actor.' She confessed that they established a rapport only in their later films, such as *Jhoola.*

By now, Sunil's money was also running out fast. At one stage he still had not received word from Nargis, despite sending her telegrams. He had no money to call her and went to a friend's house to book a call. Unfortunately for him, by the time Nargis came down from her hotel room to receive the call, it had been cut off. She did not know who had called because the call had been booked in his friend Satyavati's name. Nargis did not call back.

All sorts of fears began to haunt him. 'Are you being forced by Abbas and other people not to send me anything? I hope my telegrams did not go into their hands and they might be blackmailing you...I wait and wait at home—with every knock of the door—I run to find out if a postman (has) come with a telegram. My love I am pining away in your love...'

He waited for three evenings next to the telephone, to speak to her. When he called her again, the operator asked if he wanted to speak to Abbas since there was no reply from her room. Sunil was beset with fears as he drove all over Bombay to the places they had visited together. 'I keep roaming like a mad person, I keep on crying, sobbing like a child. My eyes are swollen and red—I don't know what will happen to me if I don't see you soon...'

His fears were mainly that Abbas and the others with her were all 'Raj's men—they will do anything for him.' He even worried that they would not give her his telegrams. He had heard a rumour that Abbas had sent Raj a telegram that 'reconciliation between you (Nargis) and Raj is possible if he comes to Russia. That he did not get a visa, but he managed through source...they (Raj and a friend) both have left India. I think—that was the reason Abbas was delaying your work. My love I worry only for this that you are alone—you are a woman, and you have to fight against these odds all alone...' He also admitted that if she did not come back to him he would not live. 'I have fought for 25 years. Now I can't fight alone. I want you.'

Obsessively he noted (much like Nargis, who was busy writing to him morning, noon and night) that he had 'sent you a telegram on 25.6.57 at 1 a.m. and again on 27.6.57 at 11.30 p.m. and again an express one on 28.6.57 at 11:30 p.m. I don't know why you did not reply to me. I am completely lost...

'Are you annoyed with me—you don't want to write to me anything—you hate me—you don't like me—you do whatever you feel like, but please tell me—write me a few lines that you are ok.'

He felt suicidal. He wanted to drive his car off a hill in Khandala after telling her 'that someone is finished. Someone who had loved you so desperately so madly.'

'Now I am nowhere,' he said. 'Earlier I had some hope in "Mother India" (of being successful). I said to myself that I will get great honours after the release of this picture and good money. But these hopes are also dashed to the ground. Mr Mehboob had cut my part completely. All my good scenes are cut... After the first editing Mr Mehboob showed the picture to Mrs Mehboob and Raaj Kumar. Mrs Mehboob was all praises for Sajid and suggested to Mr Mehboob that he can easily cut Sunil's scenes and add Sajid's scenes. Raaj Kumar also agreed with it. Because if Sajid's scenes are there, Raaj Kumar is also there. So in the second trial— I was cut—and in the final trial I was cut ruthlessly. Now everybody had changed their opinion about me—They say that Raaj Kumar and Sajid are very good. Now I am nowhere as far as "Mother India" is concerned. I have no interest left in this picture...'

He began to think that perhaps Sardar Akhtar held some grudge against him. He was upset that his scenes with Nargis, including one in which he embraced her in the jungle, were dropped. And it bothered him that no one argued against the decision to cut scenes in which he figured. He felt that 'It is only Mrs Mehboob. Because she must have warned Mr Mehboob that the rumours about our romance are still fresh in the minds of people, therefore he must keep Sunil only where he is essential.'

To add to his troubles, the rumour spread in the market that his work was only 'so-so' (i.e., average) which was why his role had been slashed.

Other worries about money began to crowd his mind. He had only one film on his hands, *Sadhana*, for which he was to be paid Rs 20,000. Unfortunately he had already taken Rs 14,000 as an advance from the producers, and now they would only pay him Rs 1500 a month. The situation was desperate because he had to run his house, send money to his mother and brother, pay for his nephew's education, pay 'income tax, life insurance'— the list went on and on.

Much of his angst was because of the way things had turned out with *Mother India*. Mehboob had not paid him anything for six months, and there were no other payments he could look forward to, either.

None of this augured well for their future plans. He had hoped that if *Mother India* did well, he would get other offers, and had asked Nargis to restrict her work to two films. With the money he made, he had planned to give at least three lakh rupees to her 'children' at Château Marine, and use the rest to send Nargis to America for her studies. Now all his plans looked in danger of going awry and he felt as though the world was laughing at him.

He sent her a last telegram with the little money he had left:

DID YOU GET MY TELEGRAMS DATED 25TH 27TH MUCH WORRIED
WIRE HEALTH
HEYJI

Lonely and depressed, he went for a long and reckless drive at night, hoping for a quick death. When that did not happen, he visited a few places where he had spent precious moments with Nargis on 28 May, just before she left for Moscow. One of these was a rather lonely spot in Thane, north of Bombay. In complete misery, he sat there waiting, almost hoping to be beaten up and killed. As if in answer to his prayers, a gang of six men came up to his car. It was raining very heavily, but to his amazement, when he rolled down his car windows and got out of the car, thinking they would rob him and perhaps kill him and take away the car, they recognized him. Instead of beating him up, they looked at his dishevelled appearance and asked him why he was so upset. Obviously he did not tell them, and they asked him to drive them to Panvel, where they got out.

It seemed to him that he had been saved only to be with Nargis.

A small glimmer of hope came in the shape of Chandran, his erstwhile boss at Radio Ceylon, who asked him if he was still interested in making radio programmes. Left with little choice, and in need of money, Sunil agreed to do the shows. Before he could slip deeper into depression, since there was still no word from Nargis in Moscow, he decided to spend some time with Dev Anand and his wife Mona on their son's birthday.

But he found it hard to be cheerful. They took him to a Chinese restaurant, Nanking, which only served to remind him of Nargis, who loved Chinese food. He felt even worse when Mona talked about Nargis, even telling Sunil that she felt Nargis had been looking 'pulled down' and was not very 'bright and cheerful'.

However, he tried to keep going. On 1 July he decided to push for some more radio work. He had not been to see Mehboob for a while and now decided to do a round of the studios with Chandran to see if any work was available. He had heard that BR Films was interested in some radio publicity for the new Dilip Kumar film, *Naya Daur*.

He also tried to borrow money unsuccessfully until finally, Chandran gave him 20 rupees, because as Sunil admitted, 'I have only one rupee.' He was 'dead broke' and could not even afford to send Nargis a telegram.

The bills arrived: he had to pay Rs 80 as school fees for his nephew, and his brother Som had written to say that the house in the village had collapsed. He needed Rs 500 to pay for the repair. He also had to pay two instalments for the car of Rs 1094 each, and he had only Rs 21 with him.

As he wrote frantically to an absent Nargis, 'I have no money, I have no friends, I have no pictures, I have no future...' He decided to sell his car as it was the only thing of value that he owned. He didn't want creditors at the door, nor did he want any interruptions in the education of his 'children' (he too was paying to educate his brother, his nephew and a cousin).

His mistake, he thought, was to fall in love with someone who was so clearly out of his league. And now his plight was such that he did not even have money to send her a telegram or phone her! It was bizarre: he was in love with one of India's most famous actors, and supposedly she returned his love. Yet he had no way of contacting her. 'If you were an ordinary woman, you would not have gone anywhere,' he reasoned with her. 'You would have always been before my eyes. You would have been only in a small world of our own. But with your name and fame it becomes impossible. Because I am poor...no name...no fame. I want my end and my death soon.'

There was obviously no way out for him. He was in love

with her and could not live without her. But their living together appeared impossible . Had he discussed his problem with someone, he may have felt better. But he still wanted to keep his romance a secret till he had built a better career for himself. Indeed, as his friend Krishen pointed out, Sunil was a very private person. He had friends, but he did not want them to feel sorry for him. He felt he could be humiliated in public because he had imagined that the great film star Nargis actually loved him. Since he had not heard from her for a while, he was convinced that death was the only way to assuage his pain, and he began to brood about it more and more.

Heartbreak Hotel
1957

While Sunil's life—and sanity—seemed to be coming apart, he did not know that his worst fears were about to come true. Raj was soon to make another appearance in Nargis's life.

Nargis had started planning her journey back to India. In those days of the Cold War, the only route she could get a ticket on was Moscow-Stockholm-Berlin-London-Geneva-Rome-Bombay. Complicated though it was, she took it. She also insisted that Abbas wrap up the shoot, forcing the Soviet team to break their rules about not shooting on Sundays. She said, 'I feel I've taught these Russians some real hard labour. I suppose this was the first Sunday in their lives that they worked. Good for them, these lazy people. I wish they knew how hard we work in India comparatively.'

After some very difficult sessions in which she had to wade through water in the freezing cold, as well as confront a blazing fire, she finally managed to negotiate her departure from Moscow. Early on the morning of 2 July, she recorded her 'terrible journey to Berlin which lasted about 8 hours. The most uncomfortable planes are these Russian Illyushins. It made two stops one at Vilna the capital of Lithuania and the other at Warsaw, the capital of Poland. Left Moscow at 7 a.m. and reached Berlin at 3 p.m.' She crossed over to West Berlin to stay at the Kempinski Hotel.

Germany was familiar territory for Nargis: she had been there with delegations and on promotional tours with Raj. She quickly found her favourite shops and began a therapeutic shopping spree which she had not been able to indulge in for many weeks because of intrusive fans asking about Raj in Moscow.

Her arrival did not go unnoticed by the Indian consulate. As the International Film Festival was on in Berlin, she was sent passes to attend the festival and the awards ceremony, at which the Bengali film *Kabuliwallah* was to receive an award for its music. Her departure was scheduled for the morning of the fifth for London, so she had time to recuperate and shop some more. She was beginning to get bored and was anxious to return soon.

As luck would have it, her ticket was waitlisted and she didn't get to fly out on the fifth. And then came a surprise.

She wrote to Sunil,

> Haven't you heard that Truth is stranger than fiction? Something most unexpected happened today. I got a call from Hamburg this morning. It was Raj on the line. He spoke to me and said he wishes to speak to me and he is coming over by the afternoon plane. So Raj came at 2 p.m. to Berlin. Came to see me at the hotel and is staying in the same hotel.
>
> I want you to understand everything before you determine anything. He behaved like a perfect gentleman. I was with him the whole afternoon and also had dinner with him. He did a lot of talking. He said that he knew that I am no more for him and that there is no going back for me. The only urge that he wanted to satisfy was to know—what is the cause of this separation. I talked a lot to him—explaining everything—what my beliefs in life are—what are my truths and what are my intentions—I was very frank as if I was talking not to Raj but to someone else—he told me I should get married and I said I want to. He was very nice and he behaved very well. We were like friends or associates, like co-workers and nothing beyond that. My talking to him or rather discussing the whole affair I think was very good for him as well as for me—There is a big load off my chest. Remember I used to tell you that I feel I should meet him and have a frank talk across the table—well it took place today and everything was said gracefully—no emotional upsets. I want you to know one thing—that I decide in life once—and if without delivering hurt to anyone I can feel clean. I would feel better. You must have faith in me and that is all I want from you. It may hurt you—but it is better to tell you the truth than to keep anything from you.

It had been an astonishing day. And it wasn't over yet. Nargis felt restless and disturbed, and she hoped that Sunil would not misunderstand her. She knew what a huge gamble she had taken by telling him everything.

The next day, she was still on the waiting list for an airline ticket. So another day was spent with Raj and a couple of other friends who also happened to be there. She told Sunil later, 'It may have looked strange to Raj—but I was not intimate with him at all. We behaved like two decent clean friends. He also mentioned once—that only six months ago we were here—who could have thought things would change so much. We all had lunch together—Bali (the friend) wanted to buy some shirts and also his wife (wanted to shop). So we all went out shopping. You might not like it and have a lot to say—but love, it is better not to have any ill feelings for people. I want you to understand that I did nothing out of any kind of politeness which I should feel ashamed of myself and you should feel degraded.

> Every night when I said good night to Raj and came into my room—I thanked God—looked at you (she still had Sunil's photograph by her bedside) and felt very proud of myself—I met Raj after five months—I was a little nervous and felt upset—but then it all passed away in a short while. The way I talked to him—he himself said that this meeting will help him—as he could never believe that things have ended. I also told him that a person dies suddenly it is difficult to believe at that moment—but the realisation comes gradually. That this parting will be good not only for me alone but good for him good for his wife and very good for his children. That he should be a responsible and loving father for his kids.
> He looked very sad and said he wanted to do everything for me and of course, it brought back old associations. I told him that whatever happens, happens for the better of all—he narrated some beautiful stories which he wants to make but can't get a girl (Raj was looking for a new actress). I told him he will get a girl, but not me, I will not work with him in his pictures or outside.
> Raj wanted to know what should he do with the money that has to be paid to me. I said I don't want it—and the land that had been bought for the house, I said I also didn't want that...

Once again Raj tried to persuade her to come to Prague for the Karlovy Vary festival, but she refused, feeling vulnerable but also sentimental. As they left the restaurant that night after dinner, Raj mentioned that it was their last supper together, and that after this they would each go their own way.

> I didn't say anything. I did not want to be rude. Why be rude to anyone? When I have decided and know what I have to do—nothing will make me change my mind. I only care for you and need your confidence and love. You must have faith in me. You must understand Pia...

Because she chose to keep quiet about these last few encounters with Raj, there was speculation that she never got over him. Most of her close friends, and even her family, knew nothing about this last dignified meeting between the two, when she finally confronted her demons and put them to rest. Not only did she sever relations with Raj, she refused the money he still owed her, and the land that he had bought for her, which again no one else seemed to know about. And it must be said that Raj, who has often been dismissed as vulgar and uncouth, especially in the way he managed his relationships, proved to be both sophisticated and sensitive in his farewell to Nargis.

Shammi says, 'Before she walked out he had almost made up his mind (to marry her), and the divorce papers were signed, and because nothing happened even after that, Nargis would have felt terrible. Naturally he would have also started feeling more guilty (that he had not been able to push the divorce through). I don't blame him at all, family pressures were there. After all this, when she told him that she was not interested, he still tried. When she went to Russia, he got in touch with her, to meet and talk to her, tried to persuade her, but once she had made up her mind she was very definite.' She wanted to marry Sunil immediately, feels Shammi, because only then would the whole Raj episode come to an end.

Finally, on the seventh, Nargis managed to get a flight to London. A tearful Raj came to see her off.

> He was very quiet and so was I. I'm sure he must be feeling bad. I myself was feeling slightly disturbed. The announcement was made, we shook hands—he said, God bless you in your mission of life and

I left for the aircraft. I saw him standing at the airport waving out to me for a long time—I had noticed slight tears in his eyes. I also felt a little pained—but I must say that whatever happened—it happened for the good. I'm glad I met him and had a very frank talk with him. Now to each his own. All is well that ends well. This ended well and gracefully without any kind of scenes—which I was afraid of.

She asked Sunil not to be upset with the information she had given him, and that they must be prepared and plan for the future, because these kind of episodes 'scared' her.

Fortunately, before Sunil allowed himself to self-destruct in her absence, Nargis, after a brief touchdown in London, returned to Bombay. They finally met on 10 July with fervent promises to never part again. 'May God unite us soon and put an end to all future separations,' she said. 'Pia is yours for ever. Pia wants to see you happy and successful...You don't know what happens to me when I am with you. I go mad with love, drunk with happiness.'

They fixed the date of their wedding, 31 December 1958. It gave them a goal to work towards. Nargis thought that 'one year will pass in the hope of being your wife...' She added her prayers of thanksgiving to all deities, especially 'Shiv and Parvati because they are the symbols of love and devotion and sublime companionship. I am very happy today.

> My darling, you keep me thinking—where were you all these years— why did we not meet earlier—was it that we were in constant search of each other—Thank God I found you—I don't know what would have become of me. I would have been a wanderer all my life looking for you, in search of you—not finding you I would have gone mad— or would have ended myself only in the hope of meeting you in a new world in a new life... My sufferings have come to an end... I was tired of living alone.

Though Nargis had managed to leave Moscow and come back home, the shoot for *Pardesi* was not yet over, and she still had another week of work left. It meant there would be another separation soon. But they made plans for the future 'when Mrs Dutt will come to stay with one Mr Dutt.'

Coming back to Bombay meant that they were in the public gaze again. A hypersensitive Sunil, ever protective of his woman, still could not bear to hear the things said about her, especially about her past. Her own grief over his unhappiness would sometimes be so acute it would result in an actual pain in her chest, and it caused her some concern, because she hoped it would not develop into anything serious.

'Both my parents died of a heart attack—my mother had a very strong heart—this is what the doctors had told her when she had it tested—at that time my father was alive. My father's death was such a big shock to her—that she had not cried when my father breathed his last—she did not even go to see him for the last time—I will never forget her words—she had told us that she can't bear to see him quiet—she will not be able to bear it if he does not call her DEAR—the result was that the unhappiness of separation became unbearable and she died within 8 months of sudden heart failure...' she explained to Sunil.

By now, they had set up a routine: they would meet every evening at eight, though they still had to keep their relationship a secret.

One of the reasons why even close friends never found out the extent of their attachment to each other may have been that like Sunil, Nargis had learnt to keep her emotions under wraps. As she put it, 'By nature I am an introvert. I can't speak like other people, act and convince that I love you—it's only to be felt—my love only you can feel—the way I cling to you—the way my heart beats for you—the way I shed tears for you—the way I smile for you when I see you happy—my moods change with your moods— like the sunflower which lives only for the sun.'

Of course, there were other hitches: 'Something or the other always comes in the way of my happiness—My family, their responsibility is on me. I don't feel like working—but if I don't, I don't leave them well secured—terrible state of mind.'

Now that they were together, the biggest 'barrier' was her 'name and fame' and she tried to set some of his fears at rest, saying, as 'regards "Mother India", you may believe it or not— but I have full faith and confidence—that this picture will take you to the top. You have worked hard and sincere labour is always repaid—God is great—it is Him you should look up to for reward—and not these mortals.'

As it turned out, Sunil's Birju would soon become the cinematic archetype of the rebellious and misunderstood young man seeking justice, a role which he himself would recreate in later films (*Mujhe Jeene Do*), as would Dilip Kumar (*Ganga Jamuna*).

A few more offers had now started trickling in for Sunil. He was also in touch with Bimal Roy again. This extremely talented director had started his career as a camera assistant in New Theatres in Calcutta. His films became especially well-known for their sensitive portrayal of women and of the social problems that plagued contemporary India. Under his own banner, Bimal Roy Productions, he had remade the classic *Devdas,* and the tragic *Do Bigha Zamin.*

Bimal Roy was in the process of casting for *Sujata.* One of the surprisingly few films made on the caste system, it was about a lower-caste orphan girl Sujata (Nutan) who is adopted by Upendranath Bose (Tarun Bose) and his wife Charu (Sulochna). They also have a daughter of their own, Rama (Shashikala). While Rama is educated and modern, Sujata is confined indoors, with little exposure. However, the man chosen to marry Rama, Adhir (Sunil Dutt), falls in love with Sujata.

The film brought out the best of Sunil Dutt's abilities as an actor. From the fierce Birju of *Mother India*, he was transformed into a well-groomed member of the Bengali bhadralok, full of idealism and reformist zeal. Social reform was in any case an ideal close to his heart and he played the part with enthusiasm. The songs, written by Majrooh Sultanpuri and set to music by S.D. Burman, had a classical appeal, especially the song that went '*Jalte hain jiske liye, teri aankhon ke diye, geet laya hoon vohi meet main tere liye* (Those songs which light up your eyes, those are the songs I bring to you)'. This was memorably filmed as a sequence in which Adhir sings his latest poem to Sujata over the telephone. She has just been told to give him up for the sake of her foster sister's happiness, but he does not know this as he serenades her. She listens to him, and the scene ends with the telephone receiver at her end dangling miserably from its wire, as she breaks down in tears. The final reconciliation comes when

Sujata donates her blood for her foster mother's cure, thus proving that caste is meaningless. Despite the melodrama, *Sujata* is one of the better films that Sunil acted in.

This was all in the future, however. On 14 July, Nargis wrote to Sunil, 'You don't know how happy I felt to know that you are going to meet Bimal Roy. I will pray day and night that you should get his picture—he is a good director and I am sure you will like working with him.' She also urged him to accept all the work he was offered, because that would ensure they were together sooner rather than later.

She was quite clear that she did not want to work after she got married, and would rather look after her husband and children. If they got married soon, she would even withdraw from the two films she had signed up for, though it was going to be difficult because she also wanted to continue helping her family financially.

Earlier, Nargis used to be out of the house from 9 a.m. till late at night, but now she felt like staying at home, waiting for it to be evening so she could go out with Sunil. Ameena, her maid since childhood, now knew that she was meeting Sunil every evening and asked her when they would get married, to which Nargis blushed and replied, 'We will as soon as I finish my work.'

As Ameena knew, it was the memory of her work-oriented childhood that made Nargis dream about a normal married life. In one of the most moving passages in her diary, she wrote:

> I did not have a very happy childhood. I always used to feel the neglected one in the house—I remember I used to hate holidays in school—I did not like staying at home. Then as I was growing up—a burden of earning for the house was put upon my shoulders—quite contrary to my wishes. All those lovely and wonderful experiences of girlhood also were snatched away from me. I developed a complex that I'm not loved in the family—because I had to earn and my brothers who were years older than me used to stay at home, go out with their friends—see pictures and enjoy life—while poor me used to get tired at the studio and never had the time for fun. My parents died just when I came into an age where every girl finds a companion in her mother and a friend in her father. I was lured away, misused and cheated of all the beautiful things of life—bitterness came into me—I became hard. I would not think of anything

beautiful—I actually used to envy people who got married and had kids especially from the films—I was robbed of every kind of love—with a lot of struggle—somebody told me 'I love you Pia—I want you for my wife'—wife—I can be a wife? A mother? A companion? It takes time for me to believe...

The intensity of their emotions often got the better of both Nargis and Sunil, though they were used to bottling things up.

In those early days, when they were unable to be with each other all the time, the distance was maddening. Just as Sunil went slightly crazy when he had no news of Nargis in Moscow, she too became hysterical when he fell ill and she was unable to go to him or comfort him.

She had been waiting for him at home, and then been told that he wasn't coming around that day because he was unwell and had gone back to his flat on Napean Sea Road.

Imagining the worst and blaming her 'moods' for his illness, a helpless Nargis decided to hurt herself. Alone and unhappy, she found no other outlet for her pain and disappointment, as she attempted to 'control' a situation over which she had little or no control.

On 19 July, after spending a restless day hoping for some news from Sunil, and not receiving any, she picked up a blade. She told him afterwards,

> I've done it—and I feel much more relaxed. You may think I'm mad but I have also felt tears in my eyes after what I did. Yes, don't get horrified—I told you I'll hurt myself—because I hurt you—I must hurt myself. I've cut all my fingers with a blade—yes they are bleeding—my hanky is full of blood—I couldn't help it, I could have done worse. Yes, I am mad, you have a mad woman in love with you—but what am I supposed to do with this restlessness that does not seem to stop.

She had done it before. In Moscow, after receiving Sunil's letters about the endless gossip concerning her, she wrote:

> I don't want this to happen, for then I know I have become hard and rigid. The same thing happened with me when I broke with Raj. The feeling comes to me at the height of suffering. As I write to you my

entire body is shaking. I am feeling very cold—though it is not yet cold tonight...

I am hurt, I'm angry, I'm very much in love. All three of them have immense strength and force—I don't know what is going to happen—who is going to win. It's like going crazy. I'm alone—I feel like banging my head against the wall so hard—that blood should ooze out that will calm me—It's funny whenever I am in this mood I must hurt myself—let myself bleed and then I feel better—Once during the shooting of 'Barsaat' I remember I had cut all my fingers with a blade—I had burnt my arm one day with a burning cigarette—you want to know about my journey...you will read about my life in these pages. I'm suddenly afraid I don't know why. I'm absolutely alone in this room—the atmosphere is so cold and frightful—as if some evil is lurking in the dark...

At this point, Nargis was intensely and frighteningly alone. She was at the peak of her career but the only people who understood her or who cared for her were Ameena, Kasam, the kids and Sunil. No one actually understood the extent of her alienation from her brothers, especially Akhtar. She kept the relationships alive for the sake of the children. But in her heart, there was only anger and loneliness and rage at being used all the time.

Some of this anger was transferred to Sunil: 'I will also not tell you even if I'm in pain, not until you, deep down within you, feel that I am yours. I am in agony right now—mentally shattered—emotionally in pieces—and also physically my hand has started paining very much. The wounds are not very deep but enough for me to feel the pain. But I won't tell you... I'll never tell you my heart's pain...'

Fortunately, in Sunil, she found a true confidante. To her immense relief, she could share her terrible emotional paralyses with him and expect him to understand. Though he may have appeared less urbane than her, Sunil was non-judgmental, and did not attach any stigma to anything she did. He accepted her for what she was, and that is why their relationship, much to the bemusement of their friends, remained on solid ground.

In fact, a few days after she shared this experience with him, they squabbled about something. Before he went to meet her the next night, Sunil deliberately cut his own fingers, so that she would know the strength of his emotion. At that point, what more could he do to express his understanding of the deep hurt she had felt, and offer his complete emotional support? The crazy but love-filled gesture reassured a distressed Nargis, and slowly she came out of her depression.

On a better day, 21 July, she would admit, 'I feel so protected with you. As if I am so weak that I need looking after, and you are there to love me, protect me against all troubles and difficulties—I love this feeling and want to live in this feeling all my life.' Even more significantly, she wrote: 'To be owned is like being in a perpetual state of drunkenness where one forgets everything, even one's own self—a state of complete oblivion. I feel hopelessly happy and intoxicated by your love. I love this state of mind...we must immerse into each other so much that even when people see us they should see you in me and me in you...'

Fortunately, over the next few days she was able to meet him and even go over to his house with a friend. He was still unwell, so she spent the day with him, had breakfast and lunch with him, and enjoyed meeting his sister, Rani. But because it was the first time they were together as a couple in the presence of others, she was 'terribly self conscious and very shy'.

Though Nargis rather wished they could be alone without the presence of Rani, she was relaxed and happy. Sunil and she talked about their future and she told him about her desire to do 'social work'. It made him nervous till she reassured him that it would not be at the cost of their marriage. She told him, 'You have only seen one side of me that is as an actress who has a lot of glamour, fame, name around her...life is all giving and sacrifice. In this giving one gains.'

It was a thought not many would have given her credit for, but over the years it would be her social work which absorbed Nargis completely, and gave her a defining identity in her later years. 'In giving one gains' became her lifelong mantra.

But even after they had made up, things continued to go a little sour once in a while. Once, for instance, Sunil was upset

when he saw her with a major star at Mehboob Studios. She
moved over to sit with him and assured Sunil, 'He was behaving
himself until you came—as soon as you came in he started
showing off. I got up from there and came and sat with you. I
want you to feel that I am all yours. Once we get married nobody
will even try to be intimate with me.'

Sunil was still trying to anchor his career, which meant the
date for the wedding kept shifting. He now felt they should
marry only after three years, out of which Nargis should be away
for two years (perhaps in America) so that everyone would forget
her star status and know her only as Mrs Dutt. It was a suggestion
that Nargis found hard to accept. A year was as long as she was
willing to wait. But Sunil did not agree, and felt that perhaps
they should stop meeting each other till he was in a position to
meet her as an equal, openly. This completely wrecked Nargis's
peace of mind. It had become impossible for her to live without
their daily meetings. She could not understand why he was
overwhelmed by what other people said.

'I feel so unfortunate,' she wrote to him, 'what is this curse
on me that I can't get love like any normal human being. Tell
me can't a film star have the same emotions as a sweeper girl on
the street. My love, any woman from a queen to a beggar has the
same desires, same emotions of wanting a home, a family to be
loved, to be possessed. Just love me. That's all and forget all the
surroundings, can't this happen?'

By now, Sunil was so upset with all the gossip that he was
seriously thinking of going away to London to start some other
work altogether. It took all of Nargis's persuasive powers to
calm him down. Again, it was Sunil's insecurity about his career
which made him so volatile. He didn't have the connections
that Nargis had and offers weren't exactly pouring in.

Luckily, a few people, such as Faredoon Irani (Mehboob's
camera person) and his wife, whom Nargis called Gool aunty,
were able to provide a ready ear for their confidences. Their home
was a safe place for them to meet.

Meanwhile, Nargis got the feeling that Akhtar was beginning
to suspect that something was up. He mentioned to common

friends that he could not understand why she wanted to sign only four films, and why work on them had to be over by 15 August. He had also started asking her to be involved in more and more story sessions. While it made her nervous that he was pushing her towards signing more films, she also felt she must be around to discuss all the terms for the new films, in case he made promises she could not fulfil. These were matters she had never really interfered in, and it made her tense all the time. 'I'm mentally very very tired because of my brother Akhtar. He keeps promising everybody that I will work in their picture. How many times have I told him that I don't have the energy to work in more than 4 pictures... I don't know why he feels I can work in 6 to 8 pictures in one year—I'm also fed up of discussing—I feel so exhausted...what kills me is that even my own people don't realize that I am tired and need rest. I was coughing today because I'm not well...'

The only time she felt she could truly relax was when she was with Sunil. The pressure was pulling her in so many directions that she wished she could leave Château Marine forever. 'I'm fed up of meeting people, tied to responsibilities, everything is the cause of my fast decay—I just can't go on like this anymore. I feel like a money earning machine—they switch me on and I keep minting—I can't—I can't—I have no energy left now. I'm surely falling ill—good—I'll have some rest at least.'

What kept them going were their meetings, which now took place past midnight. Sunil would arrive under her balcony in his car, blow the horn twice, and she would run down so they could drive away for a romantic hour or two.

But her absence from filming was short-lived because on 30 July, *Adalat* went on the floor. Unfortunately, it was not an experience she enjoyed. Indeed, her sense of professionalism was affronted. Her remarks about the film are a very blunt assessment of what happens when an actor turns into a superstar and no one has the guts to direct them any more. She said that she didn't like 'working for such people who are only commercial. I dominate the whole show—which somehow or the other I don't like—whatever I do is correct and right—and there is nobody to tell me anything or criticize—they will never take a retake—only if I want they take another shot—I feel so disgusted—but what can I do now—I'm in it and I will have to bear it—money really makes you do so many things which you don't desire.'

The one advantage was that work on the film would finish quickly, even if it wasn't up to her standards. Everything was now becoming a race: against time and against those who did not want them to be together.

For Nargis, sometimes the pain came from unexpected quarters. One day, after an evening with Sunil, she noted:

> The pain in my heart started when you told me I'll be too old to have kids of my own—and my age—oh lord—I had forgotten how many precious years of my life I have wasted without realising that time never waits for anyone—this sudden truth came to me like a shock—I started feeling old—I started feeling that I'm much older than you are—probably it is always better for a man to have a wife who is at least five years younger than him—probably then there are not so many problems as there are in my case—I became quiet for I felt at a loss—as if I was becoming older with every passing hour—Really time slipped out of my fingers—and the fool I was that I was completely blind...

Sunil had meant only to say that he too was keen they get married very soon, but Nargis, sensitive to his every remark, took it to heart. Misunderstandings such as this made Sunil think it best that they stayed away from each other for a while.

She insisted on meeting him, however, and they agreed to get together at Mehboob's house. Sunil came on time but Nargis was late because she had been called away to give a speech at St Xavier's College. By the time she arrived, a humiliated Sunil had left. This created another rift. Nargis wrote:

> This much I know that I have paid the price of my fame through my life—the bid was high and I was a fool to pay—funnily enough everyone in this house thinks that I have no heart no feelings. Today Akhtar was telling me that I am so used to a certain life that I should not try to do anything contrary to it. You see people think that I should not think of a house or of settling down—I have never heard my brother wish that I should get married, settle down and have

kids—he always grudges my position. He also said why should I be unhappy when I have everything. Why is it that these people think that if one has money one can buy happiness and contentment—I have not known of anyone who can buy happiness and contentment. My God they don't expect any human feelings from me. This is my frustration that no one understands me and feels for me. Yes, nobody. You may be right. I remember you said that I am a very complex character.

Still nursing his bruised ego, Sunil did not turn up at their usual meeting time around midnight. Nargis spent the whole night waiting for him, running up and down, mistaking each passing vehicle for his. She wondered if she had made the classic blunder of exposing her feelings too openly, and so 'losing her value'. The one consolation was that the next day she would attend the trial screening of *Mother India* at Mehboob Studios and hoped to see him at least on screen.

But when she did watch the film, she was reminded of their time together in Billimora only five months ago, when everything between them had been 'beautiful'.

By now, she was unable to sleep, eat properly or feel any happiness at all. Added to the turbulence of the past few months was the exhaustion of midnight meetings and the need to work during the day. The only way to deal with it, she realized, was to escape somewhere or become as stubborn as Sunil.

Tired, she decided she would not meet him any more. After completing her shoot for *Adalat*, she planned a quick departure for Panchgani, outside Bombay.

But Sunil, unable to stay away from her, arrived unannounced at midnight, and suddenly she forgot all her good resolutions. Once again she realized that under his feigned indifference, he too was a victim of a callous film industry. He appeared to be annoyingly thin-skinned only because he was both an object of envy—for being involved with the glamorous screen siren Nargis—and scorn because people thought he was trying to use her to push his own career forward. And then of course, there was the niggling issue of Raj: Nargis was not an easy woman to love, she came with too much baggage, and at times he could not cope with it.

Nargis finally understood how sensitive he was, and realized she would have to prioritize his needs before any other commitment: functions, lectures, awards, films—from now on everything else would take second place.

The test of this 'extra' care came the very next day. She was supposed to meet Sunil at Mehboob's house, and was late by ten minutes. She rushed in contrite and worried, but he was waiting for her. Again, she suggested an earlier wedding, even if in secret, for they could live together openly only after the magic date of 15 August 1958, after the proposed release of *Mother India*. She even wondered if they could escape to London and get married there. The date for the wedding, thanks to their impatience, was being moved closer and closer every day. From three years the wait had been reduced to one, and now it was only a matter of months or, she hoped, weeks.

Finally it seemed that their luck was turning, and in a massive breakthrough, Sunil began to sign films. Now he had three good directors: Bimal Roy, Mahesh Kaul and B.R. Chopra. The character-actor-cum-producer-cum-director Sheikh Mukhtar also wanted to sign him and was ready to pay Rs 50,000, which was more than he had ever been paid. He was tempted to accept the film, despite the fact that it might not be as good as the others, and there was a lot of pressure to do so from Mehboob as well as Nargis. As far as she was concerned, anything that contributed to their future together was welcome.

Relaxed at last, she began to talk to him about how they would need a bigger house, as his one-bedroom apartment was too small, and about how much she liked going out for drives, films and picnics. It was the kind of remark guaranteed to bring out all of Sunil's worst fears. He went to her house so they could discuss her desired lifestyle over a cup of tea, and she quickly reassured him that she would adjust to whatever lifestyle they could afford.

Rumours about them were rife once again and Lata Mangeshkar told Mehboob that she had heard Sunil and Nargis were getting married as soon as *Mother India* was released. Lata said she thought it was not true. Mehboob also said he disbelieved it. Aware that everyone was now discussing it, Faredoon Irani and his wife Gool offered to stand witness at the wedding when

Baby Rani in *Talash-e-Haq*, courtesy of
the Film Archives of India, Pune

Nargis with her mother,
courtesy of *Screen*/The Express Group

Jaddanbai, courtesy of
the Film Archives of India, Pune

Nargis and Motilal in *Taqdeer*,
courtesy the Film Archives of India, Pune

Dilip Kumar, Raj Kapoor and Nargis in *Andaaz*,
courtesy the Film Archives of India, Pune

Ashok Kumar and Nargis in *Deedar*,
courtesy the Film Archives of India, Pune

Nimmi and Dilip Kumar in *Deedar*,
courtesy the Film Archives of India, Pune

Raj Kapoor and Nargis in *Jagte Raho*,
courtesy the Film Archives of India, Pune

Pyar Hua, painting by Arpana Caur,
courtesy Osian's collection

Nargis in *Mela*,
courtesy the Film Archives of India,
Pune

Nargis and Balraj Sahni in *Lajwanti*,
courtesy the Film Archives of India,
Pune

Rajendra Kumar, Nargis and Sunil Dutt in *Mother India*,
courtesy *Screen*/The Express Group

Sunil Dutt and Mala Sinha in *Gumraah*,
courtesy *Screen*/The Express Group

Sunil Dutt in *Mujhe Jeene Do*,
courtesy *Screen*/The Express Group

Sunil and Nargis, Both pictures courtesy of *Screen*/The Express Group

Sunil, Sanjay and Nargis,
courtesy *Screen*/The Express Group

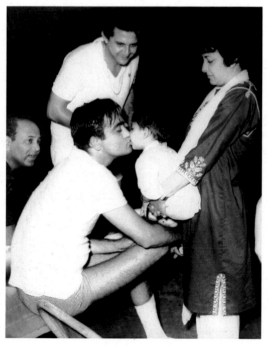

Sunil, Sanjay and Nargis,
courtesy Naseem Mukri

Nargis and Sunil at the inauguration of Ajanta Arts,
courtesy *Screen*/The Express Group

Nargis with Sanjay and Namrata,
courtesy *Screen*/The Express Group

Nargis and Sunil with their children,
courtesy *Screen*/The Express Group

Nargis and Sunil with their children,
courtesy the Film Archives of India, Pune

Nargis and Sunil with Indira Gandhi,
courtesy *Screen*/The Express Group

Nargis and Sunil entering the house allotted to her as a Rajya Sabha MP,
courtesy *Screen*/The Express Group

Sunil and Sanjay at Nargis's funeral,
courtesy *Screen*/The Express Group

Sunil and Sanjay at the premiere of *Rocky*,
courtesy the Film Archives of India, Pune

Namrata and Kumar Gaurav at their wedding,
with Rajendra Kumar (standing) and Priya (seated, front),
courtesy the Film Archives of India, Pune

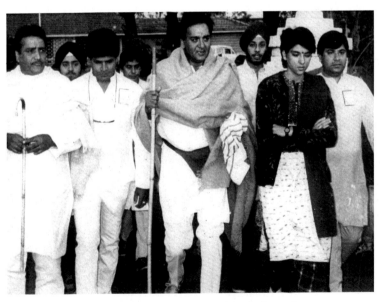

Sunil and Priya at the head of the padayatra,
courtesy *Screen*/The Express Group

Sanjay, Sunil, Priya and Namrata,
courtesy *India Today*

Sanjay Dutt,
courtesy *India Today*

Sunil in his office in Delhi,
courtesy *Screen*/The Express Group

Sunil and Sanjay in *Munnabhai MBBS*,
courtesy *Screen*/The Express Group

Sunil's funeral,
courtesy *Screen*/The Express Group

it happened, and then withdrew the offer saying Mehboob would be very hurt if he was not told about it. Naturally, neither Sunil nor Nargis wanted to risk Mehboob's wrath. Finally, it was suggested that Nemani, on whose farm *Mother India* had been shot, be called into Bombay as a witness.

But before anything could happen, Nargis and Sunil had another falling-out. Though Sunil kept admitting that he could not live without her, the gossip about her past surfaced relentlessly to ruin their evenings. He felt helpless because he could not defend her in any way without arousing suspicion. He was so upset that he almost had an accident.

She wrote to him in distress:

I could not believe that you above all had come to put an end to everything because it is my past which is more powerful and strong than my present or my future. The ghosts of the past are haunting my life and want to put an end to all plans, all sweet moments—when you banged your car I was so shocked that I lost all hold of my senses—I did not know what to believe and what not to believe. What is the reality and what is the make believe...how much you accused me, what names you called me—you said you expected a lot from me but I gave you nothing. Darling do you really believe I gave you nothing? My past all over again became fresh and living. You said you can't adjust yourself with all these things. You suffer from your complexes that I get more importance—that I don't care for you because you don't have a position because you are not Dev Anand, Dilip Kumar or Raj Kapoor—that you don't have studios and cars at your disposal.

I could not imagine that you would think like this about me. You made me feel so cheap and low as if I bother about position, name, money and cars. If I did I could get it all—but I want life, love from a man I love and above all respect for my feelings and appreciation for my character.

But she was careful to point out that she did 'command more respect than any other actress',which should make him happy. She also told him bluntly that their life would be very tough if he was continually suspicious of her, as she was used to freedom and trust.

It did not help that Akhtar kept taunting her if he saw her at home and not out working on more films. The arguments became heated, revealing Akhtar's jealousy over her stardom. He dismissed her contemptuously and advised her not to marry anyone from the film industry. She asked him how long he expected her to work, and to her horror, he said, 'till your last breath'. According to Akhtar, she was just an actress and not suited for marriage at all.

Aghast at all the hurtful things he said, she wrote to Sunil, 'They made me an actress—now they grudge me my position.' Anwar was not involved in the row. It was Akhtar alone who she felt wanted to dominate her and make her work. Matters came to a head when Iqbal took his side. Nargis told Akhtar in no uncertain terms that she would not allow him to exploit her any more. He shocked her then by saying that he was 'going to have a new car, new furniture, and wear expensive clothes and live in luxury on this very Marine Drive' even if he had to push his children into acting. 'On which I lost my temper and called him all sorts of names and said he has no right to ruin the girls and if he does anything of the sort I will go and report the matter to the police. He also threatened me that he is sending notices to their schools, and taking them around to the studios for work. These are his words "I don't have to worry, I have three Nargises with me."'

Nargis told her nieces what their father was threatening to do, upon which, to her dismay, the girls left her flat and went crying downstairs. Iqbal added to her misery by saying that she (Nargis) had no right over their children, and they would do what they were told to do.

Nargis felt totally rejected. She had expected loyalty from the children for whose sake she had carried on working, but she realized that her expectations had been built on false hopes. The sickening realization dawned once more that she had never actually been treated either as a sister or a daughter in the house, and that she was only a moneymaking machine. No feelings or sentiments were expected of her. But no matter how badly she felt she had been treated, this was the only family she had. She had brought up the children with love and affection, and even if they did not listen to her, she could not harden her heart against them.

To console herself, she sat alone in the evening in the balcony with 'Presley Junior'—a small rubber doll Sunil had given her, her own Elvis Presley, to symbolize the child they would have some day.

She had just finished reading Eugene O'Neill's *Mourning Becomes Electra*, which further depressed her. The director of *Adalat*, Kalidas, had asked her to read it, saying that if the play was ever made into a Hindi film, she ought to play Lavinia. This was the wrong time to make the suggestion, because Nargis started imagining herself in the role, as a murderess who was the cause of the ruin and death of everyone and everything she loved.

She needed Sunil more than ever—his arms around her, and his reassurance that he was going to take her away soon, very soon, from Château Marine, where life was becoming more and more unbearable every day. She sensed only greed and superficiality in its atmosphere—a well-decorated, beautiful house sans love and understanding. 'It is like living in a phantom house,' she said. 'A house which gives you the feeling of standing at the edge without any roof, without any walls, all open. Open to all storms.' She had stood there like a rock for 28 years, but could not do it any more.

Monroe and Presley
1957

On 13 August 1957, 'Marilyn Monroe' ironed a shirt for 'Elvis Presley' on the fourth floor of Prithviraj Chambers at Napean Sea Road, Bombay. It was a day Nargis would remember forever because for the first time, Sunil's home seemed like her own. They spent a blissful day together. Even Rani, Sunil's sister, had become used to Nargis's presence by now, and in her own quiet way, conveyed that she liked her. Rani had been staying with Sunil for some time now, but she was overawed by her brother and did not interfere in his life. As he had in his childhood, he continued to take good care of her and her two children.

Buoyed by a pleasant day, 'Monroe' and 'Presley' swore to get married within six months. They were increasingly impatient to begin their life together, partly worried that any enforced delay could lead them away from what 'Monroe', in her convent school fashion, called the 'pure' path.

Meanwhile, unsolicited advice from those who claimed to be close to Nargis continued to pour in, reinforcing all her insecurities, especially regarding her age and her affair with Raj Kapoor. Mehboob cautioned her that life with Sunil could turn into a nightmare. He warned her that Sunil may not forgive her past and would 'torture her' with its memories. What if, as Sunil became more famous, he lost all respect for her and behaved as though he had done her a favour by marrying her? And what if Sunil was attracted to other, younger women? Nargis saw through his grim predictions: Mehboob was trying to turn her against Sunil because Akhtar had told him about their midnight trysts. It was Mehboob's way of telling her that the world knew what she was doing and that she should be careful.

Nargis could not explain to Mehboob that the midnight meetings were actually meant to shield them from prying eyes and gossipmongers. She was shocked, once again, that her own brother could talk about her in such vulgar terms, especially at a time when she and Sunil were, like two nervous adolescents, trying to hold on to their 'purity'.

Seeing that his words had little effect on her, Mehboob tried to elicit information from her in other ways. He hinted that Sunil had confessed he cared for Nargis only as a 'mother'! He also implied that he hoped Sunil was not lying to him.

Nargis neither confirmed nor denied her relationship with Sunil. But the conversation added to her frustration. She longed even more fiercely to get away from Akhtar, and Mehboob as well.

Seeing that he could not penetrate the veil of secrecy she had drawn over her relationship with Sunil, Mehboob offered to arrange a meeting between Nargis and her estranged brother and his wife. But Nargis turned down the offer, maintaining that Akhtar and Iqbal had broken her heart. 'I don't think I'll ever talk to them,' she told Sunil that evening. 'Their attitude did hurt me a lot. Sometimes I wonder how can your own people behave like this. Can money make us forget a relationship? A sister does not remain a sister because money is more important? What is this world coming to?'

Her family's misplaced self-righteousness made her value her relationship with Sunil even more. She understood that he was the only person who did not demand anything from her, besides love and loyalty. For the first time, especially now that her beloved children had also abandoned her and were spending more time downstairs with their parents, Sunil came to her house in Château Marine at night. She waited for him until close to midnight, leaning out of the balcony, restless at the sight of every passing headlight and the sound of every horn.

As soon as he entered her room she joyfully greeted him. Sunil had been through an arduous three-day shooting schedule and was looking forward to a break. Still smarting from her family's withdrawal and Mehboob's insinuations, Nargis suggested that they advance the date of their wedding. She could complete work on her films after the wedding, instead of continuing to live miserably in a house where there was little affection for her. Neither Akhtar nor Iqbal would support her marriage plans anyway, and Anwar was not the kind to interfere. She was increasingly coming round to the view that true love and affection would only come to her from her own husband and children. So the sooner she had them, the better.

But it wasn't easy to persuade Sunil. He still wanted to have an established career before he took such a radical step.

Zahida stumbled upon their secret meetings. As she recollects, she was still a little girl and enjoyed sitting at Nargis's dressing-table, plastering on make-up. She was totally enamoured of her aunt and her glamorous lifestyle, picking up her sarees and inhaling the perfume lingering in the crisp cotton folds, wobbling dangerously in Nargis's high-heeled sandals. She would watch her aunt sail in and out and imitated her style of walking and talking. Because she was always wandering around her room, one day she found Nargis's diary and began reading it. Much to her delight, she discovered romance and Sunil in its pages. Though Nargis realized that Zahida was far too young to understand her feelings, she persuaded her to keep the affair a secret. And the curious little girl began carrying messages between the lovers.

'Her nature is identical to mine, she is a very sentimental girl, and I am sure whomever she will love, she will love sincerely,' said Nargis fondly about her niece. In fact, Zahida is the one who bears an uncanny resemblance to Nargis in her demeanour and voice, and she is the only girl in the family who became an actor. As a child, Zahida kept her aunt's secret, because it meant she could keep reading the diary as well.

Nargis was spending more time at home and with Sunil, while she vehemently resisted her brother's attempts to make her sign new films, including one by Chetan Anand. Her pleasures were simple: listening to Elvis Presley records and dreaming about Sunil. Occasionally, Rashida (there were times when she was still lucid) came upstairs with a few other cousins and they played records and sang and danced. This never failed to cheer Nargis up. Otherwise, as she wrote to Sunil, 'Without you I am like the flower that blooms in winter and withers away without the warmth of the sun. You are my warmth. You keep me alive. I love you a little too much. If I don't see you even for one day I pine away in your memory.'

Sunil had by now begun to relax his rigid stance about postponing the wedding. A new date was set: 1 March 1958.

On 20 August 1957, Nargis's cousin Sadhana (Mohan Babu's brother's daughter) arrived from Panchgani and asked to meet 'cousin Sunil'. She had heard about Nargis's interest in him, and thought that they may even be related, for the Mohiyal Brahmins were a small community and most of them were connected in some way or the other. Nargis later told Sunil triumphantly that some of the kids in her family actually wanted them to get together.

She now showed little interest in her work, for she was only biding time before she could be with Sunil. Her apathy was obvious when she attended a screening of her new film, *Miss India*, with Sadhana, Rashida and the children later that day. Usually, when she attended a screening with her family, she went incognito, disguised in a burkha, because if anyone found out that she was in the audience, there would be a riot. It was the first time she had seen *Miss India* in a public space. She was quite bored and found the film 'silly. It has no link and I could not imagine myself doing all those silly pranks on which the people were doubling up with laughter.' Her ability to critically assess herself and others never failed her, though at times her efforts to improve Sunil's acting and pronunciation were not exactly welcomed by him.

Sunil was now working fairly regularly, while she was not, so she had plenty of time to dream about him and their life together. She would wait impatiently to speak to him in the evenings when he was at the studio. Or she would drive over to his place, which was only 15 minutes away from hers, and they would spend the evening together. It was the only time she felt alive: she hardly slept at night, worrying that she was not able to spend more time with him. Occasionally they would get together at Mehboob's house, where there would be other guests as well.

Yet the thrill of meeting Sunil remained undiminished.

She confessed, 'Again as I saw you my heart started beating hard. What am I to do with this silly heart of mine. I think it beats in rhythm only when it sees you—otherwise it is quite dead for the rest of the people.' Her sense of excitement and joy when she saw Sunil created an almost uncontrollable restlessness in her. The desire to be with him constantly, to have a home and children with him, kept growing.

She also began to take more interest in his sister's family. During the day she would drop in and help Rani with her chores. Once when Rani's son, Gopal, was not well, she brought him medicines. And soon she began to take Rani's children to Château Marine to play with 'her' other children.

Nargis worried about Sunil's mother's reaction when she learnt that they planned to get married. After all, Kulwantidevi was known to be rather conservative—would she approve of a film actress as a bahu? Meanwhile, the impasse with Akhtar continued.

She wrote to Sunil,

> Do you think I bother? I am ashamed of a brother who is not happy in my happiness, who only tries to exploit me to the maximum. He talks all sorts of nonsense—after all I have done for the family there is not a word of appreciation. On the other hand he always rebukes me and makes fun of me if I tell him that I want to settle down and have a home. It hurts most when your own people misunderstand you and think low of you—I don't care about him, how much I have suffered at his hands yet I've done my duty towards my family and now I feel that I have wasted my time, my life for nothing… I wish I did not have a tender heart…

It was her own soft spot for her brothers' families that was a stumbling block. She decided to sign another film, and Sunil began to suspect that she did not want to quit cinema.

Sadness overwhelmed her. 'There are no temptations in my way,' she told him, 'only this that I am really getting very big money and if I can secure my family with enough money I will feel that I have done my duty. I'm not worried about myself. This is true that I am worried about the education and future of my kids. I want that my nieces should get married and be settled in life and I don't want that those girls who are being brought up like any other family girls should go through the same rut that I have gone through...I promise that I will finish these pictures by 15th August, 1958.' She was worried that Akhtar would make good his threat and push the girls into movies. Her protective instincts rebelled against the idea.

Initially, it had been Sunil who needed time to set himself up. But now she felt she had to complete a few projects, so she was the one who wanted to wait a year before they got married. Sunil was extremely angry: he was possessive about her and her love, while she was working ceaselessly for people who did not appreciate her.

'For God's sake,' he told her tersely. 'Don't leave anything for Akhtar—let him suffer in life—let him know that he has to fight for his bread and butter—The only thing is—that you must make those girls strong—strong in principles—in conviction—in character. Teach them that this line is no good—Teach them money is not happiness. Teach them that films are full of temptation and there are lots of people—who are waiting like hungry wolves for their prey—Quote them your example. There is no harm. They can have the biggest lesson from your life. Tell them that you have been earning for the last 14 years—you have been supporting everybody. And this is the way your brother and bhabhi treat you. Tell them that you were also tempted in life and wasted precious years of it. And now that I have money, I have name, I have fame, I have cars, flats and what not. But where is the peace of mind? Where is the contentment? Where is the happiness? This you can only find in your home, and a woman's home is her husband's home.'

It was a thought that would have cheered Nargis in other circumstances, but now she was forced to say, 'How can I displease you? But what am I to do? If I had a bank balance of lakhs I would not have bothered. But as fate would have it— with the 14 years of hard labour and struggle I have been left penniless, absolutely a pauper. I know it will be difficult for any

one to digest this—people think I have a lot of money—I alone
know what has been left for me. Any other person in my place
would have said to hell with the family, I am getting married—
maybe I am too sentimental. The way I have brought up my
kids I won't like to see them being ruined and exploited. I know
if I had left them all my poor girls would be dragged from one
studio to another...'

She said: 'I want to give them all that I didn't get in my life. I
know how much I wanted to study but because I was a girl and
had good looks I was asked, or rather forced, to be the earning
member of the family from a very tender age—an age when I also
wanted to be free and play about like other girls of my age did.
For that I sometimes wish I was a boy then the burden on my
shoulders would not be so heavy.

'I will be very happy and feel I have done my duty the day I
see the girls as good wives for their husbands. I suppose I am not
doing wrong in any way if I want to work for their happiness.'

She begged him, 'Please, my love, you must help me in this
mission of mine.'

For both of them it was a difficult decision, because by helping
the girls, they were helping Akhtar.

Nargis had given the best years of her life to the industry, but
she felt her efforts had been worthless. This was also how she
regarded the films she had made with Raj Kapoor. Years later,
she saw an RK film with Simi Garewal, the actor and TV producer.
When Simi remarked on what a wonderful screen couple they
made, she said bluntly, 'What a waste!' She did not enjoy her
celebrity status. It had become a burden she wanted to shrug
away at the earliest. She also felt, increasingly, the moral
obligation to do something socially relevant, but this would only
be possible after she was married and far from Château Marine.

In the meantime, she needed Sunil to be with her, even in this
last attempt to earn money for her family. Sunil was happy to be
around, but he would not compromise on certain things. Though
he appreciated the fact that despite her anger Nargis still loved
her brother, he felt that he had to rescue her from further
exploitation. It was very much like him to circumscribe her life,

drawing Lakshmanrekhas around her, clearly differentiating between those she could and could not meet. Nargis had finally met a man who wanted nothing more than to cherish her. Had she not been so disillusioned with her own life, she may have resisted the attempt to limit her independence, but as it was, she was prepared to accept all of Sunil's rules.

For instance, there were filmmakers and actors whom he wanted her to avoid, either because they were rogues or 'good friends'. Sunil could not bear to see her act opposite his friends.

Dev Anand was one of them. Unfortunately, the most lucrative offer she had was for a film starring Dev Anand. Sunil then told her about the time when he had been offered a part opposite Kalpana Kartik (Mona, Dev's wife). Dev had told him to drop it and he had done so. He now told her, 'I cannot tolerate my wife making love to my friend.'

Besides, he argued that she had promised she would act in only three films (as indeed she was to do in 1957-58: *Lajwanti, Ghar Sansar* and *Adalat*; only *Raat Aur Din* dragged on and was released nearly 10 years later) before the magic date of 15 August, 1958. He bluntly questioned her motive, asking her if it was wise to leave so much money behind for the girls.

He told her, 'You were getting about rupees four lakhs and fifty thousand rupees out of those three pictures. Suppose within this year you would have spent about 50 thousand rupees, and rupees one lakh would have gone to income tax and other expenses and do you think the remaining three lakhs of rupees was less for them (the family at Château Marine)—you still have to take some money from Mr Mehboob also against "Mother India".'

It is a reflection of his innate sense of correctness that even in his private correspondence, Sunil was always careful to write 'Mr Mehboob'. He was always punctilious in the way he addressed others, and those around him picked up the habit. After they were married, Nargis called him Dutt sahib in public, and she was never Nargis, always Mrs Dutt.

Nargis could not refuse the film with Dev Anand because she wanted to ensure a safe future for the girls. She signed the contract and took an advance of Rs 30,000 from the producer. Overcome with guilt, she felt she could not leave the children to 'starve', for they were looking to her 'for food, for education, for life'. She could not let them down at this time. She used all her powers to placate Sunil, but he was very deeply hurt. This was not an argument he meant to lose.

But all he could do was hold out the final threat: if she persisted with the film, he would not meet her for a whole year.

The way he saw it, it was a betrayal. She had said she was keen to marry him, and had even asked him to advance the date of the wedding time and again. She had said that she would not sign any more films. Now it seemed she had changed her mind on both counts. All the worries he had about marrying a diva came flooding back. Was he so unimportant that she could change her mind so easily?

Though Sunil was sensitive to Nargis and her needs, he was still in many ways the unsophisticated, rustic boy from Khurd. Sophistry was beyond him, and everything had to be in black and white. Only by staying away from her for a year, till she had wrapped up all her commitments, did he feel he could deal with the agony of her working when he preferred that she didn't.

Nargis went into a state of shock. Once again, she began to wonder if death was the only solution for her troubled life.

She tried to keep her spirits up. She took Rani shopping and enjoyed talking to her about her childhood in Khurd. The next day, she organized a birthday party for her brother Anwar's three-year-old daughter, as no one else had remembered to do so. Playing her usual fairy godmother role, Nargis took the child out, got her a new frock, a cake from Bombelli's, chocolates and other delicacies, and brought the family together for an impromptu celebration.

Nothing helped. That night, from her balcony, the sea seemed as dead as she felt. The moon was reflected in the still waters, shimmering like a pale woman with dark hair, a white shroud upon her. Then a small black cloud covered the moon, leaving the sea dark and desolate. It struck her as strange that such a tiny cloud could cover the moon which was so much larger, but further away. It was a metaphor for her own life.

Nargis had a large collection of dolls from all over the world and now she looked at them, inert but so beautiful, with smiles on their faces. It seemed to her that they were inviting her to join them, to be one of the dead, to 'Get locked up in a glass case and be preserved.'

Disturbed, she took out her mother's mementos: a 'cigarette case with a few cigarettes still in it, her reading glasses, her pen, her last letter which she wrote to a friend and could not post— her money purse with two annas in it.' She put them next to her on her bed, and felt her mother's presence next to her. And so she got through a very long night.

For three days afterwards, she felt feverish and stayed in bed. She sent Ameena with a letter to Sunil's house, but Ameena came back with the news that he had gone out of town.

Nargis nearly collapsed. She bought a bottle of sleeping pills and planned to drug herself everyday. If there was no news from him, she would swallow the final, lethal overdose.

Fortunately, Sunil too could not stop thinking about her. He had gone away to Panchgani, but knew she would be depressed. Unable to resist his own feelings, he called her.

The sleeping pills were thrown out as Nargis packed quickly to go to him the next morning.

Sunil had gone to Panchgani to settle his sister's son, Gopal, in a boarding school there. He used the opportunity to spend some time alone, mulling over their relationship. He walked around the hills, and as he later wrote to her, he got soaked in the rain, and cried a lot, missing her all the time. Like Nargis, he contemplated death, and even visualized his own skeleton lying at the bottom of a hill. When the rain stopped and the clouds lifted, he had an epiphany. He thought he heard a voice, perhaps the voice of God. He was consoled and told not to worry, because Nargis belonged to him, and would come to him in full agreement with what he had suggested.

When Nargis arrived, they had a wonderful reunion, though it began badly with a long and diffident silence. But slowly the passion returned and they made up. However, Sunil firmly said there would be no more films for her. He was concerned that by taking on more and more films she would jeopardize her health, as well as the health of their future children.

'Look at Mr Ashok Kumar. He worked in so many pictures. And it is reflecting on him now. He is sick. The hakeem is always with him, wherever he goes,' he told her.

He wanted her to stick to the promise she had made: 'only three films.' The fact that she had signed the fourth film without telling him made him feel 'insulted and cheated. I did not expect this from you. I always used to feel proud of you. I had that conviction that even if you go to another man you will come and tell me—but you failed me in this case—you failed me completely. I felt hurt. I felt lost and neglected and cheated. I felt so much hurt that I did not feel as much when you met Raj in Germany. It did hurt me—but I felt proud of you that you came and told me—that you wrote everything. You know I will get hurt but you wanted me to know everything about you...'

He was also distressed that she had promised Mehboob money to complete *Mother India* without first discussing it with him. He felt that the trust between them was breaking down. Other couples in the film industry had faced similar problems and their relationships had not survived the test.

Sunil reminded her of the doomed marriage plans of Madhubala and Dilip Kumar. Dilip had asked Madhubala to quit the industry; she had replied that it was not possible. At the time Nargis had felt Madhubala was wrong: if she loved him, she should have given up her career because she had made too many sacrifices for her father and sisters.

The difference here was that Sunil was not forcing her to leave films immediately—just asking her to stop working beyond the limit they had set.

More money, argued Sunil, would only spoil her 'children'. She had got them used to the good things of life—dinners at Volga restaurant, records, expensive clothes. But now she ought to show them how to stand on their own feet. Show them how families lived on less than Rs 150 a month, and discourage them from dreaming about rich husbands.

He reassured her that after she got married, her relationship with the kids in Château Marine would only improve. He would help her and she would have more time with them, since she would not be an actress any more.

But he could not hide his distaste for Akhtar who, he said, 'is used to living and eating on someone else's money. And if he knows that you are leaving some money for the children, he will adopt a lot of undue means to get that money, so you must tell the children quickly that whatever you are earning is for them, because you are sacrificing our precious year for them.'

Sunil lectured her with a missionary zeal on the spartan life he hoped they would lead after their marriage. He urged her to tell the children about his own life: 'I have starved and I have stayed in huts and I have seen palaces. This all I did on my own— and if again I go back to the ground I will not mind it because I have seen the ground already—but if I lavish all comforts upon Popy, Gopali (his sister's children), my brother, and my cousin— they will expect that always and when they are thrown to the ground one day they won't like it—because they have not seen the ground—because they have not starved and they have not seen adversity—because they were too dependent on me.'

He said in response to her niece who wanted to know if his house was nicely decorated, 'I felt very happy when you told her that there are two cane chairs and one diwan in his room and nothing else.' It demonstrated that the homes of film stars were not always luxurious.

He also reminded her of the time when a plan was hatched at Château Marine to ask her for more money—if she refused, they would throw her out of the house. At the same time, he suggested that perhaps they could try and set Akhtar up in some business. And if that did not work out by December 1958, they would offer him one last film, which would star Nargis and some other hero. They could even help him select a good story and a good director. Eventually, this idea resulted in *Raat Aur Din*, which was produced by Akhtar Hussain.

Their reunion was long and intense. He wanted her to know exactly what distressed him. He even ticked her off for behaving 'like an actress' when other men were around, casually reclining on a sofa at home or cracking 'filthy jokes' which burnt his ears when he heard someone retelling them. In Sunil's book this was unacceptable. If she had to tell dirty jokes, it had better be only to him. (It must be said in Sunil's defence that some of these 'rules' relaxed over the years as they settled into a stable relationship, and while Nargis was known for her dignity and style, she also never lost her ability to swear like a trooper or tell a ribald joke.)

After their time in Panchgani, there would have been little doubt left in Nargis's mind that living with Sunil would involve a certain discipline. She had been brought up in a household full of people, with an easy give and take between the sexes. Sunil, it seemed, had a very different gameplan in mind for their life together. Nargis found it appealing to be in a secure situation with a caring man who wanted to look after her.

Sunil had another idea: since *Mother India* was to be released the following month, he thought they should end their forced separation and get married at the end of the year.

But the fourth film she had signed, for approximately two lakh rupees, was still a matter of contention. The money would be equivalent to around fifty lakh rupees today, not a small sum by any means. Nargis said she was willing to work day and night, which made him suspect that she may be tempted to sign a fifth, sixth or seventh film.

Finally, Sunil grimly asserted that if she accepted another film, he would not marry her.

Nargis, tired of the incessant negotiations, burst into tears, then lapsed into silence.

He started getting nervous and held her close but then, to his relief, she told him, 'I will not do the fourth picture...and I will not sign any more films.'

They looked at each other finally with unalloyed joy.

Ultimately their goal was to be together, so to fight over anything else seemed meaningless. Sunil told her he did not mind if the existing contracts took a while to be completed. Relieved at her acquiescence, he again pledged to help look after her children and said that if the need arose, 'I will make you work again in films for them.' He too could not bear the idea of the girls being dragged into films. Though he did not trust Akhtar, he was willing to help Nargis in every way, even if it meant buying a house for him in Bandra.

While they were busy sorting out their future, Amarjeet called to say that Dev and Mona wanted to come up to Panchgani to visit Sunil. Thinking quickly, for he did not want his rendezvous with Nargis to become public, he said he would meet them in Khandala, which was at a safe distance. Nargis returned to Bombay, finally secure in the knowledge that no matter how many storms came their way, they would weather them.

Lajwanti

1957

After coming back from Panchgani, Nargis began work on one of her last films, *Lajwanti*, opposite the veteran actor Balraj Sahni. The mahurat was on 7 September. She put on her make-up at home and left for the studio at around 9 a.m. During the mahurat pooja, she gazed at the swirling smoke of the havan and dreamt that she was getting married. She woke from her reverie only when she realized that the 'bridegroom' was absent. Still in a happy daze, she escaped from the crowds into the make-up room and found an unexpected visitor, Meena Kumari. She had come to inform Nargis that her co-star, Raj Kapoor, would be at the studio soon. *Sharda* was Raj Kapoor's first film post-Nargis. He had asked Meena, his co-star, to convey the message to her. Perhaps he was still hoping for a reconciliation.

Meena asked Nargis if she was prepared to meet Raj. Nargis replied with a firm 'no'. As she got into her car, she realized she was a little shaken by the encounter. She did not know Meena very well at the time and was surprised at her interest in her personal life. In fact, it was only after she retired from cinema that Nargis got to know some of the other actors. In the earlier years, she met them at fundraisers, premieres and other events, but because of her preoccupation with her brothers' children, RK Studios, and now Sunil Dutt, she had very little time to spare. Later, she became close to Meena and helped her during her illness.

Meena Kumari, Madhubala and quite a few other women (including Nargis) had similar histories: they had been pushed into cinema by their ambitious families. In the case of both Madhubala and Meena, their father was the prime instigator.

Meena's original name was Mehjabeen, and she was an unusually good performer. But she could not, as time went on, shed her tragedy-queen persona. She did not try (as Nargis did) to escape the film world. She was exploited by the men in her life, first her father and then her husband, the great film writer and director Kamal Amrohi. Towards the end of her life she became an alcoholic. She was also known to have written beautiful but morbid poetry.

The difference also was that Nargis fought back for survival, while Meena Kumari allowed herself to self-destruct, bloated with drink, in full public view. Both she and Madhubala died young: Meena was only 41, while Madhubala was just 39.

Having publicly reiterated that she was not interested in Raj Kapoor, Nargis's life revolved exclusively around Sunil and their impending marriage. Realizing that his sister would be concerned about Sunil's Panchgani trip, she went to meet her. Rani, who was usually not very loquacious, confided her worries about Sunil to Nargis. All the symptoms Sunil displayed were familiar to Nargis, for she suffered from them too. Rani reported that he ate poorly and looked as though he had been crying. Nargis resisted the temptation to tell all. Instead she promised to take Rani's son Gopal shopping, and played with her daughter Popy. On another day she took Gopal back to Château Marine with her, so he could spend time with the other children.

There was open curiosity at Château Marine about her mysterious visit to Panchgani. The actress Neelam (originally Letitia), who was Akhtar's close friend, tried to chat to her about her trip. Sunil had already indicated that he did not want Nargis to confide in Neelam, so she avoided the topic and dropped a surprised Neelam back home.

Sticking to another promise, she turned down the film with Dev Anand. But disturbingly, someone warned her that they had heard of her meeting with Sunil at Panchgani. She surmised that the rumours could have only been manufactured in her own home or by those who were close to Akhtar. But the gossip and innuendo was bothering her less and less. Even the pitying looks from film industry folk when they met at programmes did not annoy her as much because she realized that no matter what they thought, she was proud of the fact that she had nothing more to do with a certain blue-eyed actor. And she was able to hold her head high about her relationship with Sunil because they were going to be married very soon.

Yet, being a famous film star meant she had little privacy. There was gossip about how she ran down from her flat in her dressing gown and got into Sunil's car in the middle of the night.

Nargis tried to ignore it all and advised Sunil to do the same. But now she strongly felt that an actor's life was not for normal people, only for those who wanted to lead an artificial existence. 'Really this "Nargis" gets on my nerves—people seem to be much more worried about the name than the person.'

Apart from Sunil, she concentrated on completing her work as fast as possible. She had a very demanding role in *Lajwanti* and it was physically tiring as well, because she had to drive every day from Marine Drive to Andheri and back.

> I was feeling quite odd and uneasy with a set of completely new people, except Balraj Sahni...the scene was one of the important scenes in this film. I wished they did not begin with this scene. I'm not yet in the role and I found it pretty difficult to act and react. The result was I had to strain myself quite a lot thus leaving myself fagged out with a head as heavy as stone. You are right...This work of acting sucks the blood out of me. All the time I am in a tension while working.

She was in bed by 9.30 at night. She no longer had any energy even for midnight trysts. Fortunately, Sunil was busy too.

He had started work on a new film opposite Waheeda Rehman, who was also to become a great friend. Nargis had heard that he was looking 'very handsome' in the film and she teasingly asked him if someday she would get the news that Waheeda had fainted while looking into his eyes. The film (*Ek Phool Char Kaante*) was released two years later. In it, Sunil is in love with Waheeda, but to win her love he has to first woo her four 'uncles' who have brought her up. It was a comic tour de force and after some fairly intense roles, it must have come as a relief to Sunil.

But for Nargis, who had also been an effortless 'natural' actor so far, things were not improving on the sets of *Lajwanti*.

I reached the studio at 9:30 a.m. and was on sets at 10 a.m. for shooting. It was extremely hot the whole day, making me feel giddy. Above all today some very emotional shots were taken. You know your Pia. I worked myself to a pitch. There was a shot (in which) they took a big close up of mine from about a 100 feet, where in the beginning I am standing expressionless, with fixed eyes and then gradually Balraj Sahni's words start playing upon me. I start reacting and tears start coming into my eyes, finally I break down into sobs…That shot took the entire energy out of me—they took 3 takes— rather I insisted because I could not get the emotions to the required pitch—by the time the 3rd shot was over I was trembling from head to foot—felt so weak in the limbs that I had to sit down and drink a cold glass of water—then for quite some time I could not come to my normal self. Really, this kind of work plays havoc with one's constitution—before I met you I never used to bother how things react on me—but after knowing that I must be a very healthy Mrs Dutt I realize that this creative and emotional work of mine takes more energy of mine than required—I was wondering that inspite of 14 years of this labour how have I managed to look a little better than I should? I should have become old much before my time. Oh yes, it has left me shattered. I have become conscious of my work…

The scene in which she is accused of being unfaithful required her to cry. The one thing that never failed to make her cry was the memory of her father's death. To this she added the recollection of the night when Sunil nearly had an accident. Tears came streaming down her cheeks effortlessly. But the impact of the scene on her and the effort involved made her seriously re-evaluate her life as an actor.

The same day, she saw the recently-wed Geeta Bali at another set close by, and was shocked that Geeta had brought her young child with her. Nargis, who was longing to be a mother herself, could not understand why the baby should be exposed to the 'dirty' studio atmosphere.

'She had brought the poor baby to the studio with his milk bottles, pram, what not—fancy bringing such a tender child into the dirty atmosphere of the studio and then also not bothering about the baby. I don't know how she could laugh and be gay knowing her child is in such an unhealthy atmosphere. I hated it… I am criticizing this but along with all this I really sincerely pray to God that I never have to see such days.'

She told Sunil: 'I'm happy and glad that my husband is a man of very strong character and will. You will never allow me to work for anything I know.'

She was right about the studios being unhealthy. Thanks to the constant turnover of sets, there was always debris lying around, and the lights used on the film sets were extremely harsh. There was very poor ventilation and few fans to provide relief from the heat and humidity. The normal diet of the average worker was not very good either and thanks to the long working hours, illness and alcoholism were common. The glamour, for what it was worth, was mainly on screen, and the romance lay in the desire to make films, not in the surroundings. It was certainly no place for a baby, and no doubt it reminded Nargis too much of her own childhood, spent on the dusty studio floors. Her discomfort helped to seal her pact with Sunil, that she would discontinue her acting career and as far as possible, not bring her own children to the studio.

Was there some truth in what Nargis had noticed? Geeta Bali was a dynamic and charming artiste of the time. She had a vivacity that grabbed your attention the moment she appeared on screen. A gutsy Punjabi, she had come from a very deprived background, but managed a break in the Bombay film world while still very young, largely due to her own drive and ambition. Like Meena Kumari, Madhubala and Nargis, she also supported her family, but fell in love with and married one of her co-stars, Shammi Kapoor (Raj Kapoor's younger brother). Tragically, she died of smallpox about six years after Nargis saw her on the sets with her child. She was 35 years old. Nearly 14 of Geeta's films were released after her marriage and she was working on yet another one, based on Rajinder Singh Bedi's famous short story, *Ek Chadar Maili Si*, when she fell fatally ill.

It is clear from Nargis's letters that though she was the earning member of the family, she was never made to feel special. In

1958

MOHAN SEGAL
Present

NARGIS — BALRAJ SAHNI
BABY NAAZ — PRABHU DAYAL & RADHA KISHEN

in

De Lux Films'

LAJWANTI

with

MANORAMA-KUSUM-MUNTAZ-LEELA MISRA-NAZIR KASHMIRI-AMRIT KUMAR
KRISHNA DUGGAL-DAYAOLVI-RAMLAL-KAMAL DUKHIYA-MANJULA
PRAVIN PAUL-CHAND EUEK-MASTER ANWAR
SHEELA KASHMIRI-PRITHVIRAJ & OTHERS.

Directed by: **NARENDRA SURI**   *Music:* S. D. BURMAN

CREDITS.

PHOTOGRAPHY :	M. N. MALHOTRA.
SOUND RECORDING :	E. M. SUBATWALLA.
SONGS RECORDING :	ISHAN GHOSH & MINOO KATRAK.
LYRICS :	MAJROOH SULTANPURI.
SCREENPLAY :	SACHIN BHAUMICK.
STORY & DIALOGUES :	UMESH MATHUR.
ADDL. DIALOGUES :	SURENDRA SHAILAJ.
ART DIRECTION :	SUDHENDU ROY.
EDITING :	PRATAP DAVE A. F. E.
PAINTINGS :	HABKISHAN LAL.
DANCE DIRECTION :	B. HIRALAL.
MAKEUP :	SUNDERJI.
HAIR STYLIST :	SALMA SIBAI.
DRESSMAN :	SHIVRAM SALVI
PUBLICITY OFFICER :	DEVENDRA PRATAP
STILL PUBLICITY :	KAMAT FOTO FLASH
PROCESSING :	ABA JOSHI.
PRODUCTION EXECUTIVE :	HAMMAD JAFRI.
GENERAL MANAGER :	J. OM PRAKASH.

ASSISTANTS.

DIRECTION :	SURENDRA SHAILAJ.
MUSIC :	JAIDEV
PHOTOGRAPHY :	YOGENDRA MALHOTRA & DHARAM CHOPRA.
ART DIRECTION :	N. M. AYTODA.
EDITING :	NAND KUMAR & D. N. PATEL
PRODUCTION :	HARISH & YAKUB PATEL.
DANCES :	RADHEY SHYAM & SHANKER
MAKEUP :	JANU MODAK.
OFFICE :	ASHOKE ROY.

Produced at : **MOHAN STUDIOS, ANDHERI, BOMBAY.**
Processed at : **FAMOUS CINE LABORATORY, TARDEO, BOMBAY.**

Gramophone Records on : **H. M. V.**

ALL RIGHTS PERTAINING TO CONTENTS HEREIN ARE RESERVED WITH
DE LUX FILMS, FAMOUS CINE BUILDING, MAHALAXMI, BOMBAY - 11.

---

* LAJWANTI *

SYNOPSIS.

"LAJWANTI" portrays a common problem–"MARRIED UNHAPPINESS". Nirmal Kumar is a successful and flourishing advocate. He has all the material comforts of life which money can buy but Nirmal's wife Kavita mother of a small child Renu, is not happy in her fabulously furnished house. She is greatly missing the love, affection, and companionship of her husband. Nirmal Kumar's most of the time is spent in his professional activities and is completely ignorant of the emotional needs of his wife.

From this state of affairs flow many emotional conflicts. Sunil an intimate friend of Nirmal and Kavita from their college days, returns from England. But unfortunately his moving about with Kavita is misunderstood by malicious and narrow-minded people and ultimately the gossip sweeps the household and eventually Nirmal Kumar, blind with suspicions and doubts, turns his wife out, separating her from her child also.

Long ten years passed away when the repentant husband quite suddenly finds his wife still alive, and is filled with abounding joy. He thinks that his life has been enriched, and that his motherless child has got a mother. But nature had still more calamities in store for Kavita. Could patience and forebearance bring her happiness ? Did Renu get her mother ? See it on the screen.

---

fact, she was the one who showered others with affection and gifts. It was something they took for granted. When she was unwell, she would make an appointment with the doctor and go alone, or dose herself with medicine without letting anyone know. Barring Sunil, no one noticed if she had a cough or a cold, or looked like she hadn't slept well. It was a peculiarly isolated life in a house crowded with no less than twenty people at any given time. The only other person who did care and fuss over her was her ayah, Ameena.

Naturally, Nargis missed her mother who had accompanied her on shoots in the early days. While she was the reason for Nargis joining the industry in the first place, she had also made sure that food was brought to her on time when she was working, and that she was allowed to leave the studio at 6.30 p.m. After Jaddanbai's death, nobody bothered. Iqbal may have tried, but it was an increasingly volatile relationship, not one Nargis could rely on. Especially now when the cold war between them was at freezing point.

However, around this time, she noticed that Akhtar was

making friendly overtures towards her, even trying to talk to her. It made her instantly suspicious because she felt he must want to use her in some way. Once his need was met, she would be dumped again.

Lajwanti was melodramatic to the core and Nargis had to maintain that dreaded high pitch in her acting throughout. She was very disciplined: she arrived at the scheduled time and working for as long as was required, even if it meant rushing out of the house without anything to eat, and remaining hungry all day. Like many other actors of the period, she was professional about her commitments. But the role was affecting her, and she found she could no longer unwind as quickly as she used to.

She felt physically unwell, and fragile. It may have been her low blood pressure or her breathlessness that caused it, but she could not sleep well at night. Finally she started taking a sleeping pill before going to bed so that she could get through the following day without becoming exhausted. Of course, we will never know if the seeds of her terrible illness were sown during this period, but it is possible that the doctors at the time had little information about cancer and the advantages of early intervention.

The atmosphere in the studio was depressing in more ways than one. She met Madhubala who was also shooting in the vicinity and who could really 'talk and talk'. She poured out all her secrets to Nargis, who felt sad that the beautiful woman was not able to settle down in any relationship, be it with Dilip Kumar or Dev Anand (who had once wanted to marry her), the veteran Ashok Kumar, or her latest love, Pradeep Kumar. Invited for lunch with her, Nargis walked in on the two of them in Madhubala's make-up room. Before she could discreetly withdraw, she saw Pradeep combing his hair and Madhubala adjusting her clothes, her lipstick all smudged. Nargis felt both embarrassed and worried because she feared the worst. There were too many lonely women like Madhubala in the industry, and she felt sorry for them, but for her it was another reason to get married quickly.

The industry, of course, thrived on gossip. There were plenty of people saying all sorts of things about her as well. And now, to make matters worse, she learnt from Sunil that they were under constant surveillance, on Akhtar's orders, no doubt. Someone followed them around every day to find out how much time they were spending together, and where. She knew that her reputation, like Madhubala's, was being torn to shreds. The situation was made even more unbearable by the fact that Sunil and she were busy with their individual films and could not meet regularly.

The only source of happiness was the news that Sunil had found their 'dream house' at Pali Hill. On 11 August, when she first heard about it, she was ecstatic and immediately began planning their life in the house. But it would be a while before they could be together in it, and the agony of living in a loveless environment grew worse every day.

Mother India
1957

Besides *Lajwanti*, Nargis was also trying to complete work on *Adalat*. But the schedule was erratic because Pran, who played the villain, was away in Madras working on another film.

Adalat and *Lajwanti* had a common thread in the plot: the woman protagonist is accused of infidelity, and struggles to wipe away the slur. Given Nargis's state of mind, the films would have been difficult to handle, but she was able to get through it all by keeping in touch with Sunil and writing regularly to him. Work on a third film would begin soon; it was a film which reflected her future dreams in its title: *Ghar Sansar* (The home is my world).

Sunil continued to be over-sensitive and unpredictable at times, but the situation had improved between them. Now they met openly at home, in the presence of her sister and her children, had dinner together, and began to feel more and more as though they were a family. After an evening of music and conversation with him, it was always difficult for her to tear herself away. She told him, 'My own house seems to be strange to me for it lacks your love. This house used to hold my childhood but now I am a stranger to my childhood. I have grown up. I want to be with my husband in his home which will be mine—in his arms—to breathe in his love—to find my life in his love—to find contentment in his kisses. Am I mad? I would love to be in this state of madness all my life.'

Their final goal was clearer now in Sunil's mind. He got the papers for the house he had found in Pali Hill. Unknown to Nargis, who had grown up with a confident capacity to generate money, he had to negotiate his way carefully to raise enough money to buy the house. It was extremely important to him that they start their married life in a home he had purchased. If she had got to know of his precarious finances, she might have sympathized, but he wanted to be the protector and look after her. He did not want her pity or her money. Nargis had no idea of his predicament. She assumed that he had enough money to buy the house. After all, she had bought several for her family. It was at moments like this when Sunil, though deeply in love with her, could see the immeasurable distance between them. There were many things she simply took for granted. For him, however, everything was still on shifting sands.

His friend Krishen remembers the transaction, which was fairly delicate: 'The bungalow belonged to an MLA, it was like a country home for him. He used to live in the city and come here to have picnics. There was nothing en route (it was a fairly uninhabited area at the time), no restaurants or anything. Sunil just decided to buy this house, because it was a big bungalow, and he wanted to maintain a certain lifestyle. The broker involved said if you want to buy a house, I will help you sign a film, they will give you the money, but don't think it will be a very stylish film or anything. And so he signed *Post Box 999*. Johnny Walker's sister-in-law Shakila was the heroine, and Sunil was the hero. And Krishnakant and others were acting in it. The house cost Rs 1,75,000. The broker told him that most of the money could be paid to him over a few years. But Sunil had to act in a few more faltu movies during that period, to pay for it.'

Post Box 999 was not as disastrous as the gloomy Sunil may have imagined initially. It was directed by Ravindra Dave, who specialized in whodunits, and had a somewhat racy appeal. Leela Chitnis played an old woman whose son has been falsely accused and convicted. She hires an investigative journalist Vikas (Sunil) to dig out the relevant evidence to save him. Vikas and his girlfriend Nilima (Shakila) track down the truth by pretending to be magicians. The film was apparently based on the Twentieth Century Fox production *Call Northside 777*, starring James Stewart and directed by Henry Hathaway.

The deal that Sunil arranged for the house remained a secret for a while. He would be moody when he met Nargis because he did not want to burden her with his troubles. And Nargis, as usual, began to fret.

They decided that an even earlier marriage would take care of their mutual insecurity. Sunil was to leave in mid-October for Mandoli with his sister and her children. The plan was that he would stay there for about fifteen days to settle some property-related issues. *Mother India* was to be released around this time. Sunil would return with Nemani after the film was released, and Nargis and he would get married.

As they had always planned, the marriage would remain confidential until they were ready to announce it to the world. Nargis even suggested that if she became pregnant during the period immediately after their marriage, she would not hesitate to have the baby as it would be a child created in love.

Meanwhile, the deal for the house ran into trouble. He had signed another 'faltu' film to pay for the house, but the role was so dreadful that he backed out. He had taken an advance of Rs 40,000 from the producer, which would now have to be returned.

Nargis came to know of his problem, partly from him and partly from Faredoon Irani and his wife, 'Gool aunty'.

Nargis immediately suggested that he should not take a loan because the interest would be high. She told him, 'I have money and I wish you would agree to take it from me—without forming any kind of complexes. It will save you interest as well as the humiliation of borrowing money. I know that Dev is a friend of yours and he will give you the money if you ask him—but why be under an obligation from a friend?... After all, you will return my money. Besides I will not tell anyone.'

She suggested that if he took the money, she would explain to everyone at home that she had put it in the bank, or given it to a friend for safe keeping. She asked him to consider it a loan from a friend. She wanted to share his troubles, she said, along with his happiness.

Sunil was not convinced, and for some time the issue kept cropping up between them, till it was overtaken by the impending release of *Mother India*.

Snippets of information started trickling out. The prints of *Mother India* had arrived. Nargis was no longer confident of her performance. 'Expectation of the people for "Mother India" is also great. I only hope and pray that if not beyond expectation, at least the picture should be up to the expectation of the people. As the day is coming nearer for the release of "Mother India" I am feeling nervous. I feel that we have all staked our best in the making of the film. Believe me Jio, I'm losing faith in my performance. Now I feel I have overacted in the picture. God help us, I am so nervous.'

As they spent more time together, she was able to persuade him to borrow the money for the house from her. One clear advantage was that this way at least his reputation would remain secure, because she would not discuss it with anyone. She successfully managed to smuggle the money (even though it belonged to her, she was always nervous that Akhtar would try to stop her) out of the house.

But before they could celebrate this big step forward in their relationship, the family at Château Marine managed to get her into trouble with Sunil.

A girl who was working in one of Kardar's films called up one evening to invite her over for a party. Nargis did not want to go, and when she was asked to send her nieces, she refused on their behalf too. But the girl turned up at the house, saying Anwar and Akhtar were also at the party and had asked their daughters to come over. As Iqbal was not at home, Nargis thought she had better go with them. 'I was so embarrassed,' she later recalled, 'her house was full of a filmi crowd and a very funny atmosphere.' Though there were quite a few well-known personalities there, including Talat Mehmood and his wife, Nargis left with the girls after five minutes.

Though she was annoyed with her brothers, and with the girl who had thrown the party, she did say, 'I don't know whom to blame. This girl is so young and her mother is using her for bait for rich people and ruining her life. I wish this sort of thing would stop.'

She also wrote to Sunil, 'Let us get married soon. I want to

start living with you because as long as I will be in this house—
these sorts of situations will keep coming and I will not know
how to avoid it. Whenever I think of that girl, I shiver. Thank
God my parents gave me proper education to know myself and
how to conduct myself in life...I don't know why Akhtar and
Anwar went there and even if they went why did they want their
kids there. Oh God, Jio darling please take me away soon.'

As she wrote those words, she did not know that the news of
her having attended the party had already been conveyed to a
furious Sunil. He arrived the next night, and she went down to
his car, unmindful of the fact that there was a group of men
sitting outside her building and watching them. Even as she
started telling him about the awful evening, she realized that he
already knew and was treating her as though 'I was unclean, as
if I had betrayed you, as if I was unfaithful to you.'

Among the list of things that Sunil had actually written out
and given her at their Panchgani pact was that he did not want
her to attend any more 'filmi' parties. So this was, for him, a
severe transgression. Sunil was always wary of the earlier influences
in her life. Knowing her background as he did, he dreaded her
further exploitation.

Nargis was at a loss:

> Your every word was like a hundred daggers piercing through me.
> You started coughing very badly, I could not hold myself back, I
> caught you but you threw me aside as if probably my touch would
> have killed you—I felt so hurt—so unwanted...On the very spot
> where we made so many plans of being together all our lives, you
> snatched the last breath of my life...you said we should not meet
> each other for you could not adjust yourself with me—we are two
> different people—and that after I have completed all my pictures and
> fulfilled all my desires—and if we still felt that we should get married
> we will, otherwise...? What could I say—the dead don't speak. The
> dead kill all their desires...

Sunil returned the wristwatch that she had recently given him
as a present. He told her that he had sold the Pali Hill house to
Mala Sinha and that she should not visit him any more at his
place on Napean Sea Road. Nargis became hysterical and finally

Sunil, who could not bear the sight of her tears, gave in. But it was a precarious moment that came back to haunt her time and again. They had been a hair's breadth away from a final break-up, and at last she realized the distance Sunil wanted her to put between the life she led with her brothers, and the world he hoped to create for them.

The next day, after a bout of weeping, she went downstairs to tell her family what she thought of them. Finally it was out in the open. She told them 'they should not expect me to keep sacrificing my life for them. I got angry with Akhtar and told him that either he should take charge of his kids and do as he pleases with them or leave them to me and not interfere.'

It was a turning point for her, and until she met Sunil later in the day, she brooded over what had happened. Then, in the evening, he took her to see the house on Pali Hill. He had not sold it, and she was thrilled. 'It was the happiest moment of my life. It is such a heaven on earth. A dream house...the moon was beautiful. Amarjeet was with us—but I was so drunk with happiness that I just didn't care what I spoke in his presence—I don't care. I found myself planning my life all over again in that house with you and with my kids. The way you had described the house I felt I knew every nook and every corner of the place. I liked it very much.'

After a magical evening, Sunil dropped her home at 3.30 a.m. She had been told by several people that she had got a new life after the fire on the sets of *Mother India*. But, she said, she felt that her new life began that night. 'Of course you love me,' she told Sunil, 'but it is a fact that it is not even a fraction of the love I have for you.'

She decided to fast for him on Karva Chauth, even though she was a Muslim. It's a very strict fast, in which no food or even water is allowed, and the woman prays for her husband's long life. She is allowed to eat very early in the morning before daybreak, and the fast is broken in the evenings only after dusk, once the moon is visible.

Meanwhile, much to her chagrin, and despite her argument with him, her brother organized another party. This time it was a mehfil with qawwalis by Shakila Bano. Nargis was worried about being accused of mixing with the wrong crowd again, but fortunately it was a 'respectable' crowd, with not too many filmi people, except a few unobjectionable ones like Lata Mangeshkar. According to an amused Nargis, Shakila's bold actions and gestures were enjoyed by all the men. However, she herself was anxious all evening: she knew she had to be on her best behaviour because of her very demanding lover.

Not long after this, Sunil's sister fell ill.

Rani remembers those days: 'I had come to visit Dutt sahib from Secunderabad only for a few months. He was in a small flat, with one live-in servant. I would sleep in the drawing room with my children, and Dutt sahib would sleep in the bedroom. Popy was around one and a half years at the time.

'I felt a severe pain whenever I put on my clothes, and was feverish quite often. A doctor came to see me because the one visible sign that I was not well was on my face—I had pimples which had turned black. The doctor gave me some lotion for my face. But I was diagnosed with tuberculosis.

'Dutt sahib was still shooting *Mother India* in Billimora. Others would also keep an eye on me—Mehboob's wife, Sardar Akhtar, came to see me after he had asked that they check on me. Rajendra Kumar dropped in, then Nargis started coming over to ask about me.

'After some time, it was decided that I would be operated on. The big problem was what would happen to my children during that period? So Nargis looked after them, and she even took the children to her own house. I stayed in the hospital for around three to four days. Dutt sahib was also there with me.'

Nargis took charge and was with her throughout. Sunil melted at the sight of her running around for his sister. And she (strange though it may seem) enjoyed being in the hospital: it reminded her of her own dreams of becoming a doctor, though her account of the surgery itself, in medical terms, may not have been the most precise.

She did everything she could: 'I went home in Gool aunty's car to get a night jacket and gown for your sister—you did show some kindness later on. You brought sandwiches for me to eat, we ate them together—we smiled. O Jio, your smile is so soothing—I really forget everything. The operation started at 3:45 p.m. I was in the theatre with your sister. The doctor was afraid I might faint—but to watch it was so exciting. I saw the glands deep in the skin. They removed the glands one by one, within 35 minutes the operation was over. I came to you and gave you the news that all is well. I stayed in the hospital and told you to go home and rest, but you stayed. I told my people at home that I am staying with a friend of mine who has been operated. Looking after Rani was like looking after my own sister-in-law. It was a duty I performed with love. At home I put Popy to sleep, you were out in the balcony. I came to you.'

Sunil had remembered that she was going to keep the Karva Chauth fast the next day, and had brought some food for her to eat early in the morning. (Normally, this meal is provided by the mother-in-law.) She woke up at four, looked at Sunil as the ritual demanded, then ate and went back to sleep. It was another peaceful glimpse into the future, free from the constant misunderstandings being created around them by their 'well-wishers' in the film world.

Later in the day, Nargis went back to Château Marine and surprised herself with her will power: she did not even have a sip of water. She could not rest either, because she had to visit Rani. For once, she did not worry that others would see her at the hospital and ask questions. While she looked after Rani in the hospital over the next three days, there were a few awkward moments when Sunil's friends, such as Mona Anand, dropped in to see Rani, but she decided that she had to do her 'duty' towards Rani and Sunil, and not be shy about gossip. She even took her nieces to meet Rani, but made them swear that they would not tell anyone.

Nargis was especially sympathetic towards Rani because she knew she was trapped in an unhappy marriage. Rani had confided in her about a particularly nasty letter her husband had sent her. Obviously, her insecurity contributed to her poor health. In the short time that Rani was with Sunil, she constantly underwent medical treatment.

Nargis was one of the few people who could appreciate Rani's uncomplicated worldview, and she hoped that once she married Sunil, she could encourage Rani to be unafraid of her husband—though Rani still does not admit that her husband ever ill-treated her.

That night, Nargis went home from the hospital with Sunil, dressed like a married woman. They gazed at the new moon, and sat down for dinner. As she wrote later, they had never felt so close to each other before. And over the next few days, they were inseparable.

Sometimes they would drive to Pali Hill and spend time in 'their house.' While Nargis was thrilled to be there, she did tell Sunil, as tactfully as she could, that it was an old-fashioned house and should be changed and redesigned. Ironically, when the house was finally redesigned nearly fifty years after Sunil bought it in 1957, neither he nor Nargis was alive to enjoy it.

Rani remembers that she had read newspaper articles linking Sunil and Nargis. She had great respect for her brother. In fact, she never even raised her eyes to look at him directly, so questioning him about the relationship was impossible. However, one day, he did ask her whether she (Rani) liked 'her'. Rani says he had his back to her, and was taking clothes out of a cupboard. He did not mention Nargis by name, but she understood who he meant. And then he wondered if his mother would like 'her'. Rani felt she would. He told her that within a few months he and Nargis would be married, but she shouldn't tell anyone, not even her husband.

According to plan, Sunil left on 20 October for Mandoli, but without Rani, who was still recuperating. It was a sad moment for Nargis, as she had become used to meeting him every day. When she came to say goodbye to Sunil, she at last knew without doubt that Rani was aware of their relationship, both from the manner in which Rani spoke to her, and the way she spoke to her about Sunil. When she asked her son Gopal to touch Nargis's feet (to show respect, and also because the irrepressible Gopal would often call her mamiji, i.e. mother's brother's wife), Nargis felt that Rani had accepted her as part of the family.

After leaving Sunil's flat, Nargis dropped in to meet Mehboob at his first wife's house. It was a convenient arrangement: Sardar Akhtar was his second wife, but he also kept a cordial relationship with his first wife, Fatima, with whom he had three sons and three daughters.

As Nargis described it, 'Raaj Kumar and Rajendra Kumar were there and a lot of other people. Mr Mehboob was talking all about his London trip and Raaj Kumar as usual saying "great" at every word. We had dinner together... Mr Mehboob said the London press were praising my work a lot.' They had brought presents for their actors: a hairpiece for Nargis, and cufflinks and a tiepin for both Sunil and Rajendra Kumar.

Mehboob and his wife clearly wanted to be on good terms with Nargis. The old acrimony was receding as the date for the premiere of *Mother India* approached. They wanted her to come to Delhi, where they were hoping to have a special show for Pandit Nehru and Dr Rajendra Prasad.

They showed her the first souvenir of *Mother India*, which she said was 'a beautiful thing and worth preserving. Mr Mehboob was very kind and presented the first copy to me with his signature. At once I thought of you and I will send it to you through Mr Amarjeet (who planned to visit Mandoli while Sunil was there). We all went along to the station to see the King off (Mehboob was going to the dargah in Ajmer to pray) on his spiritual journey... I was thinking of all those trips we made to Billimora and back and in different moods that we travelled. Our journey to Baroda and back...every place holds memories of you.'

Ignoring the impending release, Nargis kept up with her other commitments, going across every evening to pick up Rani and take her to the doctor, and then travelling to Pali Hill. Later, back in her house, she would write to Sunil, telling him every detail of the day. Rani's health was slowly improving and her husband had arrived as well. But he kept threatening to leave, insulted that Sunil had gone away without meeting him. Rani sank further into depression and Nargis began to counsel her regularly, trying to cheer her up with daily visits.

It was a difficult time for them all, because a wrong move

would mean the end of Rani's marriage, and while Nargis could privately discuss the problem with Rani and Sunil, she could not interfere or talk to Rani's husband, Bali, directly.

Sunil, meanwhile, found out that even in Mandoli he could not escape Nargis's past. But he was able to take the rumours in his stride and Nargis was happy that he could at last deal with it without becoming too morose. This time the gossip was about her mother, Jaddanbai, and it seemed that his mother had heard the stories too.

Nargis told him frankly, without hiding anything, 'Circumstances put people in places without their wanting to be there—whatever she was, she was a woman of character and I'm proud of her. She loved my father very much and so did he. They lived together without separation even for a day. He died and she couldn't wait even a year without him. They lived happily and they died contented. I am her daughter and I don't care what people say.' Fortunately, Sunil was wise enough to brush the insinuations aside, and asked his mother to do the same.

And then, the day they had been waiting for arrived—*Mother India* was finally released. After this, they could think of getting married! On 25 October 1957, *Mother India* was premiered at Liberty Theatre in Bombay. Nargis recorded every minute of that momentous day for Sunil.

> I was more nervous than ever the whole day. Specially as the hour of the first show came. My heart started beating hard. All the kids from home along with some family members left for the Liberty cinema. I was counting the minutes and seconds when they will come back to give me the news. Kasam (her driver) had also gone. At last they came back. One could see that they had cried a lot. All were just praises for the picture, for my work, and you and also Sajid. Soon after came (I.S.) Johar all panting he said that he has just come back from the show. He was so excited that he couldn't speak straight. He said that I should stop acting after this film and about you he said— that boy has established himself as first grade. I felt so happy and proud of you. Mr Mehboob rang me up and called me home. As he was nervous, too, so I went there. Johar was there so was Nemani and Dhiroo Bhai. I was more than glad to see Nemani—I gave him your message on the quiet (Sunil had wanted to bring him to Bombay

to be a witness to their wedding—but he had arrived earlier). Then came the hours of my getting ready for the premiere. My hands and feet were cold and I could feel that I was shivering.

As I arrived at Liberty theatre, I was out of breath. A huge but well managed crowd was outside. I got out amidst a lot of arc lamps and cine cameras. I passed by and entered the hall. I was told that Navketan were shooting the entire show. A lot of people came. They were all missing you—asking about you. I wish I could tell them that he is here in my heart, in my eyes, in my breath. The show started. There was a great ovation on the very first shot of mine as the old lady—people clapped. I had carried your watch next to my heart. I placed my hands on my chest and felt your warmth. People were enjoying the picture. During the interval Anwar called me out for Goldy wanted to take another shot of mine coming to the premiere. But first Anwar kissed me and I saw tears in his eyes.

Of course the congratulations of the people and hubbub of the crowd was there. I went and stood in a corner I wanted to burst with happiness. I don't know what the people of the industry will tell you about your performance but you should pay no heed to them for they are not happy at your success. You are the darling of the audience and that is what you must care for. They laugh at your light scenes and clap at your dialogues with Sukhi (the moneylender) when you come as a dacoit. You look very handsome. Oh! Jio it was a big moment in my life—sort of my prayers being heard. You were dejected with your role but people love you as Birju and that was what I was praying for.

But the past cropped up again and as always, she was honest about it.

'After the show somebody gave me a bouquet which was sent from RK Films. All met me enthusiastically...'

Nargis had stopped eating any meat or eggs, and had said she would remain a vegetarian till they were married, so at Mehboob's lavish celebratory dinner that night, she ate pickle with her bread.

Her mind throughout was on Sunil's performance, which was interesting because in reality the film belonged to her. She said nothing to Sunil about her own role, except what others had to say to her. She said, because he had been so worried that his role had been edited out substantially, 'I am proud of you. I would tell you if I didn't like your work. People do say at places Sunil is jerky but they don't know that scenes in between that connect have been cut. All my people at home like you and Kasam and others also say that Sunil has done very well. The best is that the picture is a success. Everybody says with one voice "'Mother India' is a great production." Thank God our labour was not wasted.'

It was big relief, because Mehboob had made them feel that their romance could ruin the film. 'Now when we get married,' said Nargis, 'we won't feel we have done any harm to the picture, nor can Mr Mehboob blame us.'

More importantly, Nemani had told her that he could not stay on after the premiere, but would return to Bombay on 6 November. Nargis suggested that instead of waiting, they simply go to Umra and get married there. Now that *Mother India* had had a successful release, there was no reason to wait.

Mrs Dutt?
1957

The release of *Mother India* was a relief, but also a burden
for Nargis. It became such a huge hit and Mehboob's careful
orchestration of the media created so much hype, that she could
not escape the public eye. Interviews and autographs were in
demand. Congratulatory phone calls and flowers and letters
overwhelmed her. Even other artistes such as Nadira came over
to her house to kiss and congratulate her. Never had she received
accolades of this nature.

Sunil chose to stay in Mandoli (ostensibly settling property
matters), away from all the excitement, because he was still
nervous about the public reaction to his role. His ego, unused to
the ruthless world of cinema, was a little bruised because the
woman he loved was probably going to be even more famous
after *Mother India*. He did not know that in fact, *Mother India*
was to provide an impetus for his career as well. In any case, he
wasn't around.

But Mehboob was. And Mehboob wanted to celebrate his
grand achievement. Not only that, at every celebration, he
required the presence of the woman who was at the heart of his
film. At any other time, Nargis would have relaxed and enjoyed
the attention. She would have sailed from one opening to the
other, smiling and elegant, having proven to the world that she
did not need RK Films to boost her career. She had shown
everyone that she could act and was a true professional.

However, right now it vexed her a little that the spotlight
should turn on her just when she and the man she was going to
marry had hoped that she could immediately sink into retirement.

But that was not going to happen. No one wanted to leave her alone. So, for a little while at least, she allowed herself to be carried away by the success of the film.

'I was so drunk with happiness and contentment last night that I slept peacefully as well as till late in the morning. I had a couple of appointments for interviews but I cancelled them. I lay in bed and one by one my sisters-in-law, then the servants and kids all came up and the topic of "Mother India" started. Hamida told me that she cried so much that it was disturbing other people sitting beside her. The same thing happened with one Mrs Akhtar, she says that she never cries in pictures but this picture moved her so much that she couldn't help but cry.

'Oh yes! Early in the morning at about 9 a.m. came Nadira. She had met me on the premiere night—kissed me and congratulated me—but she came in the morning, kissed me again and said she felt last night's congratulations were not enough. She too told me I should not work after this film and spoil the impression,' she wrote contentedly to Sunil.

Nadira told her that she preferred Sunil's looks to his performance, but Nargis stuck to her own view that Sunil's acting had been appreciated by all. Meanwhile, some other criticism of the film came from, surprisingly, Aga Jaani Kashmiri. He said that 80 per cent of the film's success was due to the music.

Dismissing such talk, Nargis marched Rani to the doctor for what was, fortunately, a good prognosis. The wound was healing well, though Rani had to continue taking her injections and tablets. Rani was also fretting about her husband's reaction to a stern letter Sunil had written to him. Nargis did not agree with Sunil's blunt tactics, advocating a more 'softly-softly' approach to win over Rani's husband.

Nargis now felt secure enough in their relationship to hand out advice to Sunil about how he should deal with various family members. To be fair, most of her advice was very down-to-earth, because she had grown up in a large family where daily negotiations were required to keep the rather fragile peace. Now she told him not to be too aggressive with his younger brother, Som, who had been caught gambling his tuition fees away. Sunil had written to her from Mandoli explaining some of his problems. She told him to pay the money directly to the school and not worry even if Som rebelled.

News about *Mother India* rolled out everyday, and Nargis had to go for a special press conference at Mehboob Studios as well. Pressure was building on her to go to Delhi for the opening, to which the president and the prime minister had been invited. Even though this was a great honour, Nargis was distressed for she knew that Sunil would not be happy if he came back to Bombay and found her gone. It was too late to get in touch with him because he would have started back already.

That evening, Mehboob called her over. Sheikh Mukhtar was there too, and he praised Sunil's performance. He also told Nargis what so many had already told her, that this should be her last film.

Nargis was more than willing to agree, even though she was shooting for *Ghar Sansar*, another story about marital complications. She was acting opposite one of the few people that Sunil did not disapprove of—Balraj Sahni. (She had been banned from acting with Dev Anand, Raj Kapoor and Raaj Kumar.) The film was being shot at Famous Studios, and was directed by V.M.Vyas. Vyas was a fast worker so she was hoping her part would be done soon.

Still trying to avoid the trip to Delhi, Nargis told Mehboob that she was committed to a shoot schedule and also that she was embroiled in a court case, so leaving town was out of the question. Nargis had been taken to court by the Bombay police for having allegedly shouted at a policewoman. She had to attend court every time there was a hearing. And though many felt that it had become a matter of prestige for the police, now the case became a convenient excuse for her.

She had underestimated Mehboob's determination. He spoke to Vyas and had the shooting postponed for a few days. He also persuaded the police commissioner to give her permission to go to Delhi. Nargis complained that 'Mr Mehboob is too much selfish'. When he gave her an air ticket to Delhi she realized she would have to go—it would be churlish not to. After all, this was the man who had given her the greatest role of her life.

Cornered by Mehboob, she thought that perhaps she was overreacting to a harmless trip. She would be back on the fifth, as would Sunil. She wrote to him, 'I wanted to inform you, but where? I don't know where you will be. I am rather disturbed. I don't want to go but the circumstances are confronting me in such a way that I feel I have to go. I went to Irani sahib and told him I don't want to go—but he said I should as he and aunty are also going, that they would be responsible if anything goes wrong as I told him that you won't like my being away when you are not here.'

Another issue was leaving Rani alone in Bombay, given her delicate health. Nargis met her before leaving and assured her that she would send a telegram to Sunil from Delhi as soon as she got there. She spent as much time as she could with Rani and even met her husband. But it was difficult for her to be at the Napean Sea Road flat without Sunil because everything reminded her of him. She hoped she might meet Sunil in Delhi as both Mehboob and Irani had sent telegrams to him, asking him to join them.

But her arrival in Delhi was tearful. As she feared, Sunil had misunderstood her departure from Bombay on the date that he was meant to return. From the tone of his letter, he seemed to think she would not, after the amazing success of *Mother India*, want to leave her glamorous life and live with him as a simple housewife. He thought she deserved better, 'a prince' perhaps, who could keep her in the style she was used to. It was a hurtful letter: though he was only trying to communicate his worst fears, she read in it his attempt to tell her that she was a superficial woman who would allow the adulation to go to her head.

On receiving his letter she cried without restraint, and then wrote to him from Delhi, on 31 October:

> Is it that you are trying to get rid of me, for you feel that I am not worth your family name and reputation, but then you can always tell me frankly, sweetly instead of taunting me like this. You have no faith in me. I am bad...no...I have not been so far, but tonight believe me I feel like getting drunk, misbehave, play merry hell with this damn name and prestige of mine which is bringing me so much pain. My eyes are swollen and the bar is closed—but if this is what

life wants from me, to ruin me—I will ruin myself—I know that
ultimately I will kill myself...I hate my existence...I hate humanity—
all around me are nothing but selfish people...

Though she was being treated like a queen in Delhi, Nargis
was tormented by the thought that the man she loved believed she
was unreliable, even untrustworthy. In her grief, she decided that
she might as well behave like the wicked woman she was supposed
to be. She ordered a few brandies and decided to get drunk.

To hurt him, she wrote that she would drink herself into
oblivion. Much like the time when she had cut her fingers, she
now felt that 'goodness in this world is paid back with pain. I
will give pain to myself so it will hurt less...laugh the world and
people of this world—you wanted to see me in this condition
and make fun of me—ok have your wish—laugh at me.'

Every time she read his letter, something died within her: 'you
came like a beautiful dream in my life, an episode that I thought
was to my heart's desire and contentment. In opening my eyes I
found it was a hallucination. It was Sunil Dutt that I knew and
worked with—Balraj is too good for me, an actress. A woman
with a profession that does not fit into a home. I am a woman
who desired a home but was thrown into a profession—like my
mother. But she spent her life with the man she loved and the
man who adored her made a wife and mother of this very
unfortunate woman.'

The next day, keeping up a façade of normalcy, she went
sightseeing in Delhi with a fellow artiste, Kum Kum. When she
came back, she once again sought forgetfulness in alcohol. 'I'm
going my love,' she wrote to the absent Sunil, 'very soon you
will hate Pia—and I want to—who is Pia? Nobody.' She tried to
drink during the day too, but it only brought back memories
and made her cry.

Since the alcohol brought no respite, she stopped drinking and
tried to think happier, positive thoughts. She bought a saree for
their wedding, and then cried over the hopelessness of her dreams.

There was, fortunately, no rest for her in Delhi, so she could
not fall apart. They were always on the run, from one reception
to another, talking, answering questions, 'living, though dead

within myself. They say I am loved by millions of people but I ask myself, have I ever been loved? I feel pained, a peculiar pain surrounds me, as if the coming events cast their shadows over me.' All those years of hiding her pain came in very useful now, as did her acting skills. She smiled and laughed and gave speeches and interviews, and her photographs were published everywhere: no one could have guessed the grief within her. She was the complete professional.

From Delhi they went to Calcutta, with a brief stopover at Nagpur, where a huge crowd of students greeted them. At Calcutta airport they were greeted with flowers and garlands, and then whisked off to lunch. Nargis tried to book seats for an early return but did not succeed. Calcutta was as hectic as Delhi, because Mehboob had left no stone unturned in his publicity blitz: 'Went to see the Governor, then lunch, later in the evening B.C. Roy (the Chief Minister) and the Governor came to a private showing of "Mother India". A press conference—tea—dinner and then visiting 11 cinemas, which killed me, exhausted me, tired me out. I have just finished packing, it is 3 a.m. in the morning. Thank God I will be on my way back to Bombay. Mr and Mrs Mehboob are going to Darjeeling—they wanted me to go—how can I? I don't want to. Jio, I don't know what is the matter with me—I am going insane, lost in a terrible storm of emotions...'

Sunil and Nargis met when she returned to Bombay, full of trepidation.

It was a meeting that tore her apart. He had already returned all her gifts, with a letter which confirmed that he had been looking for a wife, but found in her just a 'showgirl'. He told her bluntly that it was better that they ended everything, rather than be miserable for the rest of their lives.

They argued, and Sunil accused her of wanting to marry him on the rebound from Raj Kapoor. Nargis was aghast, but managed to calm him down. The thought of taking her life crossed her mind again. But she saw that he was as despondent as she was, so she consoled him. And it didn't take very long for them to realize once more that they were fortunate to have each other. They had found love in a world where it had little value and they had found it despite all the people who were still trying to make them doubt each other.

The scene took place in Mrs Irani's house, and both Mrs Irani and Ameena, who had accompanied Nargis, were nervously watching the argument from the sidelines. They were equally relieved with the outcome: even to them it had seemed as though the relationship was very close to being over.

Despite all that she was going through, Nargis behaved impeccably. She always tried to understand why Sunil was upset and did her utmost to placate him, though at times she may have felt that he was being childlike and unfair. She was too responsible to walk out on relationships that mattered. 'Every time I think of being no more in this world brings back the faces of my kids streaming before my eyes, of their struggling to live. Of their going through things which I have gone through with more pain. Then I say to myself how selfish I am—when I took up a mission in life for a prosperous life for my girls. I can't leave it unfinished for my own selfishness—this pain in my heart, this burning—this feeling of not being accepted, will it ever end? Will I ever be wanted and looked after? Will ever a realisation come that I have suffered bodily, emotionally and mentally?'

It was a cry from the heart, as she begged Sunil not to see her as a successful actor and a rich independent woman who could have any man she wanted, but a woman who was simple and loyal, who wanted nothing more than to be in her own home with her husband. Slowly they patched up and again agreed on a date for their wedding, brought yet closer, to 12 December. This time Nargis was not excited. After so many break-ups and reconciliations, she was unsure what to expect next.

Then came a message through Mrs Irani, probably from Mehboob, that they should postpone their wedding till at least March, since it might have a negative impact on *Mother India*. Sunil agreed, partly because he was still busy shooting, as was she. He had always hoped that she would complete work on all her films before they were married, since any association with the film world seemed to jeopardize their happiness.

But for Nargis, who was hoping for an early resolution, the postponement meant a heavy heart:

What other sacrifices does this world expect from us, why are we and our lives just a mere toy in the hands of circumstances? Why do people demand so much from us and why do we succumb to it... How I passed that day the 12th of December you can't imagine. So much pain and sorrow was around me. As the day passed into evening—I felt a pounding in my heart—I saw myself as a bride—taking the final vows at our home at Bandra—yet I was so much alone at the realisation that the day has passed—the day of marriage for which I had waited all my life has gone and very soon a new day will be born leaving me still alone. Very very much alone. I spent that night as myself, Nargis or as Tejeshwari Mohan and not as Mrs Dutt. Though I would have been a wife that night and what a beautiful morning it would have been...

Nargis began to feel unwell again: 'my condition was like a prisoner who was dragged with heavy chains to continue working even though there was no strength left.'

The doctor told her to rest before she had a nervous breakdown, because she was still going to work almost every day. There were other physical signs of her mental torment—she complained of her hands and feet feeling terribly cold, which of course, was a sign of extreme stress.

Finally, she explained to Akhtar that it was impossible for her to carry on like this, and retired to Panchgani to rest. Even in Panchgani the demons would not leave her alone, and she would wake up in the middle of the night, restless and perspiring with fear. So she decided to come back to Bombay. But she continued to be painfully sensitive to Sunil's apparent indifference. Because he did not allow his own disappointment to show, she assumed he did not care that their wedding had been postponed yet again.

The truth was that he could not bear to see her dejection or the prolonged separation from her. At the same time he was bound by his own work, and frustrated by his inability to organize an immediate wedding. The delay meant that his so-called friends kept reporting back to him about Nargis, often with details he did not want to hear. As the year drew to a close, Sunil could not decide whether it had been the saddest year of his life, or the happiest. He had met the woman of his dreams, but was she an impossible dream?

Padma Shri Nargis
1958

On 25 January 1958, Nargis was getting ready to watch *The Ten Commandments* at Regal cinema, after which she had promised to meet Sunil. Before she could leave for the show she 'got a telegram from Delhi informing me and congratulating (me) on receiving the honour of "Padma Shri", an honour given by the President to be awarded and announced on Republic day. I was so happy and yet shocked.

'I started wondering if I deserved this honour. I was also afraid that it may not take you (Sunil) away from me for you will get another complex of my being superior to you. After the show I came home to you, I couldn't sit through the picture—I wanted to come to you as soon as possible.'

As she had feared, when she showed Sunil the telegram, he didn't seem to share her joy. He appeared to be more worried about other problems, such as payments for the house, and withdrew from her. He dropped her home without commenting on the award. Nargis got into her own car, and with tears streaming down her face, began to drive around like a 'mad' person, once narrowly escaping a collision with a truck. Fortunately, Sunil, not insensitive to her distress, followed her and forced her to drive home safely.

The next day was 26 January, Republic Day. She wrote, 'The Padma Shri awards were declared in the papers—and gradually I realized that the award is quite an important one. It makes me feel quite strange—I still can't believe and I still can't understand why should this award come to me. What have I done? There are artistes other than me who have served this industry for many

more years and probably deserve it more than me. All I can do is
thank God for making me capable of this great honour—what
else is in store for me? What is it that God wants me to do? I
always pray to God to make my life sweet and honourable. I
received a lot of telephone calls from different people of the
industry and several telegrams congratulating me.'

One of the things which bemused her was that 'not one woman
of the industry bothered to congratulate me.'

Others would have been equally puzzled by her award,
because she was the first actor to receive it. It would have caused
consternation in the film industry, since many of the other
producers, directors and actors equally deserved recognition.
Could the award be attributed to the success of *Mother India*?

It was, after all, the first film to have captured the resilience
of a young country battered by all sorts of problems. In the
1950s, the Gandhian emphasis on the rural economy had not
been forgotten. At the same time, the film paid tribute to Nehru
with its opening shot, when Radha inaugurates a canal: Nehru
had called dams the temples of the new India.

The prime minister had been invited for the premiere of
Mother India in Delhi, and was probably behind the nomination,
though officially it came from the president. Because there is a
great deal of lobbying for the honours today, it is assumed that
Nargis used her influence to acquire the Padma Shri. But the fact
is, she was as surprised as anyone else.

The children wanted to celebrate, so the next morning she took
them to the Mocha Bar, just around the corner from Château
Marine, to attend a jam session. The actors David and Jairaj were
there as well, and wanted to join them. David even asked her for
a dance, but she refused as she did not want to attract attention.
They watched the 'floor show'—a rock and roll performance—
and then she took the children for a Chinese meal.

But when she met Sunil in the evening, her happiness turned
sour. 'After a long silence you told me that you have a lot of
complexes and the biggest complex was me. That you had always
wanted to marry a person who was inferior to you and that you
didn't want to marry anybody from the films. That you have a lot

of ambition but have become weak because of me. In all the ways of life I am a hindrance to you. That you will not like it if people say Nargis has married Sunil, it should be that Sunil has married Nargis, that's why you had wanted to wait for three years...'

Nargis told him, 'Love is truth, faith and hope, and when one loves why should complexes and egos create hindrances?' She did her best to reassure him that the Padma Shri would not be a road block for them, but he was not convinced.

Nargis noticed a dramatic change in his behaviour over the next few days. So far, even after major disagreements, both Sunil and she had managed to pull themselves back together.

This time, however, he felt that a decisive moment had arrived. He said he could not see her for several days because he was shooting, he could not even phone her. He needed time to think.

But an already overwrought Nargis thought otherwise. Listening to the ebb and flow of gossip around her, Nargis wondered whether it was because she was growing older and had 'neither the looks nor the youth' to attract him any longer. He suddenly seemed far too busy shooting to spend time with her, but he had the time to go to the movies with his friends. Why was he ignoring her?

She was increasingly depressed as the standoff continued for a month. By now it was almost the end of February. They were supposed to marry on 11 March. But Sunil was sounding more and more reluctant to take the final step. There were too many doubts crowding his head. She told him:

> Marriage is a serious affair and you don't want to put yourself into it with me—for you I am not the right type or the ideal woman. You are not worried about what you want or what your heart says—it's what the other people want and what they will have to say. People have already advised you against marrying a *Film Actress*, and unfortunately I am one.
>
> You yourself never wanted to be involved with a film actress. So you went against your ideals in life, against your principles, you fell in love with an actress, but you know your life better. You don't want to suffer and be miserable, which you will be with me as you presume.

Even though at the time it felt terrible, the good thing was that they were able to talk things through before they got married. With each crisis, Nargis learnt to handle him better, as most of the issues originated with an angst-driven Sunil. Through their discussions, they realized marriage did not mean that all their problems would go away, but at least they recognized the difficulties that lay ahead.

Luckily, at this juncture, Nargis refused to be pessimistic. She arranged for a pandit and bought a beautiful red and gold dupatta to wear at the wedding.

Occasionally, she did wonder whether it would be like the last time, when she dreamt of her wedding even as the appointed day dragged by without a bride or bridegroom. Did another day just like 12 December await her, when Mehboob had sent a message that they should postpone their wedding?

So far, her work had remained unaffected by her personal life. But now, as she shot for *Ghar Sansar*, she had to give up to six retakes at a time, because she was emotionally and physically drained, as well as mentally distracted. Whether she was spending her evenings with Sunil or at home, she was too restless and anxious to get enough sleep. She had almost stopped eating and felt sick most of the time. Would the marriage ever take place?

If this was a test set by Sunil Dutt, the future Mrs Dutt was passing it with flying colours, although in misery.

By 22 February Nargis had reached breaking point once again.

> It used to scare me to face another night with tears. I used to pray hard all the way from my house to yours. My steps used to be heavy climbing your stairs. To look at you and decide my fate was my life. Nights and nights I spent with pain in my heart, reaching a breaking point. I used to wonder why is it that you stay away from me. I started developing a guilt within myself. What is the use of my love for you when I bring you nothing but pain. You say you have complexes, why must you, as long as I love you and belong to you. I might be big for people who know me only as a film star and follow my activities concerned with my work, but I am not that for you... Love is immune to all complexes.

Much of Sunil's discomfort stemmed from the fact that she now received frequent invitations to receptions in her honour from people who wanted to celebrate her success. There were phone calls from the Raj Bhavan as well, and when the governor wanted to see *Mother India*, she was asked to be present. Her social calender after the Padma Shri was even more demanding and Sunil was not convinced that she would find it easy to opt out of it all once they were married.

Nargis could not help feeling hurt:

> For always I am the subject of disgust, I am the target of pain. It's me and only me who is bad—who has done nothing so far—I have not come up to your expectations. I really don't want big names or any kind of awards but I don't know why God is so pleased with me. I didn't ask for it, Jio. I didn't even know what the Padma Shri was. After getting the award a chain of responsibility got attached to me. a chain of receptions started—when they give me a reception how can I put them down. What am I to tell them? I went to Raj Bhavan for lunch—on a personal phone call. At the time I didn't think I was doing anything wrong or committing any sin. I went pale in telling you not because I was guilty but because you suffer from various complexes. I didn't know that my going to Raj Bhavan is going to hurt you so much. I was again invited to meet Mr Ho Chi Minh but I didn't go...

She stopped telling Sunil about the functions she was invited to, and hid from him the details of programmes in her honour. Or she would refuse them outright, such as a special ceremony in Patiala, and a show in Calcutta she had been asked to inaugurate.

There were even more important, career-enhancing invitations which she refused. She would tell Sunil later, 'I got a letter from America inviting me to be present for the Oscar function—I said I couldn't go. I didn't tell you these things for you develop complexes...' In 1957, *Mother India* had been nominated in the foreign language category for the Oscars. But it lost, reportedly due to inadequate lobbying, much to Mehboob's despair.

At the time Sunil tried to explain to her that he did not have a 'complex' about her, he simply had begun to doubt if she could abandon the social whirl she was so used to. He confessed that she seemed a different woman from the one he had known in Billimora.

Her fears blinded her to the fact that while Sunil had a million opportunities to leave her, he was equally incapable of actually walking out. After a particularly cold encounter on 24 February, Nargis felt she simply could not go on, and the time had come to end it all.

She took out her sleeping tablets and wrote three letters: one to Sunil, another to Akhtar, and a third to the police, exonerating others of any blame and thus ensuring that a post-mortem would not be required. This was going to be her final goodbye. As she prepared herself and was about to seal the letters, Ameena told her that Sunil had come to the house and asked Nargis to come to his place.

As always, with the very mention of Sunil, her feelings underwent a complete transformation. Though happy once more, Nargis took the letters with her. After so many miserable weeks, she was unsure of what would happen next. As on other days, she was feeling faint because she had not eaten anything since morning.

Thankfully, it turned out that Sunil too had been missing her. Her suicide attempt forgotten, they started planning their wedding with renewed vigour. A few people knew about it, including Anwar's wife Rashida, Mr and Mrs Irani, Nargis's friend Shakuntala Lal and, of course, Rani. Nargis was still visiting Rani regularly and counselling her. She was also tracking her medical progress, arranging for her doctor's appointments and x-rays. When she was unable to go because of a shoot, she would ask Mrs Irani to take Rani instead.

The wedding was to be conducted according to Arya Samaj rites. The person fixing the dates was told not to reveal the names of the people getting married. As Nargis found out, the total cost was around Rs 200, plus any donation they might want to make to the Arya Samaj. There was a suggestion that the wedding could be at Shakuntala's home, but they both wanted the ceremony to be held at the Pali Hill bungalow. It would be far more private.

For the wedding, Nargis decided to convert to Hinduism, the religion that her grandmother had been forced to abandon and that her father had given up for his own marriage.

Nargis noted, 'I will have to fill a form to confirm that I accept the religion with my own will about 2 hours earlier, and we will be married by night.'

In any case, Nargis had always had an easy familiarity with both religions and participated in all functions, whether Hindu or Muslim. Occasionally, if she felt like it, she would visit a church, or any religious shrine where she found 'peace'. Her children said later that she was always a 'seeker' deeply interested in spirituality.

At last, it seemed the wedding was going to actually take place. Nargis was excited as she prepared herself for the big day. This included buying an apron which said 'To Hell With Housework'. Her irrepressible sense of humour had returned, and with just a few days left, she could barely hide her happiness.

On 4 March, when she least expected it, she received a letter from Sunil which was like a body blow.

She wrote back to him:

> I opened it and read the contents of your letter. Again, Oh! Jio again—those sharp words that cut me through and through. 'My Dear Padma Shri' this is how you started and ended it with 'A Jr Artiste'. You made that whole noise because I didn't tell you about the Filmfare award. I thought you must have read it in the Times of India on the 2nd morning. Besides I never used to hide anything from you—till you yourself said I should not tell you these things as they create complexes in your mind, and if I tell that I had an invitation from such and such a place but I refused—you feel I say that to impress you.
>
> This is true that if I had not met you I would have continued my social activities—but I am to be your wife and naturally I will not do things which you don't want me to do.

Nargis had deliberately refrained from telling Sunil that she had won the Filmfare Best Actress award for her role in *Mother India*. With less than a week left for it, the wedding was all that she wanted to focus on.

Meanwhile, Sunil was upset because he had told her earlier that no matter how much it hurt him, he preferred to know the truth.

The next day was Holi. A few years earlier, Nargis would have celebrated it at RK where it was always a huge affair. Raj Kapoor would sing and dance and the whole film fraternity would descend on the Kapoor household. Her life today was a long way from the fun and frolic of those days, when picnics and parties ruled the day.

Zahida remembers the festivities: 'At all RK Holi functions there would be Begum Para, Nimmiji, Shammi aunty, Madhumati, Sonia Sahni. On Eid, Waheeda Rehman and others (would come to our house) so there was a fellow feeling between people. Only Suraiya, who used to stay on Marine Drive, was a total recluse. Nanda, Waheeda, Jabeen, this whole lot would go on picnics.'

Nargis had not been very close to other actors and now that Sunil had asked her to cut herself off from them, she did not even stop to chat with Raj when they met outside the studio.

Holi in 1958 was even quieter than the one she had spent the previous year with Sunil at Billimora. She remembered that she had put red colour on his face and he had put some in her hair like sindhoor, the sign of a married woman. Yet, this Holi, she was alone at home and weeping. She refused to play with the children or participate in any of the fun. She just wanted to be with Sunil, who had told her that he would only meet her now on 11 March. He was going to play Holi with his friends.

Sunil had also realized that the situation had to be resolved in the best possible manner. He did not want to raise any more issues just before their wedding, and ruin what could be a wonderful day. He thought it best to stay away.

Unaware of his decision, her eyes swollen with tears, Nargis went to the graveyard where her parents were buried: 'as it was Shab-e-Barat—put flowers on the graves of my parents. I clung to each stone of the tomb and wept bitterly. I couldn't hold myself. I didn't bother who was looking at me—I was there for about one hour—then came home. I felt as if my entire self is dead. The only solace I could find was in prayers—so I took the Quran and started reading. I prayed for who knows how many hours. It was 8:45 p.m. When I got up from prayers I was feeling a little peaceful...'

Fortunately, her prayers were going to be answered very soon. Looking back, later, they would realize that in many ways it had been both a wonderful year as well as a terrible one. In learning to deal with each other and their insecurities, they had unknowingly established the foundation of a strong and enduring relationship. In that one year they had weathered more storms than most people experience in a lifetime, and in spite of everything, the crazy rollercoaster of their relationship finally steadied.

They were married on 11 March 1958, and an ecstatic Nargis ended her record of the tumultuous year that had been:

We got married at our home, Pali Hill. All my dreams and desires have been fulfilled. Now I have nothing else to write. Nothing to say. I can only pray to God to give me the strength to bear everything smilingly and may my life be devoted in looking after my husband's happiness. Always loving him more and more.
From today I start a new chapter of life—May God help me in this new road of life.
'Pia'
Mrs Balraj Dutt
11th-3-58

She had finally found her safe harbour.

Dutt Sahib
1958

Among the guests at the small, secret marriage ceremony at
Pali Hill was Rani, who remembers, 'The day he (Sunil)
was getting married, he asked me to sing. So I told him that's
why I had asked him to call our mother. She would have known
all the wedding songs. He said we will call her later.

'I sang for him, "*Hanh ve hanh janjh teri charhdi main vekhan*
(I hope to see you astride your horse at your wedding)." Then he
went away and came back in the evening, around six. He said
we will get married at the bungalow, *she* will come there.
Bhabhiji had told her younger sister-in-law that she was getting
married. But no one came from Château Marine. Her brother had
been very against the marriage and she was trembling and scared
throughout the wedding in case he came and created trouble.

'We were all there. Bhabhiji and Shakuntala, and her husband,
Virendra Lal, and Chinnoo mama (Chiman Kant Gandhi, a former
chief assistant with Mehboob). There were two pandits. I just
wore whatever I had. But Nargis was looking very beautiful in a
red saree. And Chinnoo mama put the chuda (the wedding bangles)
on her. They were married according to Hindu rites so there was
a proper havan. Bhaiya wore a white kurta pyjama and a pink
safaa with a pink turban. He was really looking very good.

'I was very happy but wanted to tease him about the turban,
whether it reminded him of his days at Khalsa school (where he
used to wear a similar turban). He recorded the whole ceremony
which took two hours. No one got to know. There were no
photographs.'

Because there were no photographs, Nargis created a photo album with information of her wedding, and photographs of Elvis Presley and Marilyn Monroe. The album was dedicated 'To My Love From His Life'.

The wedding, she wrote, was celebrated between 'Balraj Dutt (Sunil Dutt) and Tejeshwari Mohan (Nargis)'.

The names they used in their daily lives were now in brackets. Depending on the circumstances, she would give prominence to her Muslim or Hindu identity. Since she had converted recently, her Hindu identity was in the forefront.

Tejeshwari was the name given to her by her father, and with her marriage, as she changed one home for the other, she wanted a complete transformation.

On another page she wrote:

We became Engaged on Tuesday 12th March 1957
Our Engagement Party
Was held on Tuesday night after 12 o clock
At Billimora in our small room—with the moon as our guest
The engagement gifts were:
ALL THE LOVE
EVERY BREATH OF LIFE + KISSES
GOOD WISHES
BLESSINGS
...and prayers for a very happy
life

The good wishes came from the few friends who had supported them throughout, including 'Mr Nemani, Ameena, Mr and Mrs Irani and Virendra and Shakuntala Lal': the latter were the only ones who gave a more material gift—'a tea trolley'!

On another page she wrote:

My Trousseau
Saree from Delhi—Green and red with Gota work—Red blouse
plain—Red Dupatta with Gota work on both Pallav—earrings—
Panja and red chuda

The panja was a hand ornament, and the red chuda the traditional red wedding bangles.

The bridesmaids' dresses were described thus:

Shakuntala—in thick silk Madras Mustard colour saree with green border and small green flowers all over—with green blouse —

The 'reception', she wrote in jest, was at Shakuntala's house. There was only one guest!

For the section 'Our Honeymoon', she wrote:

We spent our honeymoon at 80, Napean Sea Road, Bombay from 11th-3-58 to ————.

In the honeymoon snapshots were photographs of Presley hugging different women while Marilyn Monroe stood provocatively saying, 'Come on Presley, Press Me.' To tease Sunil, she had more photographs of Elvis than she had of Monroe.

On the final pages she listed her mother-in-law's 'gift' to her—Sunil.

Though Nargis had to leave everything she owned and move to a tiny one-bedroom house, she felt that now she had everything she had ever dreamt of. When they came home after the wedding to the small flat, there was nothing at home to celebrate the occasion, so they ordered dinner from a restaurent.

After a week, Sunil's mother and Som arrived on a visit. Soon there were ten people in the one-bedroom flat (including Ameena, Nargis's loyal domestic help, and her husband, the driver Kasam) but everyone was too happy to complain.

Rani remembers those days as Nargis euphorically embraced her new role as a housewife in her own home: 'Nargis would get up in the morning around seven and make tea for everyone. She had two movies which she was completing, *Ghar Sansar* and *Lajwanti*. She called me Lajwanti. After we stayed together for about two or three months, Mataji went back to Mandoli. Then we all shifted to Pali Hill.'

The secrecy around the Dutt wedding led to a hilarious incident, recalls Rani. 'The presswale came to Napean Sea Road. I did not know who they were, and what they wanted. They asked me, "Baby hai?" I said she is sleeping. They said they would come after a while. I thought they were asking about my daughter, Popy. Then they came back again. "Has she got up?" I got concerned and said, she hasn't got up, but what do the two of you want with my baby? They looked at each other and said they were not asking about my baby.

'Then they explained that Nargisji is known to everyone as Baby. They had come for her, not Popy! They said they would come the next day and asked when she would be available and I said I didn't know.

'Everyone knew that they had been married, but they didn't want to come in front of the press. I didn't ask why—it was up to them. But unfortunately, when the presswalle came the next day, bhabhi and bhaiya had again gone for shooting. Then the hijras arrived and they troubled me a lot. I said I am a guest, the people who live here have gone out. They said, "No, you are telling lies. You are Sunil Dutt's sister, and Sunil Dutt has got married and lives in this house. Give us the money." I gave them 101 rupees. They took it and left and went to Château Marine. They got so much more there. 1001 rupees. And sarees.'

In spite of his apparent generosity, Akhtar was furious with his sister. He felt betrayed by her all over again. Not only had she found a man, she had married him. What would happen to her career and the income from it? He had just about revived her career after all the years that she had wasted with Raj Kapoor, and now she had gone and run away.

Akhtar's children insist that he loved his sister and was only worried that she had married someone who was not good enough for her. From Nargis's personal papers, it is clear that she did not want to offend him, but that she had little respect left for him. Looking at what she wrote, it appears that the frequent fights over her independence had transformed their relationship from one based on love to mutual distrust. Now she just wanted to ensure that he did not exploit his daughters, so she kept the relationship going.

Sunil wanted very little to do with Akhtar but he had nothing against his children. He understood Nargis's fears and had promised to look after the girls as his own. So Sunil and Nargis went over to the Marine Drive flat the evening of their wedding.

Anwar met them and said he would try to placate Akhtar, who pretended to be asleep and refused to come out.

Zahida sometimes took Sunil's calls before the marriage and was the only one among the children who knew that a wedding had been planned. She remembers, 'After they got married, they came back in the night, and my father was sleeping. Anwar uncle was woken up. My uncle said, "Let Akhtar sleep because he will ruin the whole night for all us. He will drive everyone mad. I will tackle him in the morning, and then you should come again." The next morning my uncle tried , and got abused in the bargain. My father raved and ranted. And when Dutt sahib and my bua came back again, my father said, "Tell her she is to go and not to come back." The same drama was repeated for a long time.'

Rehana has other memories about the wedding. Nargis ' had bought a saree which she told us was for a wedding scene in a film, where she was playing the bride. She asked us if we liked it and then practically the next day she was married! She lived at the time in her fifth-floor flat. In the morning before going go to school, we would come to her bedroom door and wish her good morning and then go. That day she was not in the room. We checked the bathroom and her nightdress was missing, where was she? We went down and asked my mother. My mother put her head down. "Yes, she got married last night." We learnt they came at night but my father did not meet them. That was it. We went off in the school bus.'

Rehana says that though Nargis came over every day for the next three days, Akhtar would not see her. Then Iqbal started arguing: 'Why don't you meet her?' She usually didn't fight with Akhtar, but now she decided to do so. She wondered why her husband wanted his sister to stay at home at her age. 'Shouldn't she have her own home and her children?' asked an anguished Iqbal. Akhtar reportedly replied, 'Why didn't they tell me? I would have married her off in style.'

Of course, says Rehana, that was not quite the whole truth. Because when it came to marriage, he would always say, this one is too poor, that one is not nice. He said he wanted someone very well established. Yet Arif, her brother, remembers a proposal from Zulfiqar Ali Bhutto (later the prime minister of Pakistan), which too Akhtar had refused.

Shammi, who had no sympathy for Akhtar, says, 'Eventually Dutt sahib had very little to do with him. He was very unhappy with him, because he was not very nice to Nargis, especially about the wedding. Nargis and I were shooting for a film together. I had heard that she was getting married and I went to the studio to congratulate her. She said, "It's a secret, but I am getting married in one or two days." Somehow the news reached the papers the next day, so everyone got to know.

'After they got married, they had a hard time because Dutt sahib was very touchy. Not so much about Raj—one very good thing was that he never mentioned Raj Kapoor—and it must have required a lot of self-restraint. He was touchy because career-wise Nargis was a much bigger star. Till the time Sanjay was born and Dutt sahib was more mature, it was hard for them.

'If they went out together, people would abuse them and say he had married his mother. It was very bad, and they could not go out together in public for a long time.'

It was also a long time before the prodigal sister was made welcome at Château Marine. As a child, Zahida felt terribly sorry for her. 'Look at her kismet. She went through such a bad time...she lived in this one-bedroom apartment. One small bedroom, and no furniture, and if there was a cup, then the saucer was broken. A strange chair, a mattress on the floor, and a golden retriever. She used to walk up and down four flights of steps to walk that dog, and she would get the milk in the morning and heat it...and who was this? The Nargis who lived in the palatial Château Marine. Look at where she was!'

Yet, even the child Zahida noticed that the lack of luxury did not hamper her aunt's joy. 'In fact when she was on Napean Sea Road, I would make these lovely sponge cakes and cycle down with them, and then she would make trifle puddings for Sunil. She used to pamper him a lot...knit sweaters for him, you can see him wearing these in the movies, *Gumraah,* and others. She knitted them all.'

Contrary to what the world may have thought, Nargis was

happier than she had ever been. The size of the house meant nothing to her since they were soon to shift into the Pali Hill bungalow anyway. What mattered to her was that she was with Presley senior, and the much longed for 'Presley junior' that she and Sunil had joked about before their marriage was already on his way.

Sanjay was born on 29 July 1959. Nargis fell in love all over again. She could never love anyone else the way she loved her Sanju. He represented everything she had ever wanted, and life was perfect. She began to document his every move, his every smile, his slightest development, in a baby book.

A year later, she was still writing in copious detail about his birthday and other activities. Just as she had written obsessively to Sunil, she now wrote about her son. Imaginatively, she wrote as though Sanjay, just about a year old, was himself the writer.

An entry dated 21 July 1960 claims that it 'was a very exciting day for me—I travelled with my mother to Madras by an aeroplane—we went to meet Papa who was there for the shooting of a new film at AVM studio. In the plane I was crawling all over the place, and the hostess took me into the cockpit but I was soon sent back as I was becoming inquisitive and wanted to operate the plane myself—So the pilots thought the plane was more safe with me on mama's lap.'

Other important events were also noted, as on 1 January 1961: '(Today is) an important thing in my life and also my Papa's. You see he has started his own production of pictures—remember I told you about the story I heard my father tell mama about the dacoits—well at 1 p.m. I was called to Mohan studio Andheri to perform the mahurat of the said film named "Mujhe Jeene Do." It was quite an experience—I could not recognize Papa, he was dressed like a Dakoo and looked so ferocious—I only went to him when he called out to me—I switched on the camera for the first shot—and in my heart I prayed to God to take care of Papa and give him all the blessings—May I prove lucky for him.' Nargis was besotted. She had replaced her dolls with a living doll she took with her everywhere.

The launch of Ajanta Arts, the Dutt production house, was

historic because Sunil was one of the very few mainstream Hindi film stars—like Raj Kapoor—to produce socially relevant films. The India of the 1960s was struggling with issues which he wanted to portray and possibly redress through his films.

There was now a steady flow of income from the films he was working on regularly in Madras and Bombay. And thankfully, his marriage to Nargis did not seem to have had a negative impact on his career.

On 10 January 1961, she wrote, once again in the baby book, from Sanjay's point of view, 'I went to Madras by Air with mama to join papa—who was shooting there. Why I write again about this trip is because I saw my first film. It was starring papa and the name of the film was "Chhaya." I found it quite interesting as I never slept. It was a night show and also I knew Papa as soon as he appeared on the screen.'

Nargis had not forgotten her political connections. As a Padma Shri she was invited regularly to government functions, both in Delhi and in Bombay. Old hang-ups forgotten, Sunil would accompany her whenever he could. She took Sanjay with her to Delhi for the 26 January celebrations and wrote, 'I have been travelling much by Air—we went to Delhi—I was not supposed to accompany my parents but ultimately I did go—I saw the Republic Day celebrations—with all its pomp and show. I loved the pageant—with beautifully decorated elephants, camels and horses. Oh yes, and the Queen—the Queen—I saw her. She was waving out to all, and I also waved out to her. I wonder if I will remember when I grow big...' The Queen was Queen Elizabeth II, on a visit to a former colony.

Nargis kept in touch with Sunil's family, and on 27 January they went to Mandoli, 'this village where my grandmother lives. It is three hours by car from Delhi. Met Mataji, she was happy and excited to see me—though I was excited too. That's why I didn't eat anything... Everyone was very sweet to me. I think they all love me a lot. We were there till the evening then came back to Delhi. 28th morning Mama and myself we came back to Bombay.'

After Sanjay's birth, the Château Marine family had also come around, especially Akhtar. There were still occasional spats

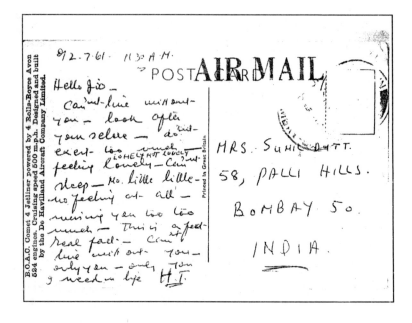

between them, usually over Sunil. Nargis refused any film offers that came her way even if it meant acting with Sunil. Some of these offers were very lucrative, and a frustrated Akhtar watched her throw away film after film.

Zahida says ruefully, 'The conditions in which she was living with this man! And they were also getting deals to act in films together for ten lakhs. That was a lot of money in those days. But Dutt sahib was very proud and said, "No, Mrs Dutt won't act." My father used to say, "What is this Duttdu, this Punjabdu?" But there was love (between Akhtar and Nargis) as well. She would get upset, he would yell, "Get out of my house," and she would retort, "I won't ever come here, bhaiya, I won't even spit in your house, I'm going." And the next day at around nine o'clock, she would be there from Pali Hill, sitting in her car downstairs.' Very reluctantly, she would allow herself to be persuaded by Iqbal and the children to come upstairs. It was a ritual that everyone got used to over the years.

However, Sunil did remember his promise that Nargis could act in one film for her brother if he asked her to.

Zahida says that the situation reminded them of when she was working more and more with Raj and the family had gone through a bad time. 'My father's films had flopped, the cars had to be sold, the jewellery was sold, the studio was sold. But after Nargis got married, my father said, "Till you were not married I had a right to your income. I worked, I took my ten per cent, I had a right, today you are married I don't want one rupee from you. But yes, I do want you to make a last film for me, and I promise you that after *Mother India* when people remember you, they will say, this woman who has done *Mother India,* this same woman has done *Raat Aur Din,* and you will get international awards for this subject."'

Raat Aur Din was said to be based on the Hollywood film, *The Three Faces of Eve.* It dealt with schizophrenia. Mental illness has rarely had a sympathetic treatment in Hindi films, and little effort has been made, till recently, to explore its cause or origin. In this film, for the first time the source of the character's illness was traced to a childhood trauma. Nargis gave an assured and sensitive performance, even though in some scenes she looks visibly older than in others.

By the time the shooting for *Raat Aur Din* began, Nargis was expecting her second child. And because she could not bear to be parted from her precious Sanju, she forgot her criticism of Geeta Bali and took the one-year-old with her to the sets.

On 12 February 1961, baby Sanjay says, 'I flew to Calcutta with Mamaji—as she was going for her shooting of "Raat Aur Din". As usual I enjoyed the flight. While in Calcutta, I was taken to the zoo to see the animals. I loved the day it was so exciting... I have travelled quite a lot for my age—what a shame that I won't remember any of these places when I grow up.'

Even after her other children came along, Nargis found the time to write in the baby books. Sanjay's first day at nursery school and then at the Cathedral and John Connon School are lovingly recorded. There is information on the children, such as their weight and height, till the age of seven. All their birthday parties are meticulously detailed, as are the presents they received.

Namrata was born on 5 January 1962. The New Year had started very well, and busily. They had attended a New Year's party hosted by Dev Anand, and Sunil also celebrated the first anniversary of Ajanta Arts. He had put up an exhibition of life-sized stills from his production *Mujhe Jeene Do* on the terrace at home. On the third was another party by Dev Anand to celebrate his wedding anniversary. They were out partying with Amarjeet when Nargis began to feel the labour pains.

In Namrata's baby book, Nargis wrote her own name as 'Fatima (Tejeshwari) Abdul (Uttamchand) Rashid (Mohan)'.

The premarital differences between Sunil and Nargis seemed to have disappeared. The enthusiastic mother continued to note every stage of her children's growth, however ordinary and normal it may have seemed, because for her each step was a miracle. For instance: the moment when Namrata first laughed out loud (1-5-62) and the time she objected loudly when a toy was taken away from her (1-6-62), and so on.

In the week that Namrata was born, Sunil signed five films. His life had been completely transformed after marriage. He no longer felt that he had married above his status because Nargis happily and lovingly took the backseat. This was not a passing phase; she had said that she would devote her life to Sunil and their children and that was exactly what she did. For the rest of her life she stuck to her promise, and except for *Raat Aur Din,* she never worked on another film.

Gia D'Cruz, who became her secretary 17 years later, remembers her determination to keep her home and her husband happy. 'I had a desk at the entrance to the house. Their bedroom was upstairs, and I would hear her coming downstairs because she had a bunch of keys in a silver keychain which would jingle as she walked. She would be in a crisp white saree or in a beautiful nightgown after her bath. She would come down to give orders to the servants. They had a family room upstairs, where Sunil would have his breakfast. She would see that everything was perfect, the tray was perfect. If a phone call came in between, she would say, "Not now, I have to give him breakfast."

'We were terrified of Dutt sahib, and the moment we knew

he was on his way everyone would be under so much stress. She would say Dutt sahib is coming—everyone would get organized. If we were chatting on the phone, the phone had to be put down. No servant would be seen walking around. It was like a schoolmaster was putting in an appearance. I don't think she did it for any other reason than out of respect for him.

'She wanted to show everyone that he is the head of the house, the master of the house. That was her own way of showing him that she cared and she loved him and gave him importance.

'The morning was run like clockwork, especially those 20 minutes that Dutt sahib was getting ready to leave, and after that she would also be more relaxed.'

However much she resisted the film world, even after she had her children, offers kept coming in. There is a suggestion that Guru Dutt had thought of casting her in his classic, *Sahib Bibi Aur Ghulam*. But this seems doubtful, because she was already pregnant with Namrata.

As a result of the pregnancy, and for other reasons, it was seven years before work on *Raat Aur Din* was finished. Instead of becoming a money-spinner, it became a trial for everyone. She began the film when she was pregnant with Namrata and completed it while she was pregnant with Priya, her third child.

Yet Akhtar was correct in his prediction that *Raat Aur Din* would be an unforgettable film; it won Nargis the national award for best actress, nearly ten years into her retirement!

For Sunil this was a very productive period. He was able to express himself as a director, producer and actor, and it helped that he had a supportive wife who knew everyone in the film business. He began to shed his reticence and his reluctance to mix with the film folk. Their social life picked up, with mehfils and parties at home, which would sometimes get out of hand. Sunil had learnt to relax some of his own rules.

Som had come to work with his brother by 1959. He remembers, 'They used to have the Ajanta Arts anniversary party, and everyone from the film industry would be there. There would be a qawwali, music, dance. And his birthday party would be celebrated in a special way on the sixth of June, when she would also have a big party. We never had to go to any film actor's house, because they would all be there. Alcohol would flow like water, and my duty was that if any person became "out" (i.e., drunk and unconscious) I should put him in my jeep (Sunil had given him one) and take him home. So I personally had to drink carefully in order to do my duty. Sunil was very *shaukeen*.'

There was a complete change in their lifestyle. Sunil, who once treasured his two kurta-pyjamas, now had an array of clothes and cars.

Som says, 'We come from a martial background, and in almost every generation there have been people who joined the army. So when he became a film actor people read about it in the papers and told my Mataji that now your son will be putting on eyeliner and lipstick and prancing in front of the camera. But she said, "I have full faith in my son, whatever he will do, he will do with dignity."

'Then a letter came saying that he was acting in a film called *Railway Platform* and he sent us some photographs as well. It is only in recent years that villagers have become smart, in those days we used to be very simple. I went to see the film and I was very happy, and I said this is a very good thing. This was the first film I had ever seen and I cycled all the way to Saharanpur to see it. It took me one and a half hours, and I took my food from home with me. I got so fond of films that whenever there was a show, even if it did not star Dutt sahib, I would be there to see it.

'Mataji also saw *Railway Platform* and was thrilled. After that as his films were released, Dutt sahib would send a copy of it to me in the village. He would book a theatre close by and all the people in the village would be invited to go there. Buses were organized and laddoos were distributed. All the Ajanta Arts films were sent there including my film *Man ka Meet* and everyone was invited, including the masterji who had taught me. He was very impressed with me, saying, "Som, yaar, you have become Dilip Kumar."

'Before Dutt sahib became such a big film star, I used to have a lot of fights in the village, but now Dutt sahib had quite a fan following. So people began to respect me a lot and also to be scared of me. Before I got spoilt in the village, he called me to Bombay.

'I still remember he had a blue Mercedes car. He had a lot of cars, but he put me in this particular car and took me all around Bombay. This must have been in '59-'60 because Sanju was born during the time I was there.

'He took me to the BEST office in Colaba and showed me the chair where he used to sit to work as a clerk in the evenings. Then he took me to Jai Hind College, where he used to study from 7 to around 10.30 in the mornings. There was an Irani restaurant on Grant Road where he would sit when he was really feeling low and depressed. Those days he would have the cheapest drink on the menu.

'After all that, he took me to the bungalow on Pali Hill and said, "Som, would you have ever thought that one day I would have such a big house in Bombay?" Then he said, "Now you sit here and enjoy yourself."'

Som did not exactly sit there and enjoy himself. For a while he was sent to college, but he did not find it easy, because Sunil had asked the lecturer to speak to him in English, which he found hard to follow. He was very embarrassed, till one day he met the teacher on a local train and explained his problem, begging her not to ask him questions in English.

Other issues also cropped up. Som remembers, 'Once in the early days when I started living with them, he tried to call home and could not get through. He tried for a while, then lost his temper and came home. He asked me, who was on the phone, and I said I was. He got upset with me, but I told him that now I had friends in Bombay and would obviously want to talk. In retaliation I stopped eating. He found out (a few days later). When he came home, at around midnight, I was asleep and he banged on my door, he said, "Open the door or I will break it down." I opened the door, and he stood there saying, "Why haven't you eaten for two days?" And then he said, "If a bloody phone is going to come between two brothers, then I don't want one in the house," and he ripped out the wire and threw the phone out. He really did love me.'

The single-minded passion with which Sunil loved and tried to protect his family meant that he also tried to make sure they were comfortable and got what they wanted. He was tough-talking but essentially soft-hearted. Because he wasn't particularly attached to wealth, he could also be very generous.

Som continues: 'But bhabhi sahiba said, "The man will become a vagabond, give him some responsibility." Dutt sahib said, "Join Ajanta Arts." The office of Ajanta Arts was at his old flat at Napean Sea Road. My duty was that whatever letters Dutt sahib had to sign, important ones, I would take from here to him at Pali Hill, and then bring them back. I was paid Rs 150 as a salary, given an air-conditioned room to sleep in, a jeep to roam around in, with unlimited petrol, and I could do what I liked.

'Then I became the production controller. *Yeh Raastey Hain Pyaar Ke*, *Mujhe Jeene Do* and *Yaadein*, these films were made under my supervision. After Dutt sahib, everyone listened to me. I learnt everything on the job. He used to give me the responsibility. He would give me the money and say, "Som, there is a set being put up in the studio and you must go there." Then slowly I picked up everything—what was required, the carpenters, booking the studio and so on.'

Sunil and Nargis also made sure that the carefree Som settled down with a 'good' girl. Nargis went all the way to Jammu to meet her future sister-in-law, Puneeta, for the first time. Som's wedding took place six years after Sunil and Nargis got married. It was proof of how well Sunil was doing by then. Apart from a comfortable lifestyle, he could now afford to be extravagant at his brother's wedding.

Som remembers, 'My mother said that she had not been able to attend her older son's wedding because he had a love marriage and she wasn't there.

'But she wanted to be present for my wedding and have it in the village and conduct all the ceremonies herself. I was in London, because Dutt sahib wanted to set up an office there. When he started looking around for a bride for me I said I don't want to get married because I don't earn anything. And I can't support children or a family. Dutt sahib said, "I will take the responsibility." So I said, no, I want to do some work. He said, what work? I said I want to become a film actor. He said, "Ask for anything else, not this." Then everybody told him, Mataji also told him, "If you can become an actor, why not him?"'

Sunil did not allow his reluctance to overshadow the wedding plans. In fact, now that he could afford to be lavish, he wanted the whole world to join the celebrations.

'The celebrations at Mandoli lasted a whole week. The food was cooked for all our guests at our home. It was open house for the whole village. Everyone came from Bombay too. From Nargis's side, Rehana, Zahida, their mother, father, all the top financiers, producers, directors. A whole compartment in the train was booked for everyone because Dutt sahib was a top producer and actor by then. Everything was organized from all over—the cooks came from Patiala, the band from somewhere else. There was a bundle of money which he gave to Mataji to do whatever she wanted, give to whomever she wanted. Clothes, jewellery, he told her not to stop at anything. But there were so many people that he turned around and asked me when a lot of cars and buses had filled up to go to Jammu as the baraat, "Are all these really our relatives and guests?" I said even I don't know who many of these people are! But it was a wedding that everyone talks about till today.'

Just before his wedding, Som had been sent to Paris. 'My bhai sahib really loved me a great deal, and at the time *Mujhe Jeene Do* was selected for the Cannes film festival. I was the co-producer of the film, so Dutt sahib said, "Dewan (to pull his leg, Sunil often called his brother by their father's title), why don't you travel abroad?" I was out of the country for three months. I also went to London. By that time I had become smart, and learnt English.'

Puneeta, his wife, says: 'Before we were married, I was told we were going to settle in UK, because Dutt sahib was going to open an office there. But Som was homesick. He missed his mother, and his daal roti.'

There were other reasons for Som to return. He could not deal with the intricacies of doing business in a strange country.

Someone even tried to dupe him of his traveller's cheques. He says, 'I was in Paris for a month and a half before Dutt sahib and bhabhi came over. I used to drink a lot, and then one day she saw me having a drink, and because I had great respect for her, I apologized. But she said, "No, Som, go ahead."' Nargis was too liberated a woman to be offended by his drinking, but it soon became obvious that Som would not be able to cope, and the drinking, perhaps, was just a symptom of this. Sunil never opened an office abroad.

On his return, Som leapt back into the film industry with enthusiasm. He found that making films was 'like a picnic. There is one person who is called the producer, who will feed you and look after you—and do everything for you. You can sit around, have your photographs taken, and in the evening put the money in your pocket and come home. This is a very enjoyable industry.'

Sunil's 1963 films *Mujhe Jeene Do* and *Yeh Raaste Hain Pyar Ke* established his banner. The controversial *Yeh Raastey Hain Pyar Ke* even celebrated a silver jubilee despite an 'A' certificate. *Mujhe Jeene Do* also generated debate because it featured a dacoit without, as Sunil was fond of pointing out, making excuses for his ruthlessness. Had Birju of *Mother India* stayed alive, he could have become the dacoit of *Mujhe Jeene Do*. Indeed, it was Sunil who introduced the angry young man to the Indian screen (Amitabh Bachchan acknowledged his debt to him in an interview to CNN-IBN on 15 August 2007), there to stay.

Mujhe Jeene Do was a film for which Sunil had done extensive research; he had even visited the Chambal Valley, then still infested with dacoits. He went so far as to collect gory photographs of dacoits shot in police encounters. The story was written by Aga Jaani Kashmiri, and Waheeda Rehman played a dancing girl, Sunil's love interest. Dacoits were attracting a lot of interest from the film industry then—Dilip Kumar had already made *Ganga Jamuna*, and Raj Kapoor had made *Jis Desh Mein Ganga Behti Hai*.

Dilip's *Ganga Jamuna* was a reworking of *Mother India*, but Raj's interpretation of the dacoits' lives and their reformation made for a far more adventurous plot. His Chaplinesque hero accidentally encounters a gang of dacoits and converts them to a life of peace through the message of love. The transformation was no doubt inspired by the venerable Vinobha Bhave, who had recently made real-life dacoits give up their arms.

Sunil won his first Filmfare award for *Mujhe Jeene Do*, as best actor. He took the film to Cannes in 1964, where he said the 'film was highly appreciated, and a copy of the film is kept in the film library in Paris.'

Yeh Raastey Hain Pyar Ke, produced in 1963 and directed by R.K. Nayyar, starred Leela Naidu and Sunil. It was loosely based on a real, well-publicized case, a crime of passion in which the lover had been 'accidentally' murdered by the cuckolded husband. Kawas Maneckshaw Nanavati, a commander with the Indian Navy, lived in Bombay with Sylvia, his British wife. During his frequent absences, Sylvia fell in love with his friend Prem Bhagwandas Ahuja. After Sylvia confessed to Nanavati, he met Ahuja on 27 April 1959, and in the ensuing quarrel, Ahuja was shot dead.

Not only did Sunil take a huge risk by playing the part of the duped husband, he also cast the beautiful but anglicized Leela Naidu. Perhaps conventional actresses would have refused the role of an acknowledged adulteress. Though the uniform-clad Sunil looked debonair, most of the screen time was taken up by the courtroom debate between the two lawyers, Ashok Kumar for the defence and Motilal for the prosecution. It is odd that Sunil, as the producer, did not demand a bigger role. Perhaps still not confident of his abilities, he was on screen for less than one-third of the film.

Keeping the sensibilities of the audience in mind, the affair between Nina (Leela Naidu) and Ashok (Rehman) is handled in a 'subtle' fashion. The romance begins with a song during which she gets drunk at home. Subsequently, she becomes a sexual pawn for Rehman who dupes her into a drunken stupor every time they meet.

Nonetheless, the film was successful—partly due to the music: in the first 15 minutes of the film, there are three songs, one after the other, all shot in Kashmir. Dialogues were obviously considered irrelevant. But with songs like '*Yeh khamoshiyan, yeh tanhaiyan, mohabbat ki duniya hai kitni jawan* (In this silence, this solitude, the world of love is young and beautiful)', a gentle duet from composer Ravi, no one was complaining. In the picturization of another favourite, '*Koi mujhse pooche ki tum mere kya ho* (If someone were to ask what you mean to me)', the cardigans Sunil wears look suspiciously like the ones Nargis used to knit for him!

The film was also helped by the huge interest the real case had generated, with the editor of the tabloid *Blitz,* R.K. Karanjia, openly supporting Nanavati. Souvenirs were sold on street corners: replicas of Ahuja Towels and toy Nanavati revolvers. Nanavati was released after three years in jail, and died only in 2003. Incidentally, it was due to this case that jury trials in India ceased, as it was concluded that the jury had been biased by the relentless media coverage.

The film did well enough for Sunil to plan his third production, the avant garde *Yaadein.*

Apart from his home productions, Sunil was also acting in a wide range of other films in the 1960s and '70s, most of which were fairly successful. A few, like B.R. Chopra's *Waqt,* were major hits. There were others that made his reputation as an actor, like *Khandaan* (1965), for which he got the Filmfare Best Actor award, *Milan* (1967) and *Padosan* (1968). He never achieved the star status of Nargis or Raj Kapoor, but he had a steady and loyal fan following and an equally devoted group of filmmakers who liked to work with him.

Khandaan, produced by Vasu Menon, was a cocktail of family histrionics and melodrama. In fact, the review in *Filmfare* in June 1965 called it a 'Marathon Limp'.

It was the tale of two brothers, one of whom, Sunil, is handicapped. The other brother was played by Soodesh Kumar. Kumar and Lalita Pawar are the villains who constantly humiliate the hapless Sunil. The reviewer notes that 'The film doesn't exactly blame Soodesh's college education for his outrageous behaviour but does make out that his brother Sunil Dutt who hasn't been to college, is the better man. The film, in fact, rests

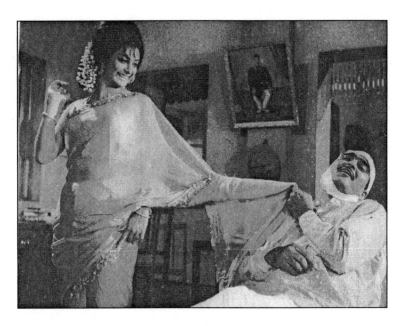

on Sunil's ample shoulders. He gives a robust and fairly
convincing portrayal of a cripple until, for no appreciable reason,
he does an about turn and starts shedding tears on Nutan's
shoulders. Lalita has only to open her sardonic mouth to send
Sunil into another tearful fit with Lalita's remarks ringing
monotonously in his ears and ours...'

Khandaan was emblematic of a society moving from a chiefly
rural to an urban structure, with many of the traditional values
breaking down. Sunil's role was packed with emotion and
required major dramatics, for which he was duly appreciated
and given an award. But his characters in *Milan* (1967) and
Padosan (1968) were more interesting and the films were among
his more successful ones.

Milan, directed by Subba Rao, depicted a relationship across
a sharp social divide. Of course, in order to show that a poor
illiterate boatman and a rich educated woman could have a
relationship at all, the device of reincarnation was used. But it
was a challenging film. Sunil had to completely deglamourize
himself for the role: he had a flat hairstyle, and rustic clothes

and manners.

Right at the start of the film, the storyline is established with the announcement that once in a million years someone remembers a past life, and all unfulfilled desires are carried into the new incarnation. The film begins with two happy college students, Sunil and Nutan, getting married. Shortly afterwards, while singing '*Hum tum yug yug se ye geet milan ke gaate rahe hain* (You and I have been singing these songs of our union through many different lifetimes)', they drive to a strangely familiar spot. It is there, by a river, that the two begin to remember their past life.

In their earlier incarnation Gopi (Sunil) was a boatman who adored the local landlord's daughter, Bibiji (Nutan). He would ferry her to, and back from, college everyday, and was extremely protective of her. She too felt a tender regard for him, but they kept their distance. These sections of the film were directed with great sensitivity by Subba Rao, who manages to make the 'love' exist for the viewer, even though there is no hint of sexuality onscreen. Eventually, she leaves the village after her marriage, and Gopi is distraught.

When she returns as a widow, he tries to help her recover from her grief. Their affection is noticed and furious villagers descend to lynch them. The two of them try to escape on Gopi's boat but are drowned in a whirlpool.

Cut to the present day, with Sunil and Nutan standing on the river bank, near the spot where they drowned in their previous life. Finally, it is a happy ending as the two lost souls have been reunited.

Stories of reincarnation have always struck a chord with Indian audiences, and because *Milan* was a clean 'family film', it did very well. The film owed its success to Subba Rao's careful direction and Laxmikant-Pyarelal's music. Some of the songs have become classics, such as '*Sawan ka mahina, pawan kare sor* (The monsoon is here, and the wind blows noisily)' when Gopi attempts to teach Bibiji a folk song for a music competition. Anand Bakshi's lyrics were equally versatile, from the teasing '*Bol gori bol tera kaun piya* (Tell us, o tell us, the name of your lover)' to the gentle lullaby '*Ram kare aisa ho jaaye, meri nindiya tohe mil jaye* (I pray that my desire to sleep becomes yours)'.

The song '*Bol gori bol*' was shot at Camp Amalapuram and was fairly energetic, as Sunil wrote to Nargis: 'I was very busy in one of the festival songs of the picture. You will be surprised that I had to dance with Yamuna and I did. I am sure you will like my dance very much. My left leg started paining terribly and we had to call the doctor. I am feeling much better now. As soon as I come back to Bombay please fix up my meeting with the doctors about my left leg...'

Obviously, the number required much more energy than Sunil had bargained for, and like Nargis, he was not known for his dancing skills, though he was game for anything.

Sunil's performance in the film made a delightful change from his scowling, red-eyed action hero look. He enjoyed the difference so much that he took on a similar role a year later, playing a rustic simpleton again, but with a comic touch. It was a role that Nargis urged him to refuse because she was worried it would ruin his romantic image forever, but the film, *Padosan* (1968) went on to become a classic.

Padosan was produced by the comic actor Mehmood and was superbly directed by Jyoti Swaroop. It was based on a Bengali story *Pasher Bari,* which had also been made into a Bengali film in 1952. Sunil played Bhola (the name translates as 'the simple one'), a devout follower of the celibate god Hanuman. Bhola comes to the city and moves in with his uncle (Om Prakash), then falls in love with his neighbour, Bindu (the very sexy Saira Bano). He forgets his vows of celibacy, but has to compete for her affections with her Carnatic music teacher, splendidly played by Mehmood. Through the machinations of his musical guru (the irrepressible Kishore Kumar), he manages to woo her successfully.

The film was a cut above the substandard comedy usually dished out, and the music, composed by the brilliant R.D. Burman with clever lyrics by Rajinder Krishen, kept the comic element alive. Songs like '*Mere saamne vaali khidki mein ek chaand ka tukda rehta hai* (In the window across lives a piece of the moon)' became mega-hits. The highlight of the film was the unforgettable and uproarious musical contest between Kishore Kumar and Mehmood (whose part was sung by Manna Dey): 'Ek *chatur naar karke singaar mere dil ke dwaar mein ghusath jaat* (A clever young woman all decked up tries to steal through the doorway of my heart)'. It was a side-splitting satire on classical music, with wonderful onscreen performances by Kishore Kumar and Mehmood.

Sunil got into his role with complete humility, playing the country bumpkin to the last beatific smile. It was a gamble that paid off.

Saira Bano was his 'heroine' in the film. Coincidentally, she became his padosan (neighbour) in real life, too. Saira was a versatile actress, the daughter of the legendary beauty and actress, Naseem Bano. She played the doe-eyed ingénue to perfection and was excellent in lightweight comic roles where she could bat her eyelashes at the camera and display her shapely legs. She eventually married Dilip Kumar. Though Dilip's romance with Madhubala ended upon his insistence that she should give up acting after their wedding, the rules were relaxed for Saira.

Saira remembers that she and Sunil had not worked together before *Padosan* because 'Dutt sahib made many very dramatic films based more on remakes of Tamil or Telugu movies. He did a spate of movies which probably suited other actresses more, *so aisa kabhi nahin hua ke hamara jum gaya. Mera zyaada* musical romantic comedy *mein raha, aur main* mainstream *mein chali gayee* (We did not become an established duo, because I went into romantic comedies, into mainstream films). And by the grace of God there was no looking back after *Jungli,* my debut film. So the first film that came to us together was *Padosan.* It seemed workable, but Mrs Dutt was quite against him doing *Padosan* because Dutt sahib's clientele were these young college-going girls and he had a romantic image from films like *Sujata* and the BR Chopra films, such as *Waqt* and *Hamraaz.* He could be very graceful, very charming, and looked good in a suit as well. Mrs Dutt *ne kaha ke "Aap ye kya* villager *ka* character *kar rahen hain aur aap ka jo* fan mail *hai vo bilkul hi kharab ho jayega, yeh aap mat kijiye* (Mrs Dutt told him that if you play this villager your fan mail will dry up, don't do it)." But he said, "*Main bezaar aa gaya hoon,* Meherbaan *mein mera ye haath toota hua hai* (I am tired of all the roles I am doing, in *Meherbaan* my hand is broken)." And in *Khandaan* he is supposed to be handicapped as well. He said, "I am fed up of dramatic and melodramatic roles, I want to do a fun film, *mujhe kuch alag karna hai* (I want to do something different)."

'(In *Padosan*) he had this poker straight hair, and dhoti kurta. When we would be going to the location, in between shots, he was always such a funster, *hanste khelte rehte the.* He said, "*Kya hai Sairaji, yeh hum kya* film *mein kaam kar rahen hai saath mein, meri haalat dekhiye mein kaisa ban raha hoon, hamari to* team *banni chahiye thi Cleopatra aur Antony ki.*" I laughed and said it doesn't matter, *iske baad Cleopatra aur Antony banayenge.* (We had a lot of fun while shooting. He told me, "Look at how I am dressed, you and I should be doing Antony and Cleopatra, not this!" And I said, after this film, that's what we will make.)'

As an actor, Saira says, 'I liked him very very much. As I said before, I never thought he would be able to do comedy, he had only worked as a serious actor. I liked him immensely in *Sujata*. Then I liked him very much in *Mujhe Jeene Do*. I really never thought he would be able to do comedy, especially in that scene, my family's favourite scene when Kishore Kumar is trying to teach him to sing and he sings "*Saaaaa, paaaa.*" And Kishore Kumar says, "*Upar se nahin, neeche se, neeche se,*" meaning, take the note up from below, and he gets off the chair and sits down on the floor and starts singing. This would always have my grandmother in splits of laughter and I would stop watching the movie and start looking at her. She would have tears of happiness streaming down her cheeks. She would literally fall off the chair and I would say, "Ammaji, please, I don't want to watch the movie, I want to see what's happening to you." *Vo* scene *mujhe itna achcha lagta hai, unke* innocent looks *thi na,* he could carry that role so well. (I really like that scene, he looked so innocent...)'

As Saira points out, *Padosan* turned out to be perennial hit, like *Mother India* and *Sholay*. But his home production, *Mujhe Jeene Do*, became important for another reason.

The film was shot in 1962, during the Sino-Indian war. In a demonstration of their patriotism, Nargis and Sunil tried to raise money for the National Defence Fund, and also thought of entertaining the troops at the border with their newly formed Ajanta Arts Troupe.

The idea of the troupe had come from Nehru. After they had raised Rs 1,00,000 for the National Defence Fund, Sunil handed over the cheque personally to Nehru. The prime minister pointed out that there was so much more Sunil and Nargis could do for the jawans as actors and performers. He told Sunil that in high-altitude areas especially, the jawans had no source of entertainment, nor access to radios. They needed a morale booster and what could be better than an actors' troupe?

Sunil and Nargis were not the first to think of entertaining the troops, or using actors to raise money for charity. Shammi remembers that Nargis and she first met at a charity cricket match in 1950. The concept was already quite popular. At that time, a committee of film artistes, which included Raj Kapoor, organized these events.

Shammi says, 'We played lots of charitable matches. We went to Patiala, Delhi, Calcutta, Amritsar.' According to Shammi, Nargis was primarily a social worker. It was this interest in social work that drew her into politics and brought Sunil along the same route as well. Perhaps the fact that she had got the Padma Shri also put her in a unique position to be able to liaise between the government and charitable causes and institutions.

Even before Ajanta Arts began visiting the border areas, C. Ramchandra had used his government connections to tour NEFA (North East Frontier Agency, now Arunachal Pradesh) and other border areas, with his musicians and other actors.

Shammi remembers the motley crowd which travelled to these distant regions. 'I along with Bhagwandada, Mahendra Kapoor and his musicians, Anwar and some other artistes went to NEFA. Initially, the army did not allow me to go, because they said those areas were not safe for women. Ramchandra persuaded them that I was required, since they needed a woman actor for the skits. That was the beginning. After the Chinese aggression, we went right inside, beyond Tezpur. We saw small groups of soldiers coming back from the war.' Her respect for the soldiers increased when she saw that 'even after starving in the jungles, they brought their guns back, they had so much discipline.' Later the group also went to Nathu La, the ancient trading pass at 14,000 feet above sea level, on the old silk route to China.

According to her, Sunil learnt the details of how to take a group around and then put together the Ajanta Arts Troupe. He even persuaded the well-known actor and singer Kishore Kumar to go with him. Shammi says, 'That is how Kishore's career started as a stage singer. On that trip there were a few other artistes such as Manohar Deepak, Madhumati. I didn't go because I had already been there...then we did a trip to Kashmir, the Rajasthan border and Leh. These days of course there is TV and people make a special effort to entertain the troops for publicity, but when we went, there was nothing and people were staying in small pockets, sometimes less than 50 people, in terrible conditions. The army used to take us in their planes, which were very uncomfortable. In certain areas there was no place to perform, and we stood on jeeps. But once the show started the jawans would start laughing and enjoying themselves.'

Sunil was still shooting for *Mujhe Jeene Do* but was preoccupied with what could be done to help the battle-weary jawans.

Nargis wrote to him on 15 November 1962 with her ideas and plans for both fundraising and the film under production:

Jan Jio
Everything is alright here. Tickly (Namrata) was ill due to teething but now she is feeling better except that she had become very weak— I went to see the IG (Inspector General of Police) last night...I also discussed the prospect of shows to be held in Indore, Bhopal, Gwalior. He thinks it would be a very good idea and that we could collect a good amount. We can play a cricket match in one of the places and have variety shows in two places—out of the entire collections 25% should go to the Police Benevolent Fund and the rest to the N.D.F

(National Defence Fund). He saw the entire rushes of our film and was very much impressed—but he had a few suggestions which are quite vital. Yash will write to you in detail about them. He wants that you should have a theme song with "Mujhe Jeene Do" in the wordings. You could bring in the present situation too. He feels and so do I feel that it will be very powerful. If you don't want to incorporate this song in this picture you should also make a two reeler with this particular song.

How are you—Sanju misses you a lot. Of course if I say the same about myself you will not believe me—but it is a fact. Please don't drive up to Amba to ring up again and again—I believe that area is very dangerous—even IG was saying that he has ordered more forces to protect you all there. He also requested you to finish your shooting as early as you can. Som rang me up last night. I am sending all the things you want from here. I gave Chinoo Mama the advance for the camera. There is hardly anything left here.

I don't think Nirupa (Roy) will be able to give the dates required as she is working with Johnny Walker here, then from the 19th at Madras, anyway they are trying—

Please look after yourself and don't worry about anything, we are alright here…

I love you and miss you
Yours
Pia

It must have been a hard time for Nargis because she was alone in Bombay with her two young children, worrying about a husband shooting under dangerous circumstances. Sunil did receive threats while he was shooting in Madhya Pradesh, but he wanted to keep the locations authentic and so dismissed all warnings.

Nargis was able to help by controlling the production arrangements and money from Bombay, as well as giving a constant flow of ideas and suggestions. For Sunil all of this was invaluable support, and he acknowledged it time and again, though he didn't always follow the well-meant advice. For instance, while he did not follow Nargis's suggestion for the opening song 'Mujhe jeene do (Allow me to live)', he did start the film with the stirringly patriotic '*Ab koi gulshan na ujde ab vatan azaad hai* (May no garden be despoiled now that the country is independent)'.

A few years later, appreciation of the Dutts' support was shown by Indira Gandhi, who after Nehru's death in May 1964 served under his successor Lal Bahadur Shastri as the Minister for Information and Broadcasting. She wrote on 25 September 1965:

> My dear Nargis,
>
> You were such a help to me at the time of the Chinese invasion that I thought I would approach you once again. I wonder if you would agree to present a 'forces programme' on All India Radio on 2nd October. This would be greatly welcomed by our officers and jawans and would be a morale booster.
>
> As I am going out on tour early tomorrow morning, I am asking the station director all India Radio, Bombay, to get in touch with you regarding the details of this programme.
>
> I hope your family is well.
>
> With every good wish,
>
> Yours sincerely,
>
> Indira Gandhi

It was an informal letter and spoke of a unique relationship which was to last through Indira's lifetime and beyond. Indira had noticed the quick response from the Dutts when her father asked them to entertain the jawans. She may have also been aware of the friendship between their families. Her relationship with Nargis had a lot to do with her commitment to social work. Many years later, when Dr Mithu Alur proposed setting up the Spastic Society of India in Bombay, Nargis was one of the 12 contacts given to Mithu by Indira, by then the prime minister.

According to various friends and family members, Nargis and Sunil did meet the Gandhi clan fairly often, especially after Nargis was awarded the Padma Shri.

Rehana, her niece, remembers a lighter side to a meeting with Indira Gandhi. At the time Nargis 'was also the president of Mahila Milan, a charity for destitute women... And she used to do a lot of fundraising. It was a very big organization. We would go with her to collect advertisements for the souvenirs. Zahida would also go along, in full make-up. Nargis aunty by then was the mother of three children and so the rest of us would all dress up. She thought that once the would-be sponsor saw her pretty looking nieces, we may be able to collect some donations for the charity!

'Once, for a Mahila Milan function, they had called Indira Gandhi, who was the Minister for Information and Broadcasting, as chief guest. Indira kept looking at us. And then she asked Nargis, "Who are these very pretty girls with you?" Nargis said, "These are my elder brother's daughters." Nargis told us later, "Mrs Gandhi was paying a lot of compliments to you, the good thing is that she has two sons!"'

Though no proposals materialized, the relationship thrived.

As Sunil wrote later, 'During the 1962 war with China and during the 1965 and 1971 wars with Pakistan, all the borders of my country, wherever the jawans were, we went to entertain them and bring a little solace and happiness in their lives. I feel that is the best thing that I did for the jawans of my country who fight selflessly for the pride and honour of our motherland. I am grateful to Pandit Jawaharlal Nehru, who inspired me to do this.'

In 1967 Sunil led a cultural delegation to the Soviet Union, sponsored by the government of India, to celebrate twenty years of India's independence. Performances were held at Tashkent, Moscow and St Petersburg, and the delegation included musicians, dancers and film artistes such as shehnai player Bismillah Khan, dancers Yamini Krishnamurthy and Gopi Krishna, singer Mahendra Kapoor—and Raj Kapoor.

Nargis was understandably nervous at the inclusion of Raj Kapoor in the delegation. In the Soviet Union, Raj and she were still remembered as a couple, so people tended to call their names out together. Second, she was still worried that Raj might say something that would upset Sunil. But Sunil by now had forged his own relationship with Raj, whom he respected as a fellow actor-producer-director. He would meet him at functions and greet him without the slightest reference to the past.

Shammi recollects, 'She had to go for a festival to Russia, and Rajji was also going to be there. She was worried about it because they used to call her Mrs Raj Kapoor there, and she thought it might happen again. Dutt sahib said, "We'll go together", and so she was prepared for a difficult time. But there was only one incident: she was coming out of the lift, and Rajji was going in. She just swept past, but Dutt sahib stopped to talk to Rajji and called out to her, "Mrs Dutt, Rajji is here," so she had to come back and talk to him. And Rajji simply asked if everything was all right. One thing great about Dutt sahib was he never a mentioned anything about all that, never, not a word.'

It was this grace and dignity which won him many friends. As he once wrote to Nargis, 'I love you, but I do not hate anyone.'

In the same year, Sunil also collected £5000 in donations from the Indo-Pak society at Southall, UK, where he had performed. He 'convinced' them to donate the money to the Bihar Relief Fund and proudly presented the cheque to Indira Gandhi.

Sunil wore his idealism and patriotism on his sleeve. In 1968, he was finally given the Padma Shri at the Republic Day honours in recognition for his efforts. Just a decade earlier, when Nargis had received her Padma Shri, he had felt overwhelmed and thought he could never be her equal. Now all those insecurities were being laid to rest, one by one.

He was increasingly confident also because he was working regularly: he acted in over 30 films in the decade between 1960 and 1970. Many of these films were produced in Chennai, where he was popular among the producers because he was not temperamental or volatile.

Fortunately, Sunil always had a devoted and large fan following as well. Even though he was not a great actor, he was always reliable and sincere. For the big studios in the south— AVM, Gemini, Prasad Productions—it was a perfect combination. Between 1965 and 1975 he had a flourishing career down south.

The southern studios had an interesting style of working: they provided all the technical facilities and often even the director, but the actors and the 'language experts' such as the script writer and the lyricist would be imported from Bombay. In 1967, Sunil delivered a hat-trick of hit films: *Milan, Meherbaan* and *Hamraaz*; the first two were Madras-based productions.

It was a time when groups had began to cluster around certain male actors. Raj Kapoor, Dilip Kumar and Dev Anand were the superstars of the period. Then came actors like Rajendra Kumar, Raaj Kumar and Sunil, and each had his own favourite producers, music directors, singers, lyricists and writers. Each film was dominated by a single male star; the multi-starrers came later, in the mid-1970s.

Meanwhile, in Bombay Sunil was cast in most B.R. Chopra films, such as *Gumraah* (1963), *Waqt* (1965) and *Humraaz* (1967). It was such a regular assignment that often Sunil would not even bother to go and collect his payment. Som would pick it up on his behalf from Shastri, the accountant at BR Studio. In 1957, when Sunil was still a struggling actor, the same Shastri had refused him money. In a letter written to Nargis on 1 July 1957, Sunil had grumbled: 'BR Films wanted me to do some radio publicity for "Naya Daur". I thought I will ask some money from Shastri—he did not give me.' He had only one rupee in his pocket then.

Now, Sunil had enough money not only to live well but also to take more risks. Which is why after on-the-edge films like *Mujhe Jeene Do* and *Yeh Raastey Hain Pyaar Ke*, he decided to make the single-actor film *Yaadein,* turning a deaf ear to advice.

Som says, '*Yaadein* was directed by Dutt sahib and he acted in it as well. At the time I was handling his production. I said, don't make these kinds of films. He started saying, "You don't know, it will definitely run." But this is a heartless media, and when this film was made and released, it was not successful at all. He was frustrated because he felt that even though this film story was so good, he probably failed in explaining it. It was the story of a man who was so attached to his wife and children that one day when he comes home to an empty house and he does not see them there, he falls apart.'

It was a film inspired by Sunil's own life. Nargis was away as a jury member of the Karlovy Vary film festival. One day, when Sunil came home, he found the eerie silence of the house after the normal hubbub of his family difficult to take. An awful desolation descended on him. Nargis had taken Sanjay and

Namrata with her as well. After that experience, he began thinking of a film in which a man, alone at home, relives the memories of his marriage.

A long letter which he wrote to Nargis from Madras on 14 July 1964, explained his feelings and his circumstances. It also shows the affection and love that continued to grow between them over the years.

Hello Jio

I am still in Madras. The work here is going on very well. Everyone is happy with my work...

I hope everything went very well at the Karlovy Vary film festival. And you have seen all the films to enable you to have an important hand during the selection. Was the festival as great as at Cannes? I have booked a call for you today. I hope I get the call. I will be able to talk to Re (Rehana), Sanju and Anju (Namrata). How are they? Have Sanju and Anju become pinkies? You must see that they eat well. Give them milk and fruits and they must put on weight by the time they come here; but not you. You must have been very busy. Are there some moments you think of me? Do you really miss me? I have started missing you and when I reach home, I don't think I will be able to stay in the house. Everything at home, every corner will be full of memories. I will feel your presence all around and when you are not there—I will feel very very lonely—I will miss you very very much. Therefore I am thinking I will stay in the hotel till you come home.

...we are working on the story of one man and his apartment. We have named the picture 'ONLY—THE LONELY'. It is turning out to be a great script and I am sure you will be proud of me when you have read the script. I am starting the picture on 29th of July and I hope I will release it this year to take this picture to Cannes next year...

1:30 a.m. Just now I heard your faint voice on the telephone, I ran down to get a better reception but to my bad luck the line went...Anyway I heard you on the phone, and I feel you are feeling fine.

It is quite late now and I have to go for work in the morning. I am shooting these days from 9 a.m. to 11 p.m. everyday and we have completed a lot of work.

The only thing I know is that I love you too much. I dream, I talk to you when I am alone. I am a lonely, lonely man—missing my wife very very much. Why do I miss you I don't know. What is that—Is that sex?—I feel not. Is that possession?—I feel not. I feel I am an

incomplete man without you. A man who has lost the most essential parts of his body. O my love—I love you, believe me. It is something much bigger than love. Because I pray that even in my next birth—if I am born again as a man—I want to get you as my woman. How are my lovers—Sanju and Anju—love them—love them too much for me. Give my love to Re.
H.T.

One of the Hindi newspapers at the time wrote a little ditty to commemorate the film, *Only the Lonely*:

Sunil Dutt! Sunil Dutt!! Sunil Dutt!!!
Duniya uski soojh par, jabki de rahi hai daad,
Kalakaar chotey karen ro ro kar fariyaad!
Ro ro kar fariyaad, haath kya unkey aaya?
Saheb ney apney matlab ka chitra banaya!

(While the world is paying tributes to his intelligence
All the junior artistes are crying and pleading before him!
For what have they got out of his film?
He has made a movie meant only for himself!)

The reviews, however, were kinder. In *Filmfare*, the headline read, 'Worthy Experiment'.

Though the film credited 'Mrs Sunil Dutt' with the story idea, the letters Sunil wrote to Nargis while she was at Karlovy Vary make it clear that he had the original idea for this immensely difficult film. The opening credits called the film a 'One actor movie monument', a statement not exactly guaranteed to woo the audience. The only other person in the film was Nargis, of whom we get a brief glimpse towards the end of the film. She played Priya, the estranged wife of the dejected husband around whom the whole film revolved.

To be fair, the film still makes intriguing viewing. Sunil puts in a stalwart performance, reliving important moments of his life. Other people he interacts with are represented through cartoons (mostly by Mario Miranda), toys and balloons with faces painted on them. While the film is surreal for the most part, it manages to make an honest and searing social comment on the superficiality of relationships. Except for the slightly shrill end, when Priya comes back to rescue her suicidal husband, the film manages to grip the viewer as the script moves swiftly between different situations, though only Sunil is on screen.

Only a very brave man would have attempted such an unconventional film. And there were some who showed their appreciation, the pleased *Filmfare* reviewer for instance: 'The woman of the home should be respected, says Sunil Dutt's unusual (one-actor, one-set) film "Yaadein" but it draws also two other, external rather delightful morals. One is that a star can make a good director. Another is that to tell a story in a film, even one with a moral, you don't need a big cast or any cast at all...' After accusing the film of occasionally indulging in melodrama, it continued that it was 'quite an experiment and one feels like cheering.'

Everyone, except Sunil, knew *Yaadein* would have a difficult time at the box office. It was barely rescued through some clever public relations strategies.

Raaj Grover, who worked on the production of *Yaadein* with Sunil, says, 'When *Yaadein* was started we were surprised. Bhabhiji (Nargis) used to say, "What is Dutt sahib doing?" I agreed with her. But he was very stubborn and he said, "I will achieve wonders with this film." The film started. It was a single actor movie and for 47 days we were stuck in Kardar studio. He had enough goodwill to raise the money. There were some financiers who were devoted to him. He had commitment but was not a businessman. He did not even know sometimes whether he had signed an actor or not. I knew, the accountant of the company also knew. Nor did he know the price of most things, even magazines. If a magazine was priced at Rs 15 he would think it was worth Rs 2. He had no idea of finance. I used to tell him, learn something from Rajendra Kumar.'

When the film was released, Sunil, Nargis and Raaj went to Delhi for the premiere, and a wonderful reception. The worry was whether it would do well in the other states. Raaj decided to find out for himself and drove down to Chandigarh. After seeing the show he called Sunil and said, '*Kamaal ho gaya* (Something amazing has happened).'

Sunil replied confidently, 'See, I told you I would achieve wonders! I've done that! What did people say?'

'I told him that a friend saw the film and said, *"Udhar Sunil akela tha parde pe, idhar main akela tha balcony mein.* (There was Sunil alone on the screen, and here I was alone in the theatre.)" He banged the phone down. Now the situation changed. We didn't even have our air tickets. Nor could we find the distributor who had welcomed us so profusely.'

Raaj went into damage control mode. 'The Plaza theatre in Delhi belonged to F.C. Mehra, the film producer, and Shammi Kapoor, the actor. They were partners and they spoke to the distributor. I came to know the film would be removed within a week. Dutt sahib and I discussed that the film should run for some more time. Otherwise our reputations would be ruined. So Dutt sahib invited F.C. Mehra for dinner. Dutt sahib was working in his film *Amrapali* and only three or four days of shooting remained.' It gave Sunil an edge, and sometime during dinner Mehra understood and declared that *Yaadein* could run a little longer.

Raaj had another plan up his sleeve. 'Then we thought we should hype it some more, invite some dignitaries for the show. I suggested the Pakistan High Commissioner, the Nepal Ambassador, Sri Lankan Ambassador. Nandani Sathpathi, the I & B minister was invited. I called everyone. I carried bouquets, brochures, and put stories in the media. It ran for five more weeks, thanks to all of this. We sent it to the Berlin Film Festival.' The hype meant that the film remained in the news.

While Sunil was busy with his work, Nargis was still attending film festivals and was also a prominent member of international juries. Obviously, he was no longer insecure about her stature.

On 12 July 1964, she wrote to him from the Karlovy Vary festival:

Darling Jan Jio
We reached here safe and sound and had no trouble on the way. Children are fine, except as I told you, they do not like the food. As a matter of fact, even we don't like the food. Since we reached here we had one Jury meeting—I am making it up by seeing all the missed pictures. It is quite a strain. I have to see at least two pictures in the private showing and two in the evening as the Festival entry. All the

same this place is really beautiful...

What bothered her the most was that the children were having a hard time settling down in an unfamiliar environment. Namrata, she says,

> is quite a craze here—everyone picks her up—kisses her and of course she is very friendly—Sanju is becoming terribly naughty and stubborn—both these children are quite a handful. Sometimes I lose my temper, they miss you and talk about you. Once I got angry with Tikku (Namrata)—she ran out of the room and said Papa is Accha and Mama is Gandi. Bimal Roy is here—his picture has been shown before I reached here. Today Abbas's picture was shown at 4 p.m. I don't think either of these pictures have much of a chance. All the pictures that are entering are a very poor selection...

She was also critical of Elia Kazan, whose film *America America* was screened unofficially. Though she was no prude, she felt that there was no need to show so much nudity on the screen. She added that people were saying that in 'world cinema, sex is essential, just as songs are a must in your cinema—sex has become a box office item for them.'

Despite meeting a host of interesting people, Nargis told Sunil:

> Believe me Jio—I am here but I feel terribly lost without you. It is not like it was in Cannes. Everyone is very kind to me but still I wish you were here. This is an honour indeed to be a member of the jury but it is more honourable to be under the shadow of your husband. Of course I won't write any other thing—because once I wrote to you what my feelings were and you came back and told me that I wrote a stupid letter—so I will not say that I miss you that I love you can't live without you because you won't believe me...
> All my love
> Pia

Nargis had already been invited to the Oscars, to Cannes and now to Karlovy Vary. It would be a long time before any Indian actor was honoured in this way.

Pali Hill
1960-1970

Just before Priya was born, Sunil was shooting on location at Camp Amalapuram for *Milan*. It was shot in a picturesque setting near the mouths of the Godavari and Krishna rivers, about 478 km from Hyderabad, where producer L.V. Prasad had created an entire village. It was a very comfortable life as all the artistes were provided with separate air-conditioned rooms powered by generators. There were boat rides in the evening after work, and fresh fish was fried for dinner. In the evening, Sunil would write passionate letters to Nargis.

Sunil had just received a telegram from Nargis, Sanjay and Anju (Namrata) congratulating him on winning the Best Actor award for *Khandaan,* in which he had played a disabled person. As he lay on a motor launch at night and looked at the stars on 20 March 1966, he was reminded of Nargis in Bombay, pregnant with their third child, and asked, 'What are you giving me this time? What will be the outcome of my most passionate, wild and demanding love this time. I must think of a lovely name, a name worthy of our love.

'I love you—I love my family—I love my children. I want my family to grow like a huge tree—with every branch protecting each other. I do believe in the growth of a huge family—not of few people—please Jio—grow them well. Grow Sanju, Anju well. I want them to grow up as human beings, as lovely children—not affected by the artificial life of today. They should grow up sweet, intelligent and not like the teenagers of today, it all depends on you, and how much time you spend for them. Their lovely growth will be your great contribution to society than any of your social work.'

He also wrote to Namrata that day:

ANJU MY SWEETY
HOW ARE YOU MY DEAR—PAPPA MISSES YOU VERY VERY MUCH. DO YOU TELL YOUR STORIES TO YOUR MAMMA AND SANJU. YOU MUST REMEMBER LOVELY STORIES AND WHEN PAPPA COMES TO BOMBAY YOU MUST TELL ALL THESE STORIES TO PAPPA.
O YES! THANK YOU VERY MUCH FOR A LOVELY TELEGRAM
LOVE
YOURS
PAPPA

He had written to Sanjay a few days earlier, on 16 March:

MY DEAREST SANJU
HOW ARE YOU MY SON. PAPPA ALWAYS REMEMBERS YOU. YOU SHOULD BE A GOOD BOY. YOU SHOULD LOVE YOUR MAMMA AND ANJU AND MATAJI—CHACHA AND CHACHIJI AND NANDITA. HOW ARE YOU IN STUDIES NOW. I AM SURE YOU MUST BE DOING WELL. GIVE MY LOVE TO YOUR MAMMA AND ANJU
YOURS
PAPPA

Sanjay was Nargis's favourite child. But they were beginning to worry about him a little, wondering whether the influences of the film world surrounding them could possibly affect him. But before they could dwell too much on their fears, their third child, Priya Darshini (another indication of how much Sunil and Nargis admired Indira Gandhi, whose middle name was Priyadarshini) was born. Coincidentally, Priya would enter active politics after her father's death just the way Indira Gandhi had followed in her father's footsteps.

Priya was born on 28 August 1966. The hospital room was full of flowers, and silver and tiny pieces of jewellery for the baby, and the list of gifts had expanded from a half a page when the older children were born, to two full pages, each name meticulously noted down by Nargis. She wrote her own name as 'Mrs Fatima Sunil Dutt (Nargis)'. She felt she was finally plain and simple Mrs Sunil Dutt, and so did the newspapers:

DAUGHTER TO SUNIL DUTT

Mrs Nargis Dutt, wife of matinee idol Sunil Dutt, gave birth to a girl on Saturday 28th August 1966 at Breach Candy Hospital.
This is the third child of the Dutts. Earlier two are a son and a daughter.

There was no mention of the matinee star Nargis. Sunil's fears about her towering over him in the film world had come to nothing. She was now just 'wife and mother'. Fortunately, it was her favourite role.

Nargis was ambitious for her children, and felt Priya could be interested in medicine when she grew up. So she was furious when Priya's teacher, Miss Lelly, suggested that Priya was a little slow to grasp and solve new problems.

Nargis fumed into Priya's baby book on 8 September 1972, 'According to me, I feel and feel very strongly—that the system of education in India (unlike that) which is observed all over the world, is very wrong. Little children of 5 and 6 are being burdened with books and too many problems to solve in school work. Std 1 work is as much as it used to be in Std III in the 50s. You don't expect every mother to produce a genius but the school expects each and every student in the class to be a genius.'

She noted the next year on 17 March, 'Priya still shows a keen interest towards medical science but also shows a lot of versatility in dancing, music and acting. She has a very strong inclination towards films—she can see pictures the whole day and not get tired. We try to keep her away from the atmosphere of films—but no getting away from the truth. She lives in her imagination of films. Loves to dress up like grown ups—styles her hair—and is very keen how she looks. Loves to go to weddings particularly to see the brides because brides are so beautifully dressed. Priya also desires to get married because she feels she will also look as pretty as all the brides...'

Incidentally, Priya did eventually work in television and documentary film making, but took her time getting married!

Nargis carried on having elaborate birthday parties for each child and celebrating their achievements. As Sunil confessed to Ameen Sayani, 'who accused' him of making Nargis abandon her film career in a mock trial on radio in 1993, 'When we got married, she herself said, "For me marriage means that I must devote time inside my home and I must build my home, that is my dream." So that is why when my children were born, I did not even know, I had no idea (what was happening at home)— I was like a soldier, shooting here and there, and I had no idea that my children had their exams, or that they were sick or that they had to be taken to the hospital. I had no idea about my relatives, that it was their children's birthdays, that there were festivals, what had to be given or taken, she used to do everything. I had no clue about any of it. For her performance as a housewife, among the Indian middle class, and the more orthodox sections and the lower middle class, where the stature of a housewife is appreciated, respect for her grew even more.'

Despite the financial rollercoaster of the film industry, Nargis tried not to let anything affect their family rituals. But 1971, the year when *Reshma Aur Shera* was made (it was to become a box office disaster), was difficult for them. They had invested all their money in the film, and the house was mortgaged. That year, Nargis wrote only occasionally in Priya's baby book. One entry reads: 'This year was a very quiet birthday. Very few children could come and there was no show of cartoons. Priya's cake was in the shape of a piano.'

The period between 1969 and 1971 was emotionally stressful as well. In 1969, they had to take the painful decision of sending Sanjay to boarding school. They could see that he was getting influenced by the larger-than-life environment around him.

Sanjay Dutt remembers the terrible time he gave his parents. He was a precocious child with a penchant for acting and melodrama. He had already been exposed to the glamorous side of filmmaking, and had been attending mahurats and film shoots since he was barely a year old. During Nargis's schooldays, making films was not considered a respectable career. So she would often feel slighted or ignored by her peers. Sanjay and Namrata experienced a very different school environment: as the children of films stars, they got too much attention from other children.

It was a difficult time for Namrata: she was shifted to a school closer home, where some of the children seemed to be overwhelmed by her status as the daughter of two film stars.

Namrata says, 'In Cathedral (her previous school) no one spoke about it. Priya came into Cathedral when I was in the seventh and she was in the first standard. Mom realized it was too much of a drive. Then we were put into an all-girls school called AF Petit School. For me it was difficult to adjust because I had now joined the eighth standard, and I guess they knew who we were. So some of the children were really in awe of us. And I remember a couple of times the boarders came to touch me and I used to get really frightened. They would feel my hair... I knew why they were doing it—but I was confused because it had never happened before. They would pack my schoolbag for me, try and do everything for me, and I would say, please, please let me be.'

Apart from this, the rest of her childhood was 'fantastic. We didn't really know that our parents were celebrities. Sanju was sent quite early to boarding school. Bandra at the time was quite different, there were just bungalows all around and we had lots of friends. We used to play on the street. My dad used to get quite upset and say, "Call all your friends inside," but we never did.

'We played with the drivers' children, the cooks' children. My parents brought us up with so much love, and it didn't matter to them who you were and where you came from. I also have beautiful memories of my mom. We travelled a lot. It was a compulsory thing, and we would go on a holiday every year, whether here in India or abroad.'

Nargis also made it a point to be home when the children came back from school so that they could have lunch together. Another ritual was for the children to stand in front of their parents and recite whatever they had learnt in school. For both Nargis and Sunil, educating their children in good schools was a dream come true. They had been equally passionate about learning but neither of them had had the luxury of an uninterrupted education. Now this, the ability to learn, was the biggest gift they could give to their children.

For Sanjay, the 'fantastic' childhood was to change soon. 'Mom and me were very very close and I used to take advantage of that definitely. I was really spoilt by her till they decided that my growing up in Bombay would have ruined me. They sent me to a boarding school and I think that was the best thing for me. I remember when they came and dropped me. I was so shattered when they left me in the dorm, and I yet remember in the night I heard Mom's voice outside. I opened the door, and she was not there.

'She was absolutely special to me. I cried like hell for many many days, you know, and she was absolutely shattered to send me to a boarding school, too. I think growing up in Bombay would have ruined me because they wanted me to be more humble and be independent.

'I have memories before that of being really naughty. Mom used to tell me. Dad was shooting in Kashmir and she took me, and I was just after her life that I want to smoke a cigarette. And because I was so small, she got mad at me. So Dad came from work and said, "If he wants to smoke let him smoke." He lit a cigarette, put it in his mouth and said, "Do exactly what I tell you." He inhaled and he thought I would choke and throw it away but I smoked the whole cigarette. I must have been six.

'In the beginning I couldn't understand why they sent me away. I felt rejected.'

Raakhi, Sunil's co-star in *Reshma Aur Shera*, had a different take on the Dutt family life. She had been chosen by Sunil to act in the film as a girl who is widowed on her wedding day. During the making of the film, she grew extremely close to the Dutt family. The children could not pronounce her name initially and called her 'Khairi Aunty.' The name stuck and Nargis and Sunil would also call her by that name. She maintains: 'I used to only say one thing to both of them (Nargis and Sunil) that the state of the house is not okay. There are two daughters and a son in the house. But you are all busy, Dutt sahib had his ambition and Mrs Dutt had hers, so, for all that, all day the children should not be left alone with these ayahs and relatives and so on. And I still feel that way.'

Sunil had also cautioned Nargis about leaving the children at

Château Marine time and again. It wasn't because the family was not loving. In fact the children were probably given far too much love. He was similarly worried about Nargis's own blind love for Sanju. Sunil believed that all relationships require boundaries and discipline. But Nargis laughed away his fears.

In reality, her love made Sanjay grow up into a gentle, slightly dreamy boy who enjoyed the good things in life. Which is probably why he did not appreciate the discipline his father wanted to impose on him. During his growing years, he was a lost child. He became the James Dean of India, drugged, drunk, and yet phenomenally successful His is the classic but tragic tale of a very bright, imaginative child slowly going astray, falling into bad company, and becoming increasingly distant from his parents.

His letters written from Lawrence School, Sanawar clearly show his development from a sweet, slightly troubled child into a fun-loving but demanding teenager. His parents, meanwhile, struggled to send him the right messages and desperately hoped that he could become an astronaut or a scientist.

On Saturday, 24 May 1969, the nine-year-old wrote from school:

> Hellow mama, papa, Anju and priya How are you? I am fine we have started football. Among the prep siwalik house is winning. We have made 2 goles while vindhya has made 1 gole. How is papa, Anju, priya and yourselve and lena Rosy and other servants? I got yours and papa's letter from Delhi and your and papas and Anju and priyas letter from Bombay. Anju's letter was full of mistakes, our house mistress even could not read it. How is my rabbit Ringo and the chicks? Are they fine? Give all the severnts my love and tell them not to worry and you too don't worry. Mama and papa when I come for my holidays we will have nice fun. I got my hockey stick and I am enjoying playing hockey here. Mama and papa I got 19/20 for my grammar and 9/10 for sums. Are you glad for that? How is priya? Is she okay or has she got measels? yet I am very sorry to trubble you, all the servants and Anju, Priya and papa. It is plesent weather here and it is very Good. Mama and papa come one day to meet me with priya Anju and Gopal Bhai. Tell Sham rao that I am alright here and give my love to him. mama and papa I am very sorry

to truble you and I am very sorry to back answer you. Did you get my first letter which I wrote to you? How is dara? If you go to Mohan Studio give Dara a kiss from me. Give yourself, papa, Anju, priya, Ringo and the rabbit a kiss. When you write a letter you give news about Bomby. And I wrote a long letter.

Bye Bye 10 kisses to

Yourself, papa, Anju, priya, rabbit, ringo and the chicks. Don't forget to come to my school. In my multipycations sums I got 10/10 and for the second I got 10/10 and on the third I got 10/10 and for my mental sums I got 5/5 plese be plesed and thank you for the letter.

Sanjay was only in his first year of boarding school when he wrote the letter, so his memories of home and everyone there are extremely vivid. He does not mention anything special about school, except the weather and the marks he got in various subjects. Like any child who has been sent away while his siblings remained home, he is concerned that perhaps it was because he was 'truble' or because he gave too many 'back answers.'

Both Sunil and Nargis were enormously relieved to receive his letter. It had been a difficult decision to send their son away, but it seemed that Sanju was actually settling down.

On 28 May Sunil wrote:

My dear Chameli JAN,

How are you. We got your letter. I am so happy that you are enjoying your school. One day you will become the best boy and we will be so proud of you. You must play the games very well—you must study well and try to be the best student. We always remember you—keep talking about you. I took anju and priya to SUN-N-SAND for a swim. We were thinking about you. Your sisters are giving lots of trouble to us. They sleep very late and get up very late. They are both too lazy... Priya is still awake. It is 11 p.m. and she is sending a flying kissy to you...

In an earlier letter, on May 20 1969, Sunil had been even more effusive, giving a sense of the excitement that pervaded 58, Pali Hill Road every time a letter came from Sanjay:

My dear Son Sanjay

You don't know how happy everybody was today. They were all expecting your letter and your letter came. Your mama read your letter to everybody. To Leena, Rosy, Kasam mama, Ameena mami, Ganga Ram, Madhaya, Ganga Ram's children and his wife, your uncle Akhtar bhai & his wife, Ronnie uncle, everybody heard your letter. They were so happy that you are doing so well in your school. Keep it up my son, one day you will become a very good man and a good son. Sanju you should not write like this that you used to trouble us. No my son—you never gave us any trouble. I think Bombay schools are not good at studies and we wanted our son to be the best student so we sent him to Sanawar... Look after yourself my son. Be a good boy. Your Ringo, Bugs Bunny and your chicks send you their love.

Yours,

Papa

For the first few years, Sanjay did find it difficult to settle down whenever he returned to the hostel after a break. In later years, he learnt to put on a brave face, and then a time came when he did not want to leave school.

But initially, the homesickness would make him cry. In 1969, the family went to London and spent a month there. Coming back to a cold hostel room must have been a nightmare for Sanjay, as it was for Nargis to leave him in Sanawar. Though she agreed with Sunil that Sanjay would be spoilt in Bombay, she was never sure if it was right to leave behind a crying child.

She wrote to him, heartbroken, on 6 August 1969 from Delhi:

Darling Son Sanjay

After I left you in school I was terribly disturbed—you were crying and I was feeling very bad. Sanjay—I know my boy that you must be missing home and me, we miss you too—the house is empty without you—but Sanjay you must try to understand that it is for your own good—you will be a good student—and study well over there—your results there are much better than what they were in Bombay. Now you have promised to do even better and I promise I will come to see you every month—You know you are our only son and we have great hopes (from) you—You must study hard and become a big man so that you can look after us in our old age. So no more crying—pay attention in your class—there is plenty of time for you to play. Please Sanjay for my sake be more attentive in your class, you must do this much to please your mother—I hope you secure

better marks... With all my love and kisses to you—
Your loving
Mama

While Nargis was almost apologetic, Sunil was firm in his letter, written on the same day. He was in Madras and shooting for a film, but Nargis had told him of the tearful scene when she dropped Sanjay back to school.

Sunil wrote:

My dearest Son,
How are you? I am sure you must be very very happy with your friends and must be telling lots of stories of London to them. I am glad that your Mama went with you to the school. But Sanjay, you are a big boy now, you should not all the time be around your mother. You must now put your mind to studies also if you want to become a scientist or an astronaut. You must love your school, your studies in the same way as you love your mama and papa. We all love you Sanju and we want you to become a good boy and a great man. Sanawar school is very very good and if you study well we will in near future put you in a good London school and we will all come to see you there...We all love you very very much.
Yours
Papa

Sanjay wrote back to thank them for taking him to London, again apologizing for having troubled them (spelt correctly this time). He also promised to improve his grades and not to cry, and asked them to keep their promise of visiting him every month.

Sanjay's letter of 20 September was the one that 'thrilled' Nargis. He wrote that his marks had improved and that he had been graded 5/5 in his mental tests and got close to full marks in his grammar, history and spellings. But the important thing was that he said, 'I am fine and Happy. I am not Home Sick any more.'

He also informed her, 'Mama I am chucked out of the English play I am in the band. Mama we went to domes pond to catch frogs and tadpoles on Friday. Mama reply soon and come on the 2nd of October for founders and send Papa soon.'

Nargis wrote back on 23 September, as soon as she got the

letter, that she was 'thrilled to get your letter written in ink—your writing was very neat and nice, of course, your progress marks were just wonderful—I was ever so happy.' Though Sanjay had stated quite casually that he had been 'chucked out of the English play', Nargis took it to heart and wrote back,

> Never mind Sanju if you are not in the English play. You should not feel sad, next time you may be taken. Remember I told you how I was always chucked out from all the plays in school. There is nothing to be ashamed. Our love for you or the love of your teachers does not depend on your being taken in plays. Just as you are so good in sports, nobody can be as good as you. Maybe the other boy may be a better actor on stage. So you must not feel bad about it. What is really most important is how good you are in your studies...

When Nargis visited Sanawar for a few days, she observed that Sanjay was very happy to see her, but when he had to go back to school, he became 'very sad and unhappy'. In a conversation with one of the teachers, she discovered that a 'change' had come over Sanjay after he had been in the school hospital following an illness.

The teacher confided to her that another female teacher was too protective of him. Also, in the course of other conversations with the staff, Nargis learnt that 'certain parents who come to visit their children try to be over friendly with Sanjay and bring things for him so that through him and their children they can be friendly with us (Nargis and Sunil) and that she felt that if she (the teacher) had my permission she should stop these things. I told her she should be firm and say politely to those parents that "Sanjay's mother does not like Sanjay receiving gifts as she (Nargis) sends him everything he needs."'

Obviously it wasn't an ideal environment for the ten-year-old, with people falling over themselves to be close to him. Unlike Namrata, who could escape the unwanted attention at the end of the day, Sanjay was completely defenceless. It was obviously affecting his work, as his class teacher, Miss Naidu, told Nargis: 'Sanjay is weak in his studies, he can do better if he tries, but he does not concentrate and keeps dreaming in class—does not finish his work and finds difficulties in written work.'

Another teacher told her that there was something important that Sanjay needed to tell Nargis.

A distraught Nargis wrote to Sunil, 'All the time Sanju was with me, he did not tell me, I even asked him, he only told me about a boy in his dormitory who teases him and bullies him, and says that your mother is an actress and you are an actor's son. I told Sanjay that he should not get upset about those things, as a matter of fact if he does not like anything what the boys tell him, he should get up and let them know that he will not tolerate their nonsense—Sanju seems to be afraid and timid, he said that this boy is a bully and he will beat him, because he is very strong but now that (he is) taking vitamin tonic he will also become strong and bash up this boy. These were just innocent things...'

But then on Sunday, after lunch, when Nargis tried to take him back to school, he started 'crying, and was very nervous. He wanted to go back with me. I tried to explain to him that how he must try hard to be the best boy in school and how proud we all will be of him, but he seemed to be very sad and upset. So I took him back to school at 2 p.m. so that I could be alone with him and talk to him. I had brought some tuck...'

During the conversation, which Nargis managed to have with Sanjay in the presence of a very sympathetic teacher, it slowly emerged that while Sanjay had been ill in hospital, there were some other older boys with him who said some 'very nasty things' which upset him.

Sanjay refused to tell Nargis anything else to begin with and became very nervous and uncomfortable as she tried to get him to talk. It was a tearful and frightening moment for both of them. But Nargis tried to handle it sensitively, for she knew that there were things no son would like to tell his mother.

Sanjay told her that some older boys, probably teenagers, had used four-letter words while talking to him in a threatening fashion. 'I asked him to tell me and with difficulty he said it is a very dirty and bad word. They were saying F— and that they used bad language and said bad things about me.' They threatened to be violent with Nargis, Sunil and his sister. 'They said that if you have a sister as big as me why don't you bring her here we would like to do things with her and they have frightened him. That next year when you (Sanjay) come to the boys school we will do things with you and if you say anything we will tell your mother that you have been abusing us and using bad language. I asked Sanjay what did he do, he said "nothing" because he was afraid of them. I have tried to put a lot of courage in him, that he should not be afraid of such things. He should have hit them and reported them... He kept on saying, Mama please take me away from here, I don't like this school, put me back in Cathedral, I don't mind repeating standard V. I kissed him and pacified him and said that when Papa comes to see you, you must talk to him. I will see what I can do about all this, he was literally begging me not to leave him there.'

Even the teacher listening to them suggested that Nargis take Sanjay away, because the atmosphere in the school was such that boys and girls were known to have run away together, older boys drank beer out of shampoo bottles, and the senior boys' school, according to her, was all 'corrupt'.

In complete confusion about what she should do, Nargis left behind a crying Sanjay. She felt that 'Sanjay is a very affectionate boy, all say so, but on the other hand he must be strong enough to fight his own battles, how long will he look to others to protect him. I am terribly worried. I just don't know what to do.

'You must go to him, talk to him,' she wrote to Sunil. She was also worried about how Sunil would interpret her fear. Would he think that the entire episode had been exaggerated because she could not bear to be away from Sanjay or he from her? She did explain to him, 'I know he loves me too much, how far it is good for him I can't say, but I can't afford him not to love me...' She was 'frightened, worried and upset.'

It was a very traumatic visit, because Nargis must have realized how helpless she actually was and that she could not protect her son from such ugly experiences. She tried to put it in perspective: the same thing could happen anywhere, after all, and Sanjay would have to fight for himself and learn to be tough. Sunil would only see it as 'pampering' if she tried to pull him out of the school.

Sunil probably thought back to his own fatherless childhood in Khurd when he learnt to use his fists to protect himself. What neither of them realized—and this became apparent only over the years—was how impressionable and soft-hearted Sanjay was, and would remain. Despite his tough, he-man image in later years, Sanjay could never become violent or aggressive, not even in self-defence.

In any case, what could he have done to protect himself from this unwanted attention and abuse at the age of ten? It was a time when he needed protection, yet no one, neither his teachers his parents, could protect him.

By now Sunil was busy with his next big home production, *Reshma Aur Shera*, set in the desert in Rajasthan. It was a very expensive film and created enormous problems. Apart from travelling to Rajasthan to help Sunil, Nargis was putting the finishing touches to the underground preview theatre being built in their compound.

Sanjay did write to Nargis, a little more cheerfully, in October, because he had met the headmaster and told him his problem. And according to Sanjay, 'He said if anyone says bad words go and tell your Housemaster that's all.'

There were other issues that were now preoccupying Sanjay. He asked rather plaintively, 'Mama why did you give my toys to Anju? Tell her to keep it back…Mama my best friend is Puneet Sikand. He has come from Hospital. He stayed there for four weeks. He gives me lots of tuck I don't give him anything but he gives me. it is quiet cold in Sanawar mama. please send me tuck my tuck nearly finishing mama send me chewing gum, chocolate, condest milk, sweets, Drinking chocolate and jam and baked beans…' As everyone who has been to boarding school knows, the importance of tuck cannot be overstated. Tuck provides friends among other things. Sanjay was learning to survive, just as his father had hoped he would.

Feeling that he was now settling down, Nargis wrote to him with ideas and thoughts that she hoped would inspire him. On the day of the moon-landing, 16 July 1969. she wrote to him, 'The splash down is going to be today—that is on Tuesday at 11 a.m. Indian time. This is a big thing in the history of the world that the men have started going to the moon—many years ago people could have never believed that man could ever step on the surface of the moon. I am sure many years from now when you will be a grown up man you might have a chance to travel up to the moon as a passenger on a moon flight. are we not lucky to be born in a time where such great things are happening in this world. This is called the Golden period of our life...'

The letter excited Sanjay enough for him to send his parents a drawing of a triumphant astronaut and a rocket landing on the moon.

As Sanjay slowly adjusted to his life in Sanawar, he stopped crying when his mother left him, and except for a few incidents, stopped complaining of homesickness. In fact, five years later, he wrote to Nargis, 'Mom I don't want to ever leave Sanawar so please don't fix me up with any other school. Mom I'll stay here till 6th form and do my Hsc exam in Sanawar...'

His letters became less and less personal and more like shopping lists. For instance, in August 1974, when he learnt that Sunil was going abroad, he wrote, 'I want a few things from there.' The 'few things' were:

Shoes, with heels
Levi jeans with a
Short Jacket
Flares (measurements to be taken from Stylo)
Pocket transistor
One good watch
Records
1)   latest of Alice Cooper if not latest of Pink Floyd
2)   latest of Black Sabboth of the 'Sabboth Bloody Sabboth.'
3)   Deep Purple 'Who do You Think You are'
4)   Jethro Tull 'Living In the Past'
5)   Doors 'LA Women'

Sanjay did not show any sign as yet of becoming the earnest student his parents wished him to be. Instead, he was a trendy cosmopolitan kid ever ready for a good time. All the things that his father had hoped he would stay away from were part of his life. To be fair, he was only 15 and could afford to be frivolous, though his parents tried to interest him in more serious things. When Sunil went to New York in October 1974, armed with yet another shopping list from Sanjay, he sent him a postcard from the United Nations:

Hello Sanju
I am writing to you from United Nations New York. This is the Security Council Chamber where Mr Bhutto and S. Swaran Singh made speeches during the war of India Pakistan during the Bangladesh problem. I am coming back reaching Bombay on 17.10.74.
Love
Papa.

While Sunil would often write about the political happenings in India and abroad, Sanjay's interests clearly lay elsewhere. The two girls, on the other hand, were growing up into caring, sober children. Though no one realized it then, the experiment of sending Sanjay away did not have the desired result. He became more and more detached from his family, and less and less interested in his studies.

The next major upheaval that awaited the Dutts was a financial crisis, but none of the three children learnt about it.

Reshma Aur Shera
1969-1970s

Ali Raza, who is a master storyteller, says that Sunil had a peculiar reason for buying the bungalow at 58 Pali Hill.

'He used to live on Napean Sea Road, but when he became a star, and had the money, he saw that all the stars had bungalows, and so he set out to find a bungalow. He was acting in quite a few films from Madras then.

'He came to Pali Hill looking for a place. All around the house, and especially where the preview theatre was built later, was a dense jungle. We were there with him and saw a big snake emerge from the undergrowth. Dutt sahib was very superstitious in certain ways and immediately, the thought came to him that if there is a naag (snake), there is bound to be a khazana (treasure). This thought obsessed him. So he bought the bungalow. But now how was he going to dig for the treasure? So he said, "I have to make a swimming pool here." So the pool was designed and the labour started working. He reached the desired depth of the swimming pool, but no treasure emerged. The work stopped but the thought was still in his heart. He said, "I've changed my mind, it's too dangerous to make a swimming pool here for the kids, because I am out for shooting most of the time. Instead, I would like to make an underground badminton court here."

So again they started digging, and then again they reached the desired depth, but nothing was found, no treasure. By then everyone was exhausted. It was quite an expense, and then the suggestion came from Rajendra Kumar, why not make an underground preview theatre. That is what they finally did.'

Nargis was also keen on building a preview theatre, because it meant that there would be an alternative source of income. They did not know how well-timed the investment was: the next Ajanta Arts production was about to bomb at the box office. That's why Ali Raza maintains that Sunil did find his khazana: the preview theatre was to earn money and rescue them from penury.

'Look at the story behind the theatre. *Allah ki karni aisi hui* (Allah willed it to happen this way). *Reshma Aur Shera* was made. The problem was that once Dutt sahib became a star, he stopped thinking rationally. He used to think he will make a great film with *Reshma Aur Shera*. When *Reshma Aur Shera* started, he was inspired by a documentary made by Sukhdev. He heard the idea, liked it and announced that the film will be completed in 15 days shooting, and then the profit made would be shared amongst everyone. Waheeda Rehman had given the dates for eight days. My problem was that I didn't like the idea at all, but I couldn't say anything because he would think I am not writing since he doesn't have the money. So I sat with Sukhdev and wrote the script. On top of the script Sukhdev wrote, "I have never seen such a great script." Dutt sahib was shooting in Madras. The script was completed and given to Mukri (the character actor) who was working on the same film as Sunil and was going to Madras. So I wrote to Sunil that this is the script and this is Sukhdev's note. My request is that you tear this script and throw it away. The next day Mukri called to say, "What have you written, he has gone mad, everything is ready for the shooting, he is going to Jaipur, how will everything happen now?" I said if he goes mad it is better than if he makes this film. But he made it.

'On the tenth day or so after he went to Rajasthan, I started getting trunk calls from Dutt sahib. "Ali sahib please come, Ali sahib please come." He told Nargis, "Bring Ali and come." So then Nargis took me to Jaipur. But the whole premise of the film was incorrect. If a man kills his whole family in the film, what are you going to do about it? When we discussed the story with the local Rajasthanis, they could not believe it. They said if the hero murders his clan, it means he is not their son, he must be a bastard. That is the way they understood it.'

In its finished form, *Reshma Aur Shera* was much more sophisticated in its style, art direction, music as well as script, than the formulaic cinema of the late 1960s and early 1970s. It is memorable for its outstanding performances, especially those of Waheeda Rehman and a very raw Amitabh Bachchan. It is, however, a relentlessly violent film, a significant instance of Sunil's latent anger against hypocritical social norms.

Unlike Raj Kapoor, who as a director and an actor playing the *aam aadmi* (common man) often used humour and satire to highlight social evils, Sunil's view was more black and white. No humour alleviates this film, which remains dark and grim throughout. Ramchandra's cinematography carefully framed the colours of Rajasthan against the white sand dunes. The long shots and the close-ups create contrasts between the stark landscape and the elaborate jewellery and clothes of the actors. Ali Raza's script is tightly constructed and shows a deep understanding of love, lust and revenge as it minutely explores the blood feud between the Kardas and the Pochinas, the Montagues and Capulets of Rajasthan. The two lovers, Reshma (Waheeda Rehman) and Shera (Sunil Dutt) are plagued by the hostility between their families. When Shera tries to reconcile them, his father orders the murder of Reshma's father and brother. The assassin is Shera's much-loved mute younger brother, an ace shot, played by Amitabh Bachchan. Shera is about to kill him in turn, when Reshma saves the boy's life by marrying him. Shera's love for her prevents him from killing her husband. The film is violent and bloody, and the audience found it difficult to sympathize with the hero-turned-villain, just as Raza had feared.

The 10-year-old Sanjay made his debut in the qawwali '*Zaalim meri sharaab mein yeh kya mila diya* (What have you put in my drink, you devil)?' with the main qawwal, Sudhir Luthra. His bit-part as a young qawwali singer is a fairly confident debut, though you can occasionally see his eyes anxiously hunting for his father's approval. After this role, he would be teased for a long time as Chameli Jaan. The film spent more time exploring the violence unleashed by the love between Reshma and Shera than on the romance itself, and the plot became a little unbalanced. Sunil, eyes menacing, eyebrows drawn over a face dark with anger, goes out looking for justice. It is a look most viewers would remember from his other films, including *Mother India*. Unfortunately, it has overshadowed his other image as the idealistic, kurta-clad young man in *Sujata*—probably his best performance.

Jaidev composed some truly memorable music for *Reshma Aur Shera*. The songs '*Ek meethi si chubhan* (This sweet tenderness)' and '*Tu chanda main chandni* (You are the moon, I am the moonlight)' sung by Lata Mangeshkar were unusual in their composition, gentle and lyrical enough to sound fresh to this day. The film was also remarkable for its large cast: Amitabh Bachchan, Raakhi, Vinod Khanna, Amrish Puri, apart from Sunil and Waheeda. It was an atypical role for Amitabh to play, because it was his voice that would become a major attraction in later films. Though mute, he puts in a marvellous cameo, certainly justifying the letter he apparently came armed with, straight from Indira Gandhi, asking Sunil to give a role to the son of a 'dear family friend'. (His mother Teji Bachchan was reputed to be a close friend of the prime minister. Raaj Grover, who worked as an assistant to Sunil Dutt, says the letter was sent to another dear friend, Nargis, so it was a request which could not be refused.)

Raakhi gave a riveting performance, also in a role without dialogue, conveying the excruciating anger and helplessness of a girl whose husband is shot within hours of their wedding. Nonetheless, the film was plagued with problems from its inception, and in some ways Raza was right: Sunil should have just torn up the script. Paradoxically, it is his best and most mature film. It is well edited, tightly scripted and beautifully shot. It also has the rudimentary 'item' number, a breathless song and dance by a bosom-heaving and hip-swivelling Padma Khanna, in '*Tauba tauba meri tauba* (I regret, I renounce)'. It is probably one of the most sexually explicit numbers seen on screen, with enough energy to run several wind turbines.

Raaj Grover says he never worked as hard as he did in *Reshma*

Aur Shera. The entire unit lived in tents in a small village called Pochina, 80 miles from the closest big town, Jaisalmer. Chiman Kant Gandhi (Chinoo mama) was the base camp manager and would have supplies sent down everyday. The mail was also picked up and delivered the same way, and some mix-ups were inevitable. Among those who sent and received letters every day was the script writer Ali Raza, who wrote regularly to his beloved Nimmi. One day Waheeda Rehman found the script had a perplexingly romantic tone, and was very amused to read it. Raza's letter to Nimmi had been given to Waheeda, and the film dialogues had been sent to Nimmi.

Ultimately, the crew had to work for over two months and not 15 days as Sunil had planned. What went wrong? Raakhi remembers with amusement, 'I went there and found that for the first 15 days we did nothing. Amitabh was new, I was newly introduced, Amrish Puri was a first-timer. We were all there, 15 days in the middle of a desert, our tents laid out in a horseshoe pattern. Dutt sahib wanted me to get into my role, so he asked me to get up at 5 o'clock, put on all my jewellery, which weighed around 15 kilos, then he made me get onto a camel, and said you must learn to ride it. I had to observe how the villagers walked, ate, for 15 days. But for the whole first schedule no shooting took place. He was also punishing himself unnecessarily, learning to ride the camels, falling off, and even getting injured. 'But all those 70 or 100 people in the crew were scared of him, not because of anything else but out of respect for him. He had set some rules…and he used to walk around and keep an eye on everyone.'

A very firm personal bond was quickly established between Raakhi and the Dutts. The green-eyed youthful Raakhi would be up to all sorts of pranks with Amitabh to amuse herself, and Sunil would usually indulge them. He celebrated her birthday on location. But when Nargis arrived, she and Raakhi began to indulge their fondness for paan, which Sunil abhorred. So the two women would find ways of getting it without his knowledge. Raakhi remembers how one day, when she was gingerly walking around in her full Rajasthani regalia, chewing her paan and trying to stay out of Sunil's way, he caught her. He was furious and dragged her to the highest sand dune and threatened to throw her down from there if he ever caught her eating paan again. It was not funny: he meant it! Raakhi was not annoyed but rather touched by his sincerity and concern for her: 'At that moment I felt so nice about it. Maybe it was something missing from my life, someone who carried the authority, even among directors, I have always felt there is hardly anyone who refuses, who says "no" firmly. If a person can distinguish between right and wrong, I am always with him. I appreciate that.'

While the team was waiting for the shoot to begin in earnest, Sunil learnt from a panicking Nargis back in Bombay that the rushes from the few days of shooting were no good. Now Sunil took over from Sukhdev. It was a major blow, but he had no choice. Raakhi notes that Sunil worked with a passion for cinema. For that he was willing to sacrifice anything. She regrets that his junoon was not appreciated enough. 'We don't have producers like V. Shantaram any more, who used to show his films in the villages before a commercial release as a pre-test, and if there was something wrong he would even burn his negatives. He could do that, but nowadays I don't think it is possible. Now filmmaking is just a business. Dutt sahib was different. His idea was, just press on regardless of the consequences or the cost. He took around a hundred people into the desert to live in tents for the shooting and tried to make things comfortable for everyone. It would have been difficult, but he had a large heart, just like Sanjay.'

His daughter Namrata also narrates how he was stubborn about details. Once, he wanted 100 camels for a scene—and refused to shoot with 99. What did this finally lead to? The cost of the film spiralled out of control. Sunil put the advances from his other films into the project, and mortgaged the house. Nargis could do nothing because she knew criticism would only upset him. She would visit the camp with the children every now and then, but she knew that her suggestions were likely to make him feel worse. Her job in most of his productions was to coordinate a steady supply of talent, material and money from Bombay. Her own knowledge of production was invaluable, and occasionally she could not help giving artistic and creative advice as well.

Sunil meanwhile concentrated on completing the film, as producer, director and actor. But her support gave him the courage to carry on. He wrote to her on 5 November 1969 from Pochina Camp.

> Jio Jio
> I love you—I love you—all my life I will be loving you. I wrote to you—Anju-Priya and Sanjay—I got all your letters—The work is going on well. We are starting today the scenes...at Reshma's village—Raakhi has done her scenes very well. Everyone is very co-operative... I get up everyday at 5 a.m.—discuss script and scenes with Ali—then do my make up and discuss with Sukhdev, do the shooting, in the evening we have early dinner and then some discussion of the film...

The film was all that really mattered at the time, but to help the crew relax, Sunil hired a projector so that the unit could occasionally watch other movies. However, the projector sent was of a poor quality, another instance of Sunil being misled by someone he trusted. Slowly, as things got worse, he began to feel more and more tense. Now he was beginning to let his anxiety show in front of Nargis, whose loving suggestions were no longer very welcome. He had to keep a restless, artistic crew in order, and no doubt the pressure was building up. After one of her slightly fraught trips to Pochina, as she reached Jaisalmer, Nargis wrote to him:

> This note is particularly to let you know and apologise if I have disturbed or annoyed you—please forgive me I did not mean to. I try my best to keep my mouth shut but I get carried away and annoy you—so I hope you have forgiven and forgotten.

But she could not resist a last attempt to help: 'I also wanted to remind you if I may to not to forget to take the last shot of the climax before the end.' One can almost imagine her screwing up all her courage to get the last line written quickly before she sent it off to Sunil. He was obviously annoyed at her suggestions but he wrote back to her on 12 December 1969:

> When you left—I went to the location and asked my apologies from Ram (the cameraman) in the presence of his assistants. Are you

happy now—I ask apologies from you also—for whatever I tell you—
not for lovely things—but for fighting things—I fight with you—
Because I love you—But Jio—you know how much agony and torture
I must be facing here—everything is so clear to you—when you come
here—I want to be happy. And you tell me about things that I already
know—I want to forget them because if I start thinking—I will not
be able to work—I thought you have been in show business—and
you understand the frustrations of an actor or actress—who does
not sell and whose pictures have been flops. If I start living in my
worries I will not be able to work—Therefore I don't think about
that part of my life—I think about today and today only—and you
come and start things that make me upset. You come and I feel these
few days you will give me lots and lots of happiness—that is what I
want from you—I am aware of my misfortunes—you have not to
keep on reminding me...

Today we have completed Mr Puri's and Vinod's work—Vinod has
done very well, the fight was good—I am sending the negative with
him.

When you came you thought you have brought raw stock—but
there were tapes (sound) only in that. We are completely bankrupt
as far as the raw stock is concerned—Do help us.

I send you Idd Mubarak—what did you do on Idd Day. I sent some
Muslim workers to Jaisalmer because they wanted to go and pray in
a Masjid—I gave them Rs 150 also. They are very happy and they
wrote a lovely letter to me—Rest of the people prayed here—Because
a Maulvi came here. In the evening we all ate together and village
singers came. Raaj Grover was the highlight. He came in Reshma's
dress and danced for hours with everyone...

Nargis had returned to Bombay and wrote to him on 15
December:

Darling Jio
Please please please don't humiliate me by asking for an apology—
why should you—I am at fault—I know I should not have mentioned
stupid things at the time when you are so worried—but let me assure
you that all these things happen in life (and) one should stand up
and fight them. Life is a constant struggle. I have that much of
confidence that from all the difficulties you will always come out
victorious. How can I ever discourage you—I am with you always
for ever. Please don't worry about all these things—

Let me tell you about 'Reshma Aur Shera'. I saw the climax and seeing it now I feel that this picture will be a picture which will also be an epic in years to come. It was very satisfying to see the end—it was ever so beautiful—I have a humble suggestion. Before 'The End' comes one feels there should be a long shot rather a crane shot, from the gun point and the dupatta fluttering. Then the camera should go back in a long shot and reveal that the bodies are completely covered and from there 'The End' should come forward and cover the screen. Without this shot the end looks incomplete. Now as the blower fans are not there with you, you could take this shot with the help of the helicopter—please do take it, if you don't like it you can throw it away later.

The raw stock must have reached you by now—we have sent 10 tins and making arrangements of another 5 tins which I will bring with me—please Jio do be a little careful with the raw stock—as after those 10 tins you will not get the same emulsion .

It was a long letter in which she described all the various arrangements she had made for actors to reach in time for their shoots in Pochina, and also about the arrangements she was making to acquire various loans to complete the film. She was clearly determined to make sure that the film was completed, but was also worried about Sunil's tendency to trust everyone.

'I am sure you will realize how difficult we are finding to include all such expenses (Sunil must have wanted to make a payment to someone). We must of course be helpful but to a certain limit. Sometimes people take a lot of advantage of your goodness. Anyway, God bless you for your tender heart it is also good to be kind to the needy. WE MUST CELEBRATE Ajanta Arts Anniversary on the 1st of Jan 1970 at Pali Hill. You must try your best.'

She was also trying to get the preview theatre ready by 1 January. 'Anyway we will definitely do our dubbing in our own theatre,' she wrote to him confidently. The children were well, she told him, and Priya even talked about him in her sleep, and carried his letter with her to school. She ended the letter on an upbeat note, which must have been very welcome to the man struggling in the desert in Pochina: 'We have made a wonderful picture. I am sure it will be among the 10 best films in the world.

Please don't get annoyed with me. I am silly but very much in love with you—I say these things to encourage you, give you strength to fight—Don't worry for anything—everything will be just fine.'

While *Reshma Aur Shera* cannot be counted among the 10 best films in the world, its artistic merit was appreciated and it did pick up at least three national awards from the Government of India: Waheeda Rehman for best actress, Ramchandra for best cameraman and Jaidev for the music. But for Sunil it was a personal blow as he always felt the film deserved more recognition than that, and he later suspected that there were people who did not want him to be honoured. Never one to admit defeat, he made an attempt to send the film abroad for participation in various festivals. It represented India at the Tashkent Film Festival in May and the Berlin Film Festival in June 1972. Nargis wrote to him on 25 April 1972, after trying to make the film's prints available for various international festivals. Money was short, which led to delays, but Nargis was somehow able to scrape together the required manpower and resources, while managing to sound cheerful:

Darling Jio
I rang you up yesterday—but was told you had gone to Leningrad. One Mr Saxena talked to me and I have informed him that the print is leaving from here by Air India on Thursday 27th. The Lab has given a lot of trouble—they have too much work and they take their own time—with great difficulty and after my running to the Lab every morning this work has been done. Regards the other two copies they say they can't take work in hand before the 5th of May. All the same we are trying to take at least one copy by Saturday so that we can shorten it and keep it ready for Berlin. Tashkent is not a competitive festival and the authorities have not yet written to us about the extension of the date. I feel we should drop Tashkent and concentrate on Berlin. We have already received the festival forms from Delhi...
I would suggest that you please go to Berlin and see that the picture is selected, we could send you the new copy with new script from here for you to subtitle into German. How will you manage money is a big problem—I just spoke to Universal Travels and they informed

me that they could send a PTA from here to travel from Moscow to
Berlin only we have to talk to Reserve Bank, so I will go there
tomorrow...
The print of *Yadein* and *Man-Ka-Meet* can be sent but not the cut
version because of the lack of money we can't buy raw stock and
have new prints made...

Sunil was nothing if not ambitious for his films. He chose
unconventional themes for his productions and was always
confident of pushing them forward. For him, each film he
produced, because it usually faced some problem or the other,
was a statement of his world view. Just as he felt that *Reshma
Aur Shera* was a classic, he felt his earlier experiment *Yaadein*
also deserved recognition. And just as *Reshma Aur Shera* won
other awards, so did *Yaadein* get a certificate of merit from the
Government of India: it won the award for best cinematography
in black and white, for Ramchandra. Sunil felt that it would do
well in festivals abroad and that was when he first discovered for
himself the difficulty of a mainstream, commercial filmmaker
trying to break into the clique of those who had been already
doing the rounds.

A few years earlier, in May 1965, Sunil had flown to Berlin,
thrilled that *Yaadein* had been officially selected by the Indian
government to represent the country at the Berlin Film Festival.
But when he arrived there he found that Satyajit Ray's *Kapurush-
O-Mahapurush* was also representing India. And waiting in the
wings was the Merchant Ivory production, *Shakespeare Wallah*.
He wrote to Nargis on 13 May 1965, from the Hotel Am Zoo
in Berlin:

It is God sent that I am in Berlin. I made inquiries and found out that
there is a very very small company which subtitles in Berlin—so we
rang up from London to Berlin festival authorities and they suggested
that we should get the subtitling done in Berlin and they can provide
all help to us.
We met Dr Baure, the director of the festival. After meeting him a lot
of things have come to light...Mr Ray actually wrote to Dr Baure
about 'Shakespeare walla...'

Sunil surmised that the festival director and the selection

committee at the Berlin Film Festival knew and had a lot of regard for Ray, who had once officiated as chairman of the jury. 'Germans feel that he is the only director who represents true India. So once again in this part of the world we have to face great, great opposition.' Sunil may have felt further disheartened by the information that only one film would be chosen from the three which had been suggested to the selection committee. He was keen to stay on in Berlin and have the film properly subtitled, but he also felt that he should simply return to his shooting schedule and a proposed trip to Kuwait with the members of Ajanta Arts Troupe. Finally he decided to return to Bombay, where he gave an interview expressing doubt about his film being chosen.

According to one news report, '"Had I known of this I would not have gone to Berlin at so much cost and expense and got a first class print made with sub titles in German. I would have stayed behind and only after being told that my film was selected, I would have gone to Berlin and spent money for sub-titling," said Sunil Dutt with an unconcealed tinge of frustration in his tone.'

It was a debate that, many years later, Nargis would bring up in parliament as a member of the Rajya Sabha: was Ray the only person who could represent India abroad, and were there not many commercial filmmakers who were equally talented? By 1965, many outstanding directors had already made their mark— Mehboob, Bimal Roy, Guru Dutt, Raj Kapoor.

Sunil did not give up, and *Yaadein* went to the Frankfurt International Film Festival where it won the Grand Prix. According to Sunil, 'It was the first one-actor feature film in the history of motion picture industry,' and therefore deserved the honour. However, when he came back from Berlin he could just about hide his unhappiness. He left almost immediately for Kuwait on 8 June with Ajanta Arts Troupe to raise money 'for the construction of a colony for cine and studio workers.' By now he had collected a few regulars for his troupe, which had been touring and staging shows for charity 'at Ludhiana, Nagpur, Baroda and Poona'. The troupe, according to one press report, comprised: Nargis, Sunil Dutt, Rajindernath, Johnny Walker,

Geeta Dutt, Mahindra Kapoor, Anwar Hussain, Shammi, Bhalla, Prem Dhawan, Manohar Deepak, Madhumati, and Gopi Krishna. They would perform skits, songs and dances. Over the years this group had become very close.

Shammi laughs helplessly remembering what a disaster it was when they reached Kuwait, because due to a mix-up, the auditorium was nearly empty! She remembers: 'We used to have a lot of fun, in India and when we went abroad as well to collect funds, like when we went to Kuwait and Beirut. But that mission did not work out, because the rumour spread that we were collecting funds for the war with Pakistan, and so the show did not take off! We did the show but there was hardly any audience. Nargis and I would perform, and then come backstage and start laughing. Dutt sahib took it much more seriously, and used to go on scolding us, and we would go on laughing. Then he would get angry, because he was in charge, and say we must have discipline. We would ask, "You mean we can't laugh and crack jokes?" He used to get very upset. Nargis and I used to laugh quite a lot, and he would say, "*Again* you've started laughing!" And she would retort, "We can say the same thing to you, *again* you've got angry."' It was this indomitable spirit, however, that saw them through the bad experiences of both *Yaadein* and *Reshma Aur Shera*.

There was no doubt that *Reshma Aur Shera* was financially a disaster. His friends remember that for the first time, the constant stream of visitors to the bungalow at 58 Pali Hill stopped. It was the one time when Sunil really felt the brunt of what he had done, because there was simply no money, and the creditors were at the door. As often happens, work also dried up because he was now perceived to be bad news. He was 40, had three children and a wife to look after, and he knew that he had to fight back. People began offering him smaller and smaller roles and he refused to take them because he felt he still had to maintain his self-respect. Fortunately, the preview theatre, their khazana, was functioning and they hired it out occasionally for dubbing and viewing. Friends like Raakhi did not desert them: she insisted on doing all the dubbing for her films at the theatre. With others using the theatre as well, slowly the situation improved, though not by much. As Sunil often said, he had been there before. He had come to Bombay with nothing, and slept on the pavement, so he had no fears for himself. But he did worry about his children who were unused to hardship, and Sanjay of course had just been sent to boarding school.

The children do not remember any change in their lifestyle. They had been brought up to live simply, not like the children of film stars, so there was never any reason to feel deprived. The necessities were always available to them. In an interview with Bhawna Somaya, Sunil said that he had been advised to declare bankruptcy at this time. His worst moment came when when he was unable to get the money together to send a new print of *Reshma Aur Shera* to Berlin and Tashkent. His financier had already lost money and refused to invest any more in the film, so the print that was finally sent was full of scratches.

A few offers finally trickled in during those lonely and dark days and he signed *Heera*, *Pran Jaaye Par Vachan Na Jaaye* and *Geeta Mera Naam*, all released in 1973-74, which slowly pulled him out of debt. Nargis showed her incomparable fortitude. She even rang up friends and castigated them for not dropping in and meeting him now that he was so depressed. She, more than anyone else, understood the vagaries of the film profession. She remembered the time in her childhood when her mother had been forced to sell her jewellery, another time when they sold their studio, and so on. Further, like Sunil, she was very down-to-earth and could adapt to any situation. Sunil remembered her darning the children's socks during this period and saving all the loose change for use in an emergency. He had signed up some films but the money was not enough. He realized that he may have to shut down his beloved Ajanta Arts office. Raaj Grover remembers that painful moment.

'One day he called everyone to the office. Sarwar Hussain (Anwar's older son) who used to handle everything, the accountant and I were there. And he said, "As an actor I am not that great. As a producer as well, there are a lot of expenses. I want to take it easy and apart from the accountant, I should let everyone else go. The circumstances are very bad." For about five minutes we were all quiet, we were all shocked, what has he said? Then I spoke up, and I said the office will remain open. Whatever work has to be done will be done, but no one will get paid. That's the only difference, and it will be no problem for us.'

Meanwhile Raaj decided to call in some favours and sniff out some good stories to film. He had a chat with K.K. Shukla, a writer who usually wrote for Manmohan Desai and had a lot of respect for Sunil. He had a story in mind. Raaj says, 'I said this is what has happened in our office yesterday. If you give this story to us...why don't I talk to Dutt sahib? I also went to Vinod Khanna, he was shooting in Modern Studio. (He had been introduced by Sunil in *Man ka Meet*.) I spoke to him and said that you were also part of this office, and this is what happened yesterday, and this is what Dutt sahib said. At four o'clock that evening, Vinod came to the office and said, "Dutt sahib, start a film." I called K.K. Shukla also, and we narrated his story to Dutt sahib. Vinod Khanna was at the top at the time. Dutt sahib got some oxygen (Bollywood speak for "breathing space") and the same night he spoke to Raj Khosla. Premnath was spoken to.'

But what about the money?

'Dutt sahib had two cars. One Mercedes and one Jaguar. He gave the Merc to Vinod and the Jaguar to Premnath, and then he made *Nehle Pe Dehla*, recovering all his money.' It was not exactly the Antony and Cleopatra he had promised her during the shooting of *Padosan*, but Sunil signed up his petite heroine from the film, Saira Bano.

Nehle Pe Dehla was an action-packed cops-and-robbers tale, a far cry from *Reshma Aur Shera*. It was also a lost-and-found story of two brothers and a blind mother. Sunil was the good brother who was on the side of the law, while Vinod played the baddie. The film was full of car chases with Sunil bashing up loads of colourful smugglers, one of them played by Premnath in a golden wig shouting 'Copacabana!' excitedly at regular intervals.

Sunil left nothing to chance. After *Reshma Aur Shera*, he decided to pull out all the stops. Saira was the 'sexy' actress at the moment and he exploited her image to the hilt. Saira had no problem with that; after all, she points out, she had the best legs in the business and Sunil was aware of that. Saira recollects: 'When I started working with Dutt sahib, I realized more and more what a wonderful man he was. *Nehle Pe Dehla* was his own home production. But in that he had all the things you see in the movies today, such as *Dhoom*. We were all on motorbikes, in black leather, Vinod, myself, Dutt sahib. I wore leather hot pants, Dutt sahib was ahead of his times! By then, I had started putting on weight, and he said, "Sairaji, what are you doing to yourself? Do you know you had the best figure in the industry? *Aap theek kijeye apne aap ko* (Please sort yourself out)."'

They were neighbours, so working together was very convenient. Her make-up room was on the terrace of her house, and the shoot was usually on the terrace of Sunil's house. When the shot was ready, someone from the unit would yell across to her from the terrace, '*Aa jaao*, REEAAAADY!' And her make-up artist would step out and say, '*Aatey hain* (We're coming).' She says, 'I told Dutt sahib there should be a straight bridge between the two homes and then I could ride across on my motorbike.'

Between *Reshma Aur Shera* and *Nehle Pe Dehla*, there were about 14 other films in which Sunil was just the actor. And he acted in another 20 before he made his next film, which was to launch his son Sanjay. For him the aftermath of *Reshma Aur Shera* also provided a much needed break to take stock and reflect. He finally knew he wanted to move on from cinema—but towards what?

The Family
1970s

In May 1969, Sunil was shooting for the film *Meri Bhabhi* in Yusmarg, Kashmir. He went out for a walk alone and when he did not return, everyone, including his co-star Waheeda Rehman, panicked. They scoured the adjoining mountains with the help of the army and the police. He returned the next morning, completely exhausted and close to tears at having found the unit after experiencing a 'rendezvous with death'. He had crossed a stream using a plank of wood, but the plank had shifted position by the time he crossed it again, and he could not find his way back. So he spent the night wandering the hillside.

On his return, Sunil went to a dargah to offer thanks. He said in newspaper interviews later that the experience made him understand that the time for death was preordained, and it would not come before its time. It was to be one of Sunil's many close encounters with death in the years to come.

Next year he returned to Yusmarg to stare down death and fear. In a letter he wrote to Nargis, it is clear that he had outgrown cinema and needed a greater arena. This philosophical letter reveals his changing vision of the world.

It was a vision inspired by the Bhagwad Gita and triggered by his memory of that dreadful night, as he wrote on 7 May 1970, at 12.30 a.m., from 'THE SAME HUT IN YUSMARG JUNGLE':

Jan Jio
It is past midnight. The night is very dark. Outside the only sound is of the stream water, when the water strikes the stones and rocks, it makes a peculiar sound—it is amazing that this same sound is

beautiful at times, painful and frightening at times.

The sound tonight is peculiar—I did not feel like this,when I was here last year. I think that night I was struggling for my survival and nothing existed for me, but for my fight to live. Tonight is different. I came prepared to spend the night here. I know it is frightening and dangerous; but Jio life itself is a constant fear and danger, then why not live dangerously, have different experiences with life.

Believe me Jio I do not do all this for my publicity or personal glory. I do it to grow myself, to find myself, we live in the world of make believe and people are all the time around you. One has lots of worldly problems and you get lost in that. You forget yourself, you are swayed away by the tides of the world. But the moments like this make you find yourself. Here I am away from civilization, away from the madding crowds, away from you, my children, my near and dear ones. Here I am by myself, finding out myself.

Who am I?

What am I?

Why am I?

And I fail to understand, because the Truth is,

I AM NOTHING

Then why these attachments, why these belongings, the feeling of possessing, feeling of authority, feeling of owning.

I feel I should not argue with you. I should not quarrel with you. I should not interfere with whatever you do. Because you are also born in this world to find yourself and I feel through your Karma, through your work, deeds, and your personal efforts alone you can find yourself. I will try, Jio, to mend myself, never to annoy you. We have to perform our duties of husband and wife.

We are not there to control, command and dictate our authority that again becomes personal, our karmas are our own, our relationship is different, that again is a karma that we are to be husband and wife, to bring to this universe children and to educate them, to marry them, to grow them and make them settle down in life. But Karma does not expect any results. My job is to perform my duty sincerely, faithfully. If I work to gain, if I do my duty with the expectations of lovely results, then I am selfish, then I am polluting the thoughts of Karma. And I feel we are all polluted people. Because I married a woman and I want that she should do everything that I like or I love my children and expect that they should also love me, then I am not sincere...

That is what Lord Krishna said to Arjun, you have to do your work (Karma) and not ask or expect any gains or victories.

When I am here all alone I am feeling a peculiar pain, a pain of humiliation. The self in me and the man is exposed and I find myself a man, who has to do, do and do, and live to do. My work, my duties, my karmas.

Jio I love you, I love you very much. But I do not hate anyone. Try to understand me Jio, think coolly about me.

What am I?

Why am I?

Who am I?

Try to find me out. I might have pained you a lot, but I am finding myself. That self that will never inflict pain on another. That self that will never lose his temper. That self that will never live for himself, that self that will never have any ego. I am finding that self in me. When will I be able to find myself? When will this search end? Will I succeed or will I die an unsatisfied man, as a man of the gutters of the world?

That is why I am here my love. I have not come away from you all. You all are with me right here. But I am not to be found. That 'me' is not there. I am here to ask from this divine atmosphere, from this pious air that I am breathing. But there is no answer. The only sound is of the stream water. It is so constant...As if the sound is the constant cry of all mankind, that we all are in search.

H.T.

1:30 a.m.

The letter gives us a profound insight into Balraj Dutt the man, more than Sunil Dutt the actor. Balraj, the idealist who had come to Bombay and wanted to do something 'important' was not enchanted by the world of cinema. The down-to-earth farmer's son knew that it was only a means of putting bread on the table. He never imagined that any of his children would actually join this world of make-believe. He wanted to educate them and give them a better life.

He was also more and more uncomfortable with the massive 'ego' one had to have to succeed in cinema. The actor, director or producer had to love themselves first, and the moment they stopped, only tragedy lay ahead. There were many examples: Guru Dutt, Meena Kumari, Madhubala. Like Nargis, he wanted to do something selfless and more meaningful.

At this point, he was still too involved in earning money and paying off his debts to think of a break from cinema. After the *Reshma Aur Shera* debacle, he had to work doubly hard to get good roles. But he managed to pull his career together again, using all the goodwill others showed him, and humility. There was no producer or director or star he was unwilling to work with. Gradually he managed to regain lost ground, and 1977 saw the release of seven of his films.

Though he had a hectic schedule, he remained close to his family and carried on looking after Rani and Som. His mother would also visit him whenever possible from the village. The support he gave to them was made possible by Nargis, who took an active interest in everyone's life. As most people were scared of Dutt sahib, she was the arbitrator.

Som remembers, 'He was a very practical person. He was a self-made man who carved out his own career by working hard, by forgoing comforts, often not even getting enough to eat. (When he arrived in Bombay) he had no one to help him, no relative, no friend, yet, he in turn wanted to help all his relatives.

'Bhabhiji used to be the one we spoke to, she was like a mother. After she died, we started talking to Dutt sahib, otherwise it was always her. No one had the guts to talk to him directly. He was actually very soft, he would not shout at anyone, but everyone respected him, and behaved themselves when he was around. Discipline was very important to him. When he was not around, everyone was relaxed, but the moment he came in, everyone would rush to take their places.

'If he was in the room, I never had the guts to try to sit on a chair, even if it was vacant. Even though I had got married, I could not do it. He would himself say, "Dewan, why don't you sit down?"'

Puneeta, Som's wife, says that it was Nargis who decided that they should live in Sunil's old flat on Napean Sea Road. Sunil's mother asked him why he couldn't let Som and his wife live with him since he had such a big bungalow on Pali Hill.

Puneeta recollects, 'Bhabhiji explained that at her parental home, her two sisters-in-law used to live together. Despite being real sisters, she said, there was so much tension that the younger one, Rashida, became mentally unstable. There is no doubt that every woman would like to run her own home, and Bhabhi felt that she would not like to see any pressure on her younger sister-in-law. She said, "Anytime you want to come, you are welcome." She had kept a room for us in that house, with an attached bath, and a cupboard for our clothes. Usually Saturdays and Sundays we would be there. They had a preview theatre there, so movies would be shown and we would go with the kids, watch films. If we didn't go there for a few days, there would be a call from her, she would usually call in the mornings and say, "Where are you?"'

Som adds, 'Dutt sahib said, "Som is a very happy-go-lucky person, and now that he has got married, he must understand his responsibility. He will always be welcome in this house, but if he remains with us he will not appreciate his responsibility."'

Sunil wanted to protect his younger brother. He hoped that he would grow up and face the real world and not get too involved in the world of cinema. However, Som, who worked with Ajanta Arts, was so carried away by the glamour of the film world he still insisted he wanted to be an actor.

It was a crisis for Sunil. The more he wanted to steer his family away from the film industry, the more deeply it seemed to embrace them. In his brusque fashion, he refused Som. He told him to ask for anything else in the world, but not this.

It was 1965, and Sunil was at the peak of his career. There was enough money in the bank, and suddenly he was under pressure from all sides. His mother also asked him why, if he was an actor, he would not help his brother become one.

Normally, Sunil could not refuse his mother anything. How could he explain to her his own constant misgivings about the industry?

Nargis, with whom Som and Puneeta came to stay for a while when Sunil was away, decided to try and persuade her recalcitrant husband and wrote to him. The letter is carefully constructed: she did not raise the topic immediately, but first asked about Sunil's health and then told him about her own slightly frail state, as she was low and depressed then. She knew that her husband would listen or 'read' better if he was feeling sympathetic towards the writer of the letter!

The letter, dated 27 August 1965, said:

The next chapter of this letter is about another big factor, that is 'Som'. Puneeta and myself, we have been talking. Jio, why can't you understand that it is Som's desire to work in films, why do you want to stop him? I don't see any harm in his working in films. Neither do you let him do anything on his own nor do you want to help him in any way. He can't pay any attention to office work because his heart is not in it. Why do you want to force him into being a clerk? You go out of your way to help people...and lose money. Why don't you establish your own brother?

Now don't get angry with me but try to understand. Som is 30 years old. He has a wife and will become a father soon, you mean to say he should have no desires to become something in life.

In his case you are acting like an absolute dictator. He does not have guts to face you and talk to you. If you ask him he will say and do as you want him to. But you are like a father to him, you must try to make him stand on his own feet. If one member becomes big in the family it is his duty to see that he settles everyone else in the family well. Not that you have not done things for the family, you have done more than anyone else could do. My only wish is that Som should have an individuality, he should be established and should be known as SOM DUTT and not as Sunil Dutt's brother.

Jio, why I write all this to you is because I love you and I don't want anyone in the family or outside to say (anything) bad about you. Let people misunderstand me, I don't care as long as you understand me, that is all I care for.

Darling Jio you have lost so much of money, people have cheated you, but even if you take a risk and lose money in this venture to make Som a star I feel you would have done your duty. As a matter of fact I have a feeling that if Som gets a good break, he will make a name for himself. Please think it over without getting angry with me.

Yours for ever and in all the births to come,

Pia

Despite all his efforts at 'detachment', Sunil could never really refuse Nargis anything. And hers was a powerful argument. He had always felt he was the head of the family since his father's death, though his mother was still alive. In the Punjabi tradition, when the father dies, the pagri or turban is transferred to the eldest son's head.

And so plans were made for a new film.

Man ka Meet (1968) had a fairly pedestrian plot, but it did well because it introduced a host of newcomers. Vinod Khanna (who was later to help Sunil out by acting in his money-making *Nehle Pe Dehla*) had met Sunil at a party, and was offered a role. Leena Chandavarkar was another newcomer, besides Som.

Raaj Grover gives an insight into how films used to be put together in those days. It was a cafeteria approach, with the producer looking around and picking his cast from those who turned up looking for work. 'At that time Subba Rao was a top filmmaker. He had made *Milan* as well as *Darpan*, and so Subba Rao was signed. Rajinder Krishen was signed as writer and then there was a new girl. The screen test was taken and she was okayed. Leena Chandavarkar. We signed Om Prakash, and Manmohan as a villain. His son is a very successful producer now, Nitin Manmohan. He was very close to Dutt sahib.

'One evening he took Dutt sahib to a party. He went reluctantly. He met Vinod Khanna at the party and asked him if he would like to work in films. He said he would. And so he called him to the office the next day. Immediately Dutt sahib made out a letter for Vinod. But his parents were very orthodox. They thought a film career was a road to self-destruction. However, his father knew my father, who was the president of the Arya Samaj and a highly respected man. Vinod took me to his house and when Vinod's father learnt that I am Master Dina Nath's son (my father was a teacher), he thought maybe this line is not all that bad. That's how the film *Man ka Meet* began.'

But before all that, Som had to be trained for cinema. Years later Sanjay would be put through the same routine. A fight-master, Veeru Devgan (Ajay Devgan's father) was hired to teach him to fight, and he was asked to go swimming, diet, lose weight, learn Urdu and join an acting class.

Puneeta remembers with dread that there was also 'dance. He hired a master called Hira Lal from Madras who made Somji cry by making him dance so much. Dutt sahib told him to break every bone in his body so that when he dances on screen it should look like he is a professional dancer. He was sent away from here to Madras in order to concentrate. Dutt sahib said, "You are not supposed to meet your wife or children."'

Som, who thought becoming an actor should have been simpler, kept begging Sunil to stop the torture and start the film. Finally, he used his old trick from childhood: he stopped eating. Sunil had to capitulate. He sent his wife and children to Madras and finally allowed work to begin.

Sunil was too busy with his acting commitments to be present throughout the shoot, but when he was, Som would invariably have a difficult time. His brother expected the best from him, which was simply not possible all the time.

Som says. 'Once we were shooting in Darjeeling and he came to see it. A song was being shot on top of a train, with dancers, and there were quite a few retakes. I could not get my steps right. Dutt sahib got really furious with me. He took a stick and started whacking me with it. He hit Sanju like that too in front of the unit, when he was shooting *Rocky*, years later.

'That evening I went for a drink with an army officer, and said, "Today I have been really humiliated, I was hit so badly." And he said, "Don't worry, he is your older brother after all." I really worked on that dance after that. Finally, I asked my dance master Hira Lal, when my brother sees this dance, what do you think he will say? He said he would "be very happy with you".'

But there were other moments when it seemed the film would never be made, largely due to Som's nervousness and Sunil's impatience at 'dangerous' shots. In the early days and indeed till even very recently, not many precautions were taken to ensure the safety of the actors when they were shooting action sequences. The actors would sometimes use a double for the stunts, but close-ups required them to do at least a few scenes, so injuries were common. (Nargis often recollected the famous swimsuit scene in *Awara* when she took a dive into a pond which had been specially constructed on the sets. One side of the pond was shallow and she seriously hurt her head. And then, of course, there was the fire on the sets of *Mother India*.)

Usually the actors would do whatever was required with the minimum fuss, but at times Som was scared. Raaj remembers an incident. 'When we were shooting in Kalimpong for *Man ka Meet*, Sanju was still a small boy. One scene was set on top of a hill. There was going to be a fight between Vinod Khanna and Som Dutt. Vinod had to punch him and Som had to go rolling down the hill. Som started suggesting alternative ways of doing the scene (not realizing that) the actors are in no position to suggest anything to the director of the film. Actually, Som was frightened.

'Dutt sahib was standing there. So Dutt sahib first thought, let Subba Rao convince him. But when he saw that he had not been able to persuade him, he asked Subba Rao if he could talk to Som. Som said, "If I roll down from here, there are stones below, and I'll get hurt." Dutt sahib didn't lose his temper with him, because after all he was the hero of the film and his brother as well. But he picked up Sanjay, twirled him around and threw him down the slope. And then asked, "Now will you do it?"'

Luckily, Sanjay was not hurt and Som gave the shot without a murmur.

Puneeta has a postscript to the traumatic shoot. 'But look at Dutt sahib's personality. If he hit Somji or upbraided him, he must have felt bad. After the film was over he sent all of us, including Bhabhiji, Anju, Sanju, me, my kids, to Darjeeling for a month-long holiday, just to relax and have a good time.'

Namrata too has many happy memories of her father. 'Dad used to be very busy, so we hardly saw him. But on every weekend, he would take us out. It was a ritual, every Sunday, Borivili National Park. We would go in this minivan, with other relatives, usually Rehana and Amarjeet (Rehana married Amarjeet, Sunil's friend and Dev Anand's publicist) and have a proper picnic, with a tent. Then sometimes we'd go for a few days to Madh Island. Some Sundays we would book a room at the Sun-n-Sand hotel and learn swimming. Horse riding on the beach. Cycling. All the sports came from my father. Mom gave us more cultural exposure.

'I took the longest to learn to swim, so he got very upset.

One day he caught me and threw me into the deep, and I just sank, I just drowned, and my mother was hysterical. I have no memory of this. He got frightened and pulled me out and I'd drunk a whole lot of water. I didn't even attempt to struggle or swim. My mother spanked me out of fright and said, "Why didn't you even try to swim?" And I said, "But Dad threw me!" I didn't care, because whatever he did was right.'

The children grew up with strict rules, especially the two girls. Shammi remembers laughingly how Sunil wanted them to dress in a salwar kameez the moment they began to grow up. His argument was that that was how girls dressed in the villages and there was nothing wrong with it. Nargis would hold her head and say, 'But this is Bombay! They can't wear salwar kameez here!' Finally, as in other things, she managed to convince him.

There were rules about the time the children had to be home—usually by sunset. They would be out playing most of the day, because the entire area around their house was open and green in those days. There were no high-rises and their friends included the kids who lived in the buildings nearby as well as the children of their driver and cook. Priya remembers helping the driver's daughter finish her housework, make rotis and sweep the house, so that they could escape for a few hours outside to play.

But it was a strict upbringing. There were no sleepovers at friends' homes. There were no TV sets in bedrooms, only one family TV set, and Sunil insisted they had to watch programmes together. There was only one air-conditioner in the house, so everyone had to sleep in the same room in summer.

Namrata says, 'I think I was closer to my dad. Like any other teenager I also had problems and I came really close to my dad when I was 13-14 years old. Because Mom was with us all the time I felt she didn't understand me. I am also very much like my dad, much more serious and disciplined. I want things organized, I want everything to be perfect. He knew that. "If I have to buy a gift or even write a thank you card," he would say, "Anju will do it." My mom used to correct me in front of friends and that used to upset me a lot. So I used to tell him, "I will confide in you, I won't confide in her." This could be things like if I haven't done well in my studies, it could be anything.

'Of course she would only criticize me in front of very, very close friends or family, but it still upset me. She didn't mean to hurt me. She was just very transparent about everything. But if I wanted to do anything, like bunk school, I wouldn't tell her, I'd tell my dad.'

Priya adds, 'My first clear memory is about us when I was seven. My father was a working dad. We knew he was in the movies but I had no idea that he was a film-star. He never took us to any shootings or anything. Neither did Mom. We were not allowed to call him on the sets. He was a very strict dad. When he came home, we all had to be there, waiting. And if we were watching TV together, we were really watching it. Mom's attention had to be there, our attention had to be there. He was never an aggressive father but he used to sulk if you ignored him or did not sit with him. He would always say, "What's the point of coming home if no one talks to me?"'

The preview theatre also became a bone of contention. Sunil had told the family that they were not supposed to watch the films screened there unless invited. They broke that rule more often than they kept it and found elaborate reasons to go down to watch films if he was not around.

Priya remembers, 'There would be trials and sometimes people would have their own private screening. Mom would go and see most of the films. We kids would also go and watch the films from the projection room. Mom had kept a guard. The guard would tell us when Dad was coming and then all of us would run back to the house.'

Nargis encouraged them to be enterprising, telling them that if they wanted pocket money, they must earn it. So Namrata and Priya got their gang of friends together and decided to have a cartoon show, with the cartoon movies their parents had got them, their projector, and the screen from the 'rich kid' next door. Tickets were sold at five rupees each to the children and their ayahs.

The family had a monthly account with a local shopkeeper, for groceries. Without informing Nargis, the gang bought Coke and wafers on this account, to have during the show. They made Rs 1600 from the show, which was shared equally among the gang members.

The kids also performed plays. Make-up and costumes were looked after by Namrata. Some of these one-act plays were adapted from books from Nargis's library. She would help with the direction occasionally. They'd sell tickets and earn more 'pocket money'.

Namrata considered her father the indulgent parent, while Priya was almost physically attached to her mother. 'I would be home for lunch around 3 p.m. and I would be really upset if she wasn't at home. She would make me do homework, and used to check it, and was very fussy about the whole thing. I would say, "All right, I will learn everything, but you read it out to me." I would lie down with my head on her lap and she would read out an English chapter to me. It was like a story, and I would go to sleep. And she would get really mad. And then books would go flying around the place. We knew our mother had a temper, she would get really mad, and then she would cool down really quickly as well.

'I would tag along with her everywhere. Maybe I was insecure. I was constantly behind her, holding her saree pallav. Didi and Bhaiya did not want to go with her. But she would say, "Come with me," and I would be ready for all her functions. I would go and not get bored.'

Meanwhile, Nargis began to expand her social work after a meeting with Dr Mithu Alur, who set up the Spastic Society of India.

Mithu was around 27 then, and 'fiery and idealistic'. Her daughter Malini is a spastic: a child born with an intelligent mind trapped in a disobedient body. She was determined to help other parents in similar situations. Some of her friends were working in the prime minister's office. Indira Gandhi was very supportive and had read an article Mithu had written for the *Illustrated Weekly of India* and understood the issue. The five minutes that Mithu had been given for a meeting with her stretched to half an hour, and shortly afterwards, P.N. Haksar gave her a list of people to meet in Bombay to push forward her project. It was a list of twelve eminent people, including Balraj Sahni and Nargis Dutt.

Mithu knew very little about Hindi cinema and had not seen *Mother India*. But she was excited by the thought that by bringing the 'Ingrid Bergman of India' into this area of social work, she could introduce some glamour into a relentlessly hard struggle. She was in for a surprise, because at her first meeting with Nargis at her Pali Hill bungalow, she realized she was meeting a very simple and professional woman. Nargis was dressed in white, with very little make-up, her trademark rudraksh around her neck. It had been given to her by Muktananda Baba, whose ashram was on the outskirts of Bombay, and whose disciple she was.

Mithu remembers what Nargis said to her: 'All my life I have wanted to be a doctor, and so this is a wonderful opportunity for me, and of course I will be patron. But I want to know everything about cerebral palsy. I want to be a worker.'

Nargis helped raise funds and brought in other celebrities as well. Eventually the Spastic Society was able to get a large plot of land and set up a school in Colaba, where it is housed today.

As often happened with Nargis, the relationship became a deeply personal one. Mithu says they were as close as sisters. Nargis helped Mithu through her messy divorce and later, was there to celebrate her happy marriage to Sathi Alur. Nargis was at the Spastic Society nearly every day, though it meant she had to travel from one end of town to the other. Mithu does not remember going to Pali Hill for any work, it was always Nargis who drove down.

Nargis was not a political person but a key social worker, says Mithu nostalgically, adding that she has rarely come across this level of sincerity. Nargis would get down on her hands and knees and teach the children. Priya went with her at times and learnt to appreciate the qualities the children possessed despite their handicap. It was a valuable lesson, as years later she too would begin regular work at the society.

Nargis usually had a very busy day. She would work with various charities or meet other commitments in the morning, then drive down to the Spastic Society and spend time there. Afterwards, she picked up Namrata from college—Namrata was studying commercial art at Sophia College—on the way back and try to make it home in time for Priya's return from school.

Gia, who became her personal secretary, says that there was always a long list of invitations addressed to Nargis, despite all the years that had passed since her last film. But she was careful about lending her support and wanted to know all the details about an organization before she got involved.

Some things, however, simply did not work out. In 1971, Nargis had been appointed president of the Indian Motion Pictures Producers' Association. The producers' association had split by then and it was felt that she had the right connections and respect in the industry to pull them together again. A united front was needed for effective lobbying for concessions, and her closeness to the Gandhi family had been noted.

The *Film Industry* newspaper said on 24 September 1971:

MOVE FOR UNITY
Once again film producers in Bombay are making a sincere effort to achieve unity among themselves. This time the lead has come from dynamic Mrs Nargis Dutt, the first and only lady president of a film organization in India. She is known for her infinite capacity for organization. She has a grace and charm which can win over any opposition.

The main issues were 'economic imbalances and unemployment in the production sector.' She also had to appeal to breakaway factions to come back to the fold but Nargis was no politician and it wasn't easy to persuade producers to behave in a way that would ensure an as yet elusive 'unity'.

Her nephew Arif says, 'In IMPPA, she did her best. She had the personality and the name, and she could stand up for anything, approach the government for anything. She was on very close terms with the Nehru/Gandhi family and they used to call her for breakfast and lunch at their home.'

Her political connections notwithstanding, Nargis found it hard. There were too many deep-seated problems between large and small production houses, not to mention sharp regional interests. It was a fulltime job.

Shammi has a different point of view: 'When she became the president of IMPPA, I told her, "Why are you taking it on?" She should not have agreed to it. Producers never combine for anything together, there are too many rivalries, and she left within six months. There was nothing she could contribute. One person would do this, and the other person would do exactly the opposite. There was never any ekta (unity).'

This did not stop her from being appointed to other positions in the 1970s: Justice of the Peace for Maharashtra in 1972, member of the Telephone Advisory Board, a juror at two international film festivals (Prague and Moscow), member of the Children's Film Society, member of the Mahila Samaj, executive chairman of the Meena Kumari Memorial for the Blind, president of the War Widows Association, member of the executive council of the Film and Television Insititute, Pune, and a life member of the Federation for the Welfare of the Mentally Retarded, New Delhi.

Over the years, the Dutts had assiduously maintained their connections in the film and political world, national and international. Nargis had a headstart over Sunil as she had very early on learnt to rub shoulders with the crème de la crème—due to Jaddanbai's training, and not, as many thought, due to Raj Kapoor.

Zahida says, trying to set the record straight: 'She knew everyone, the who's who. She mingled with the elite anyway. Raj Kapoor and she were together only when they went abroad as delegates. After all, look at Raj Kapoor's family background. Prithviraj had been a struggling stage actor. On the other hand, my grandmother, when she was a singer, had sung in the courtyards of maharajas where they were taught before being presented in the durbar, how to conduct themselves in front of royalty, how to talk, how to behave. They were sent almost into a finishing school, though they may have had very little education. So Jaddanbai knew all that, and that is perhaps where Nargis would have learnt the social graces as well. And then Nargis was in an English medium school. Queen Mary's was a very big school, and we were all properly educated. When we sat with royalty or with foreigners, we knew exactly what to do. She taught me ballroom dancing. She was a fantastic ballroom dancer, especially the waltz. See her in *Raat Aur Din* in the song '*Dil ki gerah khol do, chup na baitho* (Open up your heart, and don't be silent).' She was pregnant with Priya at the time, and she is wearing that black dress, with her hair all done up. There was in my opinion no actress of the calibre of Nargis.'

The first time that Nargis travelled abroad with a film delegation was in 1952. She went to Hollywood as part of an Indian film delegation which included Raj Kapoor, Premnath and Bina Rai. They toured the studios and met celebrities such as Greer Garson, Dana Andrews, Gregory Peck, Esther Williams, Yul Brynner, Walt Disney and Cecil B. DeMille. The experience had a huge impact on Nargis, as she said in interviews upon her return. She noticed that each studio was constructed and designed for various scenes, complete with permanent streets, houses, ponds—like a city, in fact. But everywhere she went, she was disappointed that the impression of India was still of 'a land of snakes and elephants.' And worst of all, no Indian film had been commercially released in America at the time.

In pleasant contrast was her first visit to Russia in 1954. Some of her films, *Awara* in particular, had already been released there. She found she was recognized as 'Our Rita' everywhere. In America, people had been curious about her saree, but in Russia 'people treated me like one of them'.

During her travels she began to make more friends abroad. One such star, as she said in an interview with Mohan Bawa (*Current*, 1 October 1977) was someone she met with Sunil: Sophia Loren. They met on the sets at a studio in Rome. The Dutts promptly invited her and Carlo Ponti for a chicken curry dinner. Nargis cooked the meal. Sophia came straight from the studio, make-up and all, and stretched out 'languidly' on the carpet after the meal, completely relaxed with her new Indian friends.

The Dutts were never very far from the world of global politics, either. Their friends and contacts in the political field expanded over the years. Some of these contacts had turned into deep friendship by the 1970s. In 1975, a state of Emergency had been declared by Indira Gandhi. This followed an adverse judgment against her in the Delhi High Court in a case about the misuse of official facilities during an election. She was also facing an agitation over inflation and other hardships due to the quadrupling of oil prices in late 1973. There had been a national rail strike. The situation was precarious for Indira Gandhi who only six years previously had split the Congress and created a large lobby of grumpy old men who could not bear to see the woman they had called *gungi gudiya* in 1966 take on such a commanding role.

The Emergency saw the repression of press freedom and the imprisonment of many political leaders from the Opposition, including the veteran leader Jayaprakash Narayan. She called for elections in 1977 and to her surprise lost to a motley coalition of parties which contested as the Janata Party.

There were very few Indira loyalists left by then, and among those few were Nargis and Sunil Dutt, who even campaigned for her when she contested the elections again.

Sonia Gandhi, Indira Gandhi's daughter-in-law and future president of the Congress Party, was to acknowledge this in a *Times of India* interview on 26 September 2005, after Sunil Dutt's death. 'He was a close family friend. In 1977, when my mother-in-law (Indira Gandhi) was out of power and had been harassed and humiliated, Sunil Dutt stood by her and was always at her side, at a time when most people were leaving her.'

It must have been a stressful time, because the Dutts were going against the tide. But for Nargis, who had now known the Nehru-Gandhi family personally for over two decades, it would have been difficult to take any other stand. According to Rehana, Nargis and Sunil had been among the few invitees to Sonia and Rajiv Gandhi's wedding. Nargis had bought Sonia a necklace as a wedding gift. The relationship had lasted through the generations, but it was cemented during Indira's dark days after the Emergency.

The Dutts were also moving in political circles abroad. On 22 January 1977, the newly elected president of the United States of America, Jimmy Carter, and his wife received the Dutts at the White House. M.V. Kamath's report in the *Times of India* read:

DUTTS GREETED AT CARTER'S NEW HOME

The President and Mrs Carter yesterday graciously received the Indian film star, Sunil Dutt and Nargis Dutt, the first Indians to be received at the White House since the Carters moved in.

The President remembered that Dutt had called on him at his home in Plains, Georgia, and presented him with a silk lungi and kurta.

Dutt kissed the First Lady on both cheeks while Nargis Dutt presented her with a hand knit Kulu Shawl that Mrs Carter praised as 'beautiful'.

The President introduced Dutt to newsmen present as 'the Robert Redford of India', a description originally offered by Mr Carter's mother in an interview to 'The Washington Star'.

In answer to queries by newsmen on the state of Indo-US relations, Dutt said he believed they will improve because the people of India have a great deal of affection for Mr Carter.

The President and the Dutts chatted for some time before Miss Lillian, Mr Carter's mother, offered to show the Indian couple around the White House.

The report also went on to say that the Dutts had been specially invited by Mr Carter's mother and had been received by her on their arrival at 6.30 a.m., on Inauguration Day. They then attended the Inaugural Ball as special guests of Miss Lillian.

Apart from the friends whom they meticulously kept in touch with (Nargis specially designed and printed New Year cards every year), there were regular holidays abroad. These helped provide 'cultural' exposure for the children. In 1976, they went around Europe in a ten-seater Volkswagen. Nargis took her nieces as well, though Sunil could not accompany them.

She sent him a postcard on 9 June 1976 from St Mark's Square in Venice. It was written with a certain formality that they were careful to maintain in public, conscious that the children would read the postcard too, so it was addressed to 'Dutt Sahib', and signed 'Mama'.

Dear Dutt Sahib,

It is fantastic in Venice. It is as you can see a lovely place. We are

enjoying ourselves, but missing you badly. I wish you were here with us. We have a lovely ten-seater voxwagon with us. We started from Berlin in the morning and reached Munich in the evening. From Munich to Austria, from Austria now to Italy. From Venice, we leave for FLORENZ. Overnight there and then to Rome. We will be in Rome on the 11th. Rome to Geneva then to Paris and London. It has been a lovely tour by car, something which we both love. Anju, Priya and Sanju all are fine and send you their love. One day, you, or we or you with your friends must make a trip like this. You can only see places like the way we are seeing.
Lots and lots of love
Mama

June was always a special time for Nargis, because that was when Sanjay came home from Sanawar. According to an article in *Sunday* magazine, she had once been asked to chair the feature film jury for the national film awards: 'This chairmanship is the most prestigious position that the Indian government can offer to a film luminary. Not unexpectedly, Nargis refused to accept the chairmanship. Later that year she told this correspondent that she had refused because the jury was to sit in June that year and she was not free in June when her son Sanjay would be home for vacation from his school.' (17 May 1981)

Soon after their European holiday, Sanjay finished school and came home. It would take a little while for him to fit back in. He was now used to making decisions independently and further, to his parents' disappointment, was not very serious about his college education. In fact, a few close friends believe that some undesirable influences had already found their way into Sanjay's life while he was in school.

A friend and neighbour who grew up with Nargis at Château Marine says: 'Sanjay was always playing to the gallery. He loved sympathy. Every time he left from Mumbai by train and Sunil and Nargis would see him off, he would be crying, "Mama, Papa, don't leave me." Once, they were just leaving after saying goodbye to him, and the train stopped before it left the station. They went back to take a look at him, and there he was, dancing and eating with the other boys, but the moment he saw the two, he again started crying "Mama, Papa!" He was a real drama master. He must have been around 15 at that time.'

The same friend had moved to Delhi from Bombay and Nargis would often ask her to look after Sanjay when he was passing through on his way to, or back from, Sanawar. He stayed with her occasionally and she remembers him lying on the floor, kissing his mother's photograph and crying, 'I am missing Mummy, they don't love me, they keep sending me away.' If he had come by air, he would sometimes tell her that he had fainted on the flight, and ask if he could go to school later, because he wasn't well. He would play on all their emotions, till finally one or the other parent would give in and tell her that it was fine, Sanjay could go a day later. The moment it was arranged, he would be up and about, saying, 'Let's go out and eat chaat, let's go for a movie.' And then when the phone rang and his parents called, he would instantly start crying for his mother. The friend admits that while she knew what he was up to, it was impossible to remain angry with him, because he was a lovable child.

Some of the signs were ominous, though she did not know the extent of the problem, so she indulged him, as did his parents. Only one incident caused her real worry: Sanjay suddenly appeared in Delhi, and it seemed he had come without the school's permission. Nargis was abroad and Sunil was to leave shortly.

Sanjay called her at her office and said he was not well. He needed some medicines urgently, but didn't have any money to buy them. To her relief, he said he would come and see her after a while. She then called Sunil, who said he would fly down the same day, but that Sanjay should not be told. Sanjay finally arrived and asked her for money for the medicine. He said he was hungry as well. She refused to give him any money, but looked after him and tried to keep him with her till Sunil arrived. In his usual nonchalant fashion, Sanjay went out and saw *Nehle Pe Dehla*, and then luckily for the tense friend, Sunil arrived and took over. It was obvious that Sanjay was bunking school. Another time when he came to visit her, he 'borrowed' a friend's car and had an accident while driving it.

His behaviour often caused tension between his parents. The friend remembers Nargis breaking down, unable to handle it. She and her mother had met Nargis for lunch in Bombay, and Nargis seemed very distressed. It turned out that Sunil and she were going to Dubai and Sanjay wanted to go with them. When they refused, he disappeared and didn't come home all night. Nargis stayed up, weeping and worried. She told the friend in despair: 'He will kill me, he will kill me one day.'

Matters, of course, got worse when Sanjay returned to Bombay to attend college. He was not interested in academics and informed his parents that he wanted to join the movies instead. He had also by then started using drugs. Namrata and Priya both remember that their mother suspected there was a problem. She often wondered why Sanjay was locked up for so long in his room, and who his friends were, but he always managed to assuage her fears. He could convince her about anything.

Priya thinks her mother was aware fairly soon that Sanjay had a drug problem, but she did not realize the extent of it. She used to ask about an 'agarbatti smell' coming from his room, and may have known that it was marijuana. 'She would hit him and say he had to stop, and then she would cry. She would hit him and cry and hit him and cry. Constantly.' Sanjay was not affected by any of this and sadly, he does not even remember those days clearly, for he lived in a drug induced haze.

Namrata was also aware of Sanjay's problem, but neither of the girls discussed it with Nargis. Drugs had just started becoming trendy among teenagers in India, and no one really talked about it openly, or knew much about their effects.

Priya laughs, 'Once I heard Mom say to a friend, "Why is Sanjay's room always locked when his friends are there? What is the big deal? I hope he's not gay." She didn't know for sure that it was drugs. My dad was the last to know.'

Today Sanjay admits that he picked up the habit in Bombay, and that he himself did not know what was happening to him, for many years.

Sanjay remembers an incident from those reckless days. 'I used to get up in the middle of the night, push a car out, it could be

Mom's car or Dad's car, and drive all over the place, then roll it back here. So one night I came back and the guard said, "I can't open the door because your father has given instructions that I can't let you into the house." I climbed the wall and I saw Mom and Dad sitting on the steps. They were waiting for me. I said, oh, hell, I've had it now. All of a sudden I saw Dad getting into another car and just driving off. I entered the house and she was so angry with me. It seems they had a fight over me. She said, "Let him in," and Dad said, "No, you choose between me and your son." And she said, "I want my son," and so he sat in the car and went away. He came back after two days. Mom was always there, persuading him. I've always been too headstrong and independent, but I think only as a person matures things start falling in place.'

Gia remembers how Nargis covered up for Sanjay. 'Her life was Sanjay, she ate Sanjay, drank Sanjay. It was Sanjay, Sanjay, Sanjay. You could see the passion and love in her eyes when she said, "This is my son Sanjay." He, in turn, used to drive her bananas. Drive her around the bend. She used to protect him from Dutt sahib all the time. Sanju would always have these excuses about why he was late, Dutt sahib would get furious, and Mrs Dutt would be covering up for him, and telling all the servants that "*Sahib ko kehna Baba jaldi aya* (Tell sahib that Baba came in early)." And if he ever overslept and Dutt sahib was on his way, we would knock on his door and say, "Sanju, get up fast, your father is coming." So Dutt sahib never found out.'

Nargis continued to defend her son, telling everyone that he had fallen into bad company, and would be all right in the long run. But she could not stop worrying. Neither could she share her burden with Sunil because she wanted to protect Sanjay from his father's wrath. She thought the problem would go away on its own. But she was wrong. Things were about to get worse.

Sloane Kettering
1980-81

At first, 1980 seemed like a promising year. Nargis was nominated to the Rajya Sabha and Sunil finally succumbed to Sanjay's pleas and launched him in *Rocky,* which turned out to be a blockbuster.

Gia still remembers the day when Nargis became a Rajya Sabha member. 'The speculation had been going on for a while and her name was being mentioned, but we did not know for certain. It was late evening when it was finally announced. The house was like a garden, the flowers that arrived were incredible. I came running back to the house when I heard. The flowers were still being brought in till late evening. She was very happy. Suddenly so much changed around her. The next morning, her photograph was in every newspaper and there were headlines everywhere.

'Even earlier she used to go to Delhi quite often, and yes, there were definitely meetings with the Gandhi family. After she became an MP, the interaction with them increased. I don't recall her making any requests to them. She could always pick up the phone and talk to anyone she liked. People came on the line immediately.'

Gia says that she doesn't remember discussing politics with Nargis because they spent most of their time discussing her pet obsession, Sanjay, and whether he was going to sign a film.

The first few steps towards Sanjay's entry into cinema had already been taken. Once she understood that he was not interested in studying further, Nargis had begun to look around for what he could do, while he was still in the first year of college. Sunil was still not keen on launching his career.

One day, Nargis went over to Rehana's house and told her that she was completely at her wits' end. She still suspected Sanjay was on drugs and she also knew that he was getting into brawls. She said, 'Rehana, I'm just fed up with this Sanjay, either he will send me to the madhouse or he will kill me.'

Rehana calmed her down and said that there was a solution. She suggested that he quit college and work in her husband's office in Mehboob Studio. Amarjeet had great connections in the industry and was doing very well as a publicist.

Rehana thought that working with him would appeal to Sanjay because he would meet producers, directors, watch some shooting, and it might even wean him off drugs. It also seemed like a better idea to send him to Amarjeet's office than Ajanta Arts because Sanjay could learn the business at his own pace instead of being subject to Sunil's constant scrutiny. Nargis and her niece were equally protective of Sanjay. They knew that if Sunil got a whiff of Sanjay's drug dependency, he would be furious.

They hoped he would learn some discipline at work and also that someone would 'spot' him and offer him a role, because Sanjay had inherited the best from his parents. He was tall like his father and had his mother's thin, sensitive face. Sunil was gradually getting reconciled to the fact that his son wanted to be an actor, and agreed that perhaps the best thing would be if someone made him an offer. He probably remembered his own past, when Ramesh Saigal had offered him a screen test, changing his life forever.

However, six months later, no offers had materialized for his son. As a producer, he knew what the film bosses were looking for. It was the age of the romantic action hero. He decided to work on Sanjay and train him to become an actor, as he had done for Som. In Indian cinema, acting alone is not enough. A hero has to know how to dance and how to fight. And so Sanjay was taught acting as well as kung fu and karate.

Sanjay may not have been very keen to begin with, but he went through the training. And in all probability, Nargis had explained to him that this was the only way to get his big break. It worked. Sunil was thrilled with the results.

He called up Amarjeet and said, '*Mera munda taan hun*

taiyyar ho gaya hai, te tu aa odhi audition *dekhan vaaste Ajanta Arts, Rehana nu vi liya.* (My boy is now ready to face the cameras. Come and see his audition at my office, bring Rehana too.)'

Rehana and her husband ended up enjoying a whole evening of entertainment as Sanjay acted out 15 to 20 different characters.

Obviously relishing the memory, she says, 'He gave us a full audition. He wasn't nervous, he was doing everything. He gave a first-class audition. He was totally trained. He did a nawab ka scene, chor (thief) ka scene, daku (dacoit) ka scene, everything. I hugged him. Dutt sahib said, "Launch *kariye munde nu?* (Shall we launch the boy?)" And Amarjeet said, "*Hun main apna chakker chalanda Dutt sahib. Hun tussi rest karo.* (Now it is my turn to set the wheels in motion, you take a break.)" He went straight to Gulshan Rai, the man who controlled the world rights to films such as *Deewar* and *Trishul*, and a very good friend. They would sit and drink together every evening. And he said, "*Gulshanji chaliye* peg-*veg marein,*" and they went to Rendezvous Apollo bar, in Taj. He said, "I have a boy I want to launch, how much money will you give?" So he asked, "Whose boy is this?" And he said, "*Sunil Dutt da munda, Sanjay Dutt, ki khyaal hai?* (Sunil Dutt's boy, Sanjay Dutt, what do you think?)" Gulshan Rai said, "Let's go at once."

'They went to Pali Hill. He had phoned and said, "Dutt sahib, *tussi* whisky-*shisky leaao, Gulshan sahib hain mere naal, kuch gal karni hai.* (Get some whisky, Gulshan Rai is with me, we want to discuss something with you.)" They sat on the terrace. *Munda aaya.* (The boy came.) "*Ye bhai mera munda hai*—first-class acting *karda hai, onhun assi* launch *kariye* picture *vich?* (This is my son. He is a first-class actor, shall we launch him in a film?)" Okay, done. *Ik crore rupaiya denda hain. Chalo Shri Ganesh karo.* Whisky *piyo aur* done, done-done *ho gaya uska.* (Rai agreed to give one crore rupees. Let us start the production, and celebrate with a whisky.) Set-*vet lagaya. Mahurat ki tayyari ki.* (The set was put up and preparations were made for the mahurat.) Pappo (Nargis) was very happy that her son was being launched. She hadn't come for the audition.'

The film was produced by Amarjeet's company, Nalanda

Productions. Sunil was the director. All the arrangements were made by Amarjeet.

Rehana continues, '*Rocky* happened because of the friendship between Gulshan Rai and Amarjeet. It was the fascinating idea of having Dutt sahib as director and Sanjay as hero that attracted Amarjeet. He was an advertising man. He was not interested in production. In any case, he was minting money from other producers whose films he was advertising. He was still handling all of Dev Anand's films.'

A big mahurat was planned in Mehboob Studio, and at least one hundred photographs from the film were displayed. It was a great day for Nargis, a day she had dreamt of for a long time. It was a well attended function with most of the cast present: Raakhi, Tina Munim, Amjad Khan, Shakti Kapoor, Gulshan Grover. There were many new faces and a few better-known ones.

The shooting began, amidst excitement in the Dutt household. The first schedule was in Kashmir for 23 days, where many of the songs that later became super hits were shot, such as '*Kya yehi pyaar hai?* (Is this love?)'.

It was a glorious time for Nargis. Her son was working in his first film and would hopefully settle down. Namrata was in college, studying art, and Priya was in school. Sunil was doing well in his career and was now helping to launch Sanjay. She was attending parliament and was engaged in politics and issues of social welfare. Things looked good. And then, suddenly, she started feeling unwell.

As a Rajya Sabha MP, much to the distress of her children, she was in Delhi during the weeks when parliament was in session. A bungalow had been assigned to her, though Sunil and the children visited only occasionally. They would read about her in the newspapers. Nargis was usually discreet in parliament, except once, when she spoke up bluntly enough to cause comment. (This wasn't surprising: when she heard of her nomination to the Rajya Sabha, she had quipped, 'Me and my tongue, I am bound to get into hot water!')

The controversy that did get her into a lot of hot water was her alleged statement about Satyajit Ray's films. She later maintained that she had been misunderstood. But by the time she could try and correct the impression, she was already in hospital, and events had overtaken her. According to a report, she had only spoken out in defence of commercial filmmakers from Bombay and Madras. 'We must help Indian filmmakers out. Ray merely depicts "poverty" abroad, but it is people like Manmohan Desai who keep our poor entertained.' Her words were blown out of proportion and all kinds of statements were issued against her.

In any case, soon all these issues would be pushed out of the headlines by more serious matters.

29 July 1980 was Sanjay's birthday, celebrated with a party at the Sea Rock Hotel in Bombay. There were many reasons to rejoice: Sanjay had signed a second film, *Yudh,* being made by Gulshan Rai's son Rajiv. (Sanjay would eventually abandon the film due to his drug problem.) Gulshan Rai, who had also bought the world rights for *Rocky*, had asked Amarjeet to give Rs 25,000 to Sanjay at the party as a signing amount for the new film. Happiness was in the air, because finally Sanjay was on his way to becoming a film star.

The only problem was that for a while Nargis had been plagued by constant nausea, but had ignored it. She was still feeling sick, so everyone told her not to go to Delhi for a meeting. The children tried to stop her. Namrata was worried because she felt that each time her mother came back from Delhi, she looked even more frail. They had run checks on her in a London hospital, but found nothing wrong except that she was losing weight all the time. The young Priya admonished her, 'You're not well, you don't have to go to Delhi every time they call you.' But she said, 'No, this time it's really important, let me just go and check it out. I really have to go.'

Priya, between twelve and thirteen years of age then, kept a diary and recorded the painful experience of watching a much-loved mother suffer before her eyes. In the introduction she wrote, 'I am writing this experience of mine and my family which has taught us the value of a mother and a wife.'

In Chapter 1, she gave a background to Nargis's illness. (All the spellings and expressions have been retained as in the original.)

The Dutt family is and will always be admired by everybody. My parents Mr and Mrs Dutt both are prominent figures in the film industry, though mama retired from the films long ago she was still very well known as a social worker. Mama also took keen interest in politics and was chosen a member of the Rajya Sabha, and this was from where all our problems began, mama already suffered from high blood pressure and cholestrol and was already burdened with the problems of her family and social work and about her participance in politics. She had a lot of stress on her mind and body.

Mama started getting severe pain and itching on her stomach and she started losing a lot of weight. We got mama's check ups done in London and found she had diabeties. But mama neglected this problem thinking it to be heritidary. Everything was going smoothly till one day we found out that mom had got an severe attack of jaundice, and we immediately shifted mom to the hospital on august 3.

When Nargis came back from Delhi, she was in such bad shape that she could not even walk. Rehana had booked a room for her at the Breach Candy Hospital. She picked her up at the airport and took her straight there. Namrata was in college, Priya at school, and according to Rehana, 'Sanjay was on drugs so he had no *hosh* (consciousness).'

A series of tests followed. Sunil thought it was a minor ailment and she would be all right soon, but after 15 days, the doctors gave up. They said she had to go abroad for treatment. Sunil only took it seriously when they mentioned the Memorial Sloane-Kettering Cancer Centre in New York.

The doctors were not clear what had gone wrong. Nargis became more and more anxious, as there seemed to be no answers to her questions about her illness.

Rehana adds, 'She would keep saying, "Ask them what is wrong with me and I'll face it." But they were not giving us any information. She said, "You know I am not dumb, you know I am interested in medicine, my father was a doctor," but the doctors would not say anything. Then she said, "My parents died when they were fifty, I will also go, what's the big deal about it?" I told her she should not speak like that because she had three children. She would make me cry every time we met. I would say, "Don't you understand your responsibility for these three kids?" And she would say, "No, no, yaar, *jisko jaana hai, usko jaana hai* (Whoever has to go, has to go). I am not going to live to see fifty.'"

As Priya wrote in her diary:

> Mama's jaundice became a big problem and was not coming under control because of the diabeties. Day by day mom's health started deteriorating but she kept fighting.
> The doctors did further checkups and found that mom had some kind of obstruction in the bile duct which obstructed the bile to flow and because of the accumulation of the bile in the stomach mama suffered from jaundice.

The solution was to go abroad for treatment and after getting the required Reserve Bank of India permissions (in those days it wasn't easy getting foreign exchange), Sunil and Nargis left for the US.

Priya wrote in Chapter 2 of her dairy, 'The doctors told us that mama had to go through an operation to get the obstruction out and unless it wasn't out mama would be in danger. They also told us this operation could only be done in America as it was a very major and dangerous operation and could not take place in India.'

The thought of an operation was somewhat reassuring. It meant that soon Nargis would be better. She even asked Namrata to give her a list of all the things she should buy for them while she was in America. Accordingly, Namrata and her siblings gave their lists. Seventeen-year-old Namrata especially wanted a pair of 'candy' shoes which Nargis said she would get for her.

Namrata wrote her a note to carry on the flight: 'Ma, I love you very much. You are getting better day by day. You don't feel it but the Doc's do. I had a talk with Dr Udwadia and he said you are progressing—so give a smile and cheer up. Everyone needs you so please make an effort to get well Your children need you very much. Now write back to me. Anju.'

Nargis, who was extremely unwell by then, wrote back to her while still on the flight:

> Dearest Anju

Your most affectionate letter I opened in flight but could not read right through because I started crying. I am in such a mental condition. I have gone far away from all of you and I don't know what is going to happen but I have faith in God, he is not going to be so cruel as to not send me back to all of you. I know how much all of you love me, keep praying for me that all will be well with me. Please look after Sanju and see that he does not get mixed up with those silly boys again, he is too stupid in his head, he does not realize what he is doing and how it is going to harm him.

We are heading towards London and from London there is another 7 hour journey, it is very tiring. As soon as we reach New York we will talk to you. Give my love to Nixi and tell her, her card was really sweet. I won't forget to bring your candy shoes, anything else you want, you must let me know after we give you the address.

Lots of love and look after yourself and the house.

Yours

Mom.

Priya wrote in her diary, 'On August 21, 1980 mom and dad left for New York and reached on 22 august and she was admitted on the 24th of august in the Memorial Sloan Kattering Cancer Centre. Mama had become very weak and the 22 hour journey had worsened her condition, they literally had to carry mom to her room in the hospital.'

When they reached New York, the crisis really kicked in. Sunil had booked a room at the Waldorf Astoria but Nargis was so weak that he had to carry her into the hotel. Until their room was made ready, he had to sit on the stairs with her, he could not take her up because she just could not move. The next day they admitted her to Sloane Kettering hospital.

After the initial examination, the doctors found that her system had been poisoned by the bile stored inside her body. Her pancreas had shut down. For two months they tried to drain the poisonous fluids from her body; two incisions were made on either side of her body, and two fluid collecting bags were attached. They could not operate till this poison was drained out. After about a month, Sunil called home and asked Namrata and Priya to join them. Sanjay was still shooting for *Rocky* and could not go with them.

Priya wrote:

There they started taking all sorts of tests and found out that the
obstruction was nothing else but a tumor, but they were not sure if
the tumor was mallignant or not, they would get to know this only
if they opened her up. Papa was very upset on hearing this dreadful
news, contacted in Bombay, and asked us to come to New York
immediately.

We reached Kennedy Airport on 5 September 1980 and immediately
left for the hospital. When we first saw mama we could not believe it
was the same mama, she had lost so much weight that she had
become half her size. Now was the time when we had to give
encouragement and hope to our mother and mental and physical
help to our tired father.

Namrata says, 'I remember the first time we went to hospital.
She was going to go in for her surgery, and so she wanted to
meet us. I just broke down when I saw her. She looked dark and
frail, like an old woman. The bile in her body had changed her
colour, she had glazed eyes. She said, "Don't worry, things will
be fine, you just take care of each other."'

Priya continued:

Everyday we reached the hospital around 10 am on the 16th floor
room 1606. We used to be with mama the whole day and try to
cheer her up, this went on for many days and we saw a marked
improvement in mamas health. Every day slowly and steadily mama
started walking and becoming stronger than what she was. We were
missing our school and college and had to get back to Bombay, but
after mamas first operation, in which they were supposed to drain
out the Bile and Blood accumalated in her system due to the tumor.
On Monday 15 September mama was taken to the operation theatre
and the operation lasted for 5 hours. We were so nervous and were
praying very hard, by the grace of GOD the operation was a success
BUT this was only the minor operation. Mama regained consciousness
the same night and spoke to papa and bhaiya. It was after this that
they found out that the tumor was mallignant.

Mom became more active after her first operation and the doctor
assured us that mama would become more active after her second
operation in which they would remove the tumor. Dr fortner gave
mama 3 weeks to regain her strength and become fit to withstand

the major operation.

We left for Bombay soon after mom's first operation and felt very depressed while leaving. Mama told didi and myself to concentrate on our studies and not to worry about her.

Namrata and Priya returned to Bombay, and Sunil was told that the surgery had been a success. He was enormously relieved. Back in Bombay, Priya kept noting down all the developments in her mother's health:

On Thursday 2 october 1980 mama was supposed to be taken to the operation theatre and 2 hours before going for her operation mom spoke to us in Bombay, she sounded a bit scared but was sure everything would be fine, we too gave mama courage and told her we were eagerly waiting for her to come back.

Here in Bombay there were a lot of prayers going on and all the relitives and friends were in the house waiting for the news. We were all tensed and suddenly the phone rang it was a call from New York, we were really scared till we heard the good news that the operation was a success, but they had to remove a part of the stomach which was infected , the pancreas and a portion of the intestines. Papa was very happy and celebrated this happy moment by having a small get together with his close friends in New York who had really helped him. Moid uncle his fiancee poonam and Dr Pahwa were one of dad's close friends who had helped him the most physically and mentally.

The same night after the party was over papa got a call from Dr Fortner, who gave dad the dreadful news that mama had to go back to the operation theatre as she had started bleeding, all the happiness and joy had drained out and finished.

Sunil had been told that even the removal of the pancreas would not create a problem in leading a normal life, and had just begun to relax, but now blind panic set in. Priya wrote in Chapter 3:

October 4th Saturday early in the morning just after the call papa rushed to the hospital and mama was taken to the operation theatre for the third time, this time they had to drain out the blood which was accumulated in the stomach due to the damage of a blood vessel. Dr Fortner had given mama only one per cent chance for surviving the operation as she was too weak to withstand it. This was a tense moment for papa out there and all of us in Bombay. In New York a few Indian doctors like Dr Pahwa, Dr Bains and Dr Shah were very helpful and explained the whole situation to papa at last the decision was taken and mom was operated and by the grace of god every thing was fine but you never could tell what would happen next.

Mama was cut open in the same place three times and the way mama was going through physical torture the same way papa was going through mental strain he had a lot of tension about everything first of all he worried a lot about mama and secondly about the fiancial problems.

Situation in Bombay was also very tense and we would receive the news from dad about the situation in New York. Lots of our conversation I am sure would be heard by the operaters before we knew, the news would reach everywhere press started writing all sorts of things and the next day there were headlines in the papers: 'Nargis Dutt fighting for life, Sunil Dutt shatters.'

The people all over India new about mama and we got thousands of letters and cards in Bombay as well as in New York. We children of course hated the idea of the press to write this crap but we could not do anything about it. All day long there were phone calls from friends and relatives trying to give us help in some way or the other but we did not need it as we had to be strong and face things as they come. The house would be clusttered with people, all waiting for the news from America, all waiting for the phone to ring and hear the news which was mostly bad, we never became very happy when papa would say mama is feeling better because we never knew what would happen next.

Nargis's body had received a tremendous shock and she went into a coma. Sunil was given the option of one final operation, but was unable to decide what to do. He called the children back to New York, Sanjay as well this time.

Namrata remembers the scene with horror. 'This was our second trip back to New York with Sanjay. She was on machine support, and had a tracheotomy because she could not breathe on her own. She was completely swollen, bloated. She had just shut down. She had bedsores, neck to hip, large bedsores. She was in coma for more than three months.'

Priya recorded her version in Chapter 4:

The day after mama's 3rd operation mama started bleeding again and for the fourth time mom was taken to the operation theatre. And once again once more the Doctors gave only one percent chance and told papa there was no used operating on her, but papa could not see his wife bleeding to death.

Papa know (now) had left every thing up to the hands of god and kept praying. Papa called us up in Bombay and told us to leave for New York immediately, so we caught a flight the same evening and flew to New York. We reached New York on October 10th 80 and rushed straight to the hospital on the second floor and saw mama lying there surrounded by a jungle of tubes and machines, we could not believe it, we never even dreamt that mama's condition had dituriated so much. When we reached there mama had opened her eyes and she smiled at us she couldn't speak because they had put a resperator in her throat which enabled her to breath. Mama made us feel that why had we come to meet her leaving our work and school and colleges, but we told her we had our holidays this just showed that though mama was in such a critical condition and in so much pain still she worried about us more than herself.

We started our visits to the hospital everyday and it was a torture to see mom in this condition. Mom actually did not know what was happening to her as she was in a coma and only sometimes opened her eyes. What she went through was unbelievable but she really had a will to live for her family and if there is a will there is a way.

Papa also I must say went through a lot and faced it like a brave man all the doctors were afraid that papa himself would fall ill but no papa didn't allow himself to fall ill as he had to look to the health of his wife. Didi and myself had suddenly grown up and had to take care of everything we had become very responsible.

We had some very good friends who helped us in every way and whom we cannot forget they were Moid uncle, Dr Pahwa, Dr Bains, Dr Shah, Mr and Mrs Durrani and many others.

The children were in shock. It was decided that Sanjay should go back, as in any case there was little he could do to help. He was still on drugs. He remembers with deep regret that he was unable to donate blood for his mother because of his habit. That was another reason why Sunil wanted him to get back to work.

Sanjay says, 'That drug phase of mine was very, very terrible, I yet remember before my mom fell ill, she used to think something is wrong but she couldn't pinpoint it. If anyone said anything about me, she would fight back that, "My son can never be like that. He never drinks and could never do drugs and all that."

'I remember that she was in New York and Dad asked us to come, and I was in so much of drugs that when I think about it I can't believe it. I carried something like 30 grams of heroin in my shoes, and my sisters were with me, all the way to New York City, and when I think about it today, how did I get away with it? It was so terrible. I was so dependent on something that I can't believe that I didn't care that my sisters were with me. I am alright with the thought that I would have got caught but I can't believe that I jeopardized my sisters as well. They had no idea what I had done. I remember that I used to hide the heroin under the bed in the apartment in New York, and one day I couldn't find it. I came to know that dad had it. And I had the guts to go up to him and say, "Give me my drugs back." Can you believe it?

'He was very angry but he didn't give it back to me, I went into withdrawal, but when I came back (to India) I went back into it again. She was in a coma, my mom, and dad was so angry with me he sent me back.'

For Sunil, the whole experience was a nightmare: he had a wife who was dying, two young girls to look after, a career that was on hold, debts that were mounting every day and now a son who had become a junkie. But he pulled himself together and drew on the last vestiges of his strength. He knew Nargis was dependent on him, so he focused on that: the woman he loved needed him. He refused to let any other thought come into his head. He would not leave her side. He had to somehow make her well again. It became his reason to live.

The children remember that Sunil survived on coffee and cigarettes till they arrived. Namrata was 17 then, and Priya was 13. They had never cooked or shopped for food independently. They had always had cooks and domestic help at home, and had no experience of running a household. But now they took charge and Sunil finally started getting a few decent, if often burnt or undercooked, meals. Once in a while, they would eat at the restaurant in the hospital. They would all walk the two blocks to the hospital every morning and spend the day there. They acquired a pair of binoculars through which they could see the apartment room from the hospital and vice versa, and if needed, they could signal to each other.

On bad days, Sunil would walk around the hospital praying, almost like he was doing a parikrama. The girls went to a nearby church and spent hours praying for their mother. They saw nothing of New York except the grocery shop. Once, Sunil invited some of the doctors over for dinner, and absentmindedly asked the girls to cook, forgetting their lack of culinary expertise.

In a panic, the girls tried to figure it out. Priya had announced confidently, based on her childhood experience of cooking at her friend's house, that she could make roti. But once the chicken had been burnt and the rotis had turned out looking strangely inedible, they asked one of the guests for help and managed to put a meal together. It was another lesson in growing up.

The whole experience was sobering, as Priya noted in her diary. From two carefree teenagers with a doting mother and film-star father, they became, almost overnight, grown women who could run a home, tend to a distracted and depressed father and look after a seriously ill mother—all in a strange country, without any friends. They relied on each other. They knew they could not ask Sanjay for any help. In fact, they now had to look out for him as well. Slowly they became friends with the doctors, and the other patients and their families. School and college seemed increasingly far away.

Things would soon get worse, as Priya noted in Chapter 5:

The days went by without any trouble. But one of the days was a day which a person just could not forget and that day was October 16th 80 mama once again started bleeding and the doctors gave up hope and the surgeon Dr Fotner refused to operate, and said if she would be operated again she just could not survive and it would be a big responisibilty on the surgeons, we pleaded with them to please take a chance because as it is if they would not operate mama would bleed to death. At last they agreed and once again mom was taken to the operation theatre for the 6th time. Everybody was praying very hard, this was the first time we went through this but papa went through this same thing several times. Didi and myself went to a near by church and begged god for the life of our mother we stayed in the church praying till the surgery was over that was 5 hours.

With gods grace the operation was successful but they couldn't put the stiches as the skin had become very lose and there were chances for it to tear, so they closed the operated part with a tape and stiched it after a week. All the doctors were stunned that how could mama go through all these operation and asked themselfs questions which only god could answer. We all had become very friendly with all the employees in the hospital and everybody in the hospital started calling her a MIRACLE LADY OF SLOAN KATTERING.

The next day after mom's operation her kidneys failed because of so many operations mama's body had no resistance left and every time they opened her it would effect the kidney and the liver. Mama was too weak to be dialised as she had many problems with her heart, and papa again had to make a firm dicision and so he consulted his son and told the doctor to dialise mama. Mama went through the dialisis once so we were relieved. And they started dialising mom every day till her kidneys regained strenth and start functioning again.

Because of the damage to the kidneys mamas creatnine, blood uric nitrogen (B.U.N) and the bilirubin had increased tremendously, the B.U.N. which is supposed to be in the range of 15 to 16 went upto 105, 102 and the bilirubin which is supposed to be in 0.01 went up to 70s and 80s which could even effect the brain.

There were so many complications that if you could handle one thing something else would go wrong. The dialysis went on for a long time and slowly by slowly mama started passing urine, but the liver was not functioning properly and her B.U.N. and bilirubin were still very high.

As things took a turn for the worse, Nargis remained in coma.

The doctors had told them that comatose patients could hear what was being said around them. Keeping this in mind, Priya and Namrata would go across to the hospital every day. They would talk to her all the time, even though they did not get any response. Sunil would be there as well, talking to her constantly. He left her side only if it was absolutely unavoidable, though he had commitments back home like Sanjay's half-finished film.

There were many times when, back in Bombay, Gulshan Rai would ask difficult questions about *Rocky*, but Amarjeet usually defused the situation. Somehow the film was completed, while Sunil was using all his willpower to keep Nargis alive.

Namrata remembers, 'My father was with her one day and we had gone to eat lunch. He used to always hold her hand and sit for hours. He said, "I don't want to be too optimistic about it, but I felt her pressing my hand." But the doctor said that this could be a muscle reflex.' It wasn't. Amazingly, despite everything, Nargis woke from her coma.

It was another miracle. Now the family was beginning to believe in them, and constantly praying for them. As soon as Nargis regained consciousness, she wanted to go home.

In Chapter 6, Priya struck a cautious note of optimism:

There was a little progress in mama's health and for us it was the happiest day in our lifes. We never gave up hope nor did mama, our whole family was very brave and gave encouragement to each other. Mom was in the I.C.U. for a long time and every now and then something went wrong with her, every second day mom had to go through dialisis, as she was passing very little urine and that was the period when mom regain consciousness for a little while only.

Mama started becoming better everyday soon they removed the respirator and she could talk once again this made her and all of us feel great as we had heard mom's voice after a long time. Mama had got a terrible infection called herpis—this was very painful as they are a nerve infection, during this phase our whole family had to where masks and go and meet mom due to this mom felt very bad and felt she was so sick that people could not even come to see her without wearing all this.

Mama had become very depressed as she could not walk and felt she now can never walk again, the first words that mom spoke were she said "please take me home" she hated to be in the hospital. This was the first time that mama had been in bed for such a long time she just could not believe it, we were 100 per cent sure that mama would be fine as for all these critical moments god had been very kind to us, so we felt that if god has saved mama through all these operations then he will surely make her fine we were very confident may be too confident.

Gradually we made mama walk, of course, it was very painful for her and she would cry a lot and hated to walk but she was determined to be herself again. Mama became very irritable because 24 hours papa made her do exercises and made her walk.

Papa was taping mom's voice and every day would finish one whole cassette, we loved to hear mama's voice after such a long time, and now we were just waiting for her to be fine and fly back to Bombay. Mama spoke to Swami Muktanand baba whom she really believed in. He told her to say 'Aum namh shivaye' whilst walking and all the doctors and nurses also started while taking her for her daily walks, these were the words that really encouraged her.

Nargis had lost track of time and the real world. She also had no idea that she had been slipping in and out of consciousness for nearly three months. She thought she had been in a coma for three days. She wrote to Rehana a letter dated 1 February 1980, which shows the extent of her disorientation: it was probably late 1980, or early 1981, when she was well enough to write.

Dearest Rehana

By the Grace of God I am still living and slowly I am on my way to recovery. Within 3 or 4 days I will be discharged from here and after staying in the apartment I will be on my way back home. Anju Priya are going early so they can do up my room.

Rehana everyone has been telling me how much you have been praying. Its all the love, good wishes and prayers that has brought me back from the hands (of death). After the 2nd operation which lasted for 13 hours, I was in a coma for 3 days, just hanging between life and death. Anyway the rest you can find out from Anju. One thing I want to request you, that is to tell Akhtar Bhaiya and you also to forgive Zahida. Let that Sahai be but Zahida is after all your younger sister. I don't know but I feel my life is now short.

I have lost all my hair. I can't eat anything. I have become so dark that it is difficult to recognise.

I get very tired, so I can't write to everyone, so give my love to all at home. Tell Akhtar Bhaiya that I have been missing him. Also please tell Sanju that I am coming back after a long illness he should try and understand. If she wants to marry him, he can, but he should stop her from writing silly things. People here are also talking because all magazines are available here.

All the same, God bless you all. My love to Sabrina. At this time I miss your mother and cry for her. May God give her peace in heaven.

Love

Pappo

Despite her illness, Nargis was as involved as ever with her extended family. She was worried that her niece Zahida, who had married without her father's permission, would be treated in the same way that she herself had been after marrying Sunil. Her fears were proven correct, as that is exactly what Akhtar did. He did not allow Zahida anywhere near the family home, till much later, after her first son was born.

Akhtar was reliving the Nargis-Sunil story in more ways than one. Zahida was his only daughter who had decided to become an actress. Her career was launched under the Navketan banner. Then, just when Akhtar was planning a film with her, she decided to get married. He slammed the door shut on her, but Nargis knew the agony of being an outcast, and also knew that life was really much too short, as she wrote in her letter, for these meaningless feuds.

The other message was for Sanju. He was by now in a relationship with his heroine from *Rocky*, Tina Munim. She was his first love and he was deeply involved. The petite Tina had come to Bombay to get a break in cinema. She was a very determined young woman and Sanjay was besotted with her in no time. Nargis was uneasy about the relationship from the start, possibly because she felt Sanjay was far too young to be so seriously involved, and she kept trying to wean him away. Because she wasn't there to monitor the situation, the gossip magazines were full of the couple's romance.

Nargis, when she was feeling better, read the reports and was very upset. She also worried that an early romance could derail Sanjay's fledgling career.

But despite her misgivings, her two daughters and Sunil managed to wring some happiness out of the situation. After all, she was recovering, she was coherent and talking to them, and even shouting once in a while in her old way.

Chapter 7 was written by a slightly more cheerful Priya: 'We were really happy to see mom progressing and thanked god for this. Mama's very dear friend, Shammi aunty came all the way to New York to see mom, and mom was very happy to see her

> *15th 2 - 1980*
>
> Dearest Rehana -
>
> By the Grace of God I am still living -, and slowly I am on my way to recovery- within 3 or 4 days I will be discharged from here and after staying in the apartment I will be on ~~my~~ my way back home. Anju Priya are going early so that they can do up my room.
> ~~...very~~ one has

and would always complain to her about dad saying "*Dekhiye na Dutt Saheb tho* 24 hours *mujhe exercise karathe rehte hain lekin mujhe ither se le jane ka nam he nahi lete.* (See Dutt Saheb makes me exercise for 24 hours, but doesn't say that he will take me home, away from here.)"'

Shammi remembers her trip to New York to meet Nargis. 'I went to see her. Dutt sahib met me. She was better, but still in ICU. The doctor told me to ask her something that will prove if her brain is functioning. Then finally I went inside and met her. I looked at her, and did my best acting, ever. She had completely changed, her face and everything. I asked her how she was and she said, "I am very fine," with a big smile. And Dutt sahib said to her, "Here we were trying to make you smile and laugh and now you are smiling away," and all that.

'Then she asked me, "Will I ever be all right?" And I said, "Of course you will be. In our whole life we have never talked in a pessimistic fashion." Then I told her about something that had happened a long time back, and she joined in, laughing, saying we were so bad, and then I asked her about Mehboob sahib, and she remembered everything. Her memory was absolutely fine. We also joked about some of Dutt sahib's friends. When I came out I told the doctor her memory was very good, and he said, "I wish you had come earlier, she would have laughed at least."

'Then on practically the last day before I left, I took her in a wheelchair down the corridor. We stopped at a window; it was snowing outside. We remembered a time when she had said we should come to New York when it was snowing and walk on the pavements. I said, "Here we are, as we had wanted to be." She said, 'But I am in a wheelchair, stupid." I said, "Next year when you come for your check-up, we will walk on the pavements in the snow." And then I took her back to her room.'

It took all of Shammi's acting talents to get through those days cheerfully. She knew, looking at her once beautiful friend's ravaged face and body, that they would never be together in New York again.

Nargis had never been vain, but there was a time when she had been voted the most beautiful screen siren. As an actress, she had received countless compliments. Her photographs had been on magazine covers and the front pages of newspapers since she was 14. She tried not to think about her appearance now but one day, she decided to face up to the worst. She asked Namrata for a mirror.

Thus far they had been careful not to let her know how she looked. The family treated her hair loss and dark, shrivelled skin as normal. What they saw in the hospital was sometimes far worse.

Namrata, a gentle but straightforward girl, could not argue with her mother. She gave her the mirror. Nargis did not say anything when she saw her reflection. But when Sunil came to see her, she could not stop crying. She saw what she had dreaded. She was indeed very dark, her skin had begun to wrinkle, and she had lost most of her hair.

Sunil held her and tried to inject his own indomitable spirit into her. For him, she was still the lovely woman he had married, she was going to get better, and she was going to walk out of the hospital, healthy and happy. He would help her, he would stay with her, and force the gods to make her well again.

When Sunil made her walk, she used to scream in agony because she could not hold herself upright. She would shout at Sunil, "I hate you for what you are doing to me." And he would reply patiently, "I don't care, you have to walk, you have to get all right." The ICU was oval-shaped and the nurses' centre was in the middle of that oval. There were spacious corridors in which patients could walk. The first day that she managed to walk the full circle, people came out of their rooms to applaud her courage. She kept reciting 'Aum Namah Shivaye' as Muktananda Baba had asked her to, and kept walking. Everyone, including the nurses and doctors, joined in the chant, urging her on.

Namrata took her for physiotherapy, and while she tried to exercise, Nargis would cry to her daughter in pain, "Anju, *kuchh karo* (Do something)." Nargis wanted Namrata to stop the therapists but instead, Namrata had to force herself to sit there with her eyes shut.

Priya was too young and too attached to Nargis; Sanjay was in Bombay. The onus fell on Namrata.

Priya wrote:

Mama would always feel it was up to dad to take her home as mom was very eager to get back home. After a few days mom was fit to be shifted to the 16th floor where she first was. Mama was not all that happy to get back to the 16th floor as she was dying to get back home. Didi and myself stayed in New York almost for 3 months and mom and dad for about 6 months. When mom was on the 16th floor we always tried to cheer her up, but sometimes she would get angry and start shouting at us this was the time we felt she was recovering as shouting was her old habit which she had regained. All of us really used to miss mamas screaming and shouting whenever she would go out of town there would be no noise in the house no one to play games with me and no one whom I could go and crib to, mama and me would always play games in our spare time as mom loved playing games, mama to us was more like a friend she would sometimes join our friends for a movie and mind you she was real fun being with. Mama, myself and all of us really missed home badly and all the fun our family had together and prayed to god to give those lovely days back to us. We all felt God was listening to our prayers as mom was on her way to recovery.

Every one in the I.C.U. really loved mom and visited her very often to her room. Mama could not stand the 2nd floor and referred to the i.c.u. as a dungeon. We spent our Christmas in New York it was the most beautiful sight this was the first time didi and me were seeing snow fall. Mom and dad had come to New York once before mom was dieing to go to Desney world though she got a great opportunity to go to desney world mom refused and said that if I go I will only go with my children so this time we assured mom to take her to Desney world, but mom had a peculiar feeling about her health but she never lost hope she wanted to live, live for her children to see the wedding of her daughter and the rise in the career of her son.

Papa always told us to be ready for the worst but we never got ourselves to do that as we had full confidant that mom would be perfectly fine and back to normal, we were sure our momsy would be fine.

Mama had become very weak and could not eat as the sight of food made her feel nausous. We were very worried about moms food problem the docters had to feed her through the nose and through drips.

Didi and myself tried to cheer mom by getting her many gifts and decorating her room, mom loved stuffed toys so we got her plenty of them also bought her flowers and decorated her wall with cards and big picture of bhaiya's which she would always see and admire. Bhaiya was moms weakness and mom was bhaiyas.

One day we got mom all ready for a big surprise but wasnt in a mood for surprises, she was sulking and crying and she wanted to go home, but just then dad opened the door , and there was a sudden shine on moms face seeing her son at the door we had not seen mama so happy in all these days.

Mama used to eat only if Bhaiya told and also exercise only if bhaiya told her to, as bhaiya had a way to persuade mama to do anything from the beginning.

Sanjay says, 'I was in Bombay doing my work when she came out of coma. The first thing she asked my dad was, "Where's Sanju?" He said, "I've just sent him to Washington for some work, he'll come back." He called up and asked me to come back, so I went. I went straight from the airport to the hospital. He was sitting there, and he told me not to come into her room. He went in and I heard him saying, "I've got a surprise for you, open your eyes, you can't believe it, you won't believe it." And then she opened her eyes and I walked in. I'll never forget that day. Her whole face just changed totally. Her hands were shaking and I hugged her. But those days were really bad. She just wanted to come back home and the doctors would not permit it.'

Slowly, with her family around her, Nargis started to feel better. She could walk with a stick, and even went shopping to Bloomingdales, dressed in trousers, shirt, and a thick woollen coat. The doctors were confident that she was cancer-free, but any small infection could disrupt her fragile system. So, while she was adamant that she wanted to go home, the doctors kept persuading her to rethink.

Finally, Namrata and Priya were sent home to prepare the house and make at least one room sterile for her. The idea was to recreate the hospital atmosphere as closely as possible. Nargis would stay on the first floor in her own room, with a round-the-clock nurse.

When the children reached home, Namrata found that in the six months they had been away, the house had acquired a deeply neglected look. Even the walls had turned black with dirt and had to be scrubbed clean. In Chapter 8, Priya wrote about leaving her mother in New York, and coming back to India:

> We were very happy with moms progress, taking her for walks or the recreation room where the patients could do what ever they liked and it would be a nice change for mama from the hospital atmosphere.
>
> Mom sent didi and me home to do up her room which she wanted right from the beginning. Mom was coming home soon so we had to do a quick job with the room. Staying in the hospital and in New York dad didi myself had already become half doctors, as before leaving for Bombay the doctors and nurses had taught us how to take moms blood test to test her blood suger, etc.
>
> We landed in Bombay after staying away for 6 months. Moms favourite dogs ringo and silvy had died while mom was in hospital and mom got to know about ringo by reading a letter written by one of my friends, mom was very upset about ringos death as she really loved him fortunately mom never got to know about silvy.
>
> While here in Bombay didi and myself were busy doing up moms room, we wanted it to be really new for her as she always wanted to do up her room.
>
> In New York too mom was very excited to come back home, she told

dad to take her for shopping as that was always moms best hobby mom also told him to buy her a new saree so that she can look her best on Bombay airport.

We got the super news that mom was coming back soon. We were really very excited about this fact, we made big plans about moms arrival. Dr Puri a Air India docter and a family friend made arrangements for V.I.P. treatment for mom and dad and we too were allowed to go in the air craft to receive mama.

Mom could not believe she was back home at last and she burst into tears with the joy to be back home. Mama was still very weak and tired after the long journey and so had to be brought out in a wheel chair. We had all arrangements for moms arrival at home too, there were many people waiting at home to meet mama. Before the car entered the gates of our home there were fire works and the house was all lit up to welcome the lady of the house after 8 months.

The date was 6ᵗʰ march, 1981 which was the most happiest day in moms life to be back home at last and also to her country which she loved and respected above all things.

Mama was very happy to meet all her friends and relatives whom she had really missed. The people were stunned seeing mom as she had become very weak after her prolonged sickness, they had never seen mama like this before as she was all full of fun and she was also an very active person, it was hard on mama too as she wanted to be the same one day but unfortunately that day never came.

The house was like a hospital. There was a steady stream of visitors but very few were allowed anywhere near her. Most of her friends and relatives had no idea she had become so frail, and when they saw her, they remember wondering who the old wrinkled woman was, before they realized with horror that it was Nargis.

Gia says, 'I just couldn't recognize her, there were at least a thousand people in the house when she came back from America. The news had spread that she was coming back. When the car came up, and she got out, she was so frail and dark that there was pin drop silence. I couldn't react, I didn't know whether it was her or not her. There were tubes all around her.

'When she went into the room, we all sat downstairs, Ameena Bai, her faithful ayah and all of us, and we just cried and cried. We could not believe it. Someone—I think it was her nephew

Sarwar—said, "Wipe your tears and don't go in front of her like this." There was nothing to say. But we just prayed all the time, all kinds of prayers, any kind of prayer.

'Sanju was breaking down every minute and crying all the time. He couldn't bear to see her like that. We would say she would be all right, and he would ask, "When, man, when?" Anju was a pillar of strength. She just became Mrs Dutt. She did everything perfectly, for her father, for her mother, for Sanju and Priya. She just took over. She was wonderful, though she was breaking inside. But Sanju, who was the oldest, was in a way younger, because he was always Sanju Baba. Namrata showed remarkable strength and I think this entire thing has matured her.'

Gia observed how tough it was for them as a family because earlier the whole household had revolved around Nargis. Sunil had fallen apart, though he was trying to be strong for the kids. No one ever discussed their precarious financial status. Sunil had not worked for almost a year and expenses were mounting by the day. But he pushed away all other thoughts so he could concentrate on Nargis. He was physically and mentally exhausted and he may have known that it was a losing battle. But he did not give up.

For those who believed that Raj Kapoor was the man who truly loved Nargis, seeing Sunil with her must have been an eye-opener. Raj Kapoor was far too self-centred to lavish the kind of attention or love on a dying woman that Sunil did. This was Sunil's greatest test and he proved to everyone that Nargis had made the right choice. According to Ali Raza, Sunil was a 'devi maker'. Nargis was an ordinary woman, and through his respect and devotion, Sunil turned her into a devi. It is true that no other actress in Indian cinema has been given the kind of reverential adulation that Nargis got, and while she worked hard for it, some of the credit goes to Sunil as well.

Everyone had to maintain a strict hospital regimen. Nargis had to be administered insulin thrice a day. A machine had been installed to monitor the amount of insulin in her body. She learnt to prick her fingers for the blood, asking sadly, 'Do I have to do this throughout my life?' Everything was painful, and her fingertips were sore. Sunil would encourage her by saying she was not alone in her pain, there were others like her as well. He kept encouraging her to be strong.

Though Nargis could barely walk, she was still keen to see Sanjay's film. The *Sunday* magazine reported on 17 May 1981:

On 9 March, around six in the evening, Sunil Dutt drove Nargis down to the corner of their sprawling Pali Hill bungalow where the family runs the Ajanta dubbing theatre. Mrs Dutt, as she has always been addressed after her marriage in 1958, had come to see Rocky, the first film starring her eldest child and her biggest weakness, 20-year-old Sanjay. She had seen the 'rushes' of the film while Rocky was being shot, but this was the first time she was making an attempt to see the complete film. She could only see some seven reels of it before fatigue and exhaustion forced her to return to bed.

Priya wrote in Chapter 9 of her diary:

Papa had brought along a nurse from the hospital in New York to look after mama and to train the Indian nurses as they were not used (to) the things and gadgets dad brought down from Newyork. Mom was still being fed through the nose as she had not yet gained her appetite, papa had to get a (lot) of medicines from Newyork like vivenex, it was a protein which was being fed to mom through her nose. We had to take a lot of care to what food we gave mama she was not allowed to have too much of protein and so her diet had to be controlled tremendously.

Every day mama had to go through the torture of being pricked on her fingures for blood test, her fingures has been pricked so many times that her tips had turned all blue, there were blue bruises all over moms body made by minor operations and continuos injections. As it is mom was a diabetic patient and so the wounds took a very long time to heal. There was one major wond which did not heal at all, the doctors had attached a plastic bag there as there was continuos flow of bile and blood from the wound, it was very dangerous as there were chances of infection. The wound did heal in Newyork, but back here in Bombay one night it burst and there was blood all over, mom did not (know) whats happening, all of us including the nurses became very panicy and at last every thing was taken care of by the doctors.

Fife days later after moms arrival was mamas and papas wedding anniversary on the 11th of March. That day we dressed mom up in her dulhan ka joda and she became really very happy. I gave presents to mom and dad from the money I had been collecting for this beautiful occasion. The very next day mom had a very funny feeling and she kept crying. She kept saying that 'I think this is my last anniversary'. We all consoled mama and assured her that she would be as fit as a fiddle.

Days past and mamas health started becoming unstable. Mom had now developed urine infection, it was a bit dangerous to be handled at home so once (again back to) square one we had to shift mom to the breach candy hospital. The worst thing that happened to mom was that she had given up all hope and the will which had kept her alive for so long.

Doctor Udwadia was the doctor looking after mama, he suggested that mama should be taken in the intensive care unit for special care we were very worried about mom and got all sorts of funny ideas that sombody had done something on her. People told us to go to several babas and we did and got one answer from every one that sombody had done some real strong black magic on mama. We went to all sorts of babas for their help and did everything we could to get mom alright with medicines, babas and most of all by prayers but nothing worked, but we the doctors and every one else too did not loose hope and kept trying, we could never even think that our mother can ever leave us we were still sure mom would be (fine) though dad had told us to be prepared for the worst but we never listened to him and atleast I was sure that my mother would be fine. But everything is destined for every individual and no doctor nor any baba can say what may happen tomorrow everything is left to god.

Hard Times
1981

Despite all the efforts of the doctors and the prayers of the family, Nargis was slipping away from them. After the urinary infection, hope started fading rapidly. It was exactly the sort of infection the doctors in Sloane Kettering had warned the family about.

Constantly in pain, with open bleeding sores, her fingertips aching from the daily pinpricks of the blood tests, Nargis still had other worries. Every part of her body was giving way, but her love for her children kept her going. Aside from Sanjay's movie career, she had been talking to Sunil about Namrata's wedding and how much she longed to see it. When she was finally taken back to the hospital after her urinary infection, it seemed to her that all her dreams had been snatched away from her.

Namrata remembers that even in the ICU, her mother told her that she wished she could see her getting married. Namrata was barely 18 and did not think she was ready, but she knew her mother was worried that she was running out of time.

Nargis was also anxious about Sanjay's drug abuse and kept asking everyone she met to find out the truth. She did not believe him when he denied it. When Zahida had visited her before she left for America, she had asked her niece, 'Do you know if Sanju is doing drugs?'

Zahida remembers: 'She said, "I want you to take him to a restaurant outside Breach Candy and find out, he is lying to me." I took Sanjay to the restaurant in the car. He ate a sandwich, had cold coffee. Completely relaxed. I said, "Your mother is so sick, and she says you're doing drugs." He was cool, and said, "Apa, I don't know where mother gets these ideas from. I'm not doing anything. You know Mama, she's always exaggerating." I asked him, "Sanju, swear to me." He said, "Apa, I swear to you, ma kasam (by my mother) I swear to you." I came back, completely convinced and said, "Pappo, why do you say all this?" I believed him. Sanju was like a child for us, I was 12 when he was born. We loved her kids. We used to stay in the bungalow looking after the kids when their parents went abroad.

'She said, "He's a liar, he's lying and you believe him?" The pain was eating her up.'

It was the same situation now, after nearly a year, but there was very little Nargis could do any more.

Priya wrote her saddest diary entries in Chapter 10:

> Moms condition kept deturiating day by day, once again she started passing scanty urine, with blood clots this was the sign that mom had started bleeding internerly once again. We did not want mom to go through this torture of being operated again she just could not have taken it.
>
> Mama used to get terrible pain in her back and it was just unbearible. We could not see mama in this condition she was always crying with pain, she had blisters all over her body and a little touch anywhere would make her cry.
>
> Mom started feeling scared in the I.C.U. and she was surrounded with all sorts of weird thoughts, so she wanted any one of us to always be with her. We could not hold back our tears when we saw mom in this condition she had become like a child and I can assure you she hated the idea of being like this and also hated all her things to be done by others. She did not like to be dependent on anybody but god. We people had to be strong to give hope and courage to mom and dad.
>
> Dad started becoming very lonely and spent most of his time in the hospital with mom or with the doctors. Papa went to Shirdi every second day to pray for moms recovery. Once mom wrote a letter to sai baba saying please let (me) be well soon but her prayers too were not heard and nor were ours. Dads work was on a stand still, and bhaiyas movie Rocky too as this was not the time to release it. Mama insisted that Rocky should be released as planned and also said she would be there for the premier even if she had to come on a wheel

chair, so according to moms wishes it was planned that Rocky should be released on 8th of May.

Things wernt working out in the hospital as they should have moms condition was going bad to worse, they once again had to put the respirater in her throat, and that was the first day I really felt something bad was going to happen. That night dad had gone to Shirdi and here we were all alone not knowing what to do we were just seeing our mother going in front of our eyes and could not do a thing to prevent this from happening. The(y) put the respirator and mom started bleeding from her throat where it was put she kept bleeding, mom was also in a coma we went to the baba whom at least I thought helped a lot and told him what had happened he tried to encourage us but something in his (voice) told me that she wont live long know, but I just did not want to believe it.

Namrata and Priya, who were 'half doctors' from their time in America, knew that the tracheotomy performed on Nargis could be dangerous. Since she was diabetic, wounds took a long time to heal, and the doctors in America had warned them that she could bleed to death.

Back in the hospital things were really bad. I wanted to be near my mother and try to sooth her from her pain but at the same time I did not want to see her suffer like this. Papa came at last, he went up to see mom said his prayers and came down, he told us to go home and rest but just did not feel like leaving the place, the night was the most dreadfull and scary night of my life. the atmosphere in the hospital itself was scary there were dogs howling and cats fighting and crying and all these are supposed to be bad omens.

Didi bhaiya and myself went home while dad said he would come later. Dad came home round five in the morning while we were all asleep. Suddenly the phone rang from the hospital dad picked up it was my bhaijan (Sarwar) who told us to come immediately as mom was sinking and the doctors had given up all the hope for mom. Papa hurried and left immediately and we followed in a few minutes. We reached the hospital and every one was crying. I thought moms condition had become really bad we hurried up to the I.C.U and mom had gone, gone for ever. I could not believe that my mom was no more I just could not get myself to believe it, and I still don't believe it. Many thought(s) came in my mind that how could (I) live without my mom I also wanted to kill myself and go where I could be with my mom but then thought I would be free but then what happen to my father sister and brother.

I was in a daze and just did not know what was happening, the ceremonies were going on people were pouring to console us but I just could not believe this was happening to us out of all the people. My mother was gone I had to get that through my thick skull but just cuoldn't. Mamas body was at home for a day I just did not want to leave her side at least I could feel her warmth, I wanted to cuddle up near her and sleep peacefully as I always would till this age. I wanted to do the same even now but they were taking her away from me forever to bury her, I could never see her my own mother who gave birth to me educated me by her love and effections she, she had left us and gone for ever every thing was over the ceremonies and everything.

The house where there once lived a happy family but know the family was also there the father the son and the two daughters still lived there but without a mother, the family link had broken, we all now had to learn to live without mom so all of us cooperated with each other and tried to build up a new happy family we tried to fill the gap left by my mother, we did succeed to a certain extent and it was the best we could do, our family could never be the same without mama.

The children never got a chance to 'cuddle' up with their mother, as Priya wanted to do so desperately, because as soon as word of her death got out, thousands of people descended upon them, first at Breach Candy, and then at the house. Though Nargis's frail health had been widely reported by the media, there was public hysteria over her death. Among the first statements issued was one by her old friend, Indira Gandhi:

NEW DELHI, May 3 (PTI): 'Her friendly, vivacious face will long continue to cheer our people,' the Prime Minister Mrs Indira Gandhi, said today on hearing the news of the death of Nargis Dutt.

In a touching tribute, Mrs Gandhi said she was deeply grieved to hear that Nargis had passed away after a long and heroic battle against agonising pain and prolonged illness.

'To the millions who have seen her on the screen, Nargis was a symbol of high talent and dedication. She was a person of extraordinary warmth and sympathy and extended support to numerous social causes,' she added.

On 4 May 1981, the Rajya Sabha mourned Nargis. The chairman M. Hidayatullah briefly recalled the achievements of this 'film actress of international repute' and members stood in silence for a minute as a mark of respect to her memory. Nargis had been a member of the Rajya Sabha for only three months before she fell grievously ill.

A priest, a maulvi and a pandit presided over the final ceremonies at home. Nargis was not buried according to Muslim rites alone. Sunil had not allowed anybody else, apart from the children and himself, to dress the body for its final journey. Nargis had followed the Hindu faith enthusiastically but she was afraid of fire and had told Sunil that she preferred to be buried in her mother's grave. Sunil respected her wishes and did exactly that. The body was carried on a bier Hindu style till the gate, and then transferred to a coffin.

However, when her body was about to be buried, an enthusiastic crowd of 'upholders' of the Islamic faith turned up and wanted to 'prepare' the body according to Islamic rites. While Sunil was too distraught to think of a solution, someone in his group had the presence of mind to say that the doctors had warned them not to remove the shroud.

The family, in turn, removed all the images of God from their house. They felt they had been cheated by the gods.

As Priya wrote in her final entry in Chapter 11:

This dreadful experience did teach us the value of a mother. After moms death I stopped believing in god as I felt what was the use to pray to god like a mad person and not get what you desire. but then I realised I was being selfish I then thought of the thousands of people who suffer more than what we had sufferd and could imagin what they went through, but mind you my fight with god is not yet over I just wanted one thing for my mother and she wanted it too that was a peacful death she did not get it, she also wanted to live till her daughters marraige she did not and lastly she wanted to be there and to see her sons first film she could not but died just few days before on the 3rd of May and the premier was on the 8th. I want to ask him up there only one question WHY? Why did he do this to her?

I end here praying to god and asking him not to let any one else go through the torture my mother went through and I will wait for my answers as long as I live and I doubt he will be able to give some.

After thanking everyone who helped them, Priya wrote a little poem at the end of her 'memoirs', dedicated to her mother.

Most of all I thank my mother who is not with us for what she did for us when she was alive.
THANKYOU MOTHER
Thank you mother for being wonderful you,
thank you for the beautiful moments we shared with you,
the thought that you were around made feel so good,
so why mother why had you to go so soon
Thank you mother for all the sweet memories you have left behind,
thank you mother to always be there when we wanted someone to
talk to, someone to help us solve the problem of life
But most of all I thank you mother for the love you gave us
which has helped us to stand on our own two feet
Now I can just say one thing, we love you for being wonderful you
Priya Dutt

Without Nargis, the house began to seem eerily silent. There were memories of her everywhere. Her photographs recalled their times together. Her clothes and other personal items became a source of grief, as Sunil refused to give anything away. He, like the rest of the family, found it hard to believe she had given up the fight they had fought together for so long. The miracle they had prayed for had not happened. And no one was more affected than Sunil, who now finally allowed his grief to emerge. His fighting spirit drained away and he lost interest in everything. He broke down completely.

Sunil's grief made him oblivious to everything else: that he was a father, that he had to work, that he still had a family. He spent hours crying in his room, he would forget to eat, and spent most of his time either drinking or smoking. His sister moved in for a while and tried to keep him sane, but to no avail. The children would wake up in the middle of the night and find that Sunil had gone to the graveyard to sit by their mother's grave.

Sanjay was too doped to understand or sympathize with his

father. The real tragedy is that when his much-loved mother died, Sanjay was cocooned in another world. Today, he has little memory of what happened to her. He went through the motions of grief at the time, but did not remember anything later on. He would only cry for her much later, when he finally was drug free.

Rocky was released on 8 May as planned. One seat was left empty for Nargis, symbolically, and neither Sanjay nor Sunil could hold back their tears during the screening. The woman for whom this would have meant everything was no longer there to enjoy it.

The film did extremely well and went on to establish Sanjay as an action hero. Again, Sanjay did not himself realize the importance of anything that was happening to him. All that his success meant was that there was now more money to spend on drugs and a lavish lifestyle. He had signed up other films as well and looked destined for stardom. One of his co-stars remembers how producers and directors would exploit his weakness by supplying him with whatever he wanted, so long as he continued to perform.

There was no sympathy for him, nor did any of the producers or directors he worked with attempt to help him kick the habit. There was one tragic moment witnessed by another actor when Sanjay was in the middle of a terrible withdrawal. The shoot was at a hill station. The director was worried that the schedule would be scrapped. Sanjay was trembling under the blankets, crying miserably for his mother. He was provided the drugs he needed, along with all the liquor he could drink. Soon, he was back on the high that had become his normal state. The shoot went on, regardless of the damage being done to the boy, who was not yet twenty-one.

One person in the family who decided she could not fall apart was Namrata. The burden of running the house and looking after her father fell on her; the fact that she was still a teenager did not matter. Today she feels she had no choice. She had to take on the entire onus of dealing with a withdrawn and depressed father, a junkie brother and a rebellious teenaged sister.

In her last letter to Namrata, Nargis had asked her to look

after the house. Namrata took her mother's words very, very seriously. She had to ensure that things pulled along. Money would be sent to her from the office and she thought back to how her mother had managed the home. She began to emulate her mother in every way that she could. While her friends were all out discovering the latest discotheques, Namrata was exploring the complicated world of balancing household budgets and trying to keep her father safe and sane.

Namrata remembers: 'When I went back to college, all my friends were one year ahead of me. I couldn't do many of the things they did. I couldn't go out. I was very serious about everything. I wouldn't go to a disco. Those were big at that time. I never visited a discotheque. I was serious about my work and I had to come home to look after the house. Sanju was by then deeply into drugs. He was shooting and away all night and I remember sitting and waiting all night for him to come home. It was very scary. I would be up all night, he would come back and pass out. Sometimes he would take the car out on his own, so it would (become) very frightening. I used to talk to him. I don't think it registered. And then I'd go to college. If I had to do it now, I couldn't do it.

'For years my dad shut down. He could not sleep in the same room. He was in depression, he couldn't work. He had done everything and he thought he could make her survive. He was truly finished. He didn't talk to anybody, he used to go to office, go for walks. But he was very quiet. I was leaving college, last year, that's when things became fine.'

It was two years before Sunil gathered himself together and started another production. He woke up from his depression one day, following a chance remark from Priya. They were strolling on the terrace when she pointed out a star to Sunil, saying she thought the star was her mother. She said she just could not bear the thought of her mother in the graveyard. The body lying there did not represent Nargis at all, while the star overhead, shining brightly and joyously upon her all the time, was just like 'Mama'. Sunil listened to his 14-year-old daughter and it began to dawn on him that the children had also suffered a terrible loss. He had to get back to looking after them.

It wasn't going to be easy because he was 52 and had to start all over again. Slowly he began to get back to cinema, but it was never the same after those two years he had lost.

Priya remembers those difficult days: 'As far as my sister is concerned, she became a very serious person, everything is black and white. I had more freedom to do what I wanted to do. I was very stubborn, very headstrong. In my baby book, my mother has written "very stubborn girl, she refused to apologise to her father." I always argued with my father. When Mom was alive, no one was allowed to phone him, especially while he was on a shoot. Mama had to handle everything. So now I would be constantly on the phone to him, calling him and asking, "Okay now, Dad, I have to go to my friend's place, can I go? Can I do this? Can I take the car and go there?" All the time, I would ring him up.'

Sunil's comeback film was a home production called *Dard ka Rishta* (1982), starring Smita Patil. The film was about cancer, inspired by his personal commitment to Nargis. Before she died, she had made him promise that he would try to provide better facilities for the treatment of cancer in India. She often pointed out that she had been fortunate to be able to come abroad and get the required treatment, but what about those who could not afford proper medical facilities? She wanted him to spread the message and to help the deprived. All the earnings from *Dard ka Rishta* were to go to charity. Simultaneously, the Nargis Dutt Cancer Foundation was set up to raise funds to buy equipment for cancer treatment.

The film opens with a close-up of Nargis's eyes and then slowly zooms out to her full face and the words, 'This film is our fulfilment of your last wish, and our humble homage to your evergreen memory.

'A promise to keep
A dream to fulfil
And miles to go...'

Paraphrasing the famous lines from Robert Frost, much loved by Nehru, Sunil rededicated himself to the cause of social work.

Watching *Dard ka Rishta,* it is difficult to believe that the film was made for commercial release. Since it was made for a cause, and possibly made on a low budget, it does not have any aspiration towards style beyond the bare storyline. But it does reveal Sunil's determination to move forward, without forgetting the past. Some of the hospital scenes, actually shot at Sloane Kettering, must have been particularly difficult to enact. It is a brave film with a positive message at the end, for the cancer patient survives. It failed at the box office, however.

Sunil signed up for a few outside productions as well, like *Raj Tilak, Faasle* and *Kala Dhanda Gore Log*. Essentially these were films meant to keep the money coming. A large part of their expenses so far had been managed from the amount Nargis and he had saved to rennovate the house. Still, there were debts to be paid.

Sunil's fire for cinema had burnt out. He could no longer do the facile and superficial roles required by the industry. He wanted more meaning in his life. It no longer made sense to run around trees singing songs in the rain. He wanted to do something that would heal his wounds. He could only show his love for Nargis by doing things he thought would make her happy, wherever she was. He would visit her grave as often as possible, unlike Priya, who found it too dismal to visit. He would sit there and talk to her about his life and the children.

One day, he realized what would make her really happy—if Sanjay were to be helped and brought out of his drug induced stupor.

Priya remembers that moment: 'Suddenly Papa decided, no booze, no cigarettes, he threw everything out. Because he realized Sanju had a problem, and that became a project he was working on, a mission that Sanju comes out of this, and the whole process of Sanju's treatment started. Dad approached some rehabilitation institutes here for detox. There was a tiny little hospital which Sanjay could go to, because most of the other places were run by quacks. When Sanjay was admitted, there were some strange people in the other room, and Didi and I had to stay in that hospital with him. We couldn't leave him alone. My exams were on, so I used to study in the night, and go to school from there.

It was a terrible place. He was miserable, because they were even putting electrodes on his head.

'It didn't work, then Papa said, "Forget about this, put him in hospital." But that did not help either. So he said we'll take him to Germany. He had friends there. They tried naturopathy for him there. It didn't work. Then Papa realized that all this is being done without Sanjay really wanting to become okay. It has to come from him. So he just left it till the time Bhaiya came to him and said, "Dad, I need help, and I want to chuck this now." It took Sanju ten years to come out of drugs. He was taking everything. In *Rocky* he was not that bad, but if you see his films after *Rocky*, it just started getting worse, especially after Mom died. Access to money was also easy after *Rocky*. He looked overweight and strange.'

Sanjay was finally able to come through at a very strict detoxification clinic in America, where no contact was allowed with the family. Even phone calls were rare. He lived there in a trailer near the Mississippi river, wrestling with his demons, for two years. For a while he used all his charm to take the easy way out. In the clinic, everyone was supposed to do their own work like washing and ironing their clothes. Sunil went on a brief visit and found that Sanjay was still behaving like a nawab. He had persuaded some of the girls in the clinic that he was helpless because men in India usually did not do such work. They fell for his powers of persuasion, good looks and air of innocence, and began to do all his housework.

The breakthrough came when Sunil sent some tapes to Sanjay. These were the same tapes that Priya had noticed her father recording in Sloane Kettering. Nargis had left messages for everyone in her family. There were special messages for Sanjay asking him to be 'humble' and to be a 'good man'. Sanjay broke down and wept.

It was over three years since his mother had died, but listening to her sad broken voice, Sanjay realized for the first time that his mother was actually dead, and that she had had such high hopes for him. He began to remember all the wonderful dreams she had dreamt for him.

A great sense of relief came over him, as though he realized that even from beyond the grave, his mother was reaching out to him. It gave him the strength to fight the addiction, and even today he says his mother is always with him, looking after him.

He began to take his treatment seriously and within a few months was able to come home at last. He became and still remains, drug-free.

A major concern at the time was whether Sunil would remarry. The girls remember the proposals that flooded the house. Hundreds of women wrote in offering themselves in marriage. Sunil was an eligible man and there were many who felt that the children needed a mother.

It was a topic that came up now and again. Once, Nargis appeared to Zahida in a dream and said, 'Tell that uncle of yours I will never leave him in peace if he remarries.'

Zahida says, 'I told him, and he said, "How come she came in your dream and not in mine? But how can I remarry? There will never be another Mrs Dutt in my life. Tell her to relax. I will never remarry." I am sure he still admired, and perhaps even desired some women, after all he was still a young man. But I think something like a marriage was out of the question. He said, "I've got my children and I will not remarry." It may have been a difficult decision at times because Sunil had a glamorous career and he was only in his early 50s.

It is unlikely that the children would have welcomed another woman in their father's life. In fact, they were so possessive that they could not watch their parents' films for many years without feeling upset when they romanced other actors on screen.

But they need not have worried. Sunil had other things on his mind, especially the questions he had asked himself many years ago, in Yusmarg in the middle of the night. He thought of the Gita and the message Krishna had given Arjuna, that one must do one's karma and not worry about the result. Now he took solace in that maxim, as he began to shed the life of 'make-believe' he had written about to Nargis in 1967. He began to think more and more of those less fortunate than him.

He realized that he could pick up the strands of the social

work that Nargis had started and take it forward. He joined the Spastic Society as a patron and began to expand the activities of the Nargis Dutt Cancer Foundation.

In 1981, he had been appointed the Sherrif of Bombay and that gave him a public platform outside of cinema. It was actually a great honour for him because it meant that though he had taken a break in his career, people had not forgotten him. He could be even more involved in social reform now, and the satisfaction he gained from this brought him closer to Nargis.

He too felt that she was beside him, working with the spastic children. By raising money for cancer, he felt he was actually helping her in some way. The passion he had brought to cinema when he made films like *Mujhe Jeene Do* and *Yaadein*, he now brought to the causes he championed.

Sunil Dutt, MP
1984-87

Sanjay took some time to settle down after his return from rehab. In fact, he very nearly didn't return. Once he had recovered from his addiction, he decided he wanted to invest in a cattle-ranch in America instead of coming back to India. He had met a very successful cattle-ranch owner at the detox clinic, and was going to form a partnership with him. But Sunil could never bear the thought of his children being far from him. (He felt the same way about Priya when she got a job in America.) He persuaded Sanjay to come back and try living in Bombay for a year. If things did not work out, he could always go back.

Sanjay came back, and decided he was not going to try and find any work. Sunil had already told him that he had no money to launch him in a film again, so it seemed that soon he could take that flight back to America. But one day, a film called *Jaan ki Baazi* (1985), directed by Ajay Kashyap, was offered to him with Rs 15,000 as the signing amount. He was back in business. By 1988, more than five of his films were being released every year.

For Sunil, too, life was beginning to fall into a pattern. And then came a double whammy of good luck in the same year. In 1984, Namrata decided to get married and Sunil was asked to stand for parliament. The offer came from Rajiv Gandhi and given their closeness, Sunil could not refuse. He launched his election campaign on a Congress ticket at the same time that Namrata began her wedding preparations.

It was a wonderful period. Sanjay was back as well, so the

family was together again. Their joy was compounded by the fact that Namrata was marrying the son of one of her father's oldest friends, Rajendra Kumar. Kumar Gaurav is also an actor—his debut was the silver jubilee hit *Love Story*.

Kumar Gaurav says that Nargis was the first person to come to congratulate his mother when he was born. By the time Namrata married Bunty (as Kumar Gaurav is known at home) Nargis had been dead for three years. But in a wonderful coincidence she had once gifted him a new set of clothes, twenty-four years earlier, unaware that they were for her future son-in-law!

Though Sunil was thrilled at the turn of events, he was busy with his election campaign, so like everything else in her life, Namrata arranged her own wedding. It was an emotional time. Finally, Sunil had to allow one of his children to leave home. Namrata had been so pivotal in keeping the family together that it was difficult to imagine the Pali Hill house without her.

It didn't turn out to be the dream marriage everyone had hoped for. Within a year Namrata had walked out of her marital home. It was a very brave step for someone like her, who wanted nothing more than to spend time with her husband and daughter Sakshi, then barely six months old. It was also very brave because the parents were such good friends and Namrata ran the risk of being misunderstood. But she had inherited her mother's and grandmother's genes. Social conformity was the last thing on her mind. She didn't say much about the reasons for her unhappiness, but one imagines that it was a clash of cultures in some ways, because Nargis had brought her children up to be very cosmopolitan, while Bunty's was a more traditional Punjabi family.

Namrata says she felt sorry for her father. 'After a year of marriage, I walked out of my in-laws' house. What my in-laws did not realize was that I was not a little bachcha. I had been through a lot, even though I was still very young. I was running a home, looking after my father, my brother. Maybe I was too young and headstrong. I couldn't take it after some time. I remember my dad being quite perplexed. In the Hindu tradition you go to your mother's house for around 40 days after a baby is born. I hadn't done that, so when Sakshi was about six months old I said I'd like to go to my dad's house. I took enough clothes with me for about a month.

'Coming back to my dad's house was like oxygen. He used to keep saying, "It's one month, when are you going back?" I didn't know how to break it to him. He had been through enough, he didn't need this. I said, "Dad, I need time." I didn't want to disturb him. I think one day he realized, after about two months. I said, "Dad, I don't want to go back." He said, "How can you do something like this? You are a married woman now."

'I said, "Dad, do you consider me as your daughter? This is my house also. Do you want to throw me out on the road? I am not leaving." I felt very bad because he had to go and speak to my in-laws, but it was taken for granted that I wouldn't go. They never pressurized me to come back. I think Dad realized that I had been through a lot. Six months later, when Sakshi was about to turn one, things were still not all right. But I called my in-laws up and said I am celebrating my daughter's first birthday at my father's house, so please come over.

'That was when Bunty decided that he wanted to be with me. He came over and shifted into Dad's house with me. It was such a big thing for him to walk out of his house, the only son. That was also very difficult for my dad to handle, because he was very good friends with my father-in-law and he did not want him to feel that he was encouraging this in any way.

'I went and spoke to my father-in-law on my own. I told him that my dad had nothing to do with it. And that as soon as we found a place of our own, we would shift out. Which we did. It was after around six years.'

Meanwhile, Sunil had won the parliamentary election and was now busy settling the problems of his constituency in Bandra, Bombay. Priya was at Sophia College studying sociology. The Dutt household seemed to have quietened down. And then the Punjab problem erupted. It had nothing to do with Sunil Dutt directly, but his nationalism was shaken to the core. He was, and would always be, a Punjabi first and foremost. He could not imagine his beautiful state being torn apart once again. He had already suffered the effects of Partition. Now, in front of his eyes loomed another partition, unless something was done about it.

There was a strong secessionist movement for an independent Punjab to be called Khalistan, and militants were holding innocent people to ransom.The movement had a long history, from before India was partitioned.

In Punjab there had always been three, not two communities. The Sikhs were an independent religious community straddling the two older religious communities, Hindu and Muslim. But their voices were not heard at the time of Partition in 1947.

Once Bangladesh was independent, a pro-Khalistan agitation started in Punjab. The demand was for an independent nation state for the Sikhs, to be created out of the state of Punjab. It had a lot of support from the Sikh diaspora in North America and Britain. The Government of India took a dim view of any secessionist movement, be it in Kashmir, Nagaland or Punjab. Soon the movement took to arms and Punjab became a cauldron of violence. The charismatic leader of the movement, Sant Bhindranwale, advocated a heady mix of religion and ideology. He had been encouraged in his demands by the Congress when it was briefly in the Opposition between 1977 and 1979. But on returning to power, Indira Gandhi decided to take a tough stance and there was a virtual war with the Khalistanis.

At the climax, the terrorists occupied the Golden Temple in Amritsar, the holiest Sikh shrine. Mrs Gandhi ordered troops in to flush them out.

Following the military action on the Golden Temple, codenamed Bluestar, in which many militants, including Bhindranwale, were killed, Sikhs who raged against the desecration of the temple launched a programme of revenge. In the sad aftermath, Indira Gandhi was killed by her own Sikh security guards on 31 October 1984. Rajiv Gandhi was appointed prime minister—but the situation remained volatile in Punjab.

Violent anti-Sikh riots broke out in north India, especially Delhi, in 1984, and more than 3000 Sikhs were brutally murdered. The party in power did nothing to ensure their security.

The police were by and large mute witnesses to the carnage in which thousands of Sikhs lost their lives and property. Rajiv Gandhi himself seemed to dismiss the violence, with the reported statement that the ground shakes when a big tree falls.

In his new avatar as a member of parliament, Sunil came up with a unique plan to rebuild the image of Punjab. He wanted the rest of India to know that Punjab, despite all the bloodshed, was still a part of the nation and could not, should not, secede as long as patriots like him were alive. He decided to go on a padayatra, literally a pilgrimage on foot.

Sunil never thought of himself as a politician but he did believe that he had to serve the cause of his state and the nation. He also thought that there were genuine problems in Punjab which were not being addressed. His formula of appeasement was simple: if you tell the disaffected that you love them, why should they want to kill you? He thought that the people of Punjab were being maligned because of the misguided actions of a few.

Sunil's plan wasn't supported by his own party, or any other. In fact, many within the Congress thought it was a publicity stunt. But Sunil remained committed to his padayatra because he thought with his heart rather than his head. He also felt a deeply personal attachment which drew him to Punjab. For instance, his 89-year-old schoolteacher had settled in Punjab after Partition. Many such people and memories drew him to undertake the padayatra, even though he could not have done it at a more dangerous time.

The padayatra was meticulously planned as a journey on foot between Mani Bhavan where Mahatma Gandhi had once stayed in Bombay, to Harmandir Sahib (the Golden Temple) in Amritsar, Punjab. It would take 78 days to cover the distance of 2000 kilometres. To Sunil's great surprise, Priya decided to go with him. Initially he wondered if she was trying to get out of some difficult college exams, but once she took the required permissions from her college, they set off.

Sanjay was completely at a loss. He first tried to dissuade his father. Then he tried to stop his sister, after which he gave up.

For Priya, though she did not know it at that stage, the yatra was an induction into a career in politics. Her friends had also tried to talk her out of it but her mind was made up. Her father started his padayatra on 26 January 1987. She joined him in Bhiwandi and matched him step for step in the days that followed.

Having obviously inherited her mother's passion for writing, Priya began a diary in which she noted her pride in her father, and expressed her belief that this was a historic occasion.

On the first day itself, after they had walked 20 kilometres, she observed with some astonishment the curious but enthusiastic crowds along the way. She knew then that the purpose of the padayatra had been understood by India's masses. By the time the padayatra was completed, they were clocking in more than forty kilometres a day, and everywhere they went they were rapturously received.

On 16 March, the fiftieth day of their yatra, they covered 42 kilometres, walking till 8 p.m. It had become an obsession. The crowd walking with them was a motley one including, at various stages, politicians, volunteers, Buddhists, and even acupuncturists! It ebbed and flowed as they crossed state after state, beginning in Maharashtra, going through Madhya Pradesh, Rajasthan, Uttar Pradesh, Delhi, Haryana and finally reaching Punjab. The padayatris would start every morning with a prayer and then sing the national anthem. Their destination was sometimes more than 35 kilometres away, a distance they would have to cover in a single day.

Walking in the heat and dust was not easy—especially for Priya, who had been brought up in a sheltered environment. There were instances of illness, and Sunil's back and feet caused him a lot of trouble. But he would simply bandage his blistered, swollen feet and carry on. At one stage, towards the end of the padayatra, he developed high fever and was suspected to have jaundice. But he refused to rest and in fact felt guilty that he had brought everyone with him so far only to miss the deadline of reaching Amritsar on 13 April. That date was paramount in his mind.

He could not bear the humiliation of letting the others down, so he kept walking. The only concession he made was to rest every hour and frequently drink glucose water. His determination to reach pushed everyone else on. No matter how exhausted they were at the end of the day, Sunil's complete dedication to the cause pushed them on.

Priya noted that while they used to complete one kilometre in 15 minutes, in the beginning, now they took only 12-13 minutes, even when they were climbing the ghats.

She was constantly thrilled to see people coming out to greet the padayatris, not because Sunil was a film star (at times the crowds greeting them did not even know his name) but because they had heard that someone was trying to protect the unity of the nation. At other places she saw people falling at her father's feet because they knew about him and his mission. She was particularly overwhelmed by the affection demonstrated by people in the villages, who seemed happy to share whatever little they had.

She wrote in her diary, 'Seeing all this and being exposed to these simple lives in villages and small towns has really opened my eyes and brought me out of my shell. I have seen people living in poverty and misery but yet whenever we saw and met them they had smiles on their faces and a good wish for all of us.'

And when in certain towns Sunil asked for donations towards cancer treatment, 'the response was unbelievable. All sorts of people started giving money, even the poor adivasis, some gave Rs 1, some gave 50 p, and some also gave 10 p, whatever they could afford but they also gave from the heart.

'I have noticed one thing during my journey that the poor are much more humane than the rich and they give much more than the rich, though they can hardly afford it. But if they know something is being done for a good cause they will go all out to give you whatever they can afford, even their love is greater and more pure.'

She was deeply moved by the passion demonstrated: there were some who handed over letters and messages addressed to Sunil, written in their own blood.

It was a life-changing journey for her, she wrote. 'It was something I had to do, something for my country, at least I could say I have contributed something for my country, which will of course be like a drop in (the) ocean compared to what she has given me. I have found myself changed and matured, for the first time I have felt I have taken the right decision though I have been through a lot.'

On 4 March 1987, Priya read in the newspapers that Sikh commandos had threatened to kill Sunil but, as she proudly noted, they still carried on. It was the first of many threats. The group received written death threats all along the way which they learnt to call 'Love letters from T's' (terrorists). Sunil discussed these threats with the group. If anybody wanted to go back, he would understand, he said. But everyone decided to stick it out.

During the last stretch through Punjab, they learnt of at least three attempts to disrupt the yatra, even to kill them, especially Sunil. But they persevered.

There were many exciting moments as well, as Priya noted in her diary. For instance, when they crossed the 1000-kilometre mark, which was the halfway point for their journey:

5th March
Today we left at 6:15 a.m. Dad decided that we must complete 26 km by lunch as at that point we will be completing 1000 km exactly half our long journey. We stopped for breakfast at 8:30 a.m. and we really hogged and I was feeling sick now. Dad had that pain again so we tied Dad's feet tightly with gauze and left at 10. We still had to complete 16 km more for 26 km. Dad started walking really fast and I was feeling giddy and sick, I kept thinking of sitting down and then just didn't think about it, we were getting more and more faster as we neared the milestone...each milestone passed by really fast there was just one km left, we all then started shouting out our 3 famous slogans 'Bharat Mata Ki Jai', 'Hum Sab Ek Hain' and 'Mahatma Gandhi ki Jai.' We all had our turns and Dad was the last one to say it. The milestone was about 20 feet away from us and we just couldn't wait and all of us started jogging towards it. We had completed 1001 kms from Bombay in 37 days. In half our journey we were victorious and we are sure the second half will be even better.'

The yatra provided an opportunity for Priya to hone her own

principles and values and weigh them against those of her father. She was still young enough to note that 'Papa and myself were having some real intellectual talks, papa was giving me some heavy talks and I pray to God to give me a character like dad and make me like dad when I grow older. As everyone had an idol, I idolise my father and he is my inspiration and strength. He has taught me a lot and I know that if in future I become some one great I will owe it all to dad. By great I mean I should be like dad who loves helping and serving people without any selfish purpose.'

But her idealism would clash against reality much too often and each time, she would find the real world wanting. She felt their attempt to spread the message of love and peace was defeated by the fact that they themselves were constantly surrounded by a protective barrier of the Central Reserve Police Force. It made interaction with people impossible, and it was for these people that they had travelled so far.

The stories that people told, about the brutal and utterly senseless murder of family members by the police or the terrorists made Priya feel helpless. Yet the love they showered on the padayatris made the effort worthwhile.

She wrote in her typically frank style, 'I feel really nice when the village women come to me and bless me and give me their best wishes, as I feel they can identify with me and I really feel nice about it. It is these people who give me more and more courage and will to move ahead and I really love them. Who really irritate me are the fat rich semi-educated women who meet you as no one else but Sunil Dutt's daughter.'

She felt that now, even when she was not with her father, complete strangers knew her and recognized her. 'I felt nice to know that I am not in the shadow of dad but now have an identity of my own, thanks to pop.'

The padayatra received publicity throughout, and Priya was learning to cope with the limelight with her father. There was one such occasion in Delhi when the film industry organized a function to honour the padayatris. While Shabana Azmi garlanded Priya, it was Raj Kapoor who astounded everyone as he 'gave a very emotional speech and even touched dad's feet that was really too much as he is so much senior to dad and the function went off well.'

The fact that Raj came for the function and was willing to honour Sunil was not actually surprising. Nargis had died six years earlier. And Raj, who was never one to hide his feelings, recognized that Sunil had more than proved his worth to the film industry and to the country. It was a timely reconciliation, for in a year's time, Raj would also be dead.

The idea of death had begun to haunt Sunil by now, and on 30 March he prepared his will, just in case the terrorists did manage to assassinate him. He had a meeting with a friend, Mr Wadhwa, and Priya wrote, 'later I got to know that the long meeting dad had with Wadhwa uncle was regarding his "WILL" which he prepared and dad signed in the presence of witnesses. Dad was hiding it from me all this time but I got to know somehow. It upset me a little bit and I too wanted to make my will because if anything can happen to dad it can happen to me too. I slept thinking of what I should give to whom from my treasures.'

Though Priya managed to be calm about it, the truth was that the other members of the group were also worried that the militants would get to them. In Amritsar, especially, anything could happen. They were told that when they entered the Golden Temple, they would be accompanied by plainclothes security personnel who would carry concealed pistols and revolvers. Sunil was asked to wear a bulletproof jacket 'but dad refused and I totally agree with him because why should we enter this holy place with any fear in our hearts. God is Great and is our Greatest Protector,' wrote Priya.

When they finally entered Amritsar, on the day before Baisakhi, exactly as planned, most people in the group were tearful. None of them had actually believed they would make the long 2000 km journey and arrive on schedule. The final test came the next day when they entered the Golden Temple with their heads covered by orange bandannas.

'We set off at 6:30 a.m. and roads leading to the temple were beautifully decorated and we walked quietly without shouting slogans and each step we took I felt more and more excited about reaching the temple. I felt I was being pulled towards it and my heart was beating faster as I approached it.'

It was a thrilling welcome, and the entire group was conducted safely through the temple. For Sunil, it was a moment of triumph because he felt he had managed to convey a message to the rest of the country—all that Punjab needed was a healing touch. The people needed love, not suspicion. The fact that he could enter a 'terrorist den' proved that people were mistaken, and that policies concerning Punjab needed to change.

At the time, reports in the press suggested that even the chief minister of Punjab, S.S. Barnala, did not support Sunil's efforts. Basically, there was palpable fear that if he was murdered, there could be another wave of retaliatory killings everywhere. This report upset the family so much that even the apolitical Sanjay 'went berserk'. He decided that he would go to Delhi and speak to Rajiv Gandhi about this public repudiation of Sunil's mission.

Fortunately he was dissuaded, though ultimately Sunil did have to go to Delhi to convey his strong sentiments to the prime minister personally.

The padayatra was a heroic mission, and was covered extensively by the media, but it probably did little to change the central government's policy towards Punjab.

It would take a few more years and many more killings on both sides before Punjab became peaceful again. In fact, it would finally be stringent counter insurgency, conducted by the 'iron' police officer K.P.S. Gill, which led to the demise of terrorism. In the politics of the real world, there was little room for Sunil's message of love.

The Last Days
1987-2005

In their time together during the padayatra, Sunil had seen his daughter grow up. The three months changed her irrevocably. She began to explore career options, and since she was interested in documentary filmmaking, she left for New York after college to study television and film production for a year. Sunil did not want her to go, but agreed after his old friends, the director of Sloane Kettering and his wife, agreed to 'keep an eye' on her. Like Sanjay, Priya fell in love with the Big Apple and wanted to live there. She was 'young, bohemian' and managed to get a job with Fox TV.

To earn some extra money she started working at an Indian jewellery store. She remembers that one day she was sweeping the floor and closing up for the day when her father appeared. He stood outside and watched her work, with tears in his eyes. It was so reminiscent of his difficult start in Bombay. The only difference was that his daughter could have had a pampered life in Bombay but chose to sweat it out in New York. He managed to persuade Priya to come back home and try for work in India before she took a job abroad.

She returned, and one of her first projects was a documentary on Nargis, made for the Films Division of India. She discovered her mother all over again through it. But the bureaucracy she encountered while working on the film depressed her. So her interest shifted to her father's social work, especially the Spastic Society. She also got involved in campaigns dealing with child prostitution and drug abuse.

Meanwhile, Sanjay had met and married the aspiring actress Richa Sharma, in 1987. They enjoyed a brief period of happiness but just after the birth of their child, Trishala, tragedy struck the Dutt family again. Richa was diagnosed with a brain tumour, and within weeks, was rushed to the Sloane Kettering hospital. In a dreadful déjà vu, they had to face the fact that they would lose Richa as well.

Unlike Sunil, Sanjay could not face the prospect of watching his wife slip away. He came back to Bombay and kept working. It was probably a wise if difficult decision, for he managed to keep his career and his sanity.

Richa could not be moved back to India for treatment and ultimately, when she did die, Sanjay was with her, though she could no longer see or hear anyone. Beautiful, lively Richa died blind and deaf, cut off from the world. It was a cruel twist of fate, made worse by the custody battle over Trishala. Ultimately, Trishala went to live with her maternal grandparents in America.

Fortunately, Sanjay's career was doing well. He had discovered that he could play both negative and positive roles equally well. However, his world was about to unravel once again. Sanjay's breakthrough film was Subhash Ghai's *Khalnayak* (1993), in which he played the gangster Ballu who is caught by the police and incarcerated in a high-security prison—and this was exactly what would happen to Sanjay soon.

It can be argued that Sanjay's fate was not so much due to his nexus with the underworld as it was a direct result of Sunil's politics and beliefs. He was fighting against the tide, and in the process his son was swallowed by murky political machinations.

The beginning can be traced to the communal unrest that was threatening to spin out of control in Ayodhya, Uttar Pradesh. The Ram Janmabhoomi Babri Masjid controversy was threatening the country's delicately balanced secularism. Militant Hindu organizations had been calling for the destruction of the Babri mosque to 'reinstate' a temple at the site which they believed was Ram's birthplace. Things came to a head in the early 1990s. The Congress was in power at the centre, with Narasimha Rao as prime minister, and the Hindu right-wing Bharatiya Janata

Party was at the helm in Uttar Pradesh. A clash seemed inevitable, but many like Sunil tried to resist it. He undertook another padayatra from Faizabad in UP to Ayodhya, addressing public rallies and trying to spread his message of communal harmony.

Regardless of the consequences, and in full public view, the structure was demolished by Hindu fundamentalists on 6 December 1992, leading to communal riots in Bombay. During the riots, Sunil arranged a peace rally under the statue of Mahatma Gandhi, in the city. Sanjay and Priya also pitched in to try and help the victims, mostly Muslims, and collected relief material and food for them at their own bungalow. Sanjay later noted that Sunil's life was endangered at least two times while he was out distributing relief material.

Unfazed, Sunil and his children carried white flags and toured the riot-stricken areas to distribute aid material. Then, and no one could identify the source, the Dutts started receiving frightening phone calls, with threats of rape and murder. When Sunil was away, it was often Priya or Sanjay who fielded the calls.

Sanjay later admitted that he would sit up all night with a gun, waiting for the mob to arrive. It was this attempt to protect his family which would get him into very serious trouble shortly. Was there in his mind a faint memory of the threats he had received as a child in boarding school? At that time he had been a helpless and scared 10-year-old, worried that he could not protect his mother or sisters. But now he was older and, armed with a gun, prepared for the worst. If they came to rape his sisters, he would fight back.

He admitted that he was deeply affected by 'the women and kids (who) really got damaged and raped and burnt and all that' during the Bombay riots (*To Hell and Back*, Channel 4, 1996, produced by Behroze Gandhy and Rosie Thomas). Complaints and phone calls to the police resulted in little or no help for the riot victims.

According to the Srikrishna Judicial Commission of Inquiry constituted by the Maharashtra government, 275 Hindus and over 575 Muslims were killed in the riots.

Despite the danger inherent in the situation, the Dutt family carried on with their relief work. But the riots had dealt a major blow to Sunil's secular stance. Maharashtra had a Congress government with Sharad Pawar as chief minister. Yet the proponents of Hindutva spearheaded by the Shiv Sena were allowed to operate with impunity and there was no respite from the violence. In a gesture of despair, Sunil resigned from the Lok Sabha. Though his resignation was not accepted, it was the beginning of an ambiguity concerning him within the Congress party. His resignation was treated not as an act of sorrow, but as a critique of governmental apathy. He would now have to battle foes within his own party and unfortunately, this battle continued in some form or the other till his death nearly 13 years later.

Sunil was that strange creature, an apolitical politician. It was his greatest weakness, it left him vulnerable in the cut and thrust of politics. And now, it left his family vulnerable, especially his beloved son, who would soon be shoved into a living hell.

In retrospect, he was to admit, 'Whatever my son has suffered he has suffered because of me, because of my ideologies, my thinking and whatever I did, you know, for the common people, and all the suffering went to him. That's why I feel far more sad because he's the type of guy who does not know anything about politics and who never indulged in politics.' (*To Hell and Back*, 1996)

Others also tried to bring peace to Bombay. But then, on 'Black Friday', 12 March 1993, the city was shaken by a series of bomb blasts, said to have been masterminded by Bombay don 'Tiger' Memon, the Dubai-based Dawood Ibrahim, and his brother Anees Ibrahim. The heart of Bombay—the stock exchange and the Air India building—was attacked, and the official death toll was 257.

A few weeks later, stories began appearing in the press (attributed to police sources) about Sanjay's involvement in gun procurement. When the actual explosions took place, he was shooting in Rajasthan and Priya was with him. When the accusations started appearing, he was shooting in Mauritius. Worried about the allegations, Sunil called Sharad Pawar and asked for his advice. The chief minister suggested that Sanjay return and answer the allegations in person.

Sanjay returned from Mauritius on 19 April 1993 and was immediately arrested. Over 150 people would be accused eventually of planning the terrible March explosions. Sanjay would be amongst them.

That day, Priya, Namrata and Bunty had gone to the airport to pick up Sanjay. They noticed the huge police presence and wondered which VIP was arriving. Before they realized what was happening, the police jeeps had driven up to the aircraft. Sanjay was taken directly to the police station and he was to remain in police custody under TADA (Terrorist and Disruptive Activities (Prevention) Act). TADA was a draconian anti-terrorism act which gave the police unlimited powers. In effect, if arrested under TADA, as Sanjay said, "you were guilty until proven innocent."

Bunty stayed with Sanjay that night and only left when the interrogation began the next day. All sorts of rumours about gun caches and plots started flying around. The recently released *Khalnayak* did not help. Sanjay's role of an anti-national character seemed, to the public, a reflection of reality. The publicity posters of the film carried shots of Sanjay with the lines from the film, 'Yes I am the Villain.' News television programmes (there were no 24-hour news channels at the time) and print media showed clips or photographs of Sanjay from the film, and everyone who looked at him waving a gun saw it as proof of his guilt. For Sunil, Namrata and Priya, who loved Sanjay and knew him to be a gentle, loving (if occasionally wayward) man, it was an unacceptable situation.

The next morning, the then Joint Commissioner of Police (Crime) M.N. Singh and his deputy, Rakesh Maria 'started the interrogation. Sanjay broke down and narrated the entire story. The same evening, Sunil Dutt and his daughter Priya Dutt met Sanjay in the presence of police officers. Sunil Dutt was still not ready to believe that his son could have been involved in the blasts conspiracy. Maria told Sanjay to tell his father the truth, and Sanjay conceded that he had been in possession of an assault rifle and some ammunition that he had got from Anees Ibrahim.

Sunil Dutt wanted to know the reason why. He was not prepared for the answer: "Because I have Muslim blood in my veins. I could not bear what was happening in the city." A crestfallen Sunil Dutt left the police headquarters.' (*Tehelka*, 24 March 2007)

Sunil lived for many years with the trauma of seeing his son in handcuffs. 'When they handcuffed my son I really felt that somebody is hanging all my dignity and all my honour and whatever I've done for the country and I couldn't hold my emotions at that time, which I wanted to because I felt anything I do might affect my son, he may become weaker. I couldn't hold my tears at that time and he looked at me and he understood.' (*To Hell and Back*)

The exact details of the case could not be revealed to the media or the public at the time because the investigation was still going on, but one thing was clear: Sanjay was accused of being anti-national and was allegedly involved in the 1993 bomb blasts. The central accusation which eventually emerged was that he had obtained arms illegally and could be implicated in terrorist acts. He was finally accused of acquiring, on 16 January 1993, three AK56s, nine magazines, 450 cartridges and over 20 hand grenades from Anees Ibrahim who, with his brother Dawood, was charged as one of the main conspirators in the 1993 blasts. Out of the arms cache brought to him, Sanjay reportedly admitted that he retained only one AK56 and ammunition and returned the rest of the consignment. (Sanjay was to later withdraw the 'confession'.)

Everyone who knew Sanjay realized that despite his 'bad boy' ways, he had only been trying to protect his family. He was simply not capable of 'conspiring' or planning terrorist acts. But the fact remained that it was illegal even to possess an unlicensed weapon, and his friends admitted privately that he had been a complete 'fool' to get involved in anything so dangerous.

In its final form the case, which came up for judgement after 13 years, was reported in the press as follows:

Sanjay (is) one of the accused in the 1993 Mumbai blast case who was charged by the CBI for possessing an AK 56 rifle...The weapon was delivered to him by underworld don Abu Salem, film producer

Samir Hingora and another accused Baba Moosa Chavan.

Sanjay had earlier admitted to the Mumbai police that he possessed an AK 56 rifle but later retracted his statement in court.

It is learnt that Baba Moosa Chavan, Samir Hingora and Hanif Kadawala had delivered three rifles and ammunition to Sanjay on the behest of Anees Ibrahim. Sanjay is reported to have retained one of the three rifles.

He is charged with destroying the rifle with the help of four of his friends who were granted bail. (19 October 2006, *Asian Age*)

Sunil found it difficult to believe what was happening to his son. It was incomprehensible that he could be accused of being an antinational, a traitor. How could Sanjay be a traitor when both he and Nargis had always put their country before anything else?

Sanjay would remain in jail for 15 months more. When he was shifted to the Arthur Road police station, several humiliating experiences lay in wait for the Dutt family. Despite being a member of parliament, Sunil was not accorded any special status when he went to the police station. He would sit there from seven in the morning, hoping for a glimpse of Sanjay. He would ask the police inspector, 'Please *zara andar jaane dijiye* (Please let me go in).' and often be refused.

Namrata and Priya would take food for Sanjay and be asked to taste it before giving it to him. They were horrified at the implication. Would they poison their own brother? The police search party arrived at their home, which was a temple of privacy for Sunil. The sniffer dogs and the police turned the house upside down. The news was in the papers everyday, and all their carefully built up dignity was ripped away, bit by bit.

All sorts of barbs and insults would be hurled at them. Namrata and Priya remember the strange looks they got when they went out. For Sunil, it was a gut-wrenching experience. There was no one to whom he could turn. Even if he went to Sharad Pawar, he was usually kept waiting, sometimes up to four hours. He knocked on every door. This was a very proud man, a man who refused to bend, and hated to compromise. Now for the sake of his son, he had to beg for help. But the

Bombay blasts had shocked the nation and Sanjay, rightly or wrongly, got little sympathy.

Unfortunately, Sunil could not even ask for help from the Nehru-Gandhi family because they had withdrawn from politics after the assassination of Rajiv Gandhi in 1991.

But he had to at least fight the media war for his son. In an interview he gave to the *Times Of India* on 10 November 1993, the headline read:

SUNIL DUTT SATISFIED WITH PROBE

Noted film actor and politician, Mr Sunil Dutt said here today that he was fully satisfied with the investigations related to the illegal possession of prohibited arms by his son the well known cine star, Sunjay Dutt. ...He said that the Maharashtra Chief Minister, Mr Sharad Pawar had personally been a source of great strength for him and was always available to him. 'I was going through terrible times and whenever I wanted time to meet or talk to him Mr Pawar always granted it.' He had nothing against the Bombay police or anybody in the state government for they were all performing their duty.

He said 'everybody knows that a member of the Dutt family could not have gone any further and the contribution made by me, my wife and others for the cause of national unity and integration was not forgotten by the people. Good work never goes to waste.'

Mr Dutt said that it was during the time of Sunjay's arrest that he realized he had many friends. Colleagues in the film industry, like Dilip Kumar, Shatrughan Sinha, and Subhash Ghai gave him moral support. Political leaders led by the Prime Minister, Mr P.V. Narasimha Rao, also were sympathetic. Even Mr Jaswant Singh, deputy leader of the BJP in Parliament wrote a very touching letter to him.

It went on for months. Sunil could not sleep at night any more. How could he sleep in a comfortable bed when his son was locked up in a six-by-four cell? He would drive to the jail and stand outside, staring at the thick walls all night, wishing there was some way he could get in and embrace his son.

As Sunil recalled, 'I always used to tell him that you must convince yourself mentally that behind this wall your father is there...whether you get up in the night at 12 o'clock. You feel your father is there and I will be there I guarantee you. And so many times in the dead of night I used to drive (to the jail) and I used to park my car outside the walls and sometimes I used to go around, because there's a road... I felt he must feel someone.'

Sanjay knew his father was trying very hard, but he felt completely alone, and usually kept his emotions firmly bottled up. 'You see, it's a funny kind of game between the accused who is inside and the family who is outside. It's sad and I don't know, it's funny...because you feel you don't want to emote that much for them to get worried on the outside because they can't do anything and they feel we should not cry in front of the guy because he shouldn't get upset and so we're both sitting and acting our parts.' (*To Hell and Back*)

He was kept in a high-security barrack, along with other militants, with round-the-clock patrolling by the CRPF. They were allowed out only for 15 minutes in the morning and the evening, and were locked up the rest of the time.

Sunil's neighbours, Dilip Kumar and Saira Bano, remember those days. Sunil and Dilip would constantly think of people to contact, things to do. He had to keep thinking of how he could get Sanjay out. Sometimes, Dilip would fly with him to Delhi to meet politicians who they thought might help. Saira remembers going to J.J. Hospital when Sanjay was unwell during his imprisonment. She came back and cried for hours thinking of his condition.

Priya recollects that during his jail term his lungs collapsed. 'There was an air bubble in one of them. I went to see him in J.J. Hospital and he was handcuffed to the bed. It was inhuman; one hand was handcuffed and on the other was a drip. I called my dad and said, "Papa, please come," and my dad was furious. He told the lawyers to go to court and file a case. But my brother said, "Dad, forget it, they are only doing their job." He was becoming very reconciled to his life in prison, he used to keep telling us, "Relax, forget it, it's ok." He had really started understanding life and how to get the best of what was there in order to survive. In prison, he learnt how to get his cigarettes organized, how to get that extra cup of tea organized. He just learnt to survive, no matter what happened to him.'

The chain of events led nowhere and finally one day, Sunil told Sanjay bluntly that he couldn't help him. Strangely, the words brought relief to Sanjay. All this while, he had been impatient to get out. Every time his father came to visit, he would anxiously ask, 'When am I getting out of here, dad?' The questions came to an end. He thought he would have to be reconciled to living in jail for the rest of his life, because if his father could not help him, no one could. Sanjay literally made himself stop caring. He read books which helped him re-examine his life, he read the Gita, and Nelson Mandela. He let his hair and beard grow long. In a peculiar way he actually managed to reach a level of contentment, because he met and interacted with so many others who were in a similar situation, and no one knew how long it would take to get justice.

One friend who kept visiting him, and kept his spirits up during this time, was an actress who would become an important part of his life. The elegant Rhea Pillai had come to make it big in Bollywood, and instead found love with Sanjay. Now she spent more and more time at the Arthur Road Jail, trying to cheer Sanjay up, promising him that one day soon they could be together.

Sunil was no longer optimistic, but he decided to compromise his own principles and met Bal Thackeray, the Shiv Sena chief. The militant Hindu group was thought to have been the main instigator of the Bombay riots. The Shiv Sena and the Congress party had been fierce opponents for a long time, which was why Sunil had kept his distance from the Shiv Sena supremo. But he, like Sanjay, was beyond caring about niceties. He had learnt a tough political lesson.

Now he was only a father trying to find a solution for his son. On his part, Bal Thackeray was quite supportive after their meeting. He was sympathetic and issued statements that may eventually have helped Sanjay. He also questioned how anyone could accuse the Dutt family of being antinational. Whether the statements actually made a difference or not, at last Sunil was able to get a prominent leader to speak up for his son.

In an interview given later, on 19 September 1999, to Ashish Virmani of the Sunday *Afternoon Despatch & Courier*, Sunil spoke about his relationship with Bal Thackeray:

Q: Many people thought that after you had pleaded with Thackeray to get Sanjay released, you would contest on a Sena ticket.

A: I had no contract with Thackeray to that effect. Thackeray knew that I was a Congressman and would remain one. What he did for Sanjay was on emotional grounds and there wasn't an expectation of return. Balasaheb is not a small man who does things for a friend and then expects favours in return.

In every statement I have always said that our ideologies differ. My aim has been secularism and unity of caste and creed irrespective of religion.

Q: But after the shabby treatment meted out to you and your son by Sharad Pawar, then CM of Maharashtra, weren't you tempted to cross over?

A: One individual treating me shabbily doesn't mean I'll change my philosophy of life. I adopted the philosophy because I felt it can give great service to the people of this country. People come and go, but the party remains. I hold no grudge or ill feeling towards that individual—it was his part to play at that time and my part to receive.

After about 16 months in jail, during which Sanjay was repeatedly refused bail both by the TADA court and the Supreme Court, 'a quasi-judicial committee of bureaucrats and police officers, set up to review the status of TADA detainees, granted Sanjay bail.' (*Tehelka*, 24 March 2007)

Sanjay was finally released and came home to a rapturous reception, but to a family that had been completely shaken by the strange turn of events. According to some reports, he visited the Siddhivinayak Temple and various other places of worship, and also met and thanked Bal Thackeray. Of course, the case wasn't over as yet. There were 2500 witnesses to be examined, and over 150 accused. It would take another 13 years of humiliation before Sanjay was finally exonerated of the charge of being antinational. On 28 November 2006, Judge Kode said of Sanjay Dutt, accused number 117, 'Considering the confession of the accused and other evidence, it is accepted that the arms were for self defence. Hence (he is) not guilty for possession of arms under section 5 TADA.'

Finally, the day that Sunil had hoped for arrived, but by that time, he was not around to rejoice for his son. As this book goes to press, Sanjay still awaits the final word. He has been held guilty of possessing illegal weapons under Sections 3 and 7 of the Arms Act, but with this conviction he can also file for probation, which is what the family hopes for. In any case, the joy of the initial TADA court judgement was shortlived because on 31 July 2007 he received his final sentence, six years of rigorous imprisonment, and was arrested amidst unprecedented media attention. He was first sent to the Arthur Road Jail and eventually to Yerawada Jail in Pune.

This time it is Priya, who has inherited her father's mantle as a member of parliament, who is fighting for his release. Fortunately, a Congress government is at the centre, and she has been able to avail of both advice and support from the Congress party president, the once-reticent Sonia Gandhi, who displayed her sympathy for Priya by not only meeting her but also arranging for advice from the law minister. Her sympathy has meant that other Congress ministers have also voiced their support for Sanjay, hoping he gets an early release.

Fortunately, this time the legal advice helped. After appealing to the Supreme Court, with the plea that he was yet to receive a copy of the judgement from the TADA court, Sanjay was again released on bail after 23 days in jail, in the early hours of 23 August 2007.

The situation is as precarious today as when he was released on bail in 1994. (This time round he is at the top of his profession, and an estimated Rs 70 crore are said to be riding on him.) Thirteen years ago, Sanjay had lost his foothold on the ladder, and struggled hard to find his place again. He also had to rebuild his life, because the trauma of jail changed him in many ways. He was tense and nervous, and slept badly for a long time. Sunil was with him every step of the way. His own career did not matter so much at that point. Tellingly, he did not stand against the Shiv Sena candidate in the next election. It may have been the price he paid for his political naiveté.

Everyone in the family was affected by the traumatic experience. Namrata's young daughters, Sakshi and Siya, had visited Sanjay in jail in 1993. The younger of the two, Siya, was so upset that she could not speak to Sanjay again for more than ten years.

Because the family had suffered so much, people close to them began to suggest that perhaps the bungalow that Sunil had bought so eagerly more than three decades earlier was unlucky, and that someone had put a spell on the house. Sunil was not ordinarily superstitious, but exhausted by ill fortune, he agreed that they would shift out and the bungalow rebuilt.

Accordingly, he and Priya shifted to a building close by, called Apsara. It was a heart-wrenching move, because now things had to be cleared out from 58 Pali Hill. It was something Sunil had resisted ever since Nargis died. He hated the thought of parting with anything that belonged to her. But their new flat was much smaller than the sprawling bungalow, so he agreed to finally distribute Nargis's personal effects.

The family began to scatter. Namrata had already shifted into a flat in Juhu with Bunty and their children. Sanjay had fallen in love again, with Rhea Pillai. Sunil had also met her on their jail visits. She had fallen ill during that period and Sunil suggested that she come and stay with them at Pali Hill so that she could be looked after properly. But once Sanjay came home, Sunil thought they would like to be together. So he gave up all his old-fashioned beliefs and actually rented an apartment nearby and asked Priya to do it up for the couple. The ultra-conservative Sunil was learning to move with the times.

Eventually Sanjay and Rhea had a spur-of-the-moment wedding in a temple on Valentine's Day, in 1997. Unfortunately the marriage did not last, and the couple finally divorced in 2005. On the positive side, Sanjay told his father he would handle his own career, and despite his misgivings, he was able to sign a few films in 1994 itself. Not only that, he became more and more successful each year. Sunil had been through the experience of rebuilding his career after a long hiatus, so he could appreciate what his son had achieved. Sanjay says that he knew, finally, that his father was proud of him.

For Sunil the break from active politics during this period came as a relief. He was able to concentrate again on his social work and Sanjay's rehabilitation. He kept up with his yatras and in 1995 he undertook an expedition by jeep from Singapore to New Delhi. He called it the Azad Hind Expedition. With him were two veterans of the INA, or the Azad Hind Fauj, Colonel Dhillon and Mrs Laxmi Sehgal. They covered a distance of 10,000 miles, their aim: to make the youth aware of the sacrifices of Subhash Chandra Bose and the INA.

Throughout this trying time, Sunil had not allowed his patriotism to die, though he was often puzzled by those who questioned it. Fortunately, there were many who did recognize it, and he was extremely proud of the many awards and honours he won, especially for promoting communal harmony.

He used this period also to build up the Nargis Dutt Cancer Foundation for which he travelled both in India and abroad on various missions. He was often invited to speak for the various charities, such as the Spastic Society of India, in which he was involved. Finally he was persuaded to return to politics, and won back his Lok Sabha seat from Bombay North West in 1999.

But, as noted in the press, he contested the elections in the thirteenth Lok Sabha only after Sharad Pawar had been expelled and Sonia Gandhi was brought in as party president. Sunil would always be loyal to the Gandhi family. After Sanjay's jail term, there was little love lost between Sunil and Pawar anyway. Pawar had objected to Sonia Gandhi's foreign origin when she took over as president, and he quit to form the National Congress Party with its base in Maharashtra.

There had been a break in Sunil's political career for over three years. But this time there was no return to cinema. His last film, *Phool,* was shot in 1993.

Sunil spoke about his return to politics to Ashish Virmani, in an interview for the Sunday *Afternoon Despatch & Courier* on 19 September 1999:

> Q: Considering Madhukar Sarpotdar of the Shiv Sena won the last two elections for the Lok Sabha North West constituency, what makes you think you'll make a comeback?
>
> A: People know me as a person and they know that the Congress stands for communal harmony and national integrity. Apart from my constituency, it's my commitment and the work I've done. I've always addressed people's problems – whether it was drug abuse, AIDS, spastics or cancer. When we recently drove 10,000 miles from Singapore to Delhi in the Hands Across the Borders mission, we were trying to say it's futile to spend money on weapons (the Kargil war had just taken place) when basic issues like education, healthcare, jobs for youth and water supply are not being tackled on the local level. I was the lone member of the Congress to have started a movement against my own party for better amenities for slum dwellers in '85...

But then, as he was settling down in his role as MP, the turbulence which had dogged his whole life struck again.

He had gone to Nepal on a peace mission to the SAARC countries when he suffered a slight injury on his head. He forgot about it and went for a fundraiser to the US. By the time he came back, he was in severe pain and had high fever. His condition worsened rapidly and he lost all sensation in his legs.

Priya was with him and immediately informed the doctors.

He was checked into Breach Candy Hospital. Fortunately, they injected steroids which arrested the paralysis halfway up his waist. Had it not been detected in time, he would have been completely paralysed, for his organs would have collapsed.

It was difficult for the children to see their indomitable father lying helpless in bed. But Sunil began to fight back almost immediately. The doctors had lost all hope and gave him a very slim chance of recovery; he decided otherwise.

Through sheer willpower, he began working on his legs. He began to exercise his toes all day and then slowly went into physiotherapy for the entire lower part of his body. It was a miracle when he finally began to walk. He had to use a collar and a neck brace, but he insisted on walking.

Barely had he recovered from this than he was caught in another, even more dangerous accident. He was returning from a wedding in Shirpur, when near Nasik in Maharashtra, the small aircraft he was travelling in nosedived and crashed. It caught fire and none of the doors would open. With Sunil were the young daughters of a friend. Thinking quickly, Sunil picked up his walking stick and smashed open a passage for the girls. He managed to get out after them and only then realized that his hair was burnt and he had broken his shoulder and his leg. Once again he was back in hospital and physiotherapy.

Luckily, Priya was able to take the time out from the Spastic Society, where she now worked, to help her father. She did not know it then, but it was a training period for her, because while he was unwell, she had to deal with the MLAs in his constituency, write letters for him and generally grapple with the day-to-day business of being an MP. The hospital room became a makeshift office.

Sunil had always worried about his younger daughter. He knew that Namrata was finally settled and that Sanjay's career was on a fast track. But where Priya was concerned, he knew Nargis would never forgive him. If she were looking at them (wherever she was), she would ask, 'Why is my daughter not married?' Somehow, even though he had tried to arrange a marriage for Priya, nothing had worked out.

Then she met someone who was also working with the Spastic Society. Owen Roncon owned an event management company. She says, 'I think it was Owen's simplicity which attracted me to him. I wrote a letter to my father about it. It was the first time I could relate to someone without my name overshadowing it. Someone who could relate to me as me, otherwise everyone would relate to me first as Sunil Dutt's daughter, Sanjay Dutt's sister.

'Our values matched, though he comes from a completely different background. He comes from a broken home, his parents were divorced when he was around three, he and his sister were very close, they kind of helped each other grow up. I come from a very close-knit family where family values mean everything to us, he's not had that kind of close-knit background. Yet, because of his difficult childhood, he is very attached to his mother and sister.'

Surprisingly, after all these years of wanting Priya to get married, Sunil now changed his mind. Owen was a Roman Catholic, and he was three years younger than Priya, but none of that really mattered to Sunil. He didn't really care about Owen's religion or age or financial status, though there was a visible difference between their lifestyles. He was genuinely worried about just one thing—that someone had managed, perhaps, to mislead and manipulate his beloved daughter. She was, he thought, much too innocent.

Priya tried to persuade him to meet Owen. Instead, he suggested that they should concentrate on getting married. Priya asked, 'But don't you want to meet him before we get married?' 'No,' responded Sunil. He was anxious that if he met Owen and did not like him for some reason, Priya might be pressurized into changing her mind. He did not want anything to come in the way of his daughter's happiness.

Sanjay went a step further: he said he would only meet Owen a year after the marriage, implying that he too felt there was something wrong.

Painting an amusing vignette of Sanjay, Priya says, 'My brother met Owen and he was damn happy, saying "Damn nice guy".

Then he realized that these two are actually thinking of getting married and then said, "I don't think you should get married." His reason was just, "Who is he? How can you get married just like that to anybody?" Owen went to him and said, "What can I do to convince you or to persuade you?" Sanjay said, "You want to do something? Just don't get married to her. That will be the best thing." Anyway he refused to come to my wedding. He was sitting at home, crying I think, "O god, my sister is really getting married." For him I am still the little kid sister who is always going to be a little kid. He does take me seriously, but he's very protective about me. I didn't feel bad because I know how he is. He is just a highly strung, over emotional person. Now he laughs about it all.'

Friends and family who heard of Priya's problem began to talk to Sunil. Finally, five days before the wedding, he agreed to meet Owen. And finally Sunil felt that his daughter had made a wise choice. From planning a low-key wedding he was suddenly galvanized into organizing a proper celebration. They were married on 27 November 2003, and it was Sunil who insisted that they go on a honeymoon, saying that he and Nargis never really got around to having one.

Priya shifted into Owen's home for a while till Imperial Towers, the high-rise that had come up in place of the old bungalow, was ready. Then she returned home to a flat specially earmarked for her by her father. In the same building, Sunil had reserved a flat each for Namrata, Sanjay and himself. They began moving in, except Sunil, who wanted to pack his own things, meticulously, and move only when every last screw in the house had been put in according to his instructions.

Over time, Owen and Sunil became close. Sunil was the first father figure Owen ever had and during his final election campaign, Owen managed everything. Another great bonding factor was their interest in sports. Owen is a keen swimmer, an equestrian and trekker. After Sunil was appointed the Minister for Sports and Youth Affairs in 2004, they would spend more and more time together discussing their mutual passion.

Once again it appeared that Sunil was being rehabilitated in the Congress. Sonia Gandhi personally called to tell him he had become a minister, and it was a portfolio of his choice, as he felt sports and youth affairs required special attention.

For his first day in the new office, he discarded the trademark white kurta-pyjama and wore jeans and a blue shirt and went across to meet Sonia Gandhi. She was surprised and he said, 'Why, you are the one who made me the minister for youth affairs, so I have to look the part.' And, as his assistant Shakeel Ahmed remembers, he did it in great style, sometimes even wearing a shirt over a t-shirt. He wanted to create a new image, of a minister who was completely integrated into his department.

Those were good years for Sunil, and in a happy coincidence, he and Sanjay had been cast in the same film as well. *Munnabhai MBBS* (2003), directed by Vidhu Vinod Chopra, was a light-hearted film: the young Murli Prasad Sharma aka Munnabhai (Sanjay Dutt) makes a living as a small-time mafia don in Bombay. But when his simple, rustic father (Sunil Dutt) visits him, he decides to hide his real activities and pretend he is running a hospital. The film became a phenomenal hit, with rights for a remake bought up by Mira Nair, the New York-based director. A sequel, *Lage Raho Munnabhai*, released in 2006, which popularized the idea of 'Gandhigiri', was also a super-hit.

For Sunil, who was slapping on the greasepaint after ten years, it was a joyous experience. He told Sanjay, 'I don't know why I got into politics. This is my real love.'

According to the script writer Rajkumar Hirani, Sunil was a complete professional but could not resist suggesting a few changes in the script. At the end of the film, for instance, when the father and son are reconciled, Sunil suggested the moment be reinforced with a hug and the dialogue, *'Tune apni maa ko to bahut baar jhappi daali hai. Aa aaj apne baap ke gale bhi lag ja* (You have hugged your mother many times, come now, put your arms around your father as well).' He insisted he wanted the lines included. Perhaps, said Hirani, he wanted to convey something to his son through those lines. (Rajkumar Hirani spoke to Anuradha Choudhary, *Filmfare* tribute, July 2005)

However, while on the surface things appeared to be moving

smoothly, certain unhappy events from the past caught up with Sunil again. He had won the Lok Sabha election in 2004, but it had not been an easy fight. While he enjoyed the usual wave of support, as a popular and approachable MP, the election campaign itself had been more than a little fraught. Sunil and his children had been taken aback at the virulent and vicious campaign launched by the Shiv Sena, during which certain slurs (for instance, insinuations that he hardly attended parliament) were allegedly cast at Sunil.

His opponent in the contest was the Shiv Sena MP Sanjay Nirupam. As soon as Sunil was elected, he filed a defamation suit against Nirupam.

It was a difficult case, and the matter is still under dispute even after his death. Everyone in the Congress knew about the suit but shockingly, some time later, Sanjay Nirupam was inducted into the party. This was a severe blow for Sunil. He could not imagine that the loyalty he had shown to his party would be rendered meaningless so quickly. He had managed to rebuild his life after the debacle of Sanjay's arrest, but this time the blow went far too deep and shook whatever ideals he still had left.

In the press, articles appeared about his distress and anguish. 'The last battle Sunil Dutt fought was over the induction into the Congress of ex-Shiv Sena MP, Sanjay Nirupam who had badmouthed him, Sonia Gandhi and the Congress at every available opportunity. Last fortnight when the Congress high command termed an anti-Nirupam public rally organized by Dutt's supporters as "anti-party activity", Dutt was distraught and expressed his anguish by addressing the rally himself...' (*Times of India*, 26 May 2005)

A fortnight after the rally, a broken-hearted Sunil was dead. There were other factors that caused him to be depressed towards the end. Namrata remembers that he would be in his office in Delhi from early morning till late at night. But no matter how hard he worked, he felt he was not achieving his goals. It was not as though he was not making a difference at the sports ministry. He had managed to inject enthusiasm into a largely neglected sphere. The previous year, he had been to the Olympic games in Athens and had personally met the Indian team, to find out the shortcomings in the arrangements made for them on a foreign tour and how he could make up for them.

Coming back to the Games Village from a training session one day, the Indian hockey team was surprised to see Dutt waiting patiently. He had dropped in to meet them and to take a few photographs—photographs he would take and they would pose for, not photographs in which the players would be sidekicks flanking *mantriji*.

Talking to shooter Mansher Singh, Dutt was proactive. He wondered why, instead of omnibus sports centres, India couldn't have academies bunched together for archery, shooting and similar sports that could benefit from a common sports science and psychology resource. It was only an idea, but at least the minister was thinking...

One Indian Olympian summed it up: 'I've never met a minister like him. Other sports ministers waited for us to introduce ourselves, this one was introducing himself to us...' (Ashok Malik, *Indian Express*, 22 August 2004)

Given his enthusiasm, he was saddened to find that very few were keen to move at his pace. He also discovered corruption, such as equipment being bought but not used properly. A friend who prefers to remain nameless remembers Sunil being anguished because he was constantly being stymied by the senior bureaucrats around him. The friend also points out that Sunil was replaced on the panel of the Commonwealth Games by the President of the Indian Olympic Association and MP, Suresh Kalmadi, though traditionally the sports minister is on the panel. Such jostling for power was unfamiliar for Sunil; he could not become 'political' like his fellow Congressmen.

Namrata says that just about a month before he died, he spoke to her on the phone from Delhi, sounding excessively sombre. He seemed to be talking in riddles and said that he had no control left over his own life. 'He said, "*Main bahut thak gaya hoon* (I am very tired). I think I seem to be overstraining myself. Whatever I want to do, I can't do. Whatever dreams I have of doing something, they are being shattered." I said, "I think you are getting over worked."' He used to come back to Bombay for the weekend but his weeks were spent in Delhi. She learnt after his death that he had felt increasingly isolated within the ministry.

Sunil was a doer, and not given to empty pontification, as were some of his colleagues within the Congress party. Like Nargis, if he saw an opportunity and felt he could make a difference, he leapt at it. The bureaucratic maze of Delhi was difficult for him to navigate. For years Sunil had achieved his goals because he did not have to rely on others to deliver. If he wanted to make a film, he made it. If he wanted to go on a padayatra, he did it. Now suddenly he was at the mercy of bureaucrats and politicians, most of whom cared only about their self-promotion and little else.

Perhaps to cleanse his spirit from the morass of despair in which it seemed mired, he decided to replicate Mahatma Gandhi's Dandi march between 12 March and 6 April 2005. He was still quite depressed and Namrata was upset at the decision. She was right to be so, because barely had he returned to Bombay than he fell sick. On 23 and 24 May, he was running a high temperature, but he was packing to shift into his new home at Imperial Towers. The others had all moved in. A big celebration was planned for early June.

On the morning of 25 May, Sunil woke up at about 5 a.m. He remembered he had a 9 o'clock meeting, saw it was too early, and went back to sleep. But before getting into bed, he washed, changed his clothes and brushed his teeth. It was a strange thing to do that early in the morning.

Apart from Sunil, there was only an old family retainer in the house. It was 10 o'clock when Sanjay, Namrata and Priya ran into the room, because they had been told that Sunil had not woken up. He looked peaceful and completely relaxed. Namrata and Priya were stunned and broke down, while Sanjay, who still could not believe it, started shaking his father, thinking he could wake him up. Sunil had suffered his first, and fatal, heart attack.

Soon the house was flooded with people, as the news spread. In death all the correct political procedures were followed, though in life Sunil may have been cheated. Sonia Gandhi and Prime Minister Manmohan Singh flew in that evening to pay their last respects. An official mourning period was announced and Sunil's body was wrapped in the national flag

Shocked and numb, the children tried to come to terms with Sunil's death. They did not think anything could happen to their 'superman' dad. He had risen like a phoenix over and over again. Surely he would get up once more?

Ironically, just the night before, he had shown Priya and Owen all his early photographs and papers, and had spoken to them at length about his early life and the days when he'd had hardly any money and little comfort. It was as though he was reminding them of the long way he had travelled. His work was over: the children were settled, Namrata and Priya were married, Sanjay's career was more than well established. Apart from that, his own work now left him exhausted and gave him little satisfaction.

There were few people who understood him and his old-fashioned values. All his life it had seemed that there was something to fight for. Now he realized that all the battles that could have been won were behind him.

The future seemed less enticing than the past. Perhaps it was time to lie down and dream of a life well-lived, with the one person who had always been by his side,

Epilogue

Hey there, you with the stars in your eyes,
Love never made a fool of you,
You used to be too wise.

Hey there, you on that high flying cloud
Though she won't throw a crumb to you
You think one day she'll come to you
Better forget her

Her with her nose in the air
She has you dancing on a string
Break it and she won't care
Won't you take this advice
I hand you like a brother
Or are you not seeing things too clear
Are you too much in love to hear?
Is it all going in one ear and out the other?

— 'Hey There' as sung by Johnnie Ray, 1954

Filmography

(Films made by Jaddanbai under her Sangit Movietone banner, with Nargis credited as Baby Rani)
[1] *Naachwali* (1934)
[2] *Talash-e-Haq* (1935)
[3] *Hridaya Manthan* (1936)
[4] *Madam Fashion* (1936)
[5] *Moti ka Haar* (1937)

(Films as Nargis)
[6] *Tamanna* (1942)*
[7] *Pardanasheen* (1942)*
[8] *Taqdeer* (1943)
[9] *Anban* (1944)
[10] *Ismat* (1944)
[11] *Biswi Sadi* (1945)
[12] *Humayun* (1945)
[13] *Ramayani* (1945)
[14] *Nargis* (1946)
[15] *Mehndi* (1947)
[16] *Romeo and Juliet* (1947)
[17] *Aag* (1948)
[18] *Anjuman* (1948)
[19] *Anokha Pyar* (1948)
[20] *Mela* (1948)
[21] *Andaaz* (1949)
[22] *Barsaat* (1949)
[23] *Darogaji* (1949)
[24] *Lahore* (1949)

[25] *Rumal* (1949)
[26] *Adhi Raat* (1950)
[27] *Babul* (1950)
[28] *Bhishma Pratigya* (1950)
[29] *Birhaa ki Raat* (1950)
[30] *Chhoti Bhabhi* (1950)
[31] *Josh* (1950)
[32] *Pyar* (1950)
[33] *Jaan Pehchan* (1950)
[34] *Jogan* (1950)
[35] *Khel* (1950)
[36] *Meena Bazaar* (1950)
[37] *Awara* (1951)
[38] *Deedar* (1951)
[39] *Hulchul* (1951)
[40] *Pyar ki Baaten* (1951)
[41] *Sagar* (1951)
[42] *Amber* (1952)
[43] *Anhonee* (1952)
[44] *Ashiana* (1952)
[45] *Bewafa* (1952)
[46] *Sheesha* (1952)
[47] *Aah* (1953)
[48] *Dhun* (1953)
[49] *Pehli Shadi* (1953)
[50] *Paapi* (1953)
[51] *Angarey* (1953)
[52] *Shri 420* (1955)
[53] *Chori Chori* (1956)
[54] *Jagte Raho/ Ek Din Raatre* (1956)
[55] *Miss India* (1957)
[56] *Mother India* (1957)
[57] *Pardesi* (1957)
[58] *Adalat* (1958)
[59] *Ghar Sansar* (1958)
[60] *Lajwanti* (1958)

[61] *Raat Aur Din* (1967)

(* These two films have been listed in other filmographies but are difficult to find records of.)

Sunil Dutt's Filmography:
  [1] *Railway Platform* (1955)
  [2] *Kundan* (1955)
  [3] *Ek Hi Raasta* (1956)
  [4] *Kismet ka Khel* (1956)
  [5] *Rajdhani* (1956)
  [6] *Mother India* (1957)
  [7] *Payal* (1957)
  [8] *Post Box 999* (1958)
  [9] *Sadhana* (1958)
  [10] *Didi* (1959)
  [11] *Insaan Jaag Utha* (1959)
  [12] *Sujata* (1959)
  [13] *Duniya Jhukti Hai* (1960)
  [14] *Ek Phool Char Kaante* (1960)
  [15] *Hum Hindustani* (1960)
  [16] *Usne Kaha Tha* (1960)
  [17] *Chhaya* (1961)
  [18] *Jhoola* (1962)
  [19] *Main Chup Rahungi* (1962)
  [20] *Aaj Aur Kal* (1963)
  [21] *Gumrah* (1963)
  [22] *Mujhe Jeene Do* (1963)*
  [23] *Yeh Raaste Hain Pyar Ke* (1963)*
  [24] *Nartaki* (1963)
  [25] *Beti Bete* (1964)
  [26] *Ghazal* (1964)
  [27] *Yaadein* (1964)*
  [28] *Khandaan* (1965)
  [29] *Waqt* (1965)
  [30] *Amrapali* (1966)
  [31] *Gaban* (1966)

[32] *Mera Saaya* (1966)
[33] *Hamraaz* (1967)
[34] *Meharbaan* (1967)
[35] *Milan* (1967)
[36] *Gauri* (1968)
[37] *Padosan* (1968)
[38] *Sadhu Aur Shaitan* (1968)
[39] *Man ka Meet* (1968) (only produced)*
[40] *Bhai Bahen* (1969)
[41] *Chirag* (1969)
[42] *Meri Bhabhi* (1969)
[43] *Pyaasi Shyam* (1969)
[44] *Darpan* (1970)
[45] *Bhai Bhai* (1970)
[46] *Jwala* (1970)
[47] *Reshma Aur Shera* (1971)*
[48] *Jai Jwala* (1972)
[49] *Zameen Aasman* (1972)
[50] *Zindagi Zindagi* (1972)
[51] *Heera* (1973)
[52] *Pran Jaaye Par Vachan Na Jaaye* (1973)
[53] *Man Jeete Jag Jeet* (1973)
[54] *Chhatis Ghante* (1974)
[55] *Geeta Mera Naam* (1974)
[56] *Kora Badan* (1974)
[57] *Himalay Se Ooncha* (1975)
[58] *Neelima* (1975)
[59] *Umar Qaid* (1975)
[60] *Zakhmi* (1975)
[61] *Nagin* (1976)
[62] *Nehle Pe Dehla* (1976)*
[63] *Sat Sri Akal* (1977)
[64] *Ladki Jawan Ho Gayi* (1977)
[65] *Aakhri Goli* (1977)
[66] *Darinda* (1977)
[67] *Gyaniji* (1977)
[68] *Paapi* (1977)

[69] *Charandas* (1977)
[70] *Jindri Yar Di* (1978)
[71] *Kala Aadmi* (1978)
[72] *Ram Kasam* (1978)
[73] *Daku Aur Jawan* (1978)
[74] *Ahimsa* (1979)
[75] *Jaani Dushman* (1979)
[76] *Muqabla* (1979)
[77] *Ek Gunah Aur Sahi* (1980)
[78] *Ganga Aur Suraj* (1980)
[79] *Lahu Pukarega* (1980)
[80] *Shaan* (1980)
[81] *Yaari Dushmani* (1980)
[82] *Rocky* (1981)
[83] *Badle ki Aag* (1982)
[84] *Dard ka Rishta* (1982)*
[85] *Laila* (1984)
[86] *Raj Tilak* (1984)
[87] *Yaadon ki Zanjeer* (1984)
[88] *Faasle* (1985)
[89] *Kala Dhandha Gorey Log* (1986)
[90] *Mangal Dada* (1986)
[91] *Watan ke Rakhwale* (1987)
[92] *Dharamyudh* (1988)
[93] *Yeh Aag Kab Bujhegi* (1991)*
[94] *Qurban* (1991)
[95] *Pratigyabadh* (1991)
[96] *Hai Meri Jaan* (1991)
[97] *Vidrohi* (1992)
[98] *Kshatriya* (1992)
[99] *Parampara* (1992)
[100] *Phool* (1993)
[101] *Munnabhai MBBS* (2003)

* Ajanta Arts Productions

Select Bibliography

Chatterjee, Gayatri. *Mother India*. Penguin: New Delhi, 2002.

Desai, Meghnad. *Nehru's Hero: Dilip Kumar in the Life of India*. Roli Books: New Delhi, 2004.

Dubois, Abbé J.A. *Hindu Manners, Customs and Ceremonies*. Translated from French by Henry K. Beauchamp. 3rd ed. Rupa: New Delhi, 2006.

Garga, B.D. *So Many Cinemas: The Motion Picture in India*. Eminence Designs: Mumbai, 1996.

George, T.J.S. *The Life And Times of Nargis*. Indus: New Delhi, 1994.

Kidwai, Saleem. 'The Singing Ladies Find a Voice'. Seminar, 540, August 2004.

Kinikar, Shashikant. *Nargis*. Pratik Prakashan: Pune, 2004.

Nanda, Ritu. *Raj Kapoor Speaks*. Viking: New Delhi, 2002.

Nevile, Pran. *Nautch Girls of India*. Ravi Kumar Publishers: New Delhi, 1996.

Oberai, Bodh Raj. *Indian Film Stars*. The Cinema: Lahore, 1933.

Pandey, B.N. *Nehru*. Rupa: New Delhi, 2003.

Pandya, Rajnikumar. *Aapki Parchaiyan*. Translated from Gujarati by Sarla Jagmohan. Abhiruchi Prakashan: New Delhi, 1999.

Rajdhyaksha, Ashish and Willeman, Paul. *Encyclopaedia of Indian Cinema*. Oxford University Press: New Delhi, 1994.

Reuben, Bunny. *Follywood Flashback*. Indus: New Delhi, 1993.

Sarkar, Sumit. *Modern India: 1885-1947*. Macmillan: New Delhi, 1983.

Acknowledgements

This was meant to be a book only about Nargis, but it grew into a book about Nargis and Sunil Dutt after the research began in December 2005: very soon I could not think of one without the other, especially as I discovered their passionate life-long love for each other, despite the terrible tragedies they had to face. Their lives had such immense highs and lows that the family has learnt to lead normal lives in the midst of a whirlwind. Even as this book goes to press, their son Sanjay Dutt, out on bail, awaits his final sentence under the Arms Act.

The Dutts were, in many ways, a real power couple who left an interesting legacy for their children. I hope that an insight into their lives will be found in this book, as narrated by their family and friends and indeed by Nargis and Sunil themselves, because much of this account is based on their own diaries and letters. Perhaps this is the only family in the film world with such well-archived material, where every scrap of paper has been preserved—even the cash receipt of Sunil's first radio purchase in the 1950s!

The book would not have been possible without the initial interest shown by the gentle and soft-spoken Sunil Dutt and then, after his death, the unstinting help and affection showed by Namrata and Priya Dutt. I owe them a special debt, as they shared personal papers, diaries and letters (while going through trying times themselves). Sanjay Dutt took time out from his shooting schedule (in 2006, he was still on bail under TADA) as did Kumar Gaurav (Namrata's husband) for the book. I also interviewed (sometimes with Meghnad and sometimes alone) members of their family—Rehana and Sabrina Amarjeet Singh, Zahida Sahaya, Arif and Ishrat Hussain, Rani Bali, Som and

Puneeta Dutt, and friends—Dilip Kumar and Saira Bano, Nimmi and Ali Raza, Raakhi, Shammi, Raaj Grover, Mack Mohan, Sudhir Luthra, Krishen Lal Narang, Ameen Sayani, Dr Shakeel Ahmad Khan—Director General, Nehru Yuvak Kendra—the bubbly Gia Sharan and the reticent Kusum Sethi. Simi Garewal entertained us with some delightful anecdotes about Nargis's irrepressible spirit, but then made us promise we would not use them, and I have kept that confidence. My aunt, Shanti Mahendroo and cousin, Anju Mahendroo, gave us a delightful evening and much valuable information. I thank them all for their time and their memories. And of course, special thanks are due to Dr Mithu Alur who runs the Spastic Society of India, Mumbai. The *Times of India* archives allowed us to source some very interesting press cuttings, which I am grateful for. Shekhar Gupta, as ever a good friend, helped me access *Screen,* and Vinod Dua gave us spectacular recordings of Jaddanbai: heartfelt thanks.

I travelled up and down the length and breadth of Mumbai for nearly a month and realized that with over fifty hours of interviews, the diaries and letters, photographs and film DVDs I had collected, I already had a huge book. There are still many aspects about the Dutts I could have written about, but then I would have to go into a second volume of this book, as Nargis and Sunil Dutt led very rich and varied lives.

There were very few interviews that did not end in nostalgic tears—each interviewee missed the couple, even though often the incident they were narrating had occurred several decades earlier. For me, the book also became deeply emotional as I had access to the diaries and personal letters of Nargis, Sunil Dutt, and Priya as well. And yes, I always felt the presence of Nargis, carefully reading every word! So I thank her too.

I went to the National Film Archives of India in Pune for a fortnight and along with my husband watched Nargis's first film *Taqdeer.* I gathered a wealth of material from the archives, about Jaddanbai, Nargis, Sunil Dutt and about women in early Indian cinema, some of which appears in this book. I thank K.S. Sashidharan, Director, NFAI; Arti V. Karkhanis, Library & Information Assistant; Subbalakshmi Iyer, Junior Librarian;

Acknowledgements

Urmila Joshi, Library & Information Assistant; S.R. Manohar, Projectionist; and P.A. Salam, Assistant Projectionist. I thank Tripurari Sharan, Director, Film and Television Institute of India, for his hospitality and interest in the project and Deepa and Colvyn Harris for graciously sharing their home with me for ten chaotic days in Mumbai.

My editor Karthika at HarperCollins has been invaluable as a source of strength, for her faith in the book, and of course for her excellent editing. I also thank Shivmeet Deol for her help with the edit and the photographs.

I would also like to thank Behroze Gandhy and Rosie Thomas for permitting me to use extracts from their documentary *To Hell and Back.*

And finally, my husband Meghnad: it was his patience, generosity and constant encouragement that made the book happen. It was meant to be a joint book, but he was happy to let me gather material and write the first draft—and then equally happy to say that he liked it and it could go straight to the publisher! I was overwhelmed by his confidence in me, and I thank him for it. He (like Sunil Dutt) believed in his wife, and more power to such men!

Kishwar Desai   *London/Delhi*
                                                27 September 2007

Picture Credits

1. Portrait of Dilipa at Château Marine, page 25, photograph by the author
1. Picture of Jaddanbai, page 35, courtesy of the Film Archives of India, Pune
2. Poster of *Madam Fashion,* page 39, courtesy of the Film Archives of India, Pune
3. Poster of *Taqdeer,* page 72, courtesy of Mehboob Studios, Mumbai
4. Poster of *Barsaat,* page 116, courtesy of the Film Archives of India, Pune
5. Poster of *Awara,* page 127, courtesy of the Film Archives of India, Pune
6. Poster of *Shree 420,* page 141, courtesy of the Film Archives of India, Pune
7. Poster of *Chori Chori,* page 158, courtesy of the Film Archives of India, Pune
8. Photograph of Nargis nursing Sunil after the fire, page 163, courtesy of *Screen/* The Express Group
9. Poster of *Pardesi,* page 196, courtesy of the Film Archives of India, Pune
10. Poster of *Aag,* page 215, courtesy of the Film Archives of India, Pune
11. Poster of *Mother India,* page 229, courtesy of the Film Archives of India, Pune
12. Credits and synopsis of *Lajwanti,* page 235, courtesy of the Film Archives of India, Pune
13. Postcard from Sunil to Nargis Dutt, page 276, courtesy of the Dutt family
14. Still of Sunil Dutt and Saira Bano in *Padosan,* page 287, courtesy of the Film Archives of India, Pune
15. Letter from Nargis to Rehana, page 376, courtesy of the Dutt family
16. Photograph of Sunil and Sanjay, page 418, courtesy of *Screen/* The Express Group

JACKET PHOTOGRAPHS: Courtesy of *Screen/* The Express Group